lonely planet

Discover
Costa Rica

Contents →

Throughout this book, we use these icons to highlight special recommendations:

These icons help you quickly identify reviews in the text and on the map:

The Best...
Lists for everything from bars to wildlife – to make sure you don't miss out

Don't Miss
A must-see – don't go home until you've been there

Local Knowledge   Local experts reveal their top picks and secret highlights

Detour
Special places a little off the beaten track

If you like...
Lesser-known alternatives to world-famous at...

Sights

Eating

Drinking

Sleeping

Information

Nate Cavalieri
Adam Skolnick, Wendy Yanagihara

p105 Northern Costa Rica

Península de Nicoya **p167**

San José

p77

p51

Central Valley

p283 Caribbean Coast

p205

Central Pacific Coast

p241 Southern Costa Rica

● San José

Highlights 54

○ Museums & Theaters in San José
○ Mercado Central
○ Public Parks
○ Plaza de la Cultura
○ Escazú
○ Los Yoses & San Pedro

● Central Valley

Highlights 80

○ Rafting in Turrialba
○ Volcán Irazú
○ Monumento Nacional Arqueológico Guayabo
○ Barva
○ Sarchí
○ Cartago

● Northern Costa Rica

Highlights 1

○ Monteverde & Santa Elen
○ Parque Nacional Volcán Arenal
○ La Fortuna
○ Laguna de Arenal
○ Parque Nacional Volcán Tenorio
○ La Virgen
○ Parque Nacional Santa Ro

● Central Pacific Coast

Highlights 208

○ Manuel Antonio Area
○ Dominical
○ Parque Nacional Carara
○ Jacó
○ Playa Hermosa
○ Parque Nacional Marino Ballena
○ Kayaking in Dominical & Uvita

● Southern Costa Rica

Highlights 244

○ Hiking Southern Costa Rica
○ Parque Nacional Corcovado
○ Hiking Beyond Bahía Drake
○ Pavones
○ Puerto Jiménez
○ Parque Nacional Los Quetzales
○ Zancudo

● Caribbean Coas

Highlights 2

○ Manzanillo
○ Parque Nacional Tortuguero
○ Puerto Viejo de Talamanc
○ Salsa Brava
○ Cahuita
○ Rainforest Aerial Tram

Contents

Plan Your Trip

This is Costa Rica 6

Costa Rica Map 8

**Costa Rica's
Top 25 Experiences** ... 10

**Costa Rica's
Top Itineraries** 32

Month by Month 42

What's New 46

Get Inspired 47

Need to Know 48

On the Road

● ● ●

San José   51

Highlights 54

Best... 58

Walking Tour 60

San José 62

Around San José 73

● ● ●

Central Valley   77

Highlights 80

Best... 84

Itineraries 86

Alajuela 88

*Parque Nacional
Volcán Poás* 90

Sarchí 91

*Los Ángeles Cloud
Forest Adventure Park* .. 93

Palmares 93

Heredia 93

Barva 95

Cartago 97

*Parque Nacional
Volcán Irazú* 98

Valle de Orosi 99

*Parque Nacional
Tapantí-Macizo
Cerro de la Muerte* 100

Turrialba 101

*Monumento Nacional
Arqueológico
Guayabo* 102

● Península de Nicoya

Highlights 170

○ Surfing Península de Nicoya

○ Montezuma

○ Playa Sámara

○ Playa Conchal

○ Playa del Coco

○ Playa Avellana & Playa Negra

Contents

On the Road

Northern Costa Rica 105

Highlights 108
Best... 114
Itineraries 116
La Fortuna & Around 118
Parque Nacional Volcán Arenal 125
El Castillo 127
Laguna de Arenal Area 129
Nuevo Arenal 131
Nuevo Arenal to Tilarán 132
Tilarán 133
Monteverde & Santa Elena 135
Reserva Biológica Bosque Nuboso Monteverde 146
Reserva Santa Elena 148
Liberia 148
Volcán Miravalles Area 153
Parque Nacional Rincón de la Vieja 154
Parque Nacional Volcán Tenorio 156
Parque Nacional Santa Rosa 158
Llanos de Cortés 159
La Virgen 160
La Virgen to Puerto Viejo de Sarapiquí 162
Puerto Viejo de Sarapiquí & Around 164
South of Puerto Viejo de Sarapiquí 165

Península de Nicoya 167

Highlights 170
Best... 174
Itineraries 176
Playa del Coco 178
Playa Brasilito 180
Playa Conchal 181
Playa Grande 181
Parque Nacional Marino Las Baulas de Guanacaste 182
Playa Tamarindo 183
Playas Avellana & Negra 186
Nosara Area 188
Playa Sámara 192
Montezuma 194
Reserva Natural Absoluta Cabo Blanco 198
Mal País & Santa Teresa 199

Central Pacific Coast 205

Highlights 208
Best... 214
Itineraries 216

Parque Nacional Carara 218
Jacó 218
Playa Hermosa 221
Quepos 222
Quepos to Manuel Antonio 223
Parque Nacional Manuel Antonio & Around 225
Hacienda Barú National Wildlife Refuge 230
Dominical 231
Uvita 235
Parque Nacional Marino Ballena 237
Ojochal Area 238

Southern Costa Rica 241

Highlights 244
Best... 250
Itineraries 252
Bahía Drake 254
Bahía Drake to Parque Nacional Corcovado 257
Sierpe 258
Puerto Jiménez 258
Cabo Matapalo & Carate 262
Parque Nacional Corcovado 263
Golfito 265
Zancudo & Pavones 266

Parque Nacional Isla del Cocos 268

San Isidro de El General 269

San Gerardo de Rivas 270

Parque Nacional Chirripó 271

San Gerardo de Dota . 273

Parque Nacional Los Quetzales 274

Reserva Indígena Boruca 275

San Vito 277

Parque Internacional La Amistad 281

●●●

Caribbean Coast 283

Highlights **286**

Best... .... **290**

Itineraries **292**

Puerto Limón 294

Moín 296

Cariari 296

Tortuguero Village 296

Parque Nacional Tortuguero 302

Cahuita 305

Parque Nacional Cahuita 309

Puerto Viejo de Talamanca 311

Manzanillo 315

In Focus

Costa Rica Today **320**

History **322**

Family Travel **332**

Costa Rica Outdoors .. **335**

Tico Way of Life **340**

Costa Rica Landscapes **343**

Wildlife Guide **348**

Shopping **353**

Survival Guide

Directory **356**

Accommodations 356

Business Hours 357

Climate 357

Customs Regulations 358

Discount Cards 358

Electricity 358

Food 358

Gay & Lesbian Travelers 359

Health 360

Internet Access 362

Legal Matters 362

Money 363

Safe Travel 363

Telephone 364

Time 365

Tourist Information ... 365

Travelers with Disabilities 365

Visas 365

Women Travelers 365

Transport **366**

Getting There & Away 366

Getting Around 366

Language **371**

Behind the Scenes **373**

Index **374**

How to Use this Book **383**

Our Writers **384**

This is Costa Rica

If you have long sought a piece of tropical paradise, take a deep breath, you've found it. The perfect balance of adrenaline-addled adventure destination and unplugged tropical getaway, Costa Rica is a land of dormant volcanoes, desolate beaches and dense jungle. The canopies rustle with riotous troupes of white-faced monkeys, hillsides echo with the squawk of scarlet macaws and the trees along the trail are overburdened with the day's lunch of ripe star fruit. It might seem like a wondrous tropical fantasy land, but this is Costa Rica.

Costa Rica has earned a rightful place in the cubicle daydreams of travelers around the world. Learn to surf in warm salt water and hike above the clouds; rush down white-water rivers and then hoist yourself up to a zip line to sail over jungle canopies. Sound good? That's only the beginning. Costa Rica is the preeminent eco- and adventure-tourism capital of Central America.

With a world-class infrastructure, visionary sustainability initiatives and no standing army, Costa Rica is a green, peaceful jewel of the region. Taking into account that more than a third of the country enjoys some form of environmental protection and there's greater biodiversity than the USA and Europe combined, it's a country that earns the superlative descriptions. And though the breakneck pace of American-style modernization threatens to pave over the country's cultural treasures, there's still plenty of the laid-back, heart-stopping beauty of the so-called 'Old Costa Rica'.

Then there are the people. Costa Ricans, or Ticos as they call themselves, are largely proud of their little slice of paradise. They welcome guests into the easygoing rhythms of *pura vida* – the pure life – that is as much a catchy motto as it is an enduring mantra.

> 66
>
> It might seem like a wondrous tropical fantasy land, but this is Costa Rica.
>
> 99

Red-eyed tree frog

25
Top Experiences

1. Monteverde & Santa Elena
2. Volcán Arenal
3. Parque Nacional Manuel Antonio
4. Montezuma
5. Rafting in Turrialba
6. Parque Nacional Tortuguero
7. Parque Nacional Corcovado
8. Monteverde Cloud Forest
9. Mal País & Santa Teresa
10. Parque Internacional La Amistad
11. Hiking Cerro Chirripó
12. San José
13. Surfing in Playa Grande
14. Central Valley Plantations
15. Sarapiquí Valley
16. Playa Sámara
17. Southern Caribbean
18. Hot Springs of La Fortuna
19. Nosara
20. Kayaking in the Golfo Dulce
21. Parque Nacional Santa Rosa
22. Dominical
23. Pavones
24. Parque Nacional Carara
25. Jacó

25 Costa Rica's Top Experiences

Monteverde & Santa Elena

This pristine expanse of virginal forest totaling 105 sq km is the result of private citizens – principally the Quaker settlers who left the United States to protest the Korean War and helped foster conservationist principles with Ticos of the region. But the real romance of Monteverde (p135) is in nature. For here is a mysterious Neverland of dangling vines, verdant ferns and running creeks, blooming with life and nurturing rivulets of evolution.

Canopy walkway, Reserva Biológica Bosque Nuboso Monteverde (p146)

2

Volcán Arenal

While the molten night views are gone and the volcano lies dormant, this mighty, perfectly conical giant is worthy of a pilgrimage. There are several beautiful trails, especially the magnificent climb to Cerro Chato (p119). Although Volcán Arenal (p125) is considered by scientists to be active, you'd never know it from the serene, mist-covered vistas. Even when clouds gather and the air chills, you're just a short drive from its hot springs.

Parque Nacional Manuel Antonio

Although droves of visitors pack Parque Nacional Manuel Antonio (p227) – the country's most popular (and smallest) national park – it remains an absolute gem. Capuchin monkeys scurry across its idyllic beaches, brown pelicans dive-bomb its clear waters and sloths watch over its accessible trails. It's a perfect place to introduce youngsters to the wonders of the rainforest, and splashing around in the waves you're likely to feel like a kid yourself. There's not much by way of privacy, but it's so lovely that you won't mind sharing. White-faced capuchin monkeys

The Best...
Idyllic Sunsets

MANUEL ANTONIO
Perched high on a hilltop, the restaurants en route to Manuel Antonio offer an ideal location for a sundowner. (p227)

TORTUGUERO VILLAGE
Sip an ice-cold *cerveza* (beer) and nod along to reggae beats. (p296)

PLAYA TAMARINDO
Sail on the deep-blue Pacific and watch the sun dip below the jagged coastline. (p183)

CERRO CHIRRIPÓ
Bundle up and take in the wild, windswept panoramic views from the Crestones Base Lodge atop Costa Rica's highest point. (p271)

The Best...
National Parks

PARQUE NACIONAL CORCOVADO
An untamed rainforest adventure and loads of wildlife await brave souls who make the trek. (p263)

MONTEVERDE & SANTA ELENA
Cloud forests straddle both sides of the continental divide. (p135)

PARQUE NACIONAL MANUEL ANTONIO
An excellent day at the beach with monkeys and easy hiking for the whole family. (p227)

PARQUE NACIONAL LOS QUETZALES
A cool mountain home to the elusive bird of paradise. (p274)

PARQUE NACIONAL TORTUGUERO
Sea turtles and caimans complement the Caribbean environs.(p302)

Montezuma

4

If you dig artsy beach culture, rubbing shoulders with neo-Rastas and yoga enthusiasts or have always wanted to spin fire, study Spanish or lounge on sugar-white coves, go to Montezuma (p194). As you stroll through this intoxicating town and its rugged coastline, you're never far from the rhythm and sound of the sea. From here you'll have easy access to the famed Reserva Natural Absoluta Cabo Blanco, where you can hike to a triple-tiered waterfall. The town also has some of the best restaurants in the country.
Montezuma coastline

White-Water Rafting in Turrialba

5

The dedicated adrenaline junkie could easily cover some heart-pounding river miles in the span of a few days in this compact country. Or you can make for Turrialba (p101) and join an adventure down the Río Pacuare. A range of rapids interspersed by smooth water sections allows rafters to take in the luscious jungle scenery. It's considered one of the world's best white-water runs. Rafting, Río Pacuare

CHRISTER FREDRIKSSON / GETTY IMAGES ©

JESUS OCHOA ©

Parque Nacional Tortuguero

Canoeing through the canals of Parque Nacional Tortuguero (p302) is a boat-borne safari, where thick jungle meets the water and you can get up close with shy caiman, river turtles, crowned night herons, monkeys and sloths. In the right season, under cover of darkness, watch the awesome ritual of turtles building nests and laying their eggs on the black-sand beaches.

Parque Nacional Corcovado

This vast, largely untouched rainforest (p263) is muddy, muggy and intense. Travelers with a flexible agenda and sturdy boots can thrust themselves into the unknown and leave with the story of a lifetime. Further into the jungle, down Corcovado's seldom-trodden trails is the country's best wildlife-watching, most desolate beaches and most vivid adventures. Playa Corcovado, Parque Nacional Corcovado

Zip Lining in the Monteverde Cloud Forest

The wild-eyed happiness induced by a canopy tour (p139) is self-evident. Few things are more enjoyable than clipping onto a cable and zipping above and through the seething jungle canopy. This is where kids become daredevils and adults become kids. Invented in Monteverde, zip-lining outfits quickly multiplied all over Costa Rica. The best place to try it is still Monteverde, where the forest is alive, the mist fine and swirling, and the afterglow worth savoring.

The Best...
Adrenaline Rushes

LA FORTUNA
Costa Rica's center for adventure sports, from bungee jumping to zip lining. (p118)

TURRIALBA
Home to the fiercest white water that Costa Rica has to offer. (p101)

PARQUE NACIONAL CORCOVADO
Ford rivers en route to the Sirena ranger station to spot the country's fiercest wildlife. (p263)

LA VIRGEN
Head to this northern destination if kayaking floats your boat. (p160)

NOSARA
Fly along on the world's longest zip-line canopy tour. (p188)

Mal País & Santa Teresa

Think tasty waves, creative kitchens and babes in board shorts and bikinis. It's no wonder that the rugged corner of the Península de Nicoya that is home to Mal País and Santa Teresa (p199) has become one of Costa Rica's most life-affirming destinations. The hills are lush and offer stylish boutique accommodations, while the sea is full of life and near-ideal for surfing and fishing. Follow the unpaved road to Mal País to find an authentic Tico fishing hamlet where you can cast away and score a dinner worthy of kings. Mal País

9

The Best...
Tropical Beaches

MONTEZUMA
Sprawl out on white sand in a hidden cove to take in sunset on the Península de Nicoya. (p194)

MARINO BALLENA
Scan for whales on your own deserted piece of paradise. (p237)

MANZANILLO
Swaying palms and golden sand make this the Caribbean coast's most scenic stretch of water. (p199)

MAL PAÍS
Backed by lush tropical jungle, raging surf crashes in each direction. (p199)

PLAYA CONCHAL
Crushed shells and turquoise water. (p181)

10 Parque Internacional La Amistad

Ready to rough it? Try a visit to the edge of the 'friendship' park (p281), an enormous sprawl of protected land shared by Costa Rica and Panama. Thoroughly off the beaten path, this is where the most adventurous travelers go to visit indigenous mountain villages and find utter solitude. It's no simple stroll (most trips here are multiday guided expeditions) but the rewards are on the same colossal scale as the park itself. High in the mountains, it's a wholly different world from the country's famed beaches. Strangler fig tree

Hiking Cerro Chirripó

The view from the rugged peak of Cerro Chirripó (p271), Costa Rica's highest summit – of wind-swept rocks and icy lakes – may not resemble the Costa Rica of the postcards, but the two-day hike above the clouds is one of the country's most satisfying excursions. A predawn hike holds the real prize: a chance to catch the fiery sunrise and see both the Caribbean and the Pacific in a full and glorious panoramic view.

DAVID SOUTH / ALAMY ©

San José

The heart of Tico culture and identity lives in San José (p51), as do university students, intellectuals, artists and politicians. While not the most attractive capital in Central America, it has some graceful neoclassical and colonial architecture, museums housing pre-Columbian jade and gold, nightlife that goes on until dawn, and some of the most sophisticated restaurants in the country. Street art – both officially sanctioned and guerrilla – adds unexpected pops of color and public discourse to the cityscape. Teatro Nacional (p63), San José

13 Surfing in Playa Grande

Costa Rica's east coast may move to the laid-back groove of Caribbean reggae, but the country's best year-round surfing is on the Pacific Coast, in particular at Playa Grande (p181). Here, the agenda rarely gets more complicated than the surf report, sunblock and a few cold Imperial beers. With plenty of good breaks for beginners and the country's most reliable rides, Playa Grande is home to Costa Rica's endless summer.

Coffee Plantations in the Central Valley

Take a country drive on the scenic, curvy Central Valley back roads, where the hillsides are a patchwork of varied agriculture and coffee shrubbery. If you're curious about that magical brew, tour one of the coffee plantations and learn about how Costa Rica's golden bean goes from plant to cup. One of the best places for a tour is Café Britt Finca (p96), near Barva. Coffee hacienda, Alajuela (p88)

The Best...
Bird- & Wildlife-Watching

WILSON BOTANICAL GARDEN
Very popular among bird-watchers, who keep an eye out for some rare high-altitude species. (p278)

PARQUE NACIONAL CORCOVADO
The elusive jaguar makes its home here, but you are more likely to see scarlet macaws. (p263)

PARQUE NACIONAL LOS QUETZALES
This park is named for its banner attraction, the re-splendent quetzal. (p274)

TORTUGUERO
Birds, turtles, monkeys, sloths and much more are all common at this wildlife-rich park. (p294)

The Best...
Off-the-Beaten-Path Spots

ZANCUDO
Find excellent surf, quaint bungalows and a bit of tranquillity in the far south. (p266)

PARQUE NACIONAL VOLCÁN TENORIO
Ample hiking trails, a bright-blue waterfall and little more than a few scattered footprints. (p156)

RESERVA INDÍGENA BORUCA
Difficult to access, but worth the trip if you want insight into the country's pre-Columbian past. (p275)

PUNTA MONA
Extremely remote, but the lodge is home to an amazing ongoing experiment in sustainable living. (p317)

Sarapiquí Valley

Sarapiquí (p162) rose to fame as a principal port in the nefarious old days of United Fruit dominance, before it meandered into agricultural anonymity, only to be reborn as a paddler's mecca thanks to the frothing, serpentine mocha magic of its namesake river. These days it's still a paddling paradise, and it's also dotted with fantastic ecolodges and private forest preserves that will educate you about pre-Columbian life, get you into that steaming, looming, muddy jungle, and introduce you to local wildlife up close. Above: Green violetear; Left: Río Sarapiquí (p160)

ABOVE: JUDY BELLAH © LEFT: JOHN COLETTI / GETTY IMAGES ©

Playa Sámara

Some expat residents call Playa Sámara (p192) the black hole of happiness, which has something to do with that crescent of sand spanning two rocky headlands, the opportunity to learn to surf, stand-up paddle, surf cast or fly above migrating whales in an ultralight, and the plethora of nearby all-natural beaches and coves. All of it is easy to access on foot or via public transportation, which is why it's becoming so popular with families who enjoy Sámara's palpable ease and tranquility. Surf school, Playa Sámara

Southern Caribbean

By day, lounge in a hammock, snorkel at uncrowded beaches, hike to waterfall-fed pools and visit the remote indigenous territories of the Bribrí and Kèköldi. By night, try zesty Caribbean cooking and sway to reggaetón at open-air bars cooled by ocean breezes. Cahuita (p305) and Puerto Viejo de Talamanca (p311), both outposts of this unique mix of Afro-Caribbean, Tico and indigenous culture, are perfect bases for such adventures. Rasta style bungalow, Puerto Viejo de Talamanca

CHRISTER FREDRIKSSON / GETTY IMAGES ©

Hot Springs of La Fortuna

It may no longer creep down the mountainside, but beneath La Fortuna lava heats dozens of bubbling springs. Some are free, and any local can point the way. Others are, shall we say, embellished, dressed up, luxuriated. Take Tabacón Hot Springs (p118), set in the path of Volcán Arenal's 1975 eruption. It's a cheesy but appealing set piece, with faux cliffs and a Garden of Eden motif, and water that flows and pools at a steaming and healing 40°C (104°F).

Thermal pool near Volcán Arenal, La Fortuna

The Best...
Ecolodges

ARENAL OBSERVATORY LODGE
The only lodge smack-dab in the middle of Parque Nacional Volcán Arenal. (p128)

SELVA VERDE LODGE
This former *finca* (farm) is now an elegant lodge that protects more than 200 hectares of rainforest. (p163)

ARENAS DEL MAR
This architectural stunner near Manuel Antonio has private Jacuzzis overlooking the coast. (p224)

LAPA RÍOS
A living classroom where sustainability meets eco-luxury. (p262)

Nosara

Nosara (p188) is a cocktail of international surf culture, jungled microclimes and yoga bliss, where three stunning beaches are stitched together by a network of swerving, rutted earth roads that meander over coastal hills. Visitors can stay in the alluring surf enclave of Playa Guiones – where there are some fabulous restaurants and a drop-dead gorgeous beach – or in Playa Pelada, which is as romantic as it is rugged and removed. One resident described the area as 'sophisticated jungle living,' and who wouldn't want more of that in their life? Playa Guiones

ROBERT FRANCIS / GETTY IMAGES ©

The Best...
Chill-Out Spots

SAN GERARDO DE DOTA
Fresh mountain air, trout fishing and chilly nights complement excellent high-altitude bird-watching. (p273)

CAHUITA
A low-key beach destination that moves to its own relaxed Caribbean rhythm. (p305)

NOSARA
A magical collection of remote wilderness, beaches and raging surf. (p188)

UVITA
This quiet community at the edge of a quiet marine park is a perfect place to unplug. (p235)

20 Kayaking in the Golfo Dulce

Getting out in Golfo Dulce (the 'sweet gulf') brings hardy paddlers in contact with the abundant marine life in the bay – here dolphins play, whales breech and sparkling schools of tropical fish whiz by. Leaving the open water and navigating the maze of mangrove channels (p259) is another world completely, offering a chance to glide silently past herons, crested caracaras, snakes and sloths.

BUCKWINKEL / ALAMY ©

Parque Nacional Santa Rosa

Among the oldest and largest protected areas in Costa Rica, the sprawling 386-sq-km Area de Conservacion Guanacaste is a national refuge on the Península Santa Elena. Almost all the worthy diversions can be found in the Santa Rosa sector (p158). Surfers descend to surf the legendary beach break, Witch's Rock. Biologists and naturalists come for its biological diversity and way-out hiking trails.

Dominical

A permanently chilled-out beach town where time slows to a crawl, Dominical (p231) has a way of forestalling your plans. But when the surf is crashing and the sun is blazing, few travelers seem to mind. This is an excellent place to learn how to surf, hang out with surfers from around the world and enjoy locally hooked *ceviche*. The additional bonus: its location in the middle of the central Pacific coast is perfect for visiting a handful of the country's national parks. Market, Dominical

Pavones

Pavones (p266) is the end of the road for surfers on the Pacific trail, a lovely little place in the remote southwest corner of the country. Those willing to make the trip spend their visit swaying on hammocks and taking on one of the longest left-hand surf breaks in the world. Add to the equation a suite of clean, basic *cabinas*, a number of rushing streams, and hills that are dotted with wild tropical fruit trees, and it's a difficult place to leave. Fishing, Pavones

23

The Best...
Surf Breaks

DOMINICAL
The central Pacific's hub for surfers offers excellent lessons and a chilled party scene. (p231)

PLAYAS AVELLANA & NEGRA
This is home to the on-screen surf epic *Endless Summer II*. (p186)

PAVONES
This ramshackle slice of paradise boasts one of the world's longest left-hand breaks. (p266)

PUERTO VIEJO DE TALAMANCA
Centered on Salsa Brava, one of the country's gnarliest breaks. (p311)

MAL PAÍS & SANTA TERESA
Huge swaths of prime beachfront are shaped by a variety of breaks. (p199)

Parque Nacional Carara

Carara (p218) is where two of Costa Rica's most wildlife-rich climate zones collide in an explosion of color, sound and life, and one of the best places in the country outside of the remote Península de Osa to spot the country's iconic macaws. The best part is that this park requires minimal effort: just off the Interamericana, Carara's trailheads are just a few steps from the parking lot and easy for all abilities. For bird-watchers, there's no place where big payoffs come so easily. Scarlet macaws

The Best...
Family-Friendly Spots

24

MONTEVERDE
A host of outdoor activities and fun will keep kids entertained in the cloud forest. (p135)

RÍO SARAPIQUÍ
Home to the best Class I and Class II floats that are good for kids and wildlife-watching. (p161)

PARQUE NACIONAL MANUEL ANTONIO
Highly accessible, kid-friendly trails full of a wondrous assortment of animals. (p227)

JACÓ
A kid's paradise: body boarding, canopy tours, horseback riding and family-friendly hotels with pools. (p218).

25

Jacó

Sure, with all the neon signs, tour operators and high-rise developments this might not be the 'real' Costa Rica that nostalgic old-timers reminisce about, but Jacó (p218) is a blast. With a handful of excellent restaurants, a passable surf scene and the best nightlife on the entire Pacific coast, this town should top the agenda of folks who come to Costa Rica for nocturnal fun. But it's not only for those who are ready to rage; a long history of hosting travelers has endowed the place with services for all ages. Playa Jacó

Costa Rica's
Top Itineraries

San José to Monteverde

Northern Highlights

5 DAYS

This classic route will take you through the capital and into the mountains, passing bubbling volcanoes, hot springs and tranquil cloud forests.

NICARAGUA

CARIBBEAN SEA

LA FORTUNA & VOLCÁN ARENAL

MONTEVERDE & SANTA ELENA

SAN JOSÉ

PACIFIC OCEAN

① San José (p62)

Costa Rica's sprawling capital can be a shock to the senses, but there is plenty to do here. Start with a trip to the bustling **Mercado Central** where you can bargain-hunt for anything from coffee to mangoes. If you need respite from the crowds and heat, head to the **Museo de Jade** to admire centuries-old pre-Columbian jade carvings. Architecture and culture buffs shouldn't miss the **Teatro Nacional**, a stunning colonial construction that is the heart of San José's theater scene.

SAN JOSÉ ➊ LA FORTUNA

🚗 **3½ hours** Along the Interamericana, via Alajuela. 🚌 **4½ hours** Auto-Transportes San José–San Carlos Centro arrive at La Fortuna's Comercial Adifort bus terminal.

② La Fortuna (p118) & Volcán Arenal (p125)

On the flanks of Volcán Arenal, tourist-friendly La Fortuna is a world away from the hustle and bustle of San José. Your first destination is the dark and brooding

---

Bird-watching, Reserva Biológica Bosque Nuboso Monteverde (p146)

PHOTOGRAPHER: CHRISTER FREDRIKSSON / GETTY IMAGES ©

Volcán Arenal. Ample daylight allows long hikes through the surrounding forests, while at night you can enjoy a brilliant star display. If the weather isn't cooperating, wait it out in one of the town's luxurious **hot springs**.

LA FORTUNA ➊ MONTEVERDE

🚗 **Three hours** Paved roads to Tilarán, then rougher roads complete the trip. A 4WD is required in rainy season. 🚌 **Six to eight hours** via Tilarán. ⛴ **Four hours** via boat across Laguna de Arenal, followed by a shuttle to Santa Elena.

③ Monteverde & Santa Elena (p135)

The peaceful town of Santa Elena comprises cute cafes, eclectic restaurants, attractive galleries and delicious ice cream. The main billing is **Reserva Biológica Bosque Nuboso Monteverde**, where you can search for the elusive quetzal. Nearby **Reserva Santa Elena** and the **Bosque Eterno de Los Niños** (Children's Eternal Forest) offer misty cloud-forest experiences.

MONTEVERDE ➊ SAN JOSÉ

🚗 **4½ hours** Follow mountain roads back to the Interamericana, then pass Alajuela. 🚌 **4½ hours** Via the Santa Elena bus station.

5 DAYS

Irazú to Cartago
The Mystical Central Valley

This circuit is about sleeping volcanoes, strong coffee and the spiritual core of the country. Since most tourists head to the beaches, you'll enjoy markets and squares without the crowds.

PARQUE NACIONAL VOLCÁN IRAZÚ

SAN JOSÉ

CARTAGO

TURRIALBA

OROSI VALLEY

PACIFIC OCEAN

① Irazú (p98)

This trip begins with the biggest and baddest volcano in Costa Rica, Volcán Irazú, the indigenous name of which aptly translates to 'thunder-point.' Climb to its beautifully barren volcanic landscape on a clear day – you'll spy the waters of the Pacific and the Caribbean on the distant horizons. Get to the Parque Nacional Volcán Irazú early and head straight for the center of the crater.

VOLCÁN IRAZÚ ◉ TURRIALBA

🚗 **1½ hours** Much of the trip is navigated along twisting mountain roads. Follow Rte 230 to Rte 10. 🚌 **6½ hours** via Cartago.

② Turrialba (p101)

Just down the mountain is Turrialba, an excellent hub for two very different destinations. The first is **Monumento Nacional Arqueológico Guayabo**, the country's only significant archaeological site, where visitors marvel at petroglyphs and a system of aqueducts. Second is the white water of the **Río Pacuare**, one of the country's best white-water runs, and home to some of the most scenic rafting in Central America.

TURRIALBA ◉ OROSI VALLEY

🚗 **One hour** Retrace Rte 10 east and go south on Rte 224. Follow Rte 230 to Rte 10. 🚌 **Two hours** via Cartago.

③ Orosi Valley (p99)

Swing south into the heart of the **Orosi Valley**, where pastoral villages dot the endless rolling hills. Here, road trippers take the caffeinated (and newly paved!) 60km loop through terraced hills that harbor a perfect combination of the country's two most notable economic treasures: tourism and coffee. To see the valley's untamed side, navigate to **Parque Nacional Tapantí-Macizo Cerro de la Muerte**, a wild and rugged piece of country run through with hundreds of rivers and aflutter with rare high-altitude birds.

OROSI VALLEY ◉ CARTAGO

🚗 **30 minutes**. Travel Rte 224 to Cartago city center. 🚌 **40 minutes**.

④ Cartago (p97)

End this short circuit on a spiritual note at the country's grandest colonial temple, the **Basílica de Nuestra Señora de Los Ángeles** in Cartago, which is brilliantly white among the utilitarian concrete structures of this otherwise unexciting city.

CARTAGO ◉ SAN JOSÉ

🚗 **30 minutes**. Follow the Interamericana back to San José. 🚌 **45 minutes**, departing every 15 minutes until midnight.

Suspension bridge over Río Grande de Orosi, Orosi Valley (p99)

PHOTOGRAPHER: NEIL MCALLISTER / ALAMY ©

10 DAYS

Tamarindo to Parque Nacional Corcovado
Pacific Explorer

Take in the Península de Nicoya for Costa Rica's banner attractions, then cruise south along the central Pacific coast for beach towns, and scenic parks where wilderness and wildlife abound.

① Tamarindo (p183)

From San José head to Tamarindo and kick things off with a party in the Nicoya's famous resort town, which has loads of sunny beaches, sophisticated dining and a thumping club scene. The waves of **Playa Grande** are tame, but if you're in Costa Rica for a surf safari they're a good warm up.

TAMARINDO ⊙ MAL PAÍS

🚗 **Five hours.** Follow the Pacific shore on Rte 160. 🚌 **Ten to 12 hours** Via Puntarenas with ferry connection.

② Mal País (p199)

With loads of wildlife, big waves, untouched nature and top restaurants, Mal País is worth every minute of the long journey. This is a place where visitors limber up in the morning with yoga, hit the waves in the afternoon and tuck into sophisticated plates of Latin American fusion cuisine at night.

MAL PAÍS ⊙ QUEPOS

🚗 **Four hours.** Drive up the coast to get the car ferry at Paquera, then follow coastal highways. 🚌 ⛴ **Four to five hours** Transfer after the Paquera–Puntarenas ferry.

③ Quepos & Manuel Antonio (p222)

Continuing south, public transportation leads to Quepos, a tiny Tico town bordering a chart-topping national park. At **Parque Nacional Manuel Antonio**, monkeys descend from the treetops to frolic along the palm-fringed coastline.

QUEPOS ⊙ DOMINICAL

🚗 **45 minutes** Travel along Hwy 34, the Costanera Sur. 🚌 **Two to three hours**

④ Dominical (p231)

If you haven't had enough of the postcard-perfect Pacific coast, head further south by public transportation to Dominical to catch more waves, soak up more rays and delay your return home. You don't have to try hard to get stuck in this terminally chilled-out beach town where time passes to the rhythm of the crashing surf.

DOMINICAL ⊙ PUERTO JIMÉNEZ

🚗 **2½ hours** Travel along Hwy 34, the Costanera Sur, which joins the Interamericana (Hwy 2) at Palmar Norte, then take Rte 245. 🚌 **Six hours** Via San Isidro or Palmar Norte.

⑤ Puerto Jiménez (p258)

Further down the peninsula is the official gateway to Corcovado, Puerto Jiménez (or Port Jim, as it's affectionately called by locals). Kayak around the mangroves or soak up the charm of this tiny town. Don't forget to stock up on supplies for the big adventure ahead.

PUERTO JIMÉNEZ ⊙ PARQUE NACIONAL CORCOVADO

🚗 **2½ hours** 4WD essential. 🚌 **Three hours**

⑥ Parque Nacional Corcovado (p263)

The undisputed highlight of the Península de Osa is Parque Nacional Corcovado, one of the country's top wildlife-watching spots. It's worth spending a few days exploring the trails with a backpack of supplies – well-equipped travelers can trek right across the park.

PARQUE NACIONAL CORCOVADO ⊙ SAN JOSÉ

🚗 ✈ **3½ to four hours** Return to Puerto Jiménez via 4WD or bus, then fly to San José.

Playa Santa Teresa (p199), Mal País
PHOTOGRAPHER: PAUL KENNEDY / GETTY IMAGES ©

10 DAYS

Turrialba to Tortuguero
Mountain White Water & Caribbean Escape

Spanish gives way to English, and Latin beats change to Caribbean vibes as you explore the 'other Costa Rica.' Some of the more remote coastal villages are only accessible by boat.

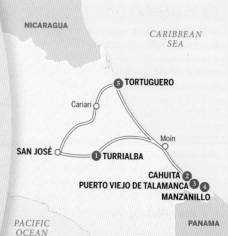

NICARAGUA

CARIBBEAN SEA

5 TORTUGUERO

Cariari

Moín

SAN JOSÉ

1 TURRIALBA

CAHUITA **2**
PUERTO VIEJO DE TALAMANCA **3** **4**
MANZANILLO

PACIFIC OCEAN

PANAMA

① Turrialba (p101)

Before you float in the turquoise waters of the Caribbean, why not squeal gleefully down Central America's best white water? Adventurers go crazy for the scenic, jungle-lined rushing water of the Río Pacuare, some of the most scenic rafting in this part of the world.

TURRIALBA ◯ CAHUITA

🚗 2½ hours Follow Hwy 10 to Hwy 32 to the coast, then take Hwy 36 along the coast. 🚌 Six hours Connect through San José

② Cahuita (p305)

Head back through San José and get on the first eastbound bus for Cahuita, capital of Afro-Caribbean culture and gateway to **Parque Nacional Cahuita**. Here, along the white-sand beaches, you can watch in awe as hungry mammals dash out of the forest to snack on scurrying crabs. Stick around Cahuita proper and get your fill of this mellow little village where the air is thick with reggae music and the scent of coconut rice.

CAHUITA ◯ PUERTO VIEJO DE TALAMANCA

🚗 20 minutes Take coastal Hwy 36 🚌 30 minutes to one hour Direct buses leave five times daily.

③ Puerto Viejo de Talamanca (p311)

It's just a quick bus or taxi ride south from Cahuita to Puerto Viejo de Talamanca, the Caribbean coast's center for surfing, nightlife and Rasta. Fronting the beach is Salsa Brava, an epic surf break that first put the town on the map. Serious surfers take note: this is Costa Rica's biggest wave. Even if you're not a proficient short-boarder, you can easily spend a few days here bar-hopping.

PUERTO VIEJO DE TALAMANCA ◯ MANZANILLO

🚗 20 mins 🚌 30 minutes

④ Manzanillo (p315)

After all the solid waves and late-night partying, rent a good old-fashioned push-bike and ride to nearby Manzanillo. This is the end of the line, where you can snorkel, kayak and take a hike in the **Refugio Nacional de Vida Silvestre Gandoca-Manzanillo**. The refuge has protected Manzanillo from developers and helped maintain its allure as an off-the-beaten-track destination, despite the newly paved road.

MANZANILLO ◯ TORTUGUERO

🚌 ⛴ 2½ hours Connect to water taxis in Puerto Viejo and transfer in Moín.

⑤ Tortuguero (p296)

For the adventurous, head north to grab a boat from Moín and travel the canal-lined coast to the village of Tortuguero, where you can watch nesting green and leather-back turtles. You can also arrange a canoe trip through the mangrove-lined canals of Parque Nacional Tortuguero, Costa Rica's mini-Amazon.

TORTUGUERO ◯ SAN JOSÉ

⛴ 🚌 Four to five hours Travel to Cariari via river, then take a bus from Cariari to San José.

Eating out in Puerto Viejo de Talamanca (p311)
PHOTOGRAPHER: CHRISTER FREDRIKSSON / GETTY IMAGES ©

2 WEEKS

The Costa Rica Circuit
The Whole Enchilada

This two-week trip around Costa Rica includes all the bells and whistles – volcanoes, waterfalls, surf towns and high mountain hikes.

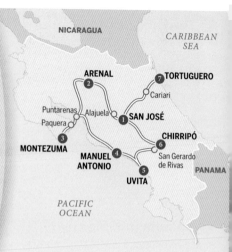

1 San José (p62)

Since you'll almost certainly fly in to San José, make the most of it, following highlights from the first itinerary and getting into the groove of Latin American life. The country's best sights lie outside the city's borders, but you'd be remiss to not spend an afternoon hanging out in Chepe.

SAN JOSÉ ➲ ARENAL

🚗 3½ hours Along the Interamericana, via Alajuela. 🚌 4½ hours Auto-Transportes San José–San Carlos Centro arrive at La Fortuna's Comercial Adifort bus terminal.

2 Arenal (p125)

With a more leisurely agenda, it's possible to venture a little deeper onto **Volcán Arenal**, with longer hikes and more soaking at **Tabacón Hot Springs** and a side trip to **La Cararata de Fortuna**, a jungle waterfall. Come down off the mountain and travel across the Laguna de Arenal.

ARENAL ➲ MONTEZUMA

🚗 Four hours Via Hwy 18 and Hwy 21 🚌 Six hours Bus to Puntarenas (three to four hours), take the ferry Paquera and another short bus ride.

3 Montezuma (p194)

Mingle with backpackers, ecotourists and surf bums in this far-flung alternative beach town. It has great beaches, scenic waterfalls and a terminally laid-back ethos. The nearby **Isla Cabo Blanco** is an excellent side trip.

MONTEZUMA ➲ MANUEL ANTONIO

🚗 Three hours Via the Paquera–Puntarenas ferry and coastal highway 🚌 Five hours Including ferry transfer.

4 Manuel Antonio (p225)

Sure, this is no secret destination – the place is loaded with visitors – but how can you blame the crowd when it is so beautiful? A place of swaying palms, playful monkeys, sparkling blue water and great bird watching; this is Costa Rica at its best.

Boat tour (p304), Parque Nacional Tortuguero

UVITA ○ CHIRRIPÓ

🚗 **One hour** Travel to San Gerardo de Rivas, the gateway village to Chirripó. 🚌 **Three hours** Change buses in San Isidro and head up the mountain.

⑥ Chirripó (p271)

Tired of the life at the beach? Get high on Chirripó, one of the highest peaks in Central America and worth every bit of bad road to get there. A two-day excursion atop the mountain presents hikers with an adventure that is wholly different from the coastal charms, and a once-in-a-lifetime sunrise.

CHIRRIPÓ ○ TORTUGUERO

🚗 ⛵ **4½ hours** Drive via the Interamericana back to San José, then to Cariari. From here, the rest of the journey is by boat.

MANUEL ANTONIO ○ UVITA

🚗 **One hour** Via the Costanera Sur. 🚌 **1½ hours** Along the coast.

⑤ Uvita (p235)

Recently connected to the rest of the world via the Costanera Sur, Uvita is coming alive as a central Pacific destination in its own right. It has passable surfing, a couple of great hostels and long deserted beaches in the **Parque Nacional Marino Ballena**, plus easy connections to Costa Rica's other outdoor hot spots.

⑦ Tortuguero (p296)

Sweep down navigable rainforest canals and into one of the country's great parks for the final stop. 'Central America's Amazon' is a memorable way to end a visit of breathtaking biodiversity.

TORTUGUERO ○ SAN JOSÉ

⛵ 🚌 **Four to five hours** Travel to Cariari via river, then take a bus from Cariari to San José.

Costa Rica Month by Month

Top Events

 Las Fiestas de Palmares,
January

 Feria de la Mascarada,
March

 Día de los Muertos,
November

 Independence Day,
September

 Dia de Juan Santamaria,
April

 ## January

Every year opens with a rush of visitors, as North American and domestic tourists flood beach towns to celebrate. January weather is ideal, with dry days and only occasional afternoon showers.

Fiesta de Santa Cruz

Held in Santa Cruz in mid-January, this festival centers around a rodeo and bullfights. It also includes the requisite religious procession, music, dances and a beauty pageant.

Las Fiestas de Palmares

(www.fiestaspalmares.com) Ten days of beer drinking, horse shows and other carnival events take over the tiny town of Palmares in mid-January. There's also a running of the bulls.

Fiesta de los Diablitos

Held from December 31 to January 2 in Boruca; February 5 to 8 in Curré. Men wear carved wooden devil masks and burlap sacks and, after roaming from house to house for free booze, re-enact the fight between the indigenous people and the Spanish. Spoiler alert: in this one, the Spanish lose.

 ## February

February is a perfect month to visit, with ideal weather and no holiday surcharges. The skies above the Nicoya are particularly clear, and it is the peak of the turtle nesting season.

Fiesta Cívica de Liberia

A beauty pageant and carnival atmosphere enlivens Liberia at the end of February.

(left) Traditional dancing, Independence Day
PHOTOGRAPHER: MEGAPRESS / ALAMY ©

March

Excellent weather continues through the early part of March. Prices shoot up at the end of the month if it corresponds with Semana Santa, the week leading up to Easter, and North American spring break.

 ### Feria de la Mascarada

Every March the little town of Barva, just north of San José, hosts the famous Feria de la Mascarada, a tradition with roots in the colonial era. People don massive colorful masks (some weigh up to 20kg), and gather to dance and parade around the town square. Demons and devils are frequent subjects, but celebrities and politicians also figure in the mix (you haven't lived until you've seen a 6m-tall Celia Cruz). The festival is usually held during the last week of the month, but dates vary from one year to the next; inquire locally.

 ### Envision Festival

(www.envisionfestival.com) Held in Dominical during the first week of March, this is a festival with a new age bent, bringing together fire dancers, yoga and jam bands.

 ### Día del Boyero

On the second Sunday in March a colorful parade is held in Escazú. It honors oxcart drivers and includes a blessing of the animals.

South Caribbean Music and Arts Festival

Manzanillo grooves to Soca and steel drums during this annual festival in the first week of March, which usually brings in some international heavy weights. Playa Chiquita in Limón and Manzanillo are usually the center of the action, with outdoor stages and a good late-night scene.

 ### Festival Imperial

(www.festivalimperial.com) In late March, 30,000 music fans fill the La Guácima outdoor venue in Alajuela, north of San José, for the country's biggest rock festival. Performers recently included TV On the Radio, Skrillex, Björk, LMFAO and The Flaming Lips.

April

Easter, and the preceding week, Semana Santa, can fall early in April, which makes beaches crowded and prices spike. Nicoya and Guanacaste are very dry and hot, with very little rain.

 ### Día de Juan Santamaría

Commemorating Costa Rica's national hero who died in battle against William Walker's troops in 1856, this week-long celebration in Alajuela includes parades, concerts and dances.

May

Wetter weather begins to sweep across the country in May, which begins the county's low-season prices. Good bargains and reasonably good weather make it an excellent season for budget travel.

 ### San Isidro Labrador's Day

Held in San Isidro de el General on May 15, this is one of the nation's largest agricultural fairs, and an opportunity to taste the bounty of the surrounding region.

June

The Pacific coast gets fairly wet during June, though this makes for good surfing swells. The beginning of the so-called 'green season' (tourist-office lingo for rainy season) means lots of discount rates.

 ### Día de San Pedro & San Pablo

Celebrations and religious processions are held in villages of the same name on June 29.

July

July is mostly wet, particularly on the Caribbean coast, but the month also occasionally enjoys a brief dry period that Ticos call *veranillo* (summer). Expect rain, particularly late in the day.

Fiesta de la Virgen del Mar

Held in mid-July, the Festival of the Virgin of the Sea involves colorful, brightly lit regattas and boat parades in Puntarenas and Playa del Coco. It is an excellent time to visit Puntarenas, as the port city really puts on a pretty ceremony.

Día de Guanacaste

This festival on July 25 celebrates the annexation of Guanacaste from Nicaragua with street vendors and lots of beer. There's also a rodeo in Santa Cruz, though this is similar to other rodeos in the country where brave (often tipsy) cowboys jump into a ring to get chased by a bull.

August

The middle of the rainy season doesn't mean that mornings aren't bright and sunny, but travelers who don't mind a bit of rain will find great deals on hotels and tour packages. This is a great month if you're visiting to surf big waves.

La Virgen de los Ángeles

The patron saint is celebrated with an important religious procession from San José to Cartago on August 2. Carago's gleaming white basilica is at the center of the action as sober ceremonies give way to nocturnal celebration.

September

The Península de Osa gets utterly soaked during September. This is the heart of the rainy season – Ticos refer to it as the *temporales del Pacífico*. It is the cheapest time of year to visit the Pacific side.

Independence Day

With events all over the country, Costa Rica's Independence Day is a fun party. The center of the action is the relay race that passes a 'Freedom Torch' from Guatemala to Costa Rica. The torch arrives at Cartago in the evening of the 14th, when the nation breaks into the national anthem.

October

Many roads become impassable as rivers swell and rain continues to fall in October, one of the wettest months in Costa Rica. Many of the lodges and tour operators are closed until November.

Día de la Raza

Columbus' historic landing on Isla Uvita has traditionally

inspired a small carnival, with street parades, live music and dancing. The party was on hiatus for a few years but returned in 2009 to a small, but enthusiastic turnout. Inquire locally – and during this time, book hotels in advance. Held on October 12.

Limón Carnival

Horsemen, beauty queens and revelers take to the streets during this week-long celebration of Columbus Day. Of course, being on Costa Rica's east coast, the festival has a distinctly Caribbean beat.

 # November

The weather can go either way in November. Some years it dries up a bit, others years see an extension of rain from El Niño. Access to Parque Nacional Corcovado is very difficult after several continuous months of rain, though by the month's end the skies clear up.

Día de los Muertos

On All Soul's Day (November 2), families visit graveyards and hold religious parades in honor of the dead – a lovely and picturesque festival.

 # December

Although the beginning of the month, with its clearer skies and relatively uncrowded attractions, is a great time to visit Costa Rica, things really ramp up toward Christmas, when travelers need to make reservations long in advance.

Las Fiestas de Zapote

This week-long celebration of all things Costa Rican (namely rodeos, cowboys, carnival rides, fried food and booze) annually draws in thousands of Ticos to the bullring in the suburb of Zapote, southeast of San José. It's worth visiting if you're in the area between Christmas and New Year's Eve.

Far left: Horse riders, Fiesta Cívica de Liberia **Left:** Dancer in traditional Guanacaste costume

What's New

For this edition of Discover Costa Rica, our authors have hunted down the fresh, the transformed, the hot and the happening. These are some of our favorites. For up-to-the-minute reviews and recommendations, see lonelyplanet.com/costarica.

1 COSTARICAPALOOZA
The Festival Imperial music festival started back up in March 2012 after a four-year hiatus, featuring headliners including The Flaming Lips, Björk and Thievery Corporation (p43).

2 OSA WILD
This new, sustainably run, community-oriented tour agency gives travelers a chance to see the undiscovered Península de Osa, by arranging family stays, local food tours and scientifically savvy visits to Parque Nacional Corcovado (p258).

3 SURFING SAFARIS
Dominical has long been known as a surfing paradise, but the disorienting number of surf schools and instructors is a bit overwhelming. We spent a couple of weeks shredding waves with a number of instructors to recommend the best (p232).

4 STADIUM KICKOFF
With retractable roof and seating capacity for 35,000, the revamped National Stadium will primarily host soccer matches, but also heavy hitters such as Pearl Jam, who played here on their 20th-anniversary tour (p63).

5 FLUTTERBY HOUSE
A few steps from the remote beaches of Parque Nacional Marino Ballena, this female-owned and operated hostel espouses visionary sustainability practices, has a couple of treehouses and is a hosteller's dream come true (p236).

6 MUSEO DE ARTE COSTARRICENSE
A complete renovation has made this museum sparkle. The highlight, of course, is the rotating exhibition of Costa Rican art, but another is the room-sized wraparound bas-relief depicting the country's history. (☎ 2256-1281; www.musarco.go.cr; east entrance of La Sabana; ☉ 9am-4pm Tue-Sun)

7 ROCK CLIMBING IN CACHI
One of the more easily accessible spots for sport climbing is gaining popularity in the Orosi Valley. The basalt wall at Escalada Cachi has more than a dozen routes ranging in difficulty. (☎ 8867-8259, 2577-1974; rockclimbingcachi@hotmail.com; 2km from fork; ☉ 8am-4pm Sat & Sun, by appointment only Mon-Fri)

8 PAPAYA
The tapas and the view at Papaya – Moana Lodge's brand-new restaurant, cantilevered high above the Mal País coast – are both magnificent (p202).

9 HOT SPRINGS RÍO NEGRO
All natural and set in a meandering pocket of dry forest along the river near the Parque Nacional Rincon de la Valle, Hot Springs Río Negro is our favorite hot spring in the country (p161).

10 VILLA DEEVENA
In Playa Negra, Villa Deevena is brand new and rocking with an incredible French kitchen. It makes its own goat cheese on its chef-operated dairy in the nearby hills (p189).

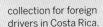

Get Inspired

 Books

- **Green Phoenix** (William Allen) Inspiring account of rainforest conservation in Guanacaste.

- **In the Rainforest: Report from a Strange, Beautiful World** (Catherine Caulfield) A riveting look at protecting the Osa rainforest.

- **Around the Edge** (Peter Ford) A travelogue about the Caribbean coast from Belize to Panama.

- **Green Dreams: Travels in Central America** (Stephen Benz) Analysis of the effect of visitors on the region and its people.

 Films

- **Agua Fría de Mar** (Cold Water of the Sea) A young couple and a girl from contrasting social backgrounds spend Christmas along the Pacific coast.

- **Jurassic Park** Michael Crichton's modern classic about the genetic resurrection of dinosaurs.

- **1492: Conquest of Paradise** Ridley Scott's epic re-enactment of Columbus' voyage to the New World.

- **The Blue Butterfly** The true story of a terminally ill boy in search of the blue morpho.

 Music

- **Sí San José** (Various Artists; 2011) A collaboration between a WFMU engineer and some of Costa Rica's hippest DIY indie rock acts.

- **Coleccion Original RCA** (Chavela Vargas; 2011) This 1946 reissue of a Costa Rican–born singer features hauntingly beautiful folk ballads.

- **Un Día Lejano** (Malpaís; 2009) These innovating and enduring rockers mix calypso, jazz and Latin American balladry.

- **La Fiesta** (Taboga Band; 1979) A classic jazz-influenced salsa and merengue record.

 Websites

- **Costa Rica Tourism Board** (www.visitcostarica.com) Website of the Instituto Costarricense de Turismo (ICT).

- **Maptak** (www.maptak.com) Essential map collection for foreign drivers in Costa Rica.

- **Guías Costa Rica** (www.guiascostarica.com) Links for entertainment, health and government websites.

Short on time?

This list will give you an instant insight into the country.

Read *Naturalist in Costa Rica* Dr Skutch weaves his philosophies into beautiful descriptions of flora and fauna in this enchanting memoir and natural-history guide.

Watch *Endless Summer II* Surfers Pat O'Connell and Robert 'Wingnut' Weaver ride Costa Rica's magical waves.

Listen *Calypsos: Afro-Limonese Music From Costa Rica* (Various) This raucous collection captures the heart of Costa Rica's Afro-Caribbean folk scene, including joyful street performers.

Log on *Tico Times* (www.ticotimes.net)

Surfer, Playa El Carmen (p199)
PHOTOGRAPHER: CHRISTIAN ASLUND / GETTY IMAGES ©

Need to Know

Money
Colones (₡) and US dollars ($)

Language
English is spoken in tourist areas and along the Caribbean coast, but Spanish prevails elsewhere.

ATMs
Widely available; machines dispense both colones and US dollars.

Credit Cards
Visa and Mastercard widely accepted, others less so.

Visas
No visa required for US, Canadian, Australian, New Zealand and many European citizens. Tourist cards (typically valid for 90 days) are issued on inbound flights or by airport immigration.

Wi-Fi
Although slow, Wi-Fi is increasingly common at restaurants and mid- to high-end accommodations.

Driving
Drive on the right; steering wheel is on the left.

Tipping
Only tip for exceptional service at top-end restaurants and hotels.

When to Go

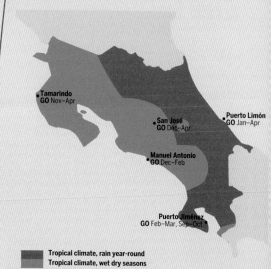

Tamarindo
GO Nov–Apr

Puerto Limón
GO Jan–Apr

San José
GO Dec–Apr

Manuel Antonio
GO Dec–Feb

Puerto Jiménez
GO Feb–Mar, Sep–Oct

Tropical climate, rain year-round
Tropical climate, wet dry seasons

High Season
(Dec–Apr)
○ Domestic tourists fill beach towns.

○ Rates are highest at Christmas, New Year and the week before Easter.

○ Book accommodations well in advance; some enforce two- or three-day stays.

Shoulder
(May–Jul, Nov)
○ Rain picks up and the stream of tourists tapers off.

○ Roads are muddy, making off-the-beaten-track travel challenging.

Low Season
(Aug–Oct)
○ Rain is heaviest, but brings swells to the Pacific and the best surfing conditions.

○ Rural roads can be impassable due to river crossings.

Advance Planning

○ **Two months before** Make accommodations reservations in advance if you're traveling during Semana Santa (the week before Easter) or the Christmas holiday season.

○ **One month before** Book car rental online before your departure so you can pick up your car at the airport and make the most of your time in Costa Rica.

Your Daily Budget

Budget less than $40

- Dorm beds: $8–15
- Eat at ubiquitous *sodas* (lunch counters) and shop from local markets, self-cater
- Go on DIY hikes without a guide
- Travel via local bus

Midrange $40–100

- Basic room with private bathroom: $20–30
- Meal at restaurants geared toward travelers: $5–10
- Travel on efficient 1st-class bus company like Interbus.

Top End more than $100

- Luxurious beachside lodges and boutique hotels start from $80
- Dine at international fusion restaurants
- Hire guides for wildlife-watching excursions
- Take short flights and rent a 4WD vehicle for local travel.

Exchange Rates

Australia	A$1	₡523
Canada	C$1	₡506
Europe	€1	₡673
Japan	¥100	₡612
Mexico	MXN10	₡396
New Zealand	NZ$	₡405
UK	£1	₡803
US	$1	₡506

For current exchange rates see www.xe.com.

What to Bring

- **Insect repellent** Make sure it contains DEET, especially if you're planning jungle adventures.
- **Refillable water bottle** The water is safe to drink from the tap and a refillable bottle helps diminish the impact to this sensitive environment.
- **Spanish phrasebook** Learning a little of the local lingo makes all the difference.
- **Sunblock** Take precautions as you don't want to get cooked by the tropical sun.
- **Proper footwear** Bring along a pair of waterproof sandals and sturdy hiking shoes.
- **Binoculars** These are requisite for proper bird-watching – a field guide also helps.
- **Miscellaneous necessities** Flashlight (torch), poncho, padlock, alarm clock.

Arriving in Costa Rica

Aeropuerto Internacional Juan Santamaria

Bus $0.75; Alajuela–San José buses run frequently and will drop you anywhere along Paseo Colón

Taxis $15–20; depart from an official stand; it's about 20 minutes to the city

Rental Car Many rental-car agencies have desks in the airport

Getting Around

- **Air** Domestic airlines and private charters can help you squeeze the most into your travels.
- **Bus** Depending on your desired level of comfort, you can choose from air-conditioned private shuttles and more economical local coaches.
- **Car** Renting a car is the best way to explore Costa Rica at your own pace though a 4WD is necessary for all but the most heavily touristed areas.
- **Taxi** In San José as well as in rural areas, a taxi is worth the cash if you don't have time to waste.

Accommodations

- **B&Bs** Midrange to top-end affairs typically run by North American and European expats.
- **Hostels** Good-value accommodations with the needs of the modern backpacker in mind.
- **Hotels** Highly variable in range, including everything from budget crash pads to lavish five-star resorts.

Be Forewarned

- **Climate** Tropical sun along the coasts, frequent precipitation in the rainforests and evening chills at high altitude – be prepared with the proper attire.
- **Rental-car fees** Mandatory national insurance is a hidden cost of car rental and can double the rate quoted online.

San José

San José might not be so pretty at first glance, but once you get the hang of it, Chepe (as San José is affectionately known) quickly reveals its charms. Soon you'll see past the concrete structures, clogged pedestrian arcades and fast-food monstrosities dominating its cityscape. Soon you'll be making sport out of dodging homicidal drivers, evading pickpockets and trying to tune out the cacophony of honking horns and ear-splitting reggaetón. Then, and only then, will Chepe's charms become evident.

In the city's historic neighborhoods, colonial mansions have been converted into contemporary art galleries, refined international restaurants and boutique hotels. Colorfully arresting murals and hipster buskers pop up on the most unexpected corners. And in the city's museums of gold and jade and national history, lie all the layers of indigenous heritage, colonial past and great minds that have made Costa Rica the environmental champion and military-free country we love today.

Teatro Nacional (p63)
RICHARD CUMMINS / GETTY IMAGES ©

Hotel Grano de Oro (p67)
LEE FOSTER ©

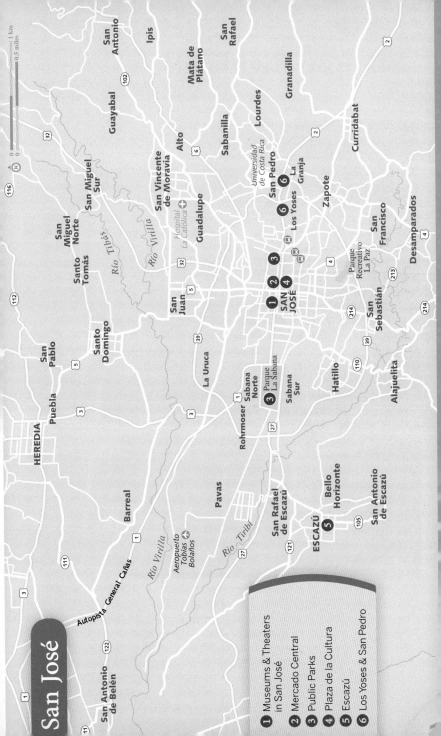

San José

Map Scale
- 1 km
- 0.5 miles

Legend
1. Museums & Theaters in San José
2. Mercado Central
3. Public Parks
4. Plaza de la Cultura
5. Escazú
6. Los Yoses & San Pedro

San José Highlights

① Museums & Theaters in San José

The cultural heart of Costa Rica lies within the San José's museums and theaters. Venues such as the Teatro Nacional (p70) and the Museo de Oro Precolombino y Numismática (p63) provide rich context for reflection.

Above: Teatro Nacional; Top right: Museo de Jade (p66), Bottom right: Pre-Columbian sculpture, Museo Nacional de Costa Rica (p66)

Need to Know

SCHEDULING San José's museums are a short stroll from one another and are an ideal way to spend your day of arrival or departure **For further coverage, see p63**

Museums & Theaters in San José Don't Miss List

BY MARIA AMALIA, MARKETING DIRECTOR FOR THE COSTA RICA TOURISM BOARD (INSTITUTO COSTARRICENSE DE TURISMO; ICT)

1 TEATRO NACIONAL

The stately national theater (p63) is a late-19th-century neoclassical architectural masterpiece. It houses a series of lavish paintings that provide visual commentary on Costa Rica's rural heritage. The theater hosts music performances and other major events.

2 MUSEO DE ORO PRECOLOMBINO Y NUMISMÁTICA

This three-in-one museum (p63) showcases a collection of pre-Columbian gold containing hand-tooled ornaments dating back to AD 400. The second part of the museum details the history of Costa Rican currency, while the third features a changing selection of temporary exhibitions.

3 MUSEO DE JADE

The world's largest collection of jade (p66) has display cases full of elaborate carvings depicting everything from frogs and serpents to shamans and fertility goddesses. The craftsmanship is superb, and the pieces are in a fine state of conservation.

4 MUSEO NACIONAL DE COSTA RICA

Costa Rica's most significant historical museum (p66) holds a collection of metates (grinding stones), an excellent gold collection, and an exhibit dedicated to Nobel Peace Prize winner Óscar Arias.

5 MUSEO DE ARTE Y DISEÑO CONTEMPORÁNEO

There's no better place to get a sense of the nation's artistic and cultural past, present and future than this museum's collection of works (p66) by contemporary Costa Rican and Latin American artists.

Mercado Central

San José's shopping action is focused on its central market (p71), a sprawling complex of stalls selling a wild mix of produce, from butchered meats to secondhand clothes and tourist souvenirs. You'll need good bargaining skills to keep the prices low – fortunately, haggling in Spanish with vendors is half the fun.

Public Parks

San José may be lacking in tree-lined promenades, but there is no shortage of leafy green parks. Two of the capital's best escapes are Parque Nacional (p60), which is studded with myriad monuments devoted to key figures in Latin American history, and Parque Metropolitano La Sabana (p63), a perfect place for a quiet stroll, a relaxed jog or a picnic with the family. Parque Metropolitano La Sabana

JESUS OCHOA ©

Plaza de la Cultura

JESUS OCHOA ©

Both the spiritual and the physical heart of the city, the Plaza de la Cultura (p63) is little more than a slab of concrete in the middle of downtown. But for the residents of San José, this is the city's greatest public space for gathering with friends and family, and indulging in a bout of people-watching. Gran Hotel Costa Rica (p68)

DAVID SANGER PHOTOGRAPHY / ALAMY ©

Escazú

A trendy suburb that is often associated with wealth and status, Escazú (p74) makes for a pleasant day trip from the capital proper. As an alternative to the urban hustle and bustle, this is where you can also bed down and dine out in relative peace and comfort. It also hosts excellent farmers markets. Hotel pool, Escazú

Los Yoses & San Pedro

Two more San José suburbs that definitely merit a glimpse are Los Yoses and San Pedro (p73), each with their own distinct character. Los Yoses is prim and proper, offering Escazú a run for its money, while the university district of San Pedro has noticeably more bohemian leanings. *Carreta* (painted oxcart)

San José's Best...

Splurges

○ **Hotel Grano de Oro**
(p67) Bed down in an
early-20th-century
'Tropical Victorian' mansion
complete with period
furniture.

○ **Restaurante Grano
de Oro** (p67) Housed
in a historic mansion,
this formal dining hall is
bedecked with fresh flowers
and wins raves for dressing
out duck and game dishes
with elegant Latin American
touches.

Shopping

○ **Mercado Central** (p70)
A traditional Latin American
shopping extravaganza
makes for fun and chaotic
browsing.

○ **Galería Namu** (p70) A
fair-trade gallery showcasing
indigenous artwork.
Proceeds go directly to
indigenous artists. The boldly
shaped tribal masks make a
particularly lovely souvenir.

○ **Biesanz Woodworks** (p75)
No need to worry about the
origin of the pieces here, this
artisan shop is arguably the
country's best woodcrafting
studio.

Entertainment

○ **Teatro Nacional** (p70)
Catch a performance in the
city's most historic theater,
which hosts the country's
finest high-culture offerings.

○ **Jazz Café** (p74) This
intimate club is a buzzing
nightspot in the San Pedro
neighborhood, and is
unmatched for its calendar
of live jazz, folk and rock
performances.

○ **Centro Comercial El
Pueblo** (p70) A complex
of dozens of bars and
clubs that attracts serious
revellers. Don't show up
early: the action gets started
well after midnight.

Eats

○ **Park Café** (p69) Michelin-starred chef Richard Neat offers visionary dishes in his romantic, atmospheric dining room.

○ **La Esquina de Buenos Aires** (p68) Crisp linens, candles and old tango enliven Costa Rica's finest steakhouse.

○ **Restaurante Tin-Jo** (p69) A pan-Asian menu and fun atmosphere make this one of Chepe's most fun date spots.

○ **Restaurant Whapin** (p73) The smell of coconut-laced Caribbean gumbos fills this Rasta-colored joint.

Need to Know

ADVANCE PLANNING

○ **One month before** Reserve car rental. Travelers touching down at Aeropuerto Internacional Juan Santamaría will be taken to their car via shuttle from the airport.

○ **Two weeks before** Scan listings and book tickets for the Teatro Nacional and Jazz Café.

RESOURCES

○ **Instituto Costarricense de Turismo** Costa Rica's main tourism board (p71).

○ **Tico Times** (www.ticotimes.net)

GETTING AROUND

○ **Air** San José is the gateway to Costa Rica for the majority of international arrivals. Aeropuerto Internacional Juan Santamaría is the main airport.

○ **Bus** The intercity bus network is comprehensive, cheap and relatively reliable.

○ **Taxi** Taxis are a safe and convenient way to move around quickly, especially at night.

○ **Walking** The compact city center is perfect for a leisurely stroll during the day.

BE FOREWARNED

○ **Crime** San José is a big city with rough areas like any other, so exercise a measure of street sense. Unsavory characters know rental cars at sight. Park in a secured lot and leave no valuables in the car.

○ **Traffic** It's not recommended you drive in the city proper. Dense traffic and a lack of public parking can quickly add up to a serious headache.

VITAL STATISTICS

○ **Area** 2366 sq km

○ **Population** City 291,100, Greater Metro Area more than 1.5 million

○ **Best time to visit** Día del Boyero (mid-March), Las Fiestas de Zapote (late December)

EMERGENCY NUMBERS

○ **Emergency** ✆911

○ **Fire** ✆118

○ **Police** ✆117

○ **Red Cross** ✆128, 2542-5000

○ **Traffic Police** ✆2222-9330

Left: Decorated carriage wheel;
Above: Museo Nacional de Costa Rica (p66).
(LEFT) BILL BACHMANN / GETTY IMAGES ©; (ABOVE) JESUS OCHOA ©

San José Walking Tour

Get to know the heart of Costa Rica's capital with this short stroll through the compact city center.

WALK FACTS
- **Start** Parque Nacional
- **Finish** Mercado Central
- **Distance** 2.5km
- **Duration** Four hours

❶ Parque Nacional

Begin at the relaxed green gem at the center of the city, the shaded Parque Nacional, where lovers stroll and old men talk politics under the watchful statues of Latin American cultural and political heroes.

❷ Museo de Arte y Diseño Contemporáneo

Although the historic National Liquor Factory was once housed here, these days the strongest stuff the building holds is the contemporary works of Costa Rican, Central American and South American artists.

❸ Museo de Jade

With the world's largest collection of precious jade, this museum's multicultural and well-preserved relics warrant an hour's worth of browsing. Jade was the most valuable trading commodity among pre-Columbian cultures, and Costa Rica's location at the center of Central America has resulted in an excellent collection.

❹ Galería Namu

If you're not planning on a deep exploration of Costa Rica's indigenous areas, stop at this fair-trade gallery and boutique for fine examples of Boruca masks, baskets, Guaymí dolls and carvings.

5 Parque Morazán

Although this park has a bit of an unsavory history as the turf of prostitutes, it's inching away from its seedy past and offers shaded benches that are perfect for rest. At the the center is the Templo de Música, a concrete bandstand that is the unofficial symbol of San José.

6 7th Street Books

English-reading visitors to the country should drop into this excellent bookstore to stock up on maps, naturalist guides and translated works by Costa Rican writers. This is the place to load up on local beach reading.

7 Plaza de la Cultura

Clowns, ice-cream vendors and lots of foot traffic make this plaza buzz with life. Sitting here for a few moments makes for excellent people-watching as suits, shoppers, tourists and dolled-up working girls whisk by.

8 Teatro Nacional

Beethoven and Calderón de la Barca (a 17th-century Spanish dramatist) peek out from the bold, gracefully columned neoclassical facade of this iconic landmark. If you catch it during opening hours, peek inside the lavish marble lobby, making sure not to miss *Alegoría al café y el banano*, an idyllic canvas portraying coffee and banana harvests that came from Italy and which once graced a Costa Rican bank note.

9 Mercado Central

If all the walking has worked up an appetite, sniff around in the Mercado Central, the exciting, chaotic, sometimes overwhelming hub of the city's commercial life. You can pick up just about anything here (bananas by the kilo, imported trinkets by the truckful) but before you start browsing make your way to one of the popular *sodas* (lunch counters) for cheap, fresh and delicious home cooking.

San José In...

ONE DAY

First, visit the city's most beautiful building, the 19th-century **Teatro Nacional**. After coffee at the theater's atmospheric cafe, head to the **Museo de Oro Precolombino y Numismática** to peruse its trove of pre-Columbian gold treasures. Stroll through **Parque Morazán** to the **Museo de Arte y Diseño Contemporáneo**, Central America's most prominent contemporary arts institution. Take lunch on the terrace of **Kalú Café & Food Shop**. Afterwards, browse the shops of historic **Barrio Amón**.

TWO DAYS

Start at the **Museo Nacional de Costa Rica**, then explore the neighborhood markets for handicrafts. Go west on Av Central to the **Catedral Metropolitana**, where *josefinos* (inhabitants of San José) pack the pews for mass. Next, head northwest to the **Mercado Central** to shop for Costa Rican coffee, cigars and cheap eats. In the evening venture east to **Los Yoses** and **San Pedro**, home to some of San José's best eateries and bars, and the city's most esteemed live-music venue, the **Jazz Café**.

Discover San José

At a Glance

○ **San José** Costa Rica's capital might not wow you, but there's plenty to love beneath the surface.

○ **Los Yoses** (p73) Modernist structures, historic inns and chilled-out eateries.

○ **San Pedro** (p73) A bohemian atmosphere and cool local shops.

○ **Escazú** (p73) This trendy neighborhood is complete with boutiques and fine dining.

Plaza de la Cultura (p63)
JESÚS OCHOA ©

SAN JOSÉ

San José's center is a grid with avenidas running east to west and calles running north to south. Av Central is the nucleus of the downtown area and is a pedestrian mall between calles 6 and 9.

◉ Sights

PARQUE ESPAÑA   Park
(Map p68; Avs 3 & 7 btwn Calles 9 & 11) Surrounded by heavy traffic and flanked by the Museo de Arte y Diseño Contemporaneo (MADC) and the Museo de Jade, Parque España may be small, but it becomes a riot of birdsong every day at sunset when the local avian population comes in to roost. In addition to being a good spot for a shady break, the park is home to an ornate statue of Christopher Columbus that was given to the people of Costa Rica in 2002 by his descendants, commemorating the quincentennial of the explorer's landing in Puerto Limón.

Just west of Parque España stands the recently remodeled Edificio Metálico, a century-old, two-story metal building that was prefabricated in Belgium. The structure was shipped piece by piece to San José and today it functions as a school and local landmark. On the Parque España's northeast corner is the Casa Amarilla, an elegant colonial-style house that is home to the Ministry of Foreign Affairs (closed to the public). The glorious ceiba tree in front was planted by John F Kennedy during his 1963 visit to Costa Rica. If you walk around to the property's northeast corner, you can see a graffiti-covered slab of the Berlin Wall standing in the rear garden.

PLAZA DE LA CULTURA Plaza
(Map p68; Avs Central & 2 btwn Calles 3 & 5) For many Ticos, Costa Rica begins here. This architecturally unremarkable concrete plaza in the heart of downtown is packed with locals slurping ice-cream cones and admiring the gamut of San José street life: juggling clowns, itinerant vendors and cruising teenagers.

TEATRO NACIONAL Notable Building
(Map p68; 2221-5341; www.teatronacional.go.cr; Av 2 btwn Calles 3 & 5; admission US$7; 9am-4pm Tue-Sun) On the southern side of the Plaza de la Cultura resides the Teatro Nacional, San José's most revered public building. Constructed in 1897, it features a columned neoclassical facade that is flanked by statues of Beethoven and Calderón de la Barca. The lavish marble lobby and auditorium are lined with paintings depicting various facets of 19th-century life. The most famous is *Alegoría al café y el banano*, an idyllic canvas showing coffee and banana harvests. The painting was produced in Italy and shipped to Costa Rica for installation in the theater, and the image was reproduced on the old ₡5 note (now out of circulation). It is clear that the painter never witnessed a banana harvest because of the way the man in the center is awkwardly grasping a bunch (actual banana workers hoist the stems onto their shoulders).

PARQUE MORAZÁN Park
(Map p68; Avs 3 & 5 btwn Calles 5 & 9) To the southwest of the Parque España is Parque Morazán, named for Francisco Morazán, the 19th-century general who attempted to unite the Central American nations under a single flag. Once a notorious center of prostitution, the park is now beautifully illuminated in the evenings.

PARQUE METROPOLITANO LA SABANA Park
(Off Map p64) Known simply as Parque La Sabana, this 72-hectare park was once the site of the country's main airport.

If You Like...
Theaters

If you like the Teatro Nacional, we think you'll like these other theaters in San José:

1 **AUDITORIO NACIONAL**
(Map p64; 2256-5876; www.museocr.com; Museo de los Niños, Calle 4 north of Av 9) A grand stage for concerts, dance, theater and plays.

2 **LITTLE THEATRE GROUP**
(8858-1446; www.littletheatregroup.org) This English-language performance troupe has been around since the 1950s.

3 **TEATRO LA MÁSCARA**
(Map p68; 2222-4574; Calle 13 btwn Avs 2 & 6) Dance performances as well as repertory theater.

4 **TEATRO MELICO SALAZAR**
(Map p68; 2233-5424; www.teatromelico.go.cr; Av 2 btwn Calles Central & 2) The restored 1920s theater has regular fine-arts performances.

Today it holds two museums, a lagoon and sports facilities. It is also home to the **Estadio Nacional de Costa Rica** (Costa Rica National Stadium; 2284-8700; Parque Metropolitano La Sabana), where major soccer matches are played.

Museums

MUSEO DE ORO PRECOLOMBINO Y NUMISMÁTICA Museum
(Map p68; 2243-4202; www.museosdelbanco central.org; Plaza de la Cultura, Avs Central & 2 btwn Calles 3 & 5; admission US$11; 9:15am-5pm) This three-in-one museum houses an extensive collection of Costa Rica's most priceless pieces of pre-Columbian gold and other artifacts, including historical currency and some contemporary regional art. The museum, housed underneath the Plaza de la Cultura, is owned by the Banco Central and its architecture brings to mind all the warmth and comfort of a bank vault. Security is tight; visitors must leave bags at the door.

San José

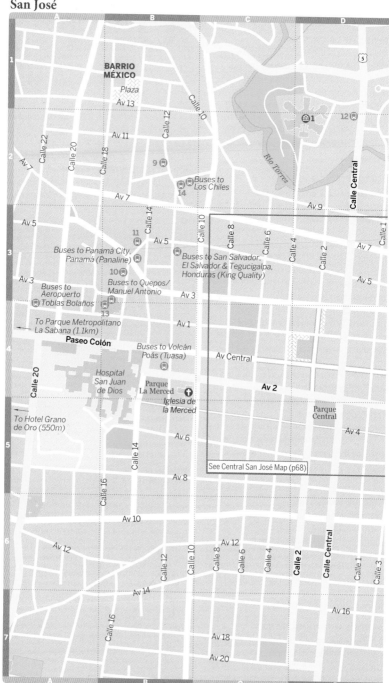

BARRIO MÉXICO

Plaza

Av 13

Calle 22
Calle 20
Calle 18
Av 7
Av 11
Calle 12
Calle 10

9

Av 7

14

Buses to Los Chiles

Calle 14
Calle 10
Calle 8
Calle 6
Calle 4
Calle 2
Calle 1

Av 5

11

Av 5

Av 9

Av 7

Av 5

Buses to Panamá City, Panamá (Panaline)

10

Buses to San Salvador, El Salvador & Tegucigalpa, Honduras (King Quality)

Av 3

Buses to Aeropuerto Toblas Bolaños

13

Buses to Quepos/ Manuel Antonio

Av 3

To Parque Metropolitano La Sabana (1.1km)

Paseo Colón

Av 1

Buses to Volcán Poás (Tuasa)

Calle 20

Hospital San Juan de Dios

Parque La Merced

Av Central

To Hotel Grano de Oro (550m)

Iglesia de la Merced

Av 2

Parque Central

Av 6

Av 4

Calle 14

Calle 16

See Central San José Map (p68)

Av 8

Av 10

Av 12

Av 16

Calle 12
Calle 10
Calle 8
Calle 6
Calle 4
Calle 2
Calle Central
Calle 1
Calle 3

Av 14

Calle 16

Av 18

Av 20

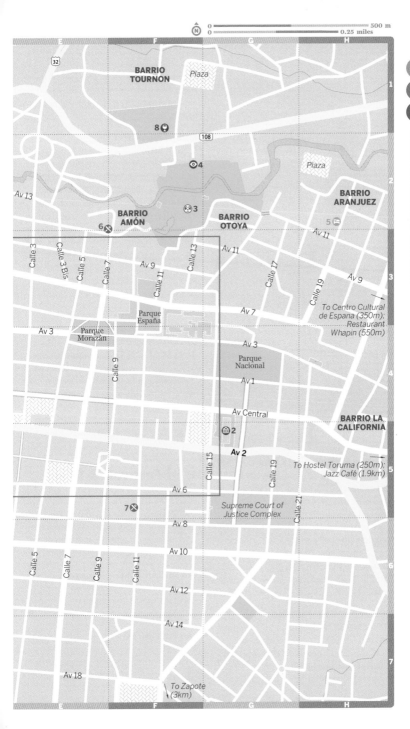

BARRIO TOURNON

Plaza

32

108

8

4

3

Av 13

BARRIO AMÓN

6

BARRIO OTOYA

Plaza

BARRIO ARANJUEZ

5

Av 11

Calle 3

Calle 3 Bis

Calle 5

Calle 7

Av 9

Calle 11

Calle 13

Av 11

Calle 17

Calle 19

Av 9

Parque España

Av 7

To Centro Cultural de Espana (350m); Restaurant Whapin (550m)

Av 3

Parque Morazán

Parque Nacional

Calle 9

Av 3

Av 1

Av Central

BARRIO LA CALIFORNIA

2

Av 2

Calle 15

Calle 19

To Hostel Toruma (250m); Jazz Café (1.9km)

Av 6

7

Calle 21

Supreme Court of Justice Complex

Av 8

Calle 5

Calle 7

Calle 9

Calle 11

Av 10

Av 12

Av 14

Av 18

To Zapote (3km)

San José

◎ Sights
1 Museo de los Niños & Galería
   Nacional...D2
2 Museo Nacional de Costa Rica...........G5
3 Parque Zoológico Nacional
   Simón Bolívar......................................F2
4 Spirogyra Jardín de Mariposas F2

◉ Sleeping
5 Hotel Aranjuez H2

⊗ Eating
6 Kalú Café & Food Shop E2
7 Restaurante Tin-Jo...............................F5

◉ Drinking
8 Centro Comercial El Pueblo.................F1

◉ Entertainment
Auditorio Nacional........................(see 1)

ⓘ Transport
Autotransportes Caribeños........(see 12)
Autotransportes Mepe...............(see 12)
9 Blanco Lobo B2
10 Empresa Cañas B3
Empresarios Guapileños............(see 12)
11 Empresas Alfaro B3
12 Gran Terminal del Caribe....................D2
13 Terminal Coca-Cola.............................B4
14 Terminal San Carlos.............................B2
Transportes Jacó........................(see 13)
Transportes Morales..................(see 13)

MUSEO DE JADE   Museum
(Map p68; ☎2287-6034; 1st fl, Edificio INS, Av 7 btwn Calles 9 & 11; adult/child under 11yr US$8/ free; ◷8:30am-3:30pm Mon-Fri, 11am-3pm Sat) The world's largest collection of American jade (pronounced 'ha-day' in Spanish) is at this small museum, including carvings that depict fertility goddesses, shamans, frogs and snakes. There is also incredible pottery, including a highly unusual ceramic head displaying a row of serrated teeth.

MUSEO DE ARTE Y DISEÑO CONTEMPORÁNEO   Museum
(Map p68; ☎2257-7202; www.madc.cr; Av 3 btwn Calles 13 & 15; admission US$3, Mon free; ◷9:30am-5pm Mon-Sat) Commonly referred to as MADC, the Contemporary Art &

Design Museum is housed in the historic National Liquor Factory building, which dates from 1856. The largest and most important contemporary-art museum in the region, MADC is focused on showing the works of contemporary Costa Rican, Central American and South American artists.

MUSEO NACIONAL DE COSTA RICA   Museum
(Map p64; ☎2257-1433; www.museocostarica. go.cr; Calle 17 btwn Avs Central & 2; adult/child US$6/3; ◷8:30am-4:30pm Tue-Sat, 9am-4:30pm Sun) The Museo Nacional is located inside the old Bellavista Fortress, which served as the old army headquarters and saw fierce fighting in the 1948 civil war. It was here that President José Figueres Ferrer announced, in 1949, that he was abolishing the country's military. The museum provides a quick survey of Costa Rican history.

MUSEO DE LOS NIÑOS & GALERÍA NACIONAL   Museum
(Map p64; ☎2258-4929; www.museocr.com; Calle 4, north of Av 9; adult/child US$2/1.50; ◷8am-4:30pm Tue-Fri, 9:30am-5pm Sat & Sun; ⍟) This unusual museum is an excellent place to bring small children, who will love the hands-on exhibits related to science, geography and natural history.

 Festivals & Events

FESTIVAL DE ARTE   Arts Festival
Every even year, San José becomes host to the biennial citywide arts showcase that features theater, music, dance and film. It's held for two weeks in March.

DÍA DE SAN JOSÉ   Religious Festival
(St Joseph's Day) Celebrated on March 19th, San José marks the day of its patron saint with Mass in some churches.

LAS FIESTAS DE ZAPOTE   Cultural Festival
Between Christmas and New Year's Eve, this week-long celebration draws tens of

thousands of Ticos to the bullring in the suburb of Zapote, southeast of the city.

Sleeping

HOTEL ARANJUEZ Hotel **$**
(Map p64; ☎ 2256-1825; www.hotelaranjuez. com; Calle 19 btwn Avs 11 & 13; incl breakfast s/d from US$32/49, s/d without bathroom US$25/30; P @ 🛜) This rambling hotel in Barrio Aranjuez consists of several nicely maintained vintage homes strung together with connecting gardens and walkways. The 36 spotless rooms come in a variety of configurations. The hotel's best attribute, however, is the lush garden patio, where a legendary breakfast buffet is served every morning. It's so popular a modern annex has been built half a block away.

HOTEL GRANO DE ORO Boutique Hotel **$$$**
(Off Map p64; ☎ 2255-3322; www.hotelgranode oro.com; Calle 30 btwn Avs 2 & 4; d US$135-205, f/garden/vista-del-oro ste US$215/265/385; P @ 🛜) Hotel Grano de Oro, a sprawling early-20th-century Victorian mansion with demure 'Tropical Victorian' rooms, is a favorite of honeymooners. Several units maintain the hotel's historic look while boasting private courtyards. If you want to experience Costa Rica's gilded age, this is the place.

San José for Kids

If you're in San José for a day with your kids, the Museo de los Niños (p66) is a hit with children who just can't keep their hands off the exhibits. Young nature-lovers will enjoy getting up close and personal with butterflies at the **Spirogyra Jardín de Mariposas** (Map p64; ☎ 2222-2937; www.butterflygardencr.com; Barrio Amón; adult/child US$7/3; ⊙ 8am-4pm; 🚻; 🚌 to El Pueblo) or checking out the exotic animals at the **Parque Zoológico Nacional Simón Bolívar** (Map p64; ☎ 2233-6701; www.fundazoo.org; Av 11 btwn Calles 7 & 9; adult/child US$5/3; ⊙ 9am-4:30pm; 🚻).

Colonial architecture, San José

OLIVER GERHARD / IMAGEBROKER ©

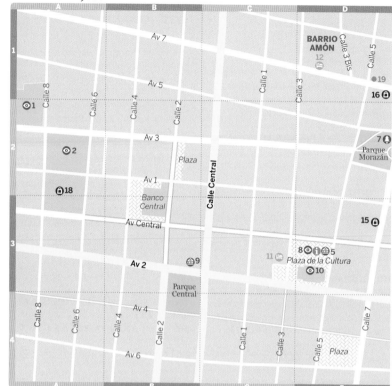

GRAN HOTEL COSTA RICA   Hotel $$$
(Map p68; ☏ 2221-4000; www.granhotelcostari
ca.com; Calle 3 btwn Avs Central & 2; d standard/
superior/deluxe $89/109/149, master ste/
presidential ste $185/250, all incl breakfast;
P ⊖ ✳ @ 🛜) The city's first prominent
hotel was constructed in 1930 and is
recognized as a national landmark (John F
Kennedy and soccer legend Pelé have both
stayed here). Frequent renovations have
kept the 107 rooms modern and comfort-
able, though they retain period touches
such as brass bed frames and wood
furnishings.

HOSTEL PANGEA   Hostel $
(Map p68; ☏ 2221-1992; www.hostelpangea.com;
Av 7 btwn Calles 3 & 3bis, Barrio Amón; dm $13-16,
d with/without bathroom $40/32, ste $60-70;
P @ 🛜 ≋) This industrial-strength, Tico-
owned hostel – 25 dorms and 25 private

rooms – has been a popular twenty-
something backpacker hangout for years.
It has a pool, a rooftop restaurant-lounge,
and a combination bar–movie theater
with a stripper pole. Needless to say, this
is a party spot.

Eating

**LA ESQUINA DE
BUENOS AIRES**   Argentine $$$
(Map p68; ☏ 2223-1909; http://laesquinadebue
nosaires.com/; cnr Calle 11 & Av 4; mains
US$10-30; ⏱11:30am-3pm & 6-11pm Mon-Fri,
noon-11pm Sat & Sun; 🍴) Spanish-tile floors,
bright white linens and old tangos evoke
the atmospheric bistros of San Telmo –
making this a top spot for a steak and a
glass of Malbec. Also tasty are the house-

Map scale:
0 — 0.2 km
0 — 0.1 miles

Central San José

◎ Sights
1 Mercado Borbón.................................A2
2 Mercado Central Annex.....................A2
3 Museo de Arte y Diseño
   Contemporáneo F2
4 Museo de Jade...................................E1
5 Museo de Oro Precolombino y
   Numismática...................................D3
6 Parque España...................................E2
7 Parque Morazán.................................D2
8 Plaza de la Cultura.............................D3
9 Teatro Melico Salazar B3
10 Teatro Nacional.................................D3

🛏 Sleeping
11 Gran Hotel Costa Rica.......................C3
12 Hostel Pangea....................................D1

✗ Eating
13 La Esquina de Buenos Aires..............E4

◎ Entertainment
14 Teatro La Máscara F4
   Teatro Nacional.......................(see 10)

🛍 Shopping
15 7th Street Books...............................D3
16 Galería Namu.....................................D1
17 Mercado Artesanal............................F4
18 Mercado Central................................A2

ℹ Information
19 Alianza Francesa D1
20 Centro de Cine...................................E1

made *empanadas* (turnovers stuffed with meat or cheese) and the extensive selection of fresh pastas, including vegetarian options such as mozzarella and fresh basil ravioli.

PARK CAFÉ   European $$$
(☎2290-6324; 100m norte de Rostipollos, Sabana Norte; mains US$26-31; ⏱noon-2pm & 7-9:30pm Tue-Sat) This anomalous (and felicitous) fusion of antique shop and French restaurant is overseen by Michelin-starred chef Richard Neat. It has an exquisite menu – crab ravioli with asparagus, artichoke and ginger sauce, for starters – and a carefully curated wine list.

RESTAURANTE TIN-JO   Asian $$
(Map p64; ☎2221-7605; www.tinjo.com; Calle 11 btwn Avs 6 & 8; mains US$10-18; ⏱11:30am-3pm & 5:30-10pm Mon-Thu, 11:30am-3pm & 5:30-11pm Fri & Sat, 11:30am-10pm Sun; ✈) The Asian standard-bearer is decorated in a riot of pan-Asian everything, just like the menu. Expect fare from various regions – from *kung pao* shrimp to spicy tuna *maki* to pad thai – and an extensive vegetarian menu.

KALÚ CAFÉ & FOOD SHOP   Cafe $$
(Map p64; ☎2221-2081; www.kalu.co.cr; cnr Calle 7 & Av 11, Barrio Amón; mains US$11-18; ⏱11:30am-6pm Mon, to 9:30pm Tue-Sat; ✈) This style-conscious cafe is run by noted chef Camille Ratton. The menu is a global fusion of salads, sandwiches and pastas, such as homemade gnocchi cooked in Malbec with wild mushrooms.

Entertainment

CENTRO COMERCIAL EL PUEBLO   Club
(Map p64; ☎ 2221-9434; www.centrocomercial
elpueblo.com; Barrio Tournon; ⏱hours vary)
This Spanish Mediterranean outdoor
mall is a warren of bars, clubs and music
venues. Things usually get going at about
9pm and shut down by 3am.

TEATRO NACIONAL   Theatre
(Map p68; ☎ 2221-5341; www.teatronacional.go.cr;
Calles 3 & 5 btwn Avs Central & 2) Costa Rica's
most important theater stages plays,
dance, opera, symphony, Latin American
music and other major events. The main
season runs from March to November,
though performances are held year-round.

Barrio Bird Walking Tours

The knowledgeable and engaging
Stacey Corrales show visitors San
José's famous and not-so-famous
sights on the **Barrio Bird Walking
Tours** (www.toursanjosecostarica.com),
providing history and insights on
the city's architecture, murals and
urban art. Specialized tours also
cater to gourmands, photographers
and bar-crawlers.

Shopping

GALERÍA NAMU   Handicrafts
(Map p68; ☎ 2256 3412; www.galerianamu.com;
Av 7 btwn Calles 5 & 7; ⏱9am-6:30pm Mon-Sat,
1-5pm Sun Jan-Apr) This fair-trade gallery
run by Aisling French does a great job
of bringing together artwork and crafts
from a diverse population of regional
ethnicities. You'll find Boruca masks,
finely woven Wounaan baskets, Guaymí
dolls, Bribrí canoes and Huetar carvings.
It can also help arrange visits to remote

Left: Lunch service, Mercado Central
Below: Vegetable stall, Mercado Central
(LEFT) JESUS OCHOA ©; (BELOW) JESUS OCHOA ©

indigenous territories in different parts of Costa Rica. See the website for details.

MERCADO CENTRAL
Market

(Map p68; Avs Central & 1 btwn Calles 6 & 8; 🕑6am-6pm Mon-Sat) This is the best and cheapest place in the city to buy just about anything, from hammocks (made in Nicaragua) and *pura vida* T-shirts (made in China), to a vast assortment of forgettable knickknacks. For something decidedly Costa Rican, export-quality coffee beans and cigars can be bought at a fraction of the price you'll pay in a tourist shop.

7TH STREET BOOKS
Books

(Map p68; Calle 7) The headquarters of all things English-language; also carries maps and music. It is a great place to stock up on beach reading.

ℹ️ Information

Canatur (Cámara Nacional de Turismo; ☎2234-6222; www.tourism.co.cr; Aeropuerto Internacional Juan Santamaría; 🕑8am-10pm) The Costa Rican National Chamber of Tourism has a small stand next to international baggage claim.

Instituto Costarricense de Turismo (ICT; ☎in USA (toll free) 800-343-6332; www.visitcostarica. com) Government tourism office has handy free maps of San José and Costa Rica.

ℹ️ Getting There & Away

San José is the country's transportation hub, and it's likely that you'll pass through. If you're only in town for a couple of days, most travel will be on foot.

Air

Two airports serve San José. There is an international departure tax of US$26 when leaving the country.

Aeropuerto Internacional Juan Santamaría (☎2437-2400; www.aeris.cr) handles international and domestic flights, including those

71

on Sansa. Aeropuerto Tobías Bolaños (📞2232-2820), in the San José suburb of Pavas, services domestic flights on NatureAir.

Car

Don't rent a car if you're not leaving San José. The traffic is heavy, the streets narrow and the meter-deep curbside gutters make parking nerve-wracking. In addition, break-ins are frequent. If you are renting a car note that there is a surcharge for renting cars at Aeropuerto Internacional Juan Santamaría.

Bus

Bus transportation in San José can be bewildering. There is no public bus system, no central terminal, and schedules and prices change regularly. Download a useful but not always up-to-date PDF copy from the ICT website.

TO NORTHWESTERN COSTA RICA

Buses to **La Fortuna** (US$6; four hours) depart from Terminal San Carlos (Map p64; Calle 12, between Avs 7 & 9) at 6:15am, 8:30am and 11:30am.

Buses to **Monteverde/Santa Elena** (US$7.50; 4½ hours) depart from Terminal San Carlos at 6:30am and 2:30pm. Book ahead as this bus fills up quickly.

TO PENÍNSULA DE NICOYA

Buses to **Montezuma** and **Mal País** (US$13; six hours) depart from Terminal Coca-Cola (Map p64) at 6am, 8am, 10am, noon, 2pm, 4pm and 6pm.

Empresas Alfaro (Map p64; 📞2256-7050; Av 5 btwn Calles 14 & 16) has buses to **Nicoya** (US$5.40; five hours) that depart at 6:30am, 10am, 1pm, 3pm and 5pm. It also runs buses to **Playa Nosara** (US$8; six hours; depart 6am) and **Playa Tamarindo** (US$9; five hours; depart 11:30am and 3:30pm).

TO THE CARIBBEAN COAST

Empresarios Guapileños (Gran Terminal del Caribe) has buses to **Cariari** (US$3.25; 2¼ hours) for transfer to **Tortuguero**, which depart every few hours until 7pm.

Autotransportes Caribeños (Gran Terminal del Caribe) runs buses to **Puerto Limón** (US$5; three hours) every 30 minutes from 5am to 7pm.

Autotransportes Mepe (Gran Terminal del Caribe) runs to **Puerto Viejo de Talamanca** (US$8.65; 4½ hours) leaving at 6am, 10am, 12pm, 2pm and 4pm.

TO THE CENTRAL PACIFIC COAST & SOUTHERN COSTA RICA

Transportes Morales (Map p64; Terminal Coca-Cola) goes to **Dominical** and **Uvita** (US$5; seven hours) at 6am & 3pm.

Foyer, Teatro Nacional (p63)

San José Cultural Centers

Various foreign institutions host film nights, art exhibits, theater, live music and academic conferences. Call ahead in January and February, when these spots tend to have limited hours.

Alianza Francesa (Map p68; 2222-2283; www.afsj.net; cnr Calle 5 & Av 7) Has French classes, a small library and rotating art exhibits in a historic Barrio Amón home.

Centro Cultural de España (✆ 2257-2919; www.ccecr.org; Rotonda del Farolito, Barrio Escalante) Offers a full roster of events, an audiovisual center and lending library.

Centro de Cine (Map p68; ✆ 2223-2127, 2223-0610; www.centrodecine.go.cr; cnr Calle 11 & Av 9) This film center holds festivals, lectures and events in outside venues.

Transportes Jacó (Map p64; ✆ 2290-2922; Terminal Coca-Cola) runs buses to **Jacó** (US$4; three hours) departing at 7:30am, 10:30am, 1pm, 3:30pm and 6:30pm. The same company also runs buses to **Quepos/Manuel Antonio** (US$7.25; four hours) at 6am, noon, 6pm and 7:30pm.

Blanco Lobo (Map p64; ✆ 2221-4214; Calle 12 btwn Avs 9 & 11) runs to **Puerto Jiménez** (US$12; eight hours) at 6am and noon. This bus will fill up quickly in high season, so book tickets in advance.

AROUND SAN JOSÉ

Over the years, San José's urban sprawl has crawled up the hillsides, blurring the lines between the heart of the city and its surrounding villages. The region now has a little bit of everything, from crowded slums to stylish residential neighborhoods. A few hundred meters east of downtown San José are the contiguous neighborhoods of Los Yoses and San Pedro, home to a number of embassies and the most prestigious university in the country, the Universidad de Costa Rica (UCR). To the west, about 7km away, is Escazú, where Americanized housing developments sit alongside old Tico homesteads.

Los Yoses & San Pedro

These two side-by-side neighborhoods may lie in close proximity to each other, but their characters are totally unique. Los Yoses is a charming residential district, dotted with modernist structures, historic inns and chilled-out eateries. San Pedro, on the other hand, houses the university district, and is brimming with bars, clubs and student activity.

Sights

MUSEO DE INSECTOS   Museum

(Insect Museum; ✆ 2511-5318; www.miucr.ac.cr; admission US$2; ⊙1-4:45pm Mon-Fri) This museum has an extensive collection of insects assembled by the Facultad de Agronomía at the UCR. Curiously, it is housed in the basement of the music building (Facultad de Artes Musicales), a brutalist structure painted Barbie pink.

Sleeping & Eating

HOSTEL TORUMA   Hostel **$**

(✆ 2234-8186; www.hosteltoruma.com; Av Central btwn Calles 29 & 33, Los Yoses; dm/s/d US$13/35/55; P @ 🛜 ❄) This graceful neoclassical home belonged to José Figueres, the Costa Rican president who abolished the army. While the Toruma contains four dormitories, it feels much more like an inn, with 17 large private rooms, wi-fi and flat-screen TVs. It's a mellow spot and one of the best budget deals in San José.

RESTAURANT WHAPIN Caribbean $$
(☎2283-1480; www.whapincr.com; cnr Calle 35 &
Av 13, Barrio Escalante; mains US$13-21; ⏰8am-
11pm Mon-Fri, 11:30am-11pm Sat) If you don't
make it to the Caribbean, eat here: an
intimate corner spot painted Rasta red,
yellow and green that serves spectacular
meals. Enjoy a steamy bowl of *rondón*
(seafood gumbo cooked in coconut milk),
a plate of rice and red beans, or fish sim-
mered in spicy coconut sauce.

 Entertainment

JAZZ CAFÉ Live Music
(☎2253-8933; www.jazzcafecostarica.com;
⏰6pm-2am) *The* destination in San José
for live music, with a different band every
night. Countless iconic Latin American
performers have taken to the stage here.
Admission charges vary, but run about
US$8 for local groups. It's 50m east of
Antiguo Banco Popular.

ⓘ Getting There & Away

From the Plaza de la Cultura in San José, take
any bus marked 'Mall San Pedro.' A taxi ride from

San José buses

downtown will cost about US$5. To get into San
José, take one of the buses along Av Central
heading west.

Escazú

You can find an unusual juxtaposition of
gringo expats, moneyed aristocrats and
old-world Tico village life in this sprawl-
ing suburb that climbs a steep hillside
overlooking San José and Heredia.

 Sleeping & Eating

POSADA EL QUIJOTE B&B $$
(☎2289-8401; www.quijote.cr; Calle del Llano,
Bello Horizonte; d standard/superior/deluxe incl
breakfast US$95/105/115; Ⓟ🐕❄🛜) This
Spanish-style *posada* (guesthouse) on
a hillside rates as one of the top B&Bs in
the San José area. Standard rooms are
simple yet homey, with wooden floors,
throw rugs, cable TV and private hot-
water bathrooms, while larger superior
units have private terraces. All guests can
take a nip at the honor bar, and then relax
on the outdoor patio with sweeping views
of the valley.

COSTA VERDE INN
Inn $$

(☎2228-4080; www.costaverdeinn.com; s/d/tr $55/65/75, d apt from $85, all incl breakfast; P @ 🛜 🏊) The sister lodge of the famous Manuel Antonio hotel, this homey stone inn is surrounded by gardens that contain a hot tub, a mosaic-tile swimming pool, a BBQ area and even a sundeck with wi-fi. Fourteen simple rooms have king-sized beds, rocking chairs and folk art. Apartments come with fully equipped kitchens.

LA CASONA DE LALY
Costa Rican $

(☎2288-5807; cnr Av 3 & Calle Central; bocas $2-5, mains $5-15; ⏱11am-midnight Mon-Sat, to 6pm Sun) At the heart of Escazú Centro, this much-loved restaurant-tavern specializes in country-style Tico fare. Locals and expats pack the joint for cheap, lip-smacking *bocas* (appetizers), ice-cold beers and a soundtrack of merengue. Try the *dados de queso* (fried cheese cubes).

 Shopping

BIESANZ WOODWORKS
Arts & Crafts

(☎2289-4337; www.biesanz.com; ⏱8am-5pm Mon-Fri, 9am-3pm Sat) Located in the hills of Bello Horizonte in Escazú, the workshop of Biesanz Woodworks can be difficult to find, but the effort will be well worth it.

If You Like...
Markets

If you like the Mercado Central (p71), we think you'll like these other markets in San José:

1 MERCADO BORBÓN
(Map p68; cnr Av 3 & Calle 8) Adjacent to the Mercado Central, the Borbón is more focused on fresh produce.

2 MERCADO CENTRAL ANNEX
(Map p68; Avs 1 & 3 btwn Calles 6 & 8) This market is less touristy and crowded with butchers, fishmongers and informal food counters.

3 MERCADO ARTESANAL
(Crafts Market; Map p68; Plaza de la Democracia, Avs Central & 2 btwn Calles 13 & 15; ⏱midmorning-sunset) This touristy open-air market sells typical handicrafts and souvenirs.

This shop is one of the finest woodcrafting studios in the nation.

🛈 Getting There & Around

Frequent buses between San José and Escazú cost about US$0.75 and take about 25 minutes. All depart San José from east of the Coca-Cola Terminal or south of the Hospital San Juan de Dios. They take several routes via San Rafael.

Central Valley

It is on the coffee-draped hillsides of the Central Valley that you will find Costa Rica's heart and soul. This is not only the geographical center of the country, it is its cultural and spiritual core. It is here that the Spanish first settled. It is here that coffee built a prosperous nation. In this mountainous region of nooks and crannies, entertainment consists of hanging out in a bustling mountain town, and watching folks gather for market days and church. That doesn't mean, however, that there is nothing to do. You can ride raging rapids, visit the country's oldest colonial church, look for trogons in mist-shrouded forests and hike myriad volcanoes. So take your time. When you explore the Central Valley, you'll not only witness great beauty, but also see the landscape that gave Costa Rica its character.

Carretas (painted oxcarts), Sarchí (p91)

Central Valley

La Virgen

Florencia

Aguas
Zarcas

Venecia

Rio Cuarto

Colonia
del Toro

San Miguel

Ciudad Quesada
(San Carlos)

Volcán
Platanar
(2183m)

El Sucre

*Laguna
Hule*

Cariblanco

Río Toro

Parque Nacional
Juan Castro Blanco

Volcán
Porvenir
(2267m)

10°15'N

Parque Nacional
Volcán Poás

Parque Nacional
Braulio Carrillo

Bajos del Toro

Volcán Poás
(2704m)

Río Sarapiquí

Los Angeles
Cloud Forest
Adventure Park

Zarcero

Poasito

Vara
Blanca

Volcán
Barva
(2906m)

Reserva
Forestal
Grecia

Concepción

Río Barranca

A l a j u e l a

Poasito

120

Fraijanes

126

San
Ramón

141

Naranjo

5 Sarchí

Sacramento

Paso Llano

Monte de
la Cruz

1

1

Grecia

San Pedro
de Poás

San José de
la Montaña

Palmares

Zona Protectora
Río Grande

Puente de
Piedra

*World of
Snakes*

130

Santa
Bárbara

El Castillo

Rosario

La Argentina

*Las Cataratas
de Los Chorros*

*The ARA
Project*

Barva

San
Rafael

135

Rincón
de Salas

ALAJUELA

San Joaquín
de Flores

3

HEREDIA

Atenas

La Garita

*Juan Santamaría
International Airport*

Santo
Domingo

La Guácima

*Butterfly
Farm*

San Antonio

3

San Juan
de Tibas

Túrrucares

Tobías Bolaños

Pavas

27

7

Río Virilla

Ciudad
Colón

Santa
Ana

Escazú

SAN JOSÉ

Alajuelita

San José

*Reserva
Indígena
Quitirrisí*

Aserri

Santiago
de Puriscal

Tarbaca

San Ignacio
de Acosta

San Gabriel

Río Candelaria

1 Rafting in Turrialba

2 Volcán Irazú

3 Monumento Nacional
Arqueológico Guayabo

4 Barva

5 Sarchí

6 Cartago

Central Valley Highlights

1

Rafting in Turrialba

A beautiful town in Costa Rica's Central Valley, Turrialba (p101) has excellent white-water rafting. With big mountains and a long rainy season, Turrialba lies close to an excellent group of fast and furious rivers. Another reason to come here on a rafting trip are the very professional and friendly local guides. Above and right: Río Pacuare, Turrialba (p100)

Need to Know
SURVIVAL TIP Only experts raft Class V Peralta and only during low-water season **WHEN TO VISIT** Rainy season for exhilarating rafting, June to October **For more, see p100**

Rafting in Turrialba Don't Miss List

BY DANIEL BUSTOS ARAYA, RIVER GUIDE
FOR EXPLORNATURA

1 RÍO REVENTAZÓN FOR BEGINNERS

The Río Reventazón is divided into four sections between the dam and the takeout point in Siquirres. Las Máquinas (Power House) is a Class II–III float that's perfect for families, while the popular Florida segment is a scenic Class III float with a little more white water to make things interesting.

2 RÍO REVENTAZÓN FOR THRILL-SEEKERS

If you've gone white-water rafting before, or you're confident in your physical prowess and quick reflexes, you might want to consider some of the more advanced runs on the Río Reventazón. The Pascua section has 15 Class IV rapids – featuring names like 'The Abyss' – and is widely considered to be the most classic run in the area. The Class V Peralta segment is extremely challenging and not for the faint of heart. Tours do not always offer it due to safety concerns, but when they do it can be some of the most exciting rafting in the country.

3 LOWER PACUARE

Not to be outdone by its top competitor, the Río Pacuare is divided into lower and upper stretches, both of which are home to an excellent variety of white-water runs. The Class III–IV Lower Pacuare is the more accessible bit, offering a 28km excursion through rocky gorges and isolated canyons, past an indigenous village, untamed jungle and lots of wildlife curious as to what the screaming is all about.

4 UPPER PACUARE

The upper reaches of the Río Pacuare are also classified as Class III–IV, but there are a few sections that can be considered Class V depending on the conditions. It's about a two-hour drive to the put-in, so you need a bit more time to access this remote stretch. It's most definitely worth the trip though, especially since you'll be able to paddle alongside the area's densest jungles.

Volcán Irazú

The roof of the Central Valley is this 3432m-tall active volcano (p98) which, in the country's brief history, has unleashed its liquid fury more than 15 times. These days things have temporarily quietened down, meaning that hiking around the summit is safer than you might imagine. When the weather is clear, you can soak up impressive views reaching out to both the Pacific Ocean and the Caribbean Sea.

2

3 Monumento Nacional Arqueológico Guayabo

Walking along the aqueducts and seeing the mysterious petroglyphs at Costa Rica's largest archaeological site (p102) offers a clear window into the past. While now only the modest remains of a pre-Columbian city, Guayabo was once inhabited by more than 20,000 sophisticated urban dwellers. The evidence is wrought in stone.

Barva

4

Lying on the edge of the city of Heredia, the historic colonial town of Barva (p95) was first settled in 1561 by the Spanish conquistadors, though many of the present buildings were constructed in the 19th century. Architecture aside, Barva is also the home of the most famous coffee roaster in Costa Rica, Café Britt Finca (p96).

Coffee berries, Café Britt Finca

JESUS OCHOA ©

JESUS OCHOA ©

Sarchí

5

Something of a shopper's paradise for authentic souvenirs, Sarchí (p91) is the birthplace of the *carreta* (painted oxcart). Beyond these colorful symbols of the Costa Rican working class, this tiny town in the Central Valley is also home to dozens of woodworking studios that fashion richly hued hardwoods into elaborate handicrafts. Church (p92), Sarchí Norte

Cartago

6

Costa Rica's second city and long-term rival to San José, Cartago (p97) has weathered its fair share of natural disasters. Cartago is the guardian of La Negrita, a venerated religious artifact that is housed in the city's grand basilica, Basílica de Nuestra Señora de Los Ángeles (p96). If your visit coincides with one of the nation's religious festivals, it makes a dramatic backdrop. La Negrita (p96), Basílica de Nuestra Señora de Los Ángeles

The Central Valley's Best...

Historical Sites

○ **Museo Juan Santamaría** (p88) Visit this historic jail to learn about Costa Rica's famous drummer boy.

○ **El Fortín** (p93) The remains of a Spanish fortress and the symbol of Heredia.

○ **Basílica de Nuestra Señora de Los Ángeles** (p96) The country's most celebrated religious monument.

○ **Monumento Nacional Arqueológico Guayabo** (p102) Costa Rica's most prominent pre-Columbian site.

Splurges

○ **Xandari Resort Hotel & Spa** (p90) Bed down in a working coffee plantation before grabbing your flight home.

○ **Casa Turire** (p103) An exceedingly elegant throwback to the colonial era.

○ **Sarchí** (p91) Bring your cash and shop 'til you drop for woodwork.

○ **Hotel Chalet Tirol** (p94) Treat yourself to a bit of surprising Alpine gingerbread quaintness.

Photo Ops

○ **Volcán Irazú** (p98) Climb to the top of the region on a clear day for a killer panorama of both coasts.

○ **Palmares** (p93) Tens of thousands of festival-goers head here for one of the biggest, baddest and rowdiest parties in the country.

○ **Cartago** (p97) The annual pilgrimage attracts devotees who walk to the white basilica on their knees.

○ **Lower Pacuare** (p100) Home to some of the most scenic rafting in Central America.

Eats & Drinks

o **Xandari** (p90) A place where the views are as impressive as the organic menu.

o **Restaurant Betico Mata** (p103) Don't miss the *gallos*, amazing open-faced tacos on corn tortillas.

o **Como en Casa** (p91) A place for excellent steaks and bold reds from south of the equator.

o **Café Britt Finca** (p96) The best spot for a freshly brewed cup of shade-grown coffee.

Left: Orchids, Lankester Gardens (p101);
Above: Volcán Turrialba (p101).
(LEFT) JESUS OCHOA ©: (ABOVE) JESUS OCHOA ©

Need to Know

ADVANCE PLANNING

o **One month before** Book car rental for collection from Aeropuerto Internacional Juan Santamaría.

o **Two weeks before** Check the *Tico Times* (www.ticotimes.net) for upcoming festivals in the region and book hotels.

o **One week before** Book rafting trips.

RESOURCES

o **Orosi Valley Guide** (www.orosivalley.com)

o **Rafting Costa Rica** (www.costasolrafting.com)

EMERGENCY NUMBERS

o **Emergency** ☏911

o **Fire** ☏118

o **Police** ☏117

GETTING AROUND

o **Air** Alajuela – not San José – is actually the closest city to the international airport.

o **Bus** Intercity bus connections are fast and frequent.

o **Car** Winding mountain roads offer expansive views over the valley, making this the best way to get around the region.

o **Walk** All of the major cities in the region are relatively safe to walk around by day.

BE FOREWARNED

o **Signage** Roads in the Central Valley are poorly signed, so it's best to bring along a good road map when setting out.

o **Flat tire scam** A scam involving flat tires on rental cars has plagued travelers to Aeropuerto Internacional Juan Santamaría for years. If your rental gets a flat immediately upon leaving the airport, be very wary of accepting 'help' from a good Samaritan.

o **Car break-ins** While the area is generally considered to be safe, there are regular reports of car break-ins. Try to use guarded parking and never leave valuables in your car.

VITAL STATISTICS

o **Population** Alajuela 43,000; Heredia 33,000; Cartago 24,000; Turrialba 27,000

o **Best time to visit** Las Fiestas de Palmares (mid-January), Feria de la Mascarada (March), pilgrimage to Cartago to honor La Virgen de los Ángeles (August 2), peak white water (June through October)

85

Central Valley Itineraries

A romp to the white water and glorious valley vistas of the Central Valley and highlands is thrilling unto itself, and a perfect way to fill a few days at the beginning or end of a trip.

3 DAYS

TURRIALBA TO PARQUE NACIONAL VOLCÁN TURRIALBA
White Water, Volcanoes & Culture

If your time is limited, this itinerary is perfect for getting an exhilarating, quick taste of what the region has to offer – white water, pre-Columbian history and scenic drives. Furthermore, if your travels started in San José, you need only hop on a quick bus to Turrialba, and then use the town as a base for exploring a couple of the Central Valley's top highlights.

After spending some time getting your bearings in **(1) Turrialba**, your first order of business is to arrange a white-water rafting trip with any of the town's recommended operators. Depending on the time of year and your skill level, your next destination will be one of the stretches along the **(2) Ríos Reventazón & Pacuare**. Day trips can take in a good sampling of rapids, though you can always extend your time out on the water with an overnight rafting trip. When you're ready to dial things down a notch, the **(3) Monumento Nacional Arqueológico Guayabo** provides a rich cultural perspective on the pre-Columbian inhabitants of the area. Finally, to catch one of the country's rarely visited volcanic peaks, make a day out of hiking into the crater of the **(4) Parque Nacional Volcán Turrialba**.

ALAJUELA TO TURRIALBA

City Hopping in the Central Valley

4 DAYS

Costa Rica's beaches and rainforests may garner most of the spotlight, but to truly understand the country, you need to understand its people. The vast majority of Ticos (inhabitants of Costa Rica) live in the cities of the Central Valley, so spending a few days here will enable you to put your finger on the pulse of the modern nation. Plus, frequent bus connections mean that moving back and forth is a snap.

As the closest city to the airport, **(1) Alajuela** provides a soft landing for bleary-eyed travelers, but it's also home to an attractive park that invites long bouts of people-watching. Home to a large university,

(2) Heredia bustles with activity, and has a few storied buildings that retell Costa Rica's history as a Spanish colony. Today it is an elegant alternative to the nearby capital. The *original* capital and long-time rival of San José (especially on the soccer field!), **(3) Cartago** is centered on one of the most impressive basilicas in Central America. Finally, though it's not much more than an oversized town in comparison to the big three, **(4) Turrialba** offers up some bucolic charm as well as stunning natural surrounds.

Excavated site at Monumento Nacional Arqueológico Guayabo (p102)
STEVE BLY / ALAMY ©

Discover Central Valley

At a Glance

○ **Alajuela** Home to Costa Rica's international airport and a lovely city park.

○ **Heredia** (p93) This peaceful alternative to the capital holds echoes of colonial history.

○ **Cartago** (p97) Proud home of one of Central America's most impressive cathedrals.

○ **Turrialba** (p101) Launching point for some of the country's best white-water adventures.

El Fortín (p93), Heredia
JOHN MITCHELL / ALAMY ©

ALAJUELA
POP 43,000

Alajuela is by no means a tourist 'destination.' Much of the architecture is unremarkable, the streets are often jammed and there isn't a lot to see here. But it's an inherently Costa Rican city, and, in its more relaxed moments, it reveals itself as such, with families having leisurely Sunday lunches and teenagers stealing kisses in the park. It's also a good base for exploring the countryside to the north.

◎ Sights

PARQUE CENTRAL   Park
(Avs Central & 1 btwn Calles Central & 2)
The shady Parque Central is a pleasant place to relax beneath the mango trees, or people-watch in the evenings.

IGLESIA LA AGONÍA   Church
(Calle 9 btwn Avs Central & 1) A Renaissance-inspired structure, built in 1941, houses the Iglesia La Agonía, a popular local spot for Mass.

MUSEO JUAN SANTAMARÍA   Museum
(☏ 2441-4775; www.museo juansantamaria.go.cr; Av 1 btwn Calles Central & 2; admission free; ⊙ 10am-5:30pm Tue-Sun) Situated in a century-old structure that has served as both a jail and an armory, the Museo Juan Santamaría chronicles the life and history of national hero Juan Santamaría. A basic exhibit area contains maps, paintings and artifacts related to the conflict that ultimately gained Costa Rica's independence.

Alajuela

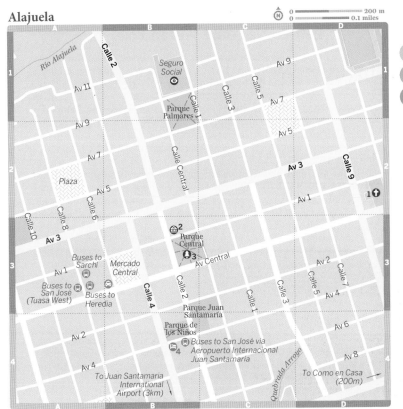

Map labels: Río Alajuela, Calle 2, Seguro Social, Av 9, Av 11, Calle 5, Calle 3, Av 7, Calle 1, Parque Palmares, Av 9, Av 5, Av 7, Calle Central, Av 3, Calle 9, Plaza, Av 5, Av 1, Calle 6, Calle 8, Calle 10, Av 3, 1, Buses to Sarchí, Mercado Central, Av 1, Parque Central, Av Central, Av 2, Calle 7, Calle 5, Buses to San José (Tuasa West), Buses to Heredia, Calle 4, Calle 2, Av 4, Parque Juan Santamaría, Calle 1, Calle 3, Parque de los Niños, Buses to San José vía Aeropuerto Internacional Juan Santamaría, Av 6, Av 2, To Juan Santamaria International Airport (3km), Av 4, Quebrada Arroyo, Av 8, To Como en Casa (200m)

DISCOVER CENTRAL VALLEY **ALAJUELA**

★ Festivals & Events

In the town that gave birth to Juan Santamaría, it would be expected that the anniversary of the **Battle of Rivas**, on April 11, would be particularly well celebrated. This momentous event is commemorated with civic events, including a parade and lots of firecrackers.

🛏 Sleeping

HOSTEL MALEKU　　　　Hostel $
(☎ 2430-4304; www.malekuhostel.com; dm US$13, s/d without bathroom US$25/35, all incl breakfast; @) This sweet little backpackers' abode has spick-and-span rooms tucked into a vintage home on a quiet

Alajuela

◉ **Sights**
1　Iglesia La Agonía..................................D2
2　Museo Juan Santamaría.....................B3
3　Parque Central.....................................B3

🛏 **Sleeping**
4　Alajuela Backpackers Boutique
　　Hostel..B4

street, 50m west of Hospital San Rafael. There are also three private rooms, with shared bathrooms, a communal kitchen, a TV lounge and free internet. It's a wonderful, serene spot and the staff is very helpful. Free shuttles to the airport leave the hostel hourly starting at 5am.

89

Detour:
Parque Nacional Volcán Poás

Just 37km north of Alajuela by a winding and scenic road is the most heavily trafficked national park in Costa Rica. And for those who want to peer into an active volcano – without the hardship of hiking one – it's ideal. The centerpiece is, of course, Volcán Poás (2704m), which had its last blowout in 1953. This event formed the eerie and enormous crater, which is 1.3km across and 300m deep – and offers the wonderful opportunity to watch the bubbling, steaming cauldron belch sulfurous mud and water hundreds of meters into the air. There are two other craters, as well, one of which contains a sapphire-blue lake ringed by high-altitude forest.

The main crater at Poás continues to be active to varying degrees. In fact, the park was briefly closed in May 1989 after a minor eruption sent volcanic ash spouting more than 1km into the air, and lesser activity closed the park intermittently in 1995. In recent years, however, Poás has posed no imminent threat, though scientists still monitor it closely.

In the meantime, the most common issue for visitors is the veil of clouds that gather around the mountain at about 10am (even in dry season). Even if the day looks clear, get to the park as early as possible or you won't see much.

ALAJUELA BACKPACKERS BOUTIQUE HOSTEL · Hotel $

(☎ 2441-7149; www.alajuelabackpackers.com; cnr Av 4 & Calle 4; dm/s/d/tr US$15/38/48/60, s/d junior ste US$55/78; ❄ @ �🛜) This four-story inn is more hotel than hostel, with private rooms and dorms surrounding a plant-draped atrium. Watch movies on the flat-screen TV in the beanbag lounge, or sip beers on the 4th-floor bar terrace and watch planes take off in the distance. Dorms house only four people per room, and each has its own bathroom. Junior suites have plasma TV and comfy king-sized bed. Credit cards accepted.

🖋 XANDARI RESORT & SPA · Hotel $$$

(☎ 2443-2020; www.xandari.com; d villa US$230-315; P ⊖ ❄ �🛜 ✈) Overlooking the Central Valley, this romantic spot north of town is the fanciful joint design of a Tico architect-designer couple. All rooms are villas, painted in tropical colors and tastefully but playfully decorated with folk art and hand-woven textiles; all include garden-view shower, minifridge and sitting area. The grounds offer more than 3km of trails for exploring, three pools, a Jacuzzi, a spa, an excellent gift shop and a restaurant specializing in organic local foods; and most of the staff are hired from the local village.

TRAPP FAMILY LODGE · Inn $$

(☎ 2431-0776; www.trappfam.com; r US$95, additional person US$15, child 3-11yr US$6, all incl breakfast; P @ �🛜 ✈) This highly recommended spot is the comfiest, most attractive option within reach of the airport landing strip. A bright, Spanish-style country inn houses 20 terra-cotta-tiled rooms with comfortable beds and a graceful hacienda vibe. The best units have balconies overlooking a lovely garden laced with bougainvillea and fig trees, and a pool. It's located 2km from the international airport; free airport transfers are provided.

Eating

🖋 XANDARI · International $$$

(☎ 2443-2020; www.xandari.com; Xandari Resort Hotel & Spa; mains US$9-20; 🖉) If you want to impress a date, you can't go wrong at this elegant restaurant with incredible views. The menu is a mix of Costa Rican and international, with plenty of vegetarian options. The restaurant utilizes the resort's homegrown organic produce, supplemented by locally grown organic produce whenever possible – making for tasty *and* feel-good gourmet meals.

COMO EN CASA Argentine **$$$**
(☎ 2441-7607; Plaza Real Alajuela; mains US$10-28; ⏱ 11am-10pm Sun-Wed, to 11pm Thu-Sat; ♫) With its white tablecloths and festive atmosphere, this Argentinean grill is a popular weekend lunch spot, serving a comprehensive round-up of grilled meats and a strong selection of pastas (including vegetarian options). A good wine list is comprised mostly of Chilean and Argentinean vintages (about US$25 a bottle).

❶ Getting There & Away

Taxis (around US$7) go to the Juan Santamaría International Airport from central Alajuela.

There is no central bus terminal; instead, a number of small terminals and bus stops dot the southwestern part of the city.

Buses go to the following destinations from Calle 8 between Avs Central and 1:

Heredia US$0.75, 30 minutes, departs every 15 minutes from 5am to 10pm.

San José (Tuasa West) US$1, 45 minutes, departs every 10 minutes from 5am to 11pm.

Sarchí US$0.75, 30 minutes, departs half-hourly from 5am to 10pm.

Buses also go to the following destinations, departing from Av 4 between Calles 2 and 4:

San José via **Juan Santamaría International Airport** Station Wagon; US$1, 45 minutes, departs every 10 minutes from 4am to midnight.

SARCHÍ

Welcome to Costa Rica's most famous crafts center, where artisans produce the ornately painted oxcarts and leather-and-wood furnishings for which the Central Valley is known. You'll know you've arrived because just about everything is covered in the signature geometric designs – even city hall. Yes, it's a tourist trap, but it's a pretty one.

Most people come in for an afternoon of shopping and call it a day.

Painting a *carreta* (oxcart), Sarchí

JESUS OCHOA ©

Sarchí is divided by the Río Trojas into Sarchí Norte and Sarchí Sur, and is rather spread out, straggling for several kilometers along the main road from Grecia to Naranjo. It's easiest to explore by private car.

In Sarchí Norte, you'll find the heart of the village, including a twin-towered **church**, some restaurants and *pulperías* (corner stores), and what is purported to be the **world's largest oxcart** (photo op!).

 ## Eating

SUPER MARISCOS Seafood $
(☎2454-4330; mains US$7-15; ⏲11am-10pm Tue-Sun; **P** 🛜) At a low-lying bend in the road in Sarchí Sur, Super Mariscos serves up good *ceviche* (seafood marinated in lemon or lime juice, garlic and seasonings), as well as pasta and a few beef dishes. Everything comes with a side of fries and a smidgen of salad. To top off the dining experience, the otherwise nondescript decor features a fake shark busting out of one wall.

 # Shopping

Most travelers come to Sarchí for one thing only: *carretas*, the elaborate, colorfully painted oxcarts that are the unofficial souvenir of Costa Rica – and official symbol of the Costa Rican worker.

Workshops are usually open from 8am to 4pm daily and they accept credit cards and US dollars. For shipping, you'll find a UPS office in Sarchí Sur. Following is a list of some of the most respected and popular spots, though with more than 200 vendors, it pays to shop around as prices and quality vary.

COOPEARSA Souvenirs
(☎2454-4196, 2454-4050; www.coopearsa. com; Sarchí Norte) Kitsch-filled paradise of *carretas*, woodwork and painted feathers. It's 200m west of the soccer field.

FÁBRICA DE CARRETAS
ELOY ALFARO Handicrafts
(☎2454-4131; Sarchí Norte) The country's oldest workshop; produced the massive

Crater of Volcán Poás (p90)

Detour:
Los Ángeles Cloud Forest Adventure Park

This private reserve, 18km north of San Ramón, is centered on a lodge and dairy ranch that was once owned by ex-president Rodrigo Carazo. Some 800 hectares of primary and secondary forest have a short boardwalk and 11km of foot trails that lead to towering waterfalls and misty cloud-forest vistas. The appeal of this cloud forest (which is actually adjacent to the reserve at Monteverde) is that it is comparatively untouristed, which means you will have a good chance of observing wildlife (jaguars and ocelots have been spotted), and the bird-watching is fantastic.

Bilingual naturalist guides are available to lead hikes (per person US$30) and guided horseback-riding trips (per hour US$20). Alternatively, you can zip along the treetops on the reserve's canopy tour (per person US$45).

A taxi to the reserve and hotel costs about US$15 from San Ramón, and the turnoff is well signed from the Interamericana.

oxcart in Sarchí's main plaza. It's 100m north of Palí Supermarket.

FÁBRICA DE CARRETAS JOAQUÍN CHAVERRI   Handicrafts
(☎ 2454-4411; Sarchí Sur) Oldest and best-known factory; watch artisans doing meticulous work in the small studio.

🛈 Getting There & Away

Buses arrive and depart from Sarchí Norte.
Alajuela US$0.80, 30 minutes, departs half-hourly from 5am to 10pm.
San José US$2, 1½ hours, departs half-hourly between 5am and 10pm.

If you're driving from San José, from the Interamericana, take the signed exit to Grecia and from there follow the road north to Sarchí.

PALMARES
POP 8900

Palmares' claim to fame is the annual **Las Fiestas de Palmares**, a 10-day beer-soaked extravaganza that takes place in mid-January and features carnival rides, a *tope* (horse parade), fireworks, big-name bands, exotic dancers, fried food, *guaro* (the local firewater made from sugarcane) and some 10,000 people. It is one of the biggest events in the country and covered widely on national TV. For the other 355 days of the year, Palmares is a tumbleweed

town, where life is centered on the ornate stained-glass **church** in the central plaza.

Buses run continuously from San José to Palmares throughout the festival. For information on the musical lineup, visit www.fiestaspalmares.com.

HEREDIA
POP 33,000

During the 19th century, La Ciudad de las Flores (The City of the Flowers) was home to a *cofetalero* (coffee grower) aristocracy that made its fortune exporting Costa Rica's premium blend. Today the historic center retains some of this well-bred air, with a leafy main square that is overlooked by a stocky cathedral and low-lying buildings that channel the architecture of the Spanish colony.

Sights

IGLESIA DE LA INMACULADA CONCEPCIÓN   Church
(east side of Parque Central) Built in 1797, this church is still in use.

EL FORTÍN   Tower
(north of Parque Central) This 1867 guard tower is the last remaining turret of a Spanish fortress and the official symbol of Heredia – it's a national historic site.

Heredia

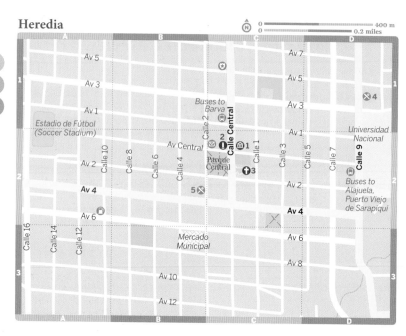

Heredia

Sights
1 Casa de la Cultura C2
2 El Fortín C2
3 Iglesia de la Inmaculada
    Concepción C2

Eating
4 Cowboy Steakhouse D1
5 Espigas B2

CASA DE LA CULTURA Museum
(☎ 2261-4485; cnr Calle Central & Av Central; admission free; ⏰hours vary) The Casa de la Cultura occupies a low-lying Spanish structure that dates back to the 18th century. The building once served as the residence of President Alfredo González Flores, who governed from 1913 to 1917. It is beautifully maintained and now houses permanent historical displays and art exhibits.

INBIOPARQUE Gardens
(☎ 2507-8107; www.inbioparque.com/en; Santo Domingo; adult/student/child US$23/17/13, parking US$3; ⏰8am-3pm Fri, 9am-4pm Sat & Sun; ♿) This wildlife park and botanical garden is run by the nonprofit National Biodiversity Institute (INBio), which catalogs Costa Rica's biodiversity and promotes its sustainable use. It's 4km south of Heredia.

Sleeping

HOTEL CHALET TIROL Inn $$$
(☎ 2267-6222; www.hotelchaleteltirol.com; d US$93-155, ste US$93-128, all incl breakfast; ℗ 🛜) Northeast of Heredia and 3km north of Castillo Country Club, you'll find this charming hotel channeling the gingerbread quaintness of the Alps (it was once covered in fake snow and used as a backdrop for a German beer advert.) The 25 suites and two-story chalets, all of which have cable TV, room service and a gorgeous mountain setting, range from minimalist to kitted out with extras such as Jacuzzis and working fireplaces. Two suites are wheelchair-accessible. On weekends the in-house restaurant hosts live music in the evenings.

HOTEL BOUGAINVILLEA Hotel $$$
(☎ 2244-1414; www.hb.co.cr; Santo Domingo; d incl breakfast US$105-130; ℗ 🛏 @ 🛜 ✱) Set

on 4 hectares about 6km outside of town, this efficient hotel is surrounded by an expansive, well-manicured garden dotted with old-growth trees, stunning flowers and plenty of statuary. Eighty-two crisp, whitewashed rooms have balconies with views of mountains or city, and several private trails wind by the swimming pool and tennis courts, through forest and orchards.

 Eating

ESPIGAS Costa Rican **$**
(☎ 2237-3275; cnr Av 2 & Calle 2; breakfast US$6.50, mains US$4-8; ⏰ 7am-9pm) One of the only, if not *the* only, eateries open on Sunday, Espigas is the go-to cafe for delicious set breakfasts. Order sit-down meals at the counter, stop by the front window to pick up fresh *batidos* (fruit shakes) or pop in for a look at the tantalizing pastry case.

COWBOY STEAKHOUSE Steakhouse **$$**
(☎ 2237-8719; Calle 9 btwn Avs 3 & 5; dishes US$4-15; ⏰ 5-11pm Mon-Sat) This yellow-and-red joint with two bars has patio seating and the best beef cuts in town. As the title suggests, steak is the focal point, making it a meat-lover's must. But the hearty salads and extensive list of *bocas* (savory bar snacks) are worth a nibble as well.

 **ⓘ Getting There & Away**
Buses go to the following destinations:

Alajuela US$0.80, 20 minutes, departs every 15 minutes from 6am to 10pm.

Barva US$0.65, 20 minutes, departs half-hourly from 5:15am to 11:30pm.

Puerto Viejo de Sarapiquí US$2.50, 3½ hours, departs at 11am, 1:30pm and 3pm.

San José US$0.90, 20 minutes, departs every 20 to 30 minutes from 4:40am to 11pm.

BARVA
POP 6100

Just 2.5km north of Heredia is the historic town of Barva, a settlement that dates back to 1561 and which has been declared a national monument. The town center is dotted with low-lying 19th-century buildings and is centered on the towering Iglesia San Bartolomé, which was constructed in 1893. Surrounded by picturesque mountains, it oozes colonial charm.

Sara Longwing butterfly

PAUL KENNEDY / GETTY IMAGES ©

JESUS OCHOA ©

Don't Miss **Basílica de Nuestra Señora de Los Ángeles**

The most important site in Cartago – and the most venerated religious site in the country – this basilica exudes airy Byzantine grace, with fine stained-glass windows, hand-painted interiors and ornate side chapels featuring carved wood altars. Though the structure has changed many times since 1635, when it was first built, the relic that it protects remains unharmed inside.

La Negrita (the Black Virgin) is a small (less than 1m tall), probably indigenous, representation of the Virgin Mary, found on this spot on August 2, 1635 by a native woman. As the story goes, when she tried to take the statuette with her, it miraculously reappeared back where she'd found it. Twice. So the townspeople built a shrine around her. Each August 2, on the anniversary of the statuette's miraculous discovery, pilgrims from every corner of the country (and beyond) walk the 22km from San José to the basilica. Many of the penitent complete the last few hundred meters of the pilgrimage on their knees.

NEED TO KNOW
Cnr Av 2 & Calle 16

◎ Sights & Activities

MUSEO DE CULTURA POPULAR
Museum
(☏ 2260-1619; Santa Lucía; admission US$3; ☉ 10am-5pm Sun) Housed in a restored 19th-century farmhouse about 1.5km southeast of Barva, this tiny museum

exhibits period pieces, such as domestic and agricultural tools.

CAFÉ BRITT FINCA
Guided Tour
(☏ 2277-1600; www.coffeetour.com; adult with/ without lunch US$37/20, student US$32/16; ☉ tours 9:30am & 11am;) The most famous coffee roaster in Costa Rica, Café Britt Finca offers a 90-minute bilingual

tour of its area plantation that includes coffee tasting, a video presentation and a hokey stage play about the history of coffee (small kids will likely dig it). More in-depth tours are available, as are packages including transport from San José; reserve ahead. Drivers won't be able to miss the *many* signs between Heredia and Barva.

Festivals & Events

Every March the town is home to the famous **Feria de la Mascarada**, a tradition with roots in the colonial era, in which people don massive colorful masks (some of which weigh up to 20kg), and gather to dance and parade around the town square. Demons and devils are frequent subjects, but celebrities and politicians also figure in the mix of characters.

ℹ Getting There & Away

Half-hourly buses travel between Heredia and Barva (US$0.85, 20 minutes), picking up and dropping off in front of the church.

CARTAGO
POP 24,900

Following major earthquake damage in the early 20th century, nobody bothered to rebuild Cartago to its former quaint specifications. As in other commercial towns, expect plenty of functional concrete structures. One exception is the Basílica de Nuestra Señora de los Ángeles, which is visible from many parts of the city, standing out like a snowcapped mountain above a plain of one-story edifices.

Sleeping & Eating

LOS ÁNGELES LODGE B&B $$
(☎ 2591-4169, 2551-0957; Av 4 btwn Calles 14 & 16; s/d incl breakfast US$35/50; P ✳ 🛜) With its balconies overlooking the Plaza de la Basílica, this decent B&B stands out with spacious and comfortable rooms, hot showers and breakfast made to order by the cheerful owners.

HOTEL DINASTÍA Hotel $
(☎ 2551-7057; Calle 3 near Av 6; r with/without bathroom US$20/15) The only budget option in town, this bare-bones spot has 27 aging rooms with thin walls. Rooms with private bathroom have hot water. It's located behind the bus station.

LA PUERTA DEL SOL Costa Rican $$
(☎ 2551-0615; Av 4 btwn Calles 14 & 16; mains US$6-10; ⊙8am-10pm Sun-Thu, to midnight Fri & Sat) Located downstairs from Los Ángeles Lodge, this pleasant restaurant has been around since 1957 and serves myriad Tico specialties as well as burgers

Farming banana plantains
CHRISTER FREDRIKSSON / GETTY IMAGES ©

and sandwiches. Don't miss the vintage photos of Cartago displayed on the walls.

🛈 Getting There & Away

Bus stops to the following destinations are scattered around town.

San José US$0.85, 45 minutes, departs every 15 minutes until midnight.

Turrialba US$1.40, 1½ hours, departs every 45 minutes from 6am to 10pm weekdays, 8:30am, 11:30am, 1:30pm, 3pm and 5:45pm weekends.

Volcán Irazú US$6, five hours round-trip, departs Cartago around 8:30am, departs Irazú 12:30pm.

PARQUE NACIONAL VOLCÁN IRAZÚ

Looming on the horizon 19km northeast of Cartago, Irazú, which derives its name from the indigenous word *ara-tzu* (thunderpoint), is the largest and highest (3432m) active volcano in Costa Rica. In 1723 the Spanish governor of the area, Diego de la Haya Fernández, watched helplessly as the volcano unleashed its destruction on the city of Cartago (one of the craters is named in his honor). Since the 18th century 15 major eruptions have been recorded.

One of the most memorable occurred in March 1963, welcoming visiting US President John F Kennedy with a rain of volcanic ash that blanketed most of the Central Valley (up to a depth of more than 0.5m). In 1994 Irazú unexpectedly belched a cloud of sulfurous gas, though it quickly quieted down. At the time of writing, the volcano was slumbering peacefully.

The national park was established in 1955 to protect 23 sq km around the base of the volcano. The summit is a bare landscape of volcanic-ash craters. The principal crater is 1050m in diameter and 300m deep; the Diego de la Haya Crater is 1000m in diameter, 80m deep and contains a small lake.

🛈 Information

Pay admission and parking fees at the ranger station (☏ 2200-5025, in Cartago 2551-9398; park admission US$10, parking US$2.20; ☉ 8am–

3:30pm) at the park's entrance. There's a basic cafe and gift shop inside the park. Note that cloud cover starts thickening, even under the best conditions, by about 10am, about the same time that the bus rolls in. If you're on one of those buses, do yourself a favor and head straight for the crater. If you have a car, make an effort to arrive early and you'll likely be rewarded with the best possible views and an uncrowded observation area.

At the summit it is possible to see both the Pacific Ocean and the Caribbean Sea, but it is rarely clear enough. The best chance for a clear view is in the very early morning during the dry season (January to April). It tends to be cold and windy up here and there's an annual rainfall of 2160mm – come prepared with warm, rainproof clothes.

From the parking lot, a 200m trail leads to a viewpoint over the craters. While hiking, be on the lookout for high-altitude bird species, such as the volcano junco.

Getting There & Away

The only public transportation (US$6) to Irazú departs from San José at 8am, stops in Cartago at about 8:30am and arrives at the summit around 10am. The bus departs from Irazú at 12:30pm.

VALLE DE OROSI

This straight-out-of-a-storybook river valley is famous for its mountain vistas, hot springs, a lake formed by a hydro-electric facility, a truly wild national park and coffee – lots and lots of coffee. A 60km scenic loop (freshly paved in 2009) winds through a landscape of rolling hills terraced with shade-grown coffee plantations and expansive valleys dotted with pastoral villages. This is too time consuming on a bus, but those who have a rental car (or a good bicycle) are in for a treat.

The loop road starts 8km southeast of Cartago in Paraíso, and then heads south to Orosi. At this point you can either continue south into Parque Nacional Tapantí-Macizo Cerro de la Muerte or loop back to Paraíso via Ujarrás.

99

PARQUE NACIONAL TAPANTÍ-MACIZO CERRO DE LA MUERTE

This 580-sq-km **national park** (admission US$10; ☉8am-4pm) protects the lush northern slopes of the Cordillera de Talamanca, and has a rainy claim to fame: it is the wettest park in the country, getting almost 8000mm of precipitation a year. In 2000 it was expanded to include the infamous Cerro de la Muerte – otherwise known as the 'Mountain of Death.' This precipitous peak is the highest point on the Interamericana, a highland shrub and tussock grass habitat that's common to the Andes and is home to a variety of rare bird species.

Known simply as Tapantí, the park also protects wild and mossy country that's fed by, literally, hundreds of rivers. Waterfalls abound, vegetation is thick and the wildlife is prolific, though not always easy to see because of the rugged terrain.

There is an **information center** (☎2200-0090; ☉6am-4pm) near the park

White-Water Rafting in the Central Valley

There are two major rivers in the Turrialba area that are popular for rafting – the Río Reventazón and the Río Pacuare. The following is a quick guide to the ins and outs (and ups and downs) of each.

RÍO REVENTAZÓN

This storied rock-lined river has its beginnings at the Lago de Cachí, an artificial lake created by a dam of the same name. It begins here, at 1000m above sea level, and splashes down the eastern slopes of the cordilleras to the Caribbean lowlands. It is one of the most difficult, adrenaline-pumping runs in the country, with more than 65km of rapids.

Tour operators divide the river into four sections between the dam and the take-out point in Siquirres.

○ **El Carmen** A Class II float that's perfect for families.

○ **Florida** The final and most popular segment is a scenic Class III with a little more white water to keep things interesting.

○ **Pascua** Has 15 Class-IV rapids and is considered to be the classic run.

○ **Peralta** Rated Class V, this section is the most challenging; tours do not always run it due to safety concerns.

RÍO PACUARE

The Río Pacuare is the next major river valley east of the Reventazón, and has arguably the most scenic rafting in Costa Rica, if not Central America. The river plunges down the Caribbean slope through a series of spectacular canyons clothed in virgin rainforest, through runs named for their fury. The Pacuare can be run year-round, though June to October are considered the best months.

○ **Lower Pacuare** With Class II–IV rapids, this is the more accessible run: 28km through rocky gorges, past an indigenous village and untamed jungle.

○ **Upper Pacuare** Also classified as Class III–IV, but a few sections can go to Class V, depending on conditions. It's about a two-hour drive to the put-in, after which you'll have the prettiest jungle cruise on earth all to yourself.

entrance where you can pick up a simple park map to a couple of trails leading to various attractions. The 'dry' season (January to April) is generally considered the best time to visit.

 Getting There & Away

If you have your own car, you can take a bumpy gravel road (4WD recommended) from Purisil to the park entrance.

TURRIALBA

27,000

When the railway shut down in 1991, commerce slowed down, but Turrialba nonetheless remained a regional agricultural center, where local coffee planters could bring their crops to market. And with tourism on the rise in the 1990s, this modest mountain town soon became known as the gateway to some of the best white-water rafting on the planet. By the early 2000s, Turrialba was a hotbed of international rafters looking for Class-V thrills.

⊙ Sights

CATIE   Gardens

(Centro Agronómico Tropical de Investigación | Center for Tropical Agronomy Research & Education; 2556-2700; www.catie.ac.cr/jardinbotanico; admission US$10, guided tours US$25-50; ⏰7am-4pm Mon-Fri, 8am-4pm Sat & Sun) About 4km east of Turrialba, Catie consists of 1000 hectares dedicated to tropical agricultural research and education. Agronomists from all over the world recognize this as one of the most important centers in the tropics.

👉 Tours

Plenty of operators offer either kayaking or rafting in the area.

COSTA RICA RÍOS   Rafting

(in USA & Canada 888-434-0776; www.costaricarios.com) Week-long rafting trips must be booked in advance.

 If You Like…
Flora & Fauna

If you like the natural wonders of flora and fauna at INBioparque, we think you'll like these other glimpses into the astounding nature of the Central Valley:

1 BUTTERFLY FARM
(2438-0400; www.butterflyfarm.co.cr; La Guácima de Alajuela; adult/child 4-11yr $19/12.50, with transportation from San José $40/25; ⏰tours 8:30am, 11am, 1pm & 3pm) Started in 1983, this farm offers a fascinating look at the life cycles of these delicate and beautiful creatures.

2 WORLD OF SNAKES
(2494-3700; adult/child US$11/6; ⏰8am-4pm) Grecia's premiere attraction is a well-run breeding center focused on supporting endangered snake populations. It's a slithering delight for families.

3 ARA PROJECT
(8389-5811; www.thearaproject.org; Río Segundo de Alajuela; suggested per person donation US$20; ⏰by appointment) Richard and Margot Frisius founded this crucial and successful green and scarlet macaw breeding program in 1992 and continue the effort to reintroduce these magnificent birds into the wild.

4 LANKESTER GARDENS
(2511-7939; www.jbl.ucr.ac.cr; adult/student US$7/5; ⏰8:30am-4:30pm) The University of Costa Rica runs this exceptional garden, a tranquil 11-hectare spot, with more than 1100 orchids. There is also a new Japanese garden, as well as areas full of bromeliads, palms, heliconias and other tropical plants. Find it 5km west of Paraíso on the road to Cartago.

EXPLORNATURA   Adventure Tour
(2556-2070, in USA & Canada 866-571-2443; www.explornatura.com; Av 4 btwn Calles 2 & 4)

RÍO LOCOS   Rafting
(2556-6035; www.whiteh2o.com)

RAINFOREST WORLD   Rafting
(2556-0014; www.rforestw.com)

Detour:
Monumento Nacional Arqueológico Guayabo

Nestled into a patch of stunning hillside forest 19km northeast of Turrialba is the largest and most important **archaeological site** (☏559 1220; admission US$4, camp site US$2; ⊙information and exhibit center 8am-3:30pm) in the country. Guayabo is composed of the remains of a pre-Columbian city that was thought to have peaked at some point in AD 800, when it was inhabited by as many as 20,000 people. Today visitors can examine the remains of old petroglyphs, residential mounds, an old roadway and an impressive aqueduct system – built with rocks hauled in from the Río Reventazón along a cobbled 8km road. Amazingly, the cisterns still work.

The settlement may have been occupied as early as 1000 BC but was mysteriously abandoned by AD 1400. For centuries it lay largely untouched under the cover of the area's thick highland forest. But in 1968 archaeologist Carlos Aguilar Piedra of the University of Costa Rica began excavations of Guayabo, finding pottery and gold artifacts that are now exhibited at San José's Museo Nacional.

In 1973, as the site's importance became evident, Guayabo was declared a National Monument. The site occupies 232 hectares, most of which remains unexcavated. It's a small place – don't expect Mayan pyramids.

By car, head north out of Turrialba and follow the signs.

Buses from Turrialba (US$0.85, one hour) depart at 11:15am, 3:10pm and 5:20pm Monday through Saturday and at 9am, 3pm and 6:30pm on Sunday. Buses travel from Guayabo to Turrialba at 5:15am, 7am, 12:30pm and 4pm Monday through Saturday; 7am, 12:30pm and 4pm on Sunday. You can also take a taxi from Turrialba (from US$16).

TICO'S RIVER ADVENTURES   Rafting
(☏2556-1231; www.ticoriver.com)

Sleeping & Eating

CASA DE LIS HOSTEL   Hostel $
(☏2556-4933; www.hostelcasadelis.com; Av Central near Calle 2; dm US$10, d/tr/q US$40/45/50, without bathroom US$25/35/40; ☏) Just what Turrialba needed – a bright, new hostel right in the center of town. This sweet four-room place is spotless, with a fully equipped kitchen, roof terrace for enjoying volcano views, a small garden in the back and a distinctly friendly atmosphere. Inexpensive breakfasts (topping out at US$4) and laundry service are available.

TURRIALTICO LODGE   Lodge
(☏2538-1111; www.turrialtico.com; d incl breakfast US$64-75; P☏) Off the highway to Siquirres, 8km east of Turrialba, this Tico-run lodge has been owned and managed by the García family since 1968. There are 14 attractive, polished-wood-panel rooms in an old farmhouse that have paintings by local artists. Rooms in the reception building share a large terrace and sitting area, and a pleasant open-air restaurant (mains US$3 to US$15) serves up country cooking. Best of all are its fantastic, dramatic views.

HOTEL INTERAMERICANO   Hotel $
(☏2556-0142; www.hotelinteramericano.com; Av 1 near Calle 1; s/d/tr/q US$25/35/50/65, without bathroom US$11/22/33/44; P☏) On the south side of the old train tracks is this basic 22-room hotel, regarded by rafters

as *the* meeting place in Turrialba. The showers are clean, the tiled rooms are bright, and Luis, the bilingual manager, is a great source of local information.

TURRIALBA B&B
B&B

(☎2556-6651; akius@hotmail.com; Calle 1 north of Av 6; s/d/tr US$40/60/80; ❄️🛜) This tranquil spot has clean, bright, well-appointed rooms, a cozy living-room area, a lovely garden patio equipped with a Jacuzzi and a library chock-full of travel guides on Latin America. There is also a shared kitchen and a small bar. Excellent value.

🖊️CASA TURIRE
Luxury Hotel $$$

(☎2531-1111; www.hotelcasaturire.com; d standard/ste/master ste incl breakfast US$135/210/350, additional person US$25-55, child under 6yr free; 🅿️❄️@🛜♨️) From the highway, take the turnoff to La Suiza/Tuis, head south for 2km and you'll see signs leading to Casa Turire. An elegant three-story plantation inn, it has 16 graceful well-appointed rooms with high ceilings, wood floors and wrought-iron beds; a massive master suite comes with a Jacuzzi and excellent views of the coffee and macadamia-nut plantations in the distance. Spa services are available among a suite of activities.

PANADERÍA LA CASTELLANA
Bakery $

(☎2556-9090; www.lacastellanacr.com; cnr Calle 2 & Av 4; breakfast US$2.50-5, pizzas US$8-13; ⏱️24hr) Whether it's pizza by the slice, *gallo pinto* (a common meal of blended rice and beans) and eggs or coffee and a pastry, La Castellana does it well and at all hours. It even offers half-orders for smaller appetites. Dine in, or pick up some whole-wheat bread or desserts for eats on the road.

RESTAURANT BETICO MATA
Barbecue $

(☎2556-8640; Hwy 10; gallos US$1.25-1.75; ⏱️11am-midnight, until later Sat & Sun) This carnivore's paradise at the south end of town specializes in *gallos* (open-faced tacos on corn tortillas) piled with succulent, fresh-grilled meats including beef, chicken, sausage or pork. The restaurant has a counter that faces the street – making it easy to pick up a snack if you're driving through town.

ℹ️ Getting There & Away

A modern bus terminal is located on the western edge of town off Hwy 10. Buses run to the following destinations:

San José via Paraíso & Cartago US$2.60, two hours, departs every 45 minutes from 5am to 6:30pm.

Siquirres, for transfer to Puerto Limón US$2.25, 1¾ hours, departs every 60 to 90 minutes from 6am to 6pm.

Northern Costa Rica

Perfect waves, lush jungles, glowering volcanoes: this is Northern Costa Rica. Whether hiking in the shadow of Volcán Arenal; catching a flash of green from a quetzal's wing or riding the perfect barrel at Witch's Rock, the region is heavily traveled for good reason. From the blazing, dry beaches of the Guanacaste coast to the mist-shrouded heights of Volcán Miravalles, this is the turf that has long held the banner attractions for Costa Rica's eco-minded adventure travelers.

Beyond the touristed areas lie the northern lowlands, where plantations of bananas, sugarcane and pineapples roll across the humid plains from the Cordillera Central to the Nicaraguan border. And though it might rarely enter a daydream, this is real-life Costa Rica, where the balance of agricultural commerce and ecological conservation converge to create a contemporary work in green progress.

Canopy walkway, Reserva Biológica Bosque Nuboso
Monteverde (p146)

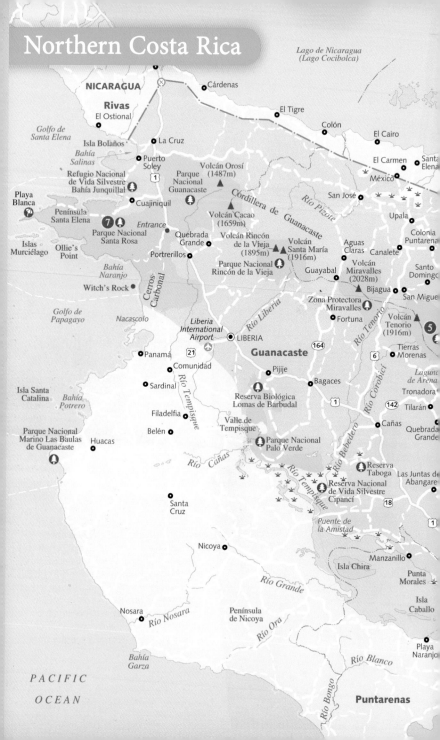

Northern Costa Rica

Lago de Nicaragua
(Lago Cocibolca)

NICARAGUA

Rivas
El Ostional

Cárdenas

El Tigre

Colón

El Cairo

El Carmen

Santa Elena

México

Golfo de
Santa Elena

Isla Bolaños

La Cruz

San José

Bahía
Salinas

Puerto
Soley

Refugio Nacional
de Vida Silvestre
Bahía Junquillal

Parque
Nacional
Guanacaste

Volcán Orosí
(1487m)

Córdillera de Guanacaste

Río Pizote

Upala

Playa
Blanca

Península
Santa Elena

Cuajiniquil

Volcán Cacao
(1659m)

Colonia
Puntarena

Islas
Murciélago

Entrance

Parque Nacional
Santa Rosa

Quebrada
Grande

Volcán Rincón
de la Vieja
(1895m)

Volcán
Santa María
(1916m)

Aguas
Claras

Canalete

Ollie's
Point

Portrerillos

Parque Nacional
Rincón de la Vieja

Guayabal

Volcán
Miravalles
(2028m)

Santo
Domingo

Cerros Carbonal

Bahía
Naranjo

Witch's Rock

Río Liberia

Bijagua

San Miguel

Golfo de
Papagayo

Nacascolo

Zona Protectora
Miravalles

Fortuna

Volcán
Tenorio
(1916m)

Liberia
International
Airport

LIBERIA

Guanacaste

164

Río Tenorio

Tierras
Morenas

Río Corobicí

6

Panamá

Comunidad

Pijije

Bagaces

Laguna
de Arena

Tronadora

Isla Santa
Catalina

Bahía
Potrero

Sardinal

Río Tempisque

Reserva Biológica
Lomas de Barbudal

1

142

Tilarán

Cañas

Quebrada
Grande

Parque Nacional
Marino Las Baulas
de Guanacaste

Huacas

Filadelfia

Belén

Valle de
Tempisque

Parque Nacional
Palo Verde

Río Cañas

Reserva
Taboga

Las Juntas de
Abangare

Reserva Nacional
de Vida Silvestre
Cipancí

18

Santa
Cruz

Río Tempisque

Puente de
la Amistad

1

Nicoya

Manzanillo

Isla Chira

Punta
Morales

Nosara

Río Nosara

Península
de Nicoya

Río Grande

Río Ora

Isla
Caballo

Playa
Naranjo

Bahía
Garza

Río Bongo

Río Blanco

Puntarenas

PACIFIC

OCEAN

21

7

5

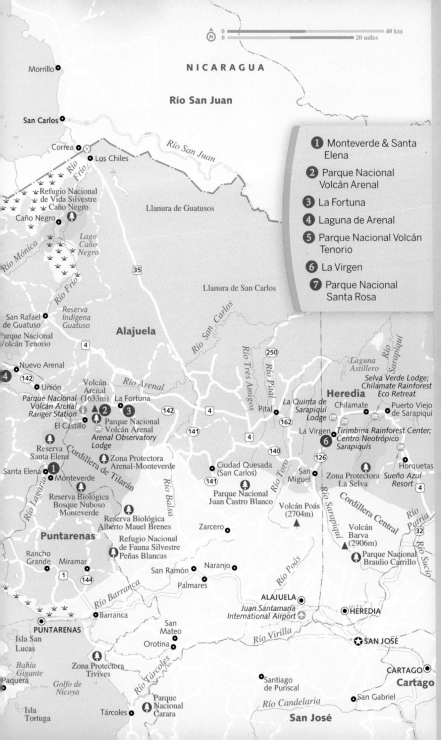

NICARAGUA

Río San Juan

Morrillo

San Carlos

Correa

Los Chiles

Río San Juan

Río Frío

Refugio Nacional
de Vida Silvestre
Caño Negro

Caño Negro

Lago
Caño
Negro

Llanura de Guatusos

Río Mónica

35

Llanura de San Carlos

San Rafael
de Guatuso

Reserva
Indígena
Guatuso

Alajuela

Río San Carlos

Parque Nacional
Volcán Tenorio

4

Río Tres Amigos

Río Pital

250

Laguna
Astillero

Río Sarapiquí

Selva Verde Lodge;
Chilamate Rainforest
Eco Retreat

Nuevo Arenal

142

Unión

Volcán
Arenal
(1633m)

Río Arenal

La Fortuna

Parque Nacional
Volcán Arenal
Ranger Station

El Castillo

142

Parque Nacional
Volcán Arenal
Arenal Observatory
Lodge

141

Pital

162

Chilamate

Heredia

Puerto Viejo
de Sarapiquí

La Quinta de
Sarapiquí
Lodge

La Virgen

Tirimbina Rainforest Center;
Centro Neotrópico
Sarapiquís

Reserva
Santa Elena

Cordillera de Tilarán

Zona Protectora
Arenal-Monteverde

Río Balsa

4

140

126

Horquetas

Santa Elena

Monteverde

Ciudad Quesada
(San Carlos)

San
Miguel

Zona Protectora
La Selva

Sueño Azul
Resort

4

Reserva Biológica
Bosque Nuboso
Monteverde

141

Parque Nacional
Juan Castro Blanco

Río Toro

Río Sarapiquí

Cordillera Central

Río Patria

Reserva Biológica
Alberto Mauel Brenes

Zarcero

Volcán Poás
(2704m)

32

Puntarenas

Refugio Nacional
de Fauna Silvestre
Peñas Blancas

Río Poás

Volcán
Barva
(2906m)

Río Sucio

Rancho
Grande

Miramar

San Ramón

Naranjo

Parque Nacional
Braulio Carrillo

1

144

Palmares

Río Barranca

San
Mateo

ALAJUELA

Juan Santamaría
International Airport

HEREDIA

PUNTARENAS

Barranca

Orotina

Río Virilla

SAN JOSÉ

Isla San
Lucas

CARTAGO

Cartago

Bahía
Gigante

Paquera

Zona Protectora
Tivives

Golfo de
Nicoya

Río Tárcoles

Santiago
de Puriscal

San Gabriel

Isla
Tortuga

Tárcoles

Parque
Nacional
Carara

Río Candelaria

San José

① Monteverde & Santa
Elena

② Parque Nacional
Volcán Arenal

③ La Fortuna

④ Laguna de Arenal

⑤ Parque Nacional Volcán
Tenorio

⑥ La Virgen

⑦ Parque Nacional
Santa Rosa

0   40 km
0   20 miles

Northern Costa Rica Highlights

1

Monteverde & Santa Elena

Monteverde and Santa Elena (p135) are a destination for biologists, and ongoing research has broadened knowledge of tropical ecosystems. They are also popular tourist destinations, with lodgings and restaurants for every taste. Activities include family-oriented tours, wilderness treks and cloud-forest zip lines. Above: Mountains, Monteverde; Above right: Zip lining in Monteverde; Below right: Quetzal, male

Need to Know

WHEN TO VISIT Clouds blanket the forest in mid-November to February, the misty season **FITNESS** Trail lengths from 300m allowing all hiking abilities **For more, see p135**

Monteverde & Santa Elena Don't Miss List

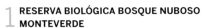

BY J ANDRÉS VARGAS, DIRECTOR OF EUFORIA EXPEDITIONS

1 RESERVA BIOLÓGICA BOSQUE NUBOSO MONTEVERDE

One of the country's most famous biological reserves, Monteverde is a bird-watching paradise. Although the list of recorded species exceeds 400, the one most visitors want to see is the quetzal. The Maya bird of paradise is most often spotted during the March and April nesting season, but you could get lucky any time. For mammal-watchers, commonly sighted species include coatis, howler monkeys, capuchins, sloths, agoutis and squirrels.

2 MONTEVERDE BACKCOUNTRY TREKKING

Longer, less developed trails stretch out east across the reserve and down the Peñas Blancas river valley to lowlands north of the Cordillera de Tilarán and into the Bosque Eterno de los Niños (Children's Eternal Forest). If you are strong and have time to spare, these hikes are highly recommended as you'll maximize your chances of spotting wildlife. If you're serious about visiting the backcountry, hire a reliable guide – you'll be entering rugged terrain.

3 RESERVA SANTA ELENA

This community-managed reserve is slightly higher in elevation than Monteverde. Since some of the forest is secondary growth, there are sunnier places for spotting birds and other animals throughout. This place is moist, and almost all the water comes as fine mist. More than 25 percent of all the biomass in the forest consists of epiphytes (mosses and lichens), for which this is a humid haven. Ten percent of species here aren't found in Monteverde, which is largely on the other side of the continental divide.

4 CANOPY TOURS

Wondering where the whole Costa Rican zip line craze was born? Here in Santa Elena, the site of Costa Rica's first canopy tour. You won't be spotting quetzals or coatis as you whoosh over the canopy, but this is the best way to burn your holiday buck on some adrenaline-soaked thrills.

Parque Nacional Volcán Arenal

The most obvious reason to visit this park is Volcán Arenal. Since erupting in 1968 it has been one of the world's most active volcanoes (though it has recently calmed down). Surrounded by jungle, waterfalls and hardened lava flows, the area is home to over 350 bird species, abundant mammals and fascinating insects. Below: Volcán Arenal; Above right: Mantled howler monkey; Below right: Trekking to Volcán Arenal

Need to Know

ACCESS Parque Nacional Volcán Arenal is easily accessed from the town of La Fortuna **ONLINE** Check out all things Arenal at www.arenal.net **For more, see p125**

2

Parque Nacional Volcán Arenal Don't Miss List

BY CHRISTIAN CAMPOS, NATURALIST GUIDE FOR THE ARENAL OBSERVATORY LODGE

1 VOLCÁN ARENAL

Even though the degree of activity has lessened and you can no longer see the spectacular display of flowing red-hot lava, Costa Rica's most famous volcano is still one of the region's monumental sights that cannot be missed. As you drive through the region, you'll catch amazing views of the mist-capped mountain and surrounding jungle. It is an awe-inspiring testament to the power of mother nature, even without the glow.

2 WILDLIFE-WATCHING

This area is rugged and varied, and the biodiversity is very high; roughly half the species of land-dwelling vertebrates known in Costa Rica can be found here. Bird-life is very rich in the park, and includes species such as trogons, rufous motmots, fruitcrows and lancebills. Commonly sighted mammals include howler monkeys, white-faced capuchins and coatis.

3 ARENAL OBSERVATORY LODGE

Even if you're not staying here, the lodge (p128) is worth visiting as there are 6km of trails in total. A handful of short hikes include views of a nearby waterfall, while sturdy souls could check out recently cooled lava flows (2½ hours), old lava flows (three hours) or climb to Arenal's long-dormant partner, Volcán Chato (four hours), the crater of which holds a 1100m-high lake. The lodge also has a 4.5km bike trail that winds through secondary forest, as well as a 1km sidewalk trail that is completely wheelchair-accessible.

4 HIKING IN THE NATIONAL PARK

From the ranger station and the park headquarters there is an extensive network of trails. Independent exploration is permitted, but you'll get the most out of the experience if you bring along a knowledgeable guide.

La Fortuna

The closest town to Volcán Arenal, La Fortuna (p118) welcomes visitors with its well-developed tourist infrastructure. After a good night's sleep and a delectable meal, check out the incredible number of activities on offer. True hedonists can spend days soaking in the hot springs, while adventure buffs will want to go bungee jumping, canyoning, horseback riding and zip lining. La Cataratade la Fortuna (p119)

3

4 ## Laguna de Arenal

Although you're going to need a car to make the most of this stunningly beautiful region, Laguna de Arenal (p129) has all the makings of a classic road trip. First of all, there is the vibrant nature on display, prompting many to make the comparison to Switzerland. Add to the mix boutique hotels and gourmet restaurants, and suddenly you have a multistop itinerary that can take a couple of days to complete.

Parque Nacional Volcán Tenorio **5**

One of the region's hidden treasures, this national park (p156) is centered on a series of volcanoes, but the undisputed highlight is the Río Celeste, a milky-blue river complete with a dramatic cascade. The vibrant hues are the result of the rich mineral deposits that collect in high concentrations in the waterway.

Waterfall, Río Celeste (p156)

CRAIGE BEVIL / ALAMY ©

6
La Virgen

If you're an avid kayaker – or if you've ever thought about going kayaking – the far-flung town of La Virgen (p160) in the northern lowlands should make an appearance on your itinerary. With a whole slew of crisscrossing rivers to choose from, the area around La Virgen has the country's most diverse offering of kayak runs. Rafting on Río Sarapiquí (p161), La Virgen

7
Parque Nacional Santa Rosa

Lying just south of the Nicaraguan border, this remote national park (p158) takes some serious commitment to access. But if you're interested in surfing two legendary breaks – namely Witch's Rock and Ollie's Point (p159) – it's most definitely worth the long boat ride out to the country's extreme northwestern corner. Surf break at Witch's Rock

Northern Costa Rica's Best...

Splurges

○ **Tabacón Grand Spa Thermal Resort Lodge** (p123) Admire the rainforest from the Jacuzzi.

○ **Arenal Observatory Lodge** (p128) The only lodge within Parque Nacional Volcán Arenal.

○ **Hidden Canopy Treehouses** (p142) Indulge your inner child in a luxury tree house.

○ **Tenorio Lodge** (p157) Relax in volcano-view bungalows.

○ **Rancho Margot** (p128) This self-sufficient farm offers a luxurious connection with the land.

Vistas

○ **Monteverde and Santa Elena** (p135) The cloud-forest panoramas are everything you expect them to be: lush, misty and full of wildlife.

○ **Volcán Arenal** (p125) It's hard to top the dramatic sight of this geological monster – impressive even without the lava.

○ **Laguna de Arenal** (p129) Find a Switzerland-like vista in the middle of Central America.

○ **Volcán Chato** (p119) Peer into the crater of Arenal's long-dormant partner, which holds a sparkling lake, Cerro Chato.

Eats

○ **Restaurant Don Rufino** (p123) Eatery blending continental and Tico (Costa Rican) influences.

○ **Gingerbread Hotel and Restaurant** (p131) Menu changes weekly, ensuring the freshest fare.

○ **Sofia** (p144) Nuevo Latino spot transforming the Monteverde restaurant scene.

○ **Finca Artesana** (p129) Drop in for homemade hot sauces and baked goods.

○ **Copa de Oro** (p150) Don't miss the delectable seafood house specialty, *arroz copa de oro*.

Activities

- **Hiking** (p139) Monteverde and Santa Elena are within easy walking distance of some of the country's greatest hiking trails.

- **Kayaking** (p161) Head to La Virgen with oar in hand for excellent river kayaking.

- **Surfing** (p159) Parque Nacional Santa Rosa is an undisputed surfing mecca, with a variety of breaks for beginners and experts alike.

- **Zip lining** (p139) Santa Elena is home to Costa Rica's favorite high-speed jungle zip lines.

Need to Know

ADVANCE PLANNING

- **One month before** Book a rental car, as it increases your ability to move around this large and fairly spread-out region. Also make hotel reservations, since this corner of the country is always busy.

- **Two weeks before** Although Volcán Arenal is technically still active, lava flows are not expected again any time soon. Look online to get a sense of what to expect from the mountain.

RESOURCES

- **Arenal Tourism Information** (www.arenal.net)

- **Costa Rica Tourism Board** (www.visitcostarica.com)

- **Tico Times** (www.ticotimes.net)

GETTING AROUND

- **Air** An increasing number of international flights are touching down at and taking off from Liberia's Aeropuerto Internacional Daniel Oduber Quirós.

- **Bus** Distances are long, but intercity bus connections are reliable.

- **Car** The roads surrounding Laguna de Arenal are perfectly conducive to road-tripping.

- **Jeep-boat-jeep** This unique transportation combination connects La Fortuna to Monteverde.

- **Walk** The cloud forests of the northern reaches attract both casual hikers and serious trekkers.

BE FOREWARNED

- **Signage** Roads in northern Costa Rica are poorly signed, so it's best to bring along a good road map before setting out.

VITAL STATISTICS

- **Population** La Fortuna 10,000; Liberia 63,000

- **Best time to visit** Guanacaste has little rain November to April and bakes in the tropical sun. At higher elevations, such as in Monteverde and Santa Elena, temperatures are cooler and rainfall is fairly constant year-round. This region is popular all year though, so expect plenty of other visitors.

EMERGENCY NUMBERS

- **Emergency** 911

- **Fire** 118

- **Police** 117

Left: Rain-filled flower
Above: Giant grasshopper

Northern Costa Rica Itineraries

Even if your time is short, a romp through northern Costa Rica will present the country's vivid charms. From three days to a week or more, these itineraries bring you to the best the region has to offer.

LAGUNA DE ARENAL ③

LA FORTUNA ①

PARQUE NACIONAL VOLCÁN ARENAL ②

RESERVA SANTA ELENA ③

MONTEVERDE & SANTA ELENA ①

RESERVA BIOLÓGICA BOSQUE NUBOSO MONTEVERDE ②

3 DAYS

MONTEVERDE TO RESERVA SANTA ELENA
Monteverde & Santa Elena

Northern Costa Rica is an enormous region that takes time to access but, by focusing on Monteverde and Santa Elena, three days is just long enough to visit the top highlights and get a sense of the region. Truth be told, you could easily spend a week here and not exhaust the huge number of hiking and trekking opportunities on offer. There are also activities galore and plenty of boutique hotels, restaurants and galleries. Still, in three days you'll get the best of the best.

Base yourself in the adjacent towns of **(1) Monteverde & Santa Elena**, though make sure you allow time for coming and leaving as the access roads are largely unpaved and very slow-going. Make the most of your brief time here by staying busy around the clock – night tours through the Bosque Eterno de los Niños (Children's Eternal Forest) provide face-to-face encounters with nocturnal wildlife. During the daylight hours, a diverse range of hiking is available at both **(2) Reserva Biológica Bosque Nuboso Monteverde** and **(3) Reserva Santa Elena**, two of the country's most famous protected spaces. By the time you board the flight back home, you'll have seen some of the best the country has to offer.

 5 DAYS

LA FORTUNA TO LAGUNA DE ARENAL

La Fortuna & Around

Monteverde and Santa Elena garner their fair share of the spotlight, but the area around La Fortuna is a close contender when it comes to the country's top attractions. This tiny Tico town has one of the country's best tourist infrastructures, as well as a remarkable number of luxurious hot-spring resorts and tons of activities. Of course, the main reason you're here is to stand in awe of the Volcán Arenal, one of the world's most active volcanoes.

Everything centers on **(1) La Fortuna**, and with good reason – even if the weather isn't cooperating and Arenal is shrouded in clouds, you'll still enjoy yourself

immensely here. Hedonists can't seem to pry themselves away from Tabacón Hot Springs, while more outdoorsy types can hike to waterfalls or zip line through the forest canopy. If the weather is good, clear your agenda and make a beeline to **(2) Parque Nacional Volcán Arenal**. By day, you can hike along hardened lava flows. As an added bonus, the roads surrounding the nearby **(3) Laguna de Arenal** are perfect for road-tripping.

Laguna de Arenal (p129)

Discover Northern Costa Rica

At a Glance

○ **La Fortuna** Heavily traveled hub with hot springs and canopy tours galore.

○ **Parc Nacional Volcan Arenal** (p125) A volcano towers over the country's largest lake.

○ **Monteverde and Santa Elena** (p135) At the edge of the cloud forest, an ecotour destination.

○ **Liberia** (p148) This busy international airport offers quick access to Península de Nicoya.

LA FORTUNA & AROUND

POP 10,000

You'll be forgiven if your first impression of La Fortuna is somewhat lacking, what with all the tourists and uninspired cinder-block architecture. But with time its charms will be revealed. Here, horses graze in unimproved lots, spiny iguanas scramble through brush, sloth eyes peer from the riverside canopy, and sunny, eternal spring mornings carry just a kiss of humidity on their breath. Then there's that massive volcano looming on clear days. Yes, the influx of tourism has altered the face, fame and fortunes of this former one-horse town, and it's true that tour operators have set up shop on every block, but despite all the noise, the longer you linger, the more you'll see that La Fortuna has managed to retain an underlying, small-town *sabanero* (cowboy) feel.

◎ Sights & Activities

TABACÓN HOT SPRINGS Spring

(Map p120; ☎2519-1900; www. tabacon.com; day pass adult/child incl lunch or dinner US$85/40, evening pass incl dinner US$70/35, day pass without meals US$65/45; ☺10am-10pm; **P**) If a movie director ever needed a setting for a cheesy Garden of Eden dream sequence, Tabacón Hot Springs would be it. Here, broad-leaf palms, rare orchids and other florid tropical blooms part to reveal a 40°C (104°F) waterfall pouring over a (fake) cliff, and caves complete with camouflaged cup holders. Lounged across each well-placed stone-

Green iguana
MARK NEWMAN / GETTY IMAGES ©

La Fortuna

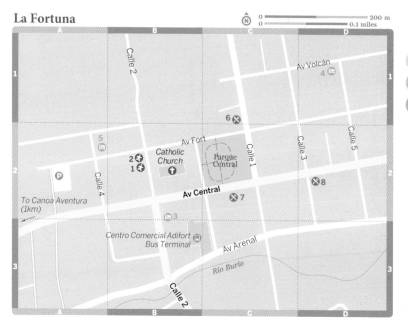

like substance, overheated tourists of various shapes and sizes relax.

The spa, 14km west of La Fortuna, is actually the site where a volcanic eruption ripped through in 1975, and the former village of Tabacón was destroyed in the 1968 eruption, killing 78. Don't, ahem, sweat it. The mountain is once again dormant. For now.

LA CATARATA DE LA FORTUNA Waterfall
(Map p120; admission US$10; ⏰ **8am-5pm)**
You can glimpse the sparkling 70m ribbon of clear water that pours through a sheer canyon of dark volcanic rock with minimal sweat equity. But it's worth the climb down and out to see it from the jungle floor. Though it's dangerous to dive beneath the thundering falls, a series of perfect swimming holes with spectacular views tiles the canyon in aquamarine. Keep an eye on your backpack.

From the turnoff on the road to San Ramón, it's about 4km uphill to the falls. If you decide to walk up, you'll enjoy spectacular views. You might appreciate a stop at **Neptune's House of Hammocks** (☎ 2479-8269; hammocks US$50-170). You can

La Fortuna

🟢 **Activities, Courses & Tours**
1 Desafío Adventure Company B2
2 Wave Expeditions B2

🔵 **Sleeping**
3 Arenal Hostel Resort B2
4 Cabinas Arsol D1
5 La Choza Inn A2

⬛ **Eating**
  Flying Tomato Cafe .... (see 4)
6 La Cascada C1
7 My Coffee C2
8 Restaurant Don Rufino D2

also get to the waterfall on horseback or by car or taxi.

CERRO CHATO Hiking
(Map p120) The La Catarata de la Fortuna (p119) falls are the trailhead for this seriously strenuous five- to six-hour climb of Volcán Chato to the beautiful lake-filled volcanic crater that is Cerro Chato. Starting from here, you'll have to pay a US$10 fee for crossing the *finca* (farm) leading to Cerro Chato.

119

Around La Fortuna

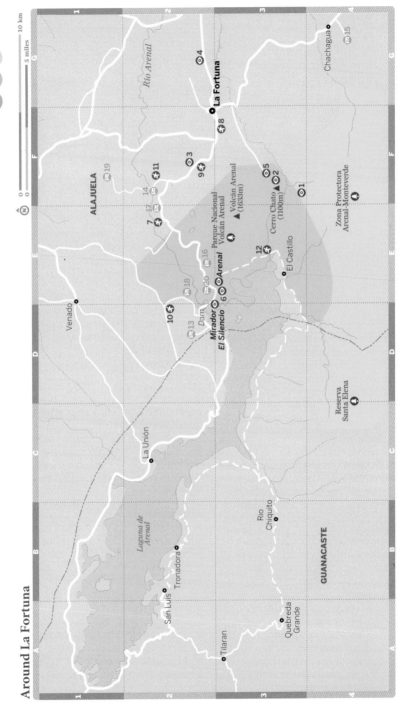

Around La Fortuna

◎ Sights

1	Arenal Observatory Lodge	F3
2	Cerro Chato	F3
3	Eco Thermales Hot Springs	F2
4	Ecocentro Danaus	G2
5	La Catarata de la Fortuna	F3
6	Tabacón Hot Springs	E3

◆ Activities, Courses & Tours

7	Arenal Paraíso Canopy Tours	E2
8	Canoa Aventura	F3
9	Ecoglide	F2
10	Puentes Colgantes de Arenal	D2
11	PureTrek Canyoning	F2
12	SkyTrek	E3

☺ Sleeping

13	Arenal Lodge	D2
14	Arenal Nayara Hotel & Gardens	F2
15	Chachagua Rainforest Hotel	G4
16	Erupciones Inn B&B	E2
17	Hotel Campo Verde	E2
18	Lost Iguana Resort	E2
19	Springs Resorts & Spa	F1
20	Tabacón Grand Spa Thermal Resort Lodge	E2

Tours

CANOA AVENTURA   Canoeing

(Map p120; ☏2479-8200; www.canoa-aventura. com; full-day trip to Caño Negro incl breakfast & lunch US$131; ☻6:30am-9:30pm) About 1.5km west of town on the road to Arenal, Canoa Aventura specializes in canoe and float trips led by bilingual naturalist guides. Most are geared toward wildlife and bird-watching. Popular paddles include the full-day trip to Caño Negro.

ECOGLIDE   Canopy Tour

(Map p120; ☏2479-7120; www.arenalecoglide. com; adult/student & child 5-12yr US$45/35; ☻8am-4pm; 🐾) Opened in 2008, Ecoglide is the biggest canopy game in town, featuring 12 cables, 14 platforms and a 'Tarzan' swing. The dual-cable safety system provides extra security and peace of mind.

ARENAL PARAÍSO CANOPY TOURS   Canopy Tour

(Map p120; ☏2479-1100; www.arenalparaiso. com; adult/student & child US$45/35) Popular two-hour tours along 12 zip lines.

PURETREK CANYONING   Canyoning

(Map p120; ☏1-866-569-5723, 2479-1315; www. puretrek.com; 4hr incl transportation & lunch US$98; ☻7am-10pm) Reputable PureTrek leads guided rappels down four waterfalls, one of which is 50m high. It's located several kilometers west of town. Children as young as five years old can participate, but there's no price break.

DESAFÍO ADVENTURE COMPANY   Rafting, Horse Riding

(Map p119; ☏2479-9464; www.desafiocos tarica.com; Calle 2; horse tour to Arenal US$65; ☻6:30am-9pm) Desafío has the widest range of river trips in La Fortuna, and offers paddling trips on the Río Balsa and, occasionally, the Sarapiquí.

It also offers horse-riding treks to Volcán Arenal, adventure tours rappelling down waterfalls and mountain-bike expeditions. Look for the crenelated new build.

WAVE EXPEDITIONS   Rafting, Kayaking

(Map p119; ☏2479-7262; www.waveexpeditions. com; cnr Calle 2 & Av Fort; river trips US$65-85; ☻7am-9pm) A rafting shop in the center of town, Wave Expeditions runs the wild Toro and mellower Balsa. You can also run the smooth Río Arenal on an inflatable kayak or pair a canopy zip-line tour with the rafting experience.

AGUAS BRAVAS   Rafting, Kayaking

(☏2479-7645; www.aguas-bravas.co.cr; safari float trip US$50, Class III/Class IV trips US$65/85; ☻7am-7pm) Aguas Bravas, 2km east of Fortuna, offers a gentle safari float trip on Peñas Blancas that's a good choice for families, plus Class III and IV trips.

Festivals & Events

The big annual bash is **Fiestas de la Fortuna**, held in mid-February and featuring two weeks of Tico-rules bullfights, colorful carnival rides, greasy food, craft stands and unusual gambling devices. It's free, except for the beer (which is cheap) and you'll have a blast getting down to *reggaetón* or the rough and wild tents with live *ranchero* and salsa music.

Sleeping

There are loads of places to stay in town. If you're driving, consider staying on the pastoral road to Cerro Chato, a few kilometers south of town, where several appealing hotels have cropped up, or closer to the volcano in El Castillo.

In the low season room rates plummet by as much as 40%.

In Town

CABINAS ARSOL B&B $
(Map p119; ✆ 2479-9913; www.cabinasarsol.com; Calle 5 & Av Volcan; s/d US$20/30, incl breakfast; @) A recently refurbished, American-Tica owned B&B with cramped and somewhat oddly situated rooms that also happen to have charms like pastel paint jobs and beamed ceilings. Beds are new, and digs are quite clean and come with cable TV.

There's an attached vegetarian cafe here too.

LA CHOZA INN Inn $
(Map p119; ✆ 2479-9361; www.lachozainn. com; Av Fort btwn Calles 2 & 4; dm US$8, d US$30-35, all incl breakfast; P @ 🛜) This popular budget inn 100m west of Parque Central has a great variety of rooms – from spotless doubles in a pink-washed concrete section to airy, palm-wood dorm rooms. There's a well-stocked communal kitchen, extremely personable staff and it's consistently packed.

ARENAL HOSTEL RESORT Hostel $
(Map p119; ✆ 2479-9222; www.paraisotropical. org; Av Central; dm/s/d US$14/44/52; P ❄ 🛜) A hotel under new, ambitious management. The lodge rooms sprinkled around the garden are spacious with stone floors. Upstairs rooms have balconies, and all have air-con. The dorm wasn't up and running when we visited, but should be open by the time you visit.

Outside Town

HOTEL CAMPO VERDE Bungalow $$
(✆ 2479-1080; www.hotelcampoverde. com; s/d $75/90) An absolutely darling

La Catarata de la Fortuna (p119)

family-owned property. Canary yellow wooden bungalows have vaulted beamed ceilings, two double beds, lovely drapes and chandeliers, and a sweet tiled patio blessed with two rockers waiting. Book the wooden bungalows furthest from the road at the foot of the mountain.

ERUPCIONES INN B&B   B&B $$
(Map p120; ☎2479-1400; www.erupcionesinn. com; d incl breakfast US$60-65; Ⓟ❄) The colorful *cabinas* (cabins) at this quaint B&B, off the highway and by the riverside, are adorned with ornamental tiles and windows facing the volcano. Some have vaulted, beamed ceilings, and each comes with its own private patio with chairs. It's 9km west of La Fortuna.

CHACHAGUA RAINFOREST HOTEL   Hotel $$$
(Map p120; ☎2468-1010; www.chachaguarain foresthotel.com; d incl breakfast from US$135; Ⓟ⊖❄🛜❄) This hotel is a naturalist's dream, situated on a private reserve that abuts the Bosque Eterno de Los Niños in Chachagua. Part of the property is a working orchard, cattle ranch and fish farm, while the rest is humid rainforest that can be accessed either through a series of hiking trails or on horseback. The cheaper rooms aren't really worth the splurge but for $10 extra you can have a spacious dark-wood bungalow with wood floors, exquisite bathrooms and wide decks with a rocker out front.

ARENAL NAYARA HOTEL & GARDENS   Hotel $$$
(Map p120; ☎2479-1600; www.arenalna yara.com; r/ste incl breakfast US$232/350; Ⓟ❄@🛜❄) This intimate hotel has 24 *casitas* (cottages) with Asian-inspired architecture and minimalist decor. All rooms have exquisite furnishings and bedding, rich woods, flat-screen TV, DVD player, iPod dock, an outdoor shower and a private outdoor Jacuzzi where you can soak up views of Arenal volcano. The only thing missing are the hot springs – you'll have to leave the property for those.

TABACÓN GRAND SPA THERMAL RESORT LODGE   Lodge $$$
(Map p120; ☎2256-1500; www.tabacon.com; d incl breakfast US$245-450; Ⓟ⊖❄@🛜❄) The original and still one of the finest luxury resorts in the area, this classy complex features 114 recently remodeled rooms and suites. Amenities include a gym, restaurant, bar, pool and onsite transportation. Tabacón lodge guests have unlimited access to the hot springs, which is where you'll want to spend most of your time if you stay here. The hot springs also offers the best dining options. Tabacón is 13km west of La Fortuna.

THE SPRINGS RESORT & SPA   Resort $$$
(☎2401-3313; www.springscostarica.com; d from US$435; Ⓟ❄@🛜❄) Arenal's swankiest hot-springs property is set 4km from the highway amidst pueblo pasture land and perched on a precipice with spectacular volcano and valley views. Rooms are plush with all of the four-star amenities. There are eight thermal pools and an indulgent top-shelf spa as well as four restaurants, four bars and a private zoo. It is very much the American package-tourist scene, but it is lovely.

 Eating

RESTAURANT DON RUFINO   Restaurant $$$
(Map p119; ☎2479-9997; www.donrufino. com; cnr Av Central & Calle 3; mains US$16-39; ◷10am-11pm) In almost every way this trendy, hopping indoor-outdoor bar and grill is light years ahead of the competition. In addition to the amazing grilled porterhouse with gorgonzola sauce, it offers tilapia and crab risotto, a ginger-glazed grilled tuna, and a Bengali chicken in coconut curry. Tables book up with the well-coifed in high season. Break out the smell goods and reserve ahead.

LA CASCADA   Restaurant $$
(Map p119; ☎2479-9145; cnr Av Fort & Calle 1; mains US$6-26; ◷11am-late) This thatched-roof landmark has been around so long

that the *palapa* roof is almost as big an institution as the volcano it mimics. It has a small bar and acquires a drinking crowd at night but tourists consider it a lunch and dinner option too. It has roast and grilled meat dishes, pastas, sandwiches and three veggie options.

MY COFFEE   Cafe $

(Map p119; 📞2479-8749; Av Central; mains US$6-9; ⏰8am-8pm; 📶) Doubtless the best breakfast in town. Even if the lounge is a bit overdone, it's a cool concept spot where the coffee comes naturally filtered Tico-style and is fantastic. It offers omelets, eggs al gusto, French toast and pancakes.

FLYING TOMATO CAFE   Vegetarian $

(Map p119; 📞2479-9913; www.cabinasarsol.com; Calle 5 & Av Volcan; mains US$3-5; ⏰8am-9pm; 🍴) An exclusively veggie kitchen, it does pasta, veggie burgers, stir-frys and soups, and it is the only place in Fortuna to offer soy milk for espresso drinks and *batidos* (fruit shakes). Hours can be iffy.

❶ Getting There & Away

Bus

All domestic buses stop at the Centro Comercial Adifort bus terminal (Av Arenal). The Tica Bus to Nicaragua (US$27) passes by El Tanque between 6:30am and 7am daily; to catch the bus you'll have to take a taxi to El Tanque (15 minutes, US$12).

Keep an eye on your bags, particularly on the weekend San José run.

Monteverde US$3.60, six to eight hours, departs 8am (change at Tilarán at 12:30pm for Monteverde).

San José (Auto-Transportes San José–San Carlos) US$4.25, 4½ hours, departs 12:45pm and 2:45pm. Alternatively, take a bus to Ciudad Quesada and change to frequent buses to the capital.

Tilarán (Auto-Transportes Tilarán) US$2.60; 3½ hours, departs 8:30am and 5:30pm.

Jeep-Boat-Jeep

The fastest route between Monteverde-Santa Elena and La Fortuna is the sexy-sounding jeep-

boat-jeep combo (US$12 to US$18, three hours) – the 'jeep' is actually a minivan with the requisite yellow 'turismo' tattoo. It's still a terrific transportation option and can be arranged through almost any hotel or tour operator in either town. The minivan from La Fortuna takes you to Laguna de Arenal, meeting a boat that crosses the lake, where a 4WD taxi on the other side continues to Monteverde. This is increasingly becoming the primary transportation between La Fortuna and Monteverde as it's incredibly scenic, reasonably priced and it'll save you half a day of travel.

PARQUE NACIONAL VOLCÁN ARENAL

Arenal was just another dormant volcano surrounded by fertile farmland from about AD 1500 until July 29, 1968, when huge explosions triggered lava flows that destroyed three villages, killing about 80 people and 45,000 cattle. The area was evacuated and roads throughout the region closed. Eventually the lava subsided to a relatively predictable flow and life got back to normal. Sort of.

Although it occasionally quieted down for a few weeks or even months, Arenal produced menacing ash columns, massive explosions and streams of glowing molten rock almost daily from 1968 until it all quite abruptly ended in 2010, leaving the alarmed local tourist industry to gasp and spew in its place. Still, any obituary on the Arenal area is premature given the fact that the volcano has retained its picture-perfect conical shape despite the volcanic activity, and there is still plenty of forest on its lower slopes and in the nearby foothills.

While the molten night views are gone for now, this mighty mountain is still worthy of your time. Though clouds may shroud her at any time, there are several beautiful trails to explore, and even if it rains or there is a chill in the air, you are just a short drive away from hot springs.

🏃 Activities

Arenal was made a national park in 1995, and it is part of the Area de Conservación Arenal, which protects most of the Cordillera de Tilarán. This area is rugged and varied, and the biodiversity is high; roughly half the species of land-dwelling vertebrates (birds, mammals, reptiles and amphibians) known in Costa Rica can be found here.

The park is rich in wildlife. Resident bird species include trogons, rufous motmots, fruitcrows and lancebills, while commonly sighted mammals include howler monkeys, white-faced capuchins and surprisingly tame coatis.

CERRO CHATO TRAIL　　Hiking
(arenalobservatorylodge.com; Arenal Observatory Lodge; day use fee per person $4) The ultimate hike in the national park, the Cerro Chato Trail meanders through pasture before climbing quite steeply through remnant forest and into patches of virgin growth reaching into misty sky.

Eventually the trail crests Volcán Chato, Arenal's dormant partner, and ends in the stunning 1100m-high volcanic lake, Cerro Chato. It takes two to three hours each way, though the hike is only 8km round trip.

WATERFALL TRAIL　　Hiking
(www.arenalobservatorylodge.com; Arenal Observatory Lodge; day pass per person US$4) This scenic hike departing from the Arenal Observatory Lodge is an easy, 2km round-trip hike, which will take about an hour to complete. The terrain starts out flat before descending into a grotto where you'll find a thundering gusher of a waterfall that's about 12m high. You'll feel the mist long before you see its majesty.

SENDERO LOS HELICONIAS　　Hiking
From the ranger station (which has trail maps available), you can hike this 1km circular track, which passes by the site of the 1968 lava flow (vegetation here is slowly sprouting back to life). A 1.5km-long path branches off this trail and leads to an overlook.

SENDERO LAS COLADAS　　Hiking
This track branches off the Heliconias trail and wraps around the volcano for 2km past the 1993 lava flow before connecting with the **Sendero Los Tucanes** (US$4), which extends for another 3km through the tropical rainforest at the base of the volcano. To return to the car-parking area, you will have to turn back. You'll get good views of the summit on the way to the car park.

SENDERO LOS MIRADORES　　Hiking
From the park headquarters (not the ranger station), is the 1.3km Sendero Los Miradores, which leads down to the shores of the

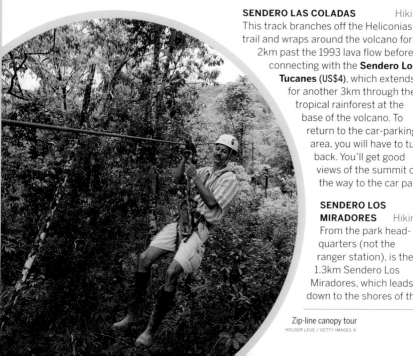

Zip-line canopy tour
HOLGER LEUE / GETTY IMAGES ©

volcanic lake, and provides a good angle for volcano viewing.

OLD LAVA FLOW TRAIL   Hiking
Branching from park headquarters is this interesting and strenuous lower-elevation trail. It follows the flow of the massive 1992 eruption, and the 4km round trip takes two hours to complete. If you want to keep hiking, combine it with the 1.8km **El Ceibo trail**.

ℹ Information

The ranger station is on the western side of the volcano. Most people arrive as part of a group tour, but you can easily reach it independently. To get here by car, head west from La Fortuna for 15km, then turn left at the 'Parque Nacional' sign and take the 2km good dirt road to the entrance on the left side of the road.

EL CASTILLO

The tiny mountain village of El Castillo is a wonderful alternative to staying in La Fortuna – it's bucolic, reasonably untouristed (although there is a tight expat community), and has easy access to Parque Nacional Volcán Arenal. There are also some delightful accommodations options. It's best to have your own wheels out here, as buses don't serve this little enclave.

◎ Sights & Activities

SKYTREK   Canopy Tour
(Map p120; ☏2479-9944; www.skyadventures.travel; adult/child Sky Tram only US$42/29, Sky Walk US$33/21, Sky Trek & Sky Tram US$73/46; ⊙7:30am-4pm) El Castillo's entry in the canopy-tour category has zip lines (Sky Trek), a tram (Sky Tram) and a series of hanging bridges (Sky Walk). It's well run, safe and visitors tend to leave smiling. It also offers night tours.

APPALOOSA FARMS   Horse Riding
(☏2479-1140; per person US$35) A fabulous horseback-riding option. Tours depart

♥ **If You Like...**

Secluded Mountain Lodges

If you like staying in secluded mountain lodges such as the Arenal Observatory Lodge, try some of these remote alternatives:

1 **EL ESTABLO MOUNTAIN RESORT**
(Map p136; ☏2645-5110; www.hotelelestablo.com; d deluxe/ste incl breakfast US$250/325; P ⊜ @ ⊠) This is a seriously upscale lodge offering open-plan suites that are A-frame lofts with private terraces.

2 **LA CAROLINA LODGE**
(☏2466-6393; www.lacarolinalodge.com; per person incl meals & horse rides US$70-90; P ⊠) Flanked by a roaring river and tucked in the trees is this gloriously rustic retreat.

3 **RIO CELESTE HIDEAWAY**
(☏2206-5114; www.riocelestehideaway.com; d incl breakfast US$249-299) This luxury property has huge, 90-sq-m thatched *casitas* (cottages) with antique furnishings, flat-screen TVs and lush landscaped grounds.

from a working dairy aboard well-maintained horses. Your humble and knowledgable guide, Lelander Alvarez, will lead you on a four-hour tour through the rainforest to a hidden waterfall. Call to reserve at least a day ahead.

EL CASTILLO-ARENAL BUTTERFLY CONSERVATORY   Wildlife Reserve
(☏2479-1149; www.butterflyconservatory.org; adult/student US$14/10; ⊙8am-4pm) This conservatory has one of the largest butterfly exhibitions in Costa Rica, and raises all the butterflies and frogs on exhibit. Altogether there are six domed habitats, a ranarium (for breeding frogs), an insect museum, a medicinal herb garden, and an hour's worth of trails through a botanic garden and along the river. The center is always looking for a few good volunteers.

SIEPMANN / IMAGEBROKER ©

Don't Miss **Arenal Observatory Lodge**

The Arenal Observatory Lodge was built in 1987 as a private observatory for the Universidad de Costa Rica. Scientists chose to construct the lodge on a macadamia-nut farm on the south side of Volcán Arenal due to its proximity to the volcano (only 2km away) and its relatively safe location on a ridge. Since its creation volcanologists from all over the world, including researchers from the Smithsonian Institute in Washington, DC, have come to study the active volcano. Today the majority of visitors are tourists, though scientists regularly visit the lodge, and a seismograph in the hotel continues to operate around the clock. The lodge is the only place inside the park where you can legally bed down.

In addition to beds, it offers massages (from US$60), guided hikes and all the usual tours at good prices, has an excellent trail network, including the leisurely Waterfall Trail and the challenging-but-worth-it Cerro Chato Trail. You can swim in the pool, wander around the macadamia-nut farm or investigate the pine forest that makes up about half of the 347-hectare site. You can also rent horses for US$8 per hour.

NEED TO KNOW

Map p120; ☎lodge 2479-1070, reservations 2290-7011; www.arenalobservatorylodge.com; day pass per person US$4, museum admission free; P

 Sleeping & Eating

RANCHO MARGOT   Resort, Lodge $$$
(☎8302-7318; www.ranchomargot.org; s/d bunkhouse US$90/150, bungalow US$152/230; P ⊛ ≋) Rancho Margot, part resort lodge, part 152-hectare, self-sufficient organic farm, is set along the rushing Río Cano Negro, surrounded by rainforested mountains. Choose from tiny bunkhouse accommodations, or the far better bungalows with sweet mosaic-tiled washbasins, Spanish tile, and a deck strung

with a hammock blessed with views of hulking mountains, weeping jungle and that placid lake. All meals are included as is yoga and a complimentary tour where you can see how this off-the-grid, sustainable organic ranch works. There is a full-service spa too.

ESSENCE ARENAL Hostel $

(☏ 2479-1131; www.essencearenal.com; dm/d US$14/28; P @ ☎ ☒) Perched on a 100-acre hilltop with incredible volcano and lake views, this 'boutique hostel' is the best cheap sleep in the Arenal region. The basic but clean rooms have orthopedic mattresses and hypo-allergenic pillows. Or you might enjoy a fine hippified tent, done up with plush bedding and wood furnishings. Possibly the best reason to stay is the onsite restaurant, with lovingly prepared vegetarian meals (US$10) that will delight even the most hardcore carnivore. It's not easy getting here without your own wheels, but the hostel can arrange transportation from La Fortuna.

HUMMINGBIRD NEST B&B B&B $$

(☏ 2479-1174, 8835-8711; www.hummingbird nestbb.com; d incl breakfast US$75; P) At the entrance to town, you'll see a small path that leads up the (steep) hill to one of our favorite B&Bs. Also known as Nido del Colibri, it's owned by a former Pan Am stewardess. Her quaint complex has two guest rooms with private hot showers, access to a fabulous communal kitchen, and enough frilly pillows to make you miss home. Soak the night away in a huge outdoor Jacuzzi in the garden.

NEPENTHE Hotel $$

(☏ 8892-5501, 8760-0412; Krisaray21@hotmail.com; s/d $70/85; P ❄ ☎ ☒) The highlight of the newest nest in El Castillo is its spectacular infinity pool overlooking the lake. Lodgelike rooms are simple tiled numbers with colorful artisanal accents set in a gentle arc of a ranch-style building. There are hammocks on the patio and its Blue Lagoon spa (by appointment only, treatments from $35) comes highly recommended.

FINCA ARTESANA Deli, Bakery $

(☏ 8533-7902) Meet Thomas and Hannah. He's Czech and makes the hot sauce and the vinegar, she's American and bakes cookies and breads. Although you can find their creations throughout El Castillo, the fiery hot sauces and vinegars are cheapest at the source and made from peach palm, the ancient indigenous cash crop in Costa Rica. Breads and cookies are made to order. They sell their wares out of their house, uphill from Essence Arenal in the heart of El Castillo.

LAGUNA DE ARENAL AREA

About 18km west of La Fortuna, you'll arrive at a 750m-long causeway across the dam that created Laguna de Arenal, an 88-sq-km lake and the largest in the country. A number of small towns were submerged during its creation, but the lake now supplies valuable water to Guanacaste, and produces hydroelectricity for the region. High winds also produce power with the aid of huge, steel windmills, though windsurfers and kitesurfers frequently steal a breeze or two.

If you have your own car (or bicycle), this is one of the premier road trips in Costa Rica. The road is lined with odd and elegant businesses, many run by foreigners who have fallen in love with the place, and the scenic views of lakeside forests and Volcán Arenal are about as romantic as they come. Strong winds and high elevations give the lake a temperate feel, and you'll be forgiven if you suddenly imagine yourself in the English Lakes District or the Swiss countryside.

But, things are changing – quickly. Gringo baby boomers, lured to the area by the eternal spring climate, are snapping up nearly every spot of land with a 'For Sale' sign on it.

Dam to Nuevo Arenal

This beautiful stretch of road is lined on both sides with cloud forest, and a number of fantastic accommodations are strung along the way.

⊙ Sights & Activities

PUENTES COLGANTES
DE ARENAL   Forest
(Arenal Hanging Bridges; Map p120; ☎2290-0469; www.hangingbridges.com; adult/student/child under 12yr US$25/22/free; ☺7:30am-4:30pm) Unlike the fly-by view you'll get on a zip-line canopy tour, a walk through Puentes Colgantes de Arenal allows you to explore the rainforest and canopy from six suspended bridges and 10 traditional bridges at a more natural and peaceful pace. The longest swaying bridge is 97m long and the highest is 25m above the earth. All are accessible from a single 3km trail that winds through a tunnel and skirts a waterfall. Reservations are required for guided bird-watching tours (three hours, from 6am) or informative naturalist tours (9am and 2pm).

Sleeping

ARENAL LODGE   Lodge $$$
(Map p120; ☎2290-4232; www.arenallodge.com; d standard/superior US$89/140, f US$167, junior ste US$175, chalet US$184, all incl breakfast; P ✳ ☻) If you want to stay in the area, Arenal Lodge is 400m west of the Laguna de Arenal, at the top of a steep 2.5km ascent, though the entire lodge is awash with views of Arenal and the surrounding cloud forest. Standard rooms are just that, but junior suites are spacious, tiled and have wicker furniture, a big hot-water bathroom and a picture window or balcony with volcano views. The lodge also has a Jacuzzi, a billiards room, a sophisticated restaurant (mains US$8 to US$18), complimentary mountain bikes and private stables.

LOST IGUANA RESORT   Resort $$$
(Map p120; ☎2479-1331, 2267-6148; www.lostiguanaresort.com; standard/deluxe incl breakfast US$245/275; P ✳ @ ☎ ☻) This stylish and splashy tropical resort, just 1.5km from the dam, is set amongst lush rainforest and rushing streams and there are glorious volcano views. Even the standard rooms have private balconies looking out on Arenal, beds boasting Egyptian cotton

sheets, flat screens with Apple TV, a terracotta wet bar, and an invaluable sense of peace and privacy.

Unión Area

The following accommodations and restaurants are listed in order of their distance from the Laguna de Arenal dam.

You can't miss **Hotel Los Héroes** (☎2692-8012/3; www.hotellosheroes.com; d with/without balcony US$65/55, tr/apt US$80/115, all incl breakfast; P ☻), a more than slightly incongruous alpine chalet 13.5km west of the dam. Large, immaculate rooms with wood paneling and hot-water bathrooms are decorated with wood furniture that may make Swiss-Germans a little homesick, particularly when viewing paintings of tow-headed children in lederhosen. There are also two apartments (each sleeps up to five) with full kitchen, huge bathroom and balcony overlooking the lake. Facilities include a Jacuzzi, swimming pool and a church complete with Swiss chimes. The owners have even built a miniature train (US$11) that brings you up a hill to an underground station beneath the **Rondorama Panoramic Restaurant** (mains US$10-20), a revolving dining room (seriously!) that's reportedly one-of-a-kind in Central America. There's also a hiking trail that is great for wildlife-watching.

Rates for the gorgeous cottages at **La Mansion Inn Arenal** (☎2692-8018; www.lamansionarenal.com; r/cottages incl breakfast US$175/200) include a champagne breakfast, fruit basket, welcome cocktail, canoe access and horse rides. They feature huge split-level rooms with loud paint jobs, private terraces, lake views, high ceilings and Italianate painted walls and arches. There's also a formal restaurant (four-course dinner excluding wine US$22 to US$38) with a bar shaped like the bow of a ship. It's 15.5km west of the dam.

A serene, German-run escape, **La Ceiba Tree Lodge** (☎2692-8050; www.ceibatree-lodge.com; s/d US$63/84; P ✳ ☎) is 22km west of the dam and centered on a magnificent 500-year-old ceiba tree. Its

Laguna de Arenal (p129) with Volcán Arenal in the background

CHRISTER FREDRIKSSON / GETTY IMAGES ©

five spacious, cross-ventilated Spanish-tiled rooms are entered through Maya-inspired carved doors and decorated with original paintings. It's one of the best-value places on the lake.

Another accommodation option is **Villa Decary B&B** (☎2694-4330, from US or Canada 1-800-556-0505; www.villadecary. com; r/casitas incl breakfast US$109/164; **P ❄ 🛜**), an all-round winner with bright, spacious, well-furnished rooms, and two massive Cape Cod–style *casitas* that sleep up to four. The elegance extends from the clumps of slender palms to the delicious full breakfasts and, of course, to the fabulous hosts. Rooms have private hot showers, a queen and a double bed, bright serape bedspreads and artwork. They also have balconies with excellent views of the woodland immediately below and the lake just beyond. The *casitas* have epic views from wide porches, and a kitchenette. It's 24.5km west of the dam, and 2km east of Nuevo Arenal.

Make absolutely sure to book dinner reservations at the **Gingerbread Hotel & Restaurant** (☎2694-0039, 8351-7815; www. gingerbreadarenal.com; mains US$9-40; ⏱5-

9pm Tue-Sat, lunch by reservation only), one of the best restaurants in northwestern Costa Rica. You may even choose to stay at the charming boutique hotel built into the same stone house as the restaurant, but the thing here is the kitchen. With the freshest local fare providing the foundation for his weekly menus, Chef Eyal turns out transcendent meals and is choosy about his wine list. Portions are big enough to split and share; we loved the blackened tuna salad and the mushrooms smothered in creamy, parsley-flecked gravy. A word to the wise: do not pass up dessert. Come prepared – credit cards are not accepted, and don't be alarmed if Eyal shouts, sweats, dances and raps along to Naughty By Nature. It happens.

Nuevo Arenal

The only good-sized town between La Fortuna and Tilarán, it's 27km west of the dam, or a one hour drive from La Fortuna. In case you were wondering what happened to old Arenal, it's about 27m below the surface of Laguna de Arenal. In order to create a large enough reservoir for the dam, the government had to make certain, er, sacrifices, which ultimately resulted in the forced relocation of 3500 people. Today the humble residents of Nuevo Arenal don't seem to be fazed by history, especially since they now own premium lakeside property.

Eating

SUNSET GRILL   Restaurant $
(2694-4557; www.sunsetgrillcostarica.com; mains US$5-9; 7am-11pm;) American owned and patronized, Sunset Grill does big breakfasts, burgers and Philly-style cheesesteaks. The attached internet cafe offers internet service (US$1 per hour), and it occasionally stays open until 2am depending upon the bar crowd.

MOYA'S PLACE   Pizzeria $$
(2694-4001; mains US$6-12; 11am-10pm) A new and savory smelling pizza joint, it also does an assortment of wraps, pastas and salads, and a lovely, fresh stuffed trout steamed in banana leaf. It doesn't serve alcohol.

NUEVO ARENAL TO TILARÁN

West and around the lake from Nuevo Arenal, the scenery becomes even more spectacular just as the road gets progressively worse. Tilarán is the next 'big' city, with a reasonable selection of hotels and restaurants, plus roads and buses that can take you to Liberia, Monteverde or beyond.

Activities

Some of the world's most consistent winds blow across northwestern Costa Rica, and this consistency attracts wind riders. Laguna de Arenal is rated one of the best windsurfing spots in the world and kitesurfers flock here too, especially from late November to April when **Tico Wind** (8813-7274, 2692-2002; www.ticowind. com; windsurf/kitesurf half-day US$50/58, full day incl lunch US$85/86) sets up camp on the shore. It has state-of-the-art boards and sails, with equipment to suit varied wind conditions. First-timers should consider the 'Get on Board' package (US$120). Lessons are offered in English, Spanish, German, Italian and Portuguese. The launch is located 15km west of Nuevo Arenal, about 400m after the Equus bar-restaurant. The entrance is by the big white chain-link fence with 'ICE' painted on it. Follow the dirt road 1km to the shore.

Laguna de Arenal is also now attracting wakeboarders. **Paradise Adventures Costa Rica** (2479-8159, 8856-3618; www.paradise-adventures-costa-rica.com; per hr US$200), based in La Fortuna, has the latest wakeboarding equipment. Rates are for

Black-necked stilts
RICK DALEY / ALAMY ©

up to seven people including equipment, lessons and boat ride.

Sleeping & Eating

BLUE ZONE SPA B&B **$$**
(2694-4713; www.bluezonespa.com; d incl breakfast US$75; P 🛜 ♨) The sounds of nature will lull you to sleep at this intimate B&B on the banks of the rainforest-shaded Río Cote. Four simple, tiled rooms feature queen beds and creative bathrooms. The property was recently rebranded as a full-service spa, which is set downstairs. It does facials, massages and body scrubs. Treatments range from US$75 to US$125.

LUCKY BUG B&B B&B **$$**
(2694-4515; www.luckybugcr.net; r incl breakfast US$89-120; P ❄ 🛜 ♨) Set on a rainforest lagoon, the bungalows at the Lucky Bug are not only blissfully isolated but feature unique art and decorative details by local artisans, including the owner's big-eyed, blonde triplets. Blonde wood floors, wrought-iron butterflies, hand-painted geckos, mosaic washbasins and end tables make each room unique and captivating. Plus, there's onsite **Caballo Negro Restaurant** (mains US$8-14) and the fabulously quirky Lucky Bug Gallery. Should you fall in love with a painting of a bug or something bigger, they can ship it for you. It's 3km west of Nuevo Arenal.

ECOLODGE ANDAMAYA Lodge **$$**
(2694-4306; www.ecolodgecostarica.com; r/cabins incl breakfast US$75/125; P ❄ 🛜) This aging, environmentally friendly lodge has been done up with hip touches such as draped scarves, retro door numbers and stylish floral motifs. Built in 1990 with an endowment from the World Bank, the hotel is committed to preserving its 250 hectares of primary forest and 50 hectares of secondary-growth forest. There are 14km of trails, and even if you don't stay here you can join its indigenous guides on a guided hike (per person US$20). Go 4.5km west of Nuevo Arenal, then turn 3km down an unpaved road.

EQUUS BAR-RESTAURANT Restaurant **$$**
(mains US$6-14; ⏰3-9pm Fri, 11am-2am Sat, 11am-9pm Sun) Set on its own little cove, this groovy tavern specializes in grilled meat plates and is perennially popular among wind riders looking to swap stories over an icy Imperial. There's a good mix of Tico and Western dishes, and on some nights there's live music. This is what passes for a night scene on the lake. It's 14.5km west of Nuevo Arenal.

VOLCANO BREWING Hotel **$$**
(2653-1262, 2695-5050; www.volcanobrewing company.com; r US$60-75; P ➡ ❄ @ 🛜 ♨) Is it a brewery? A hotel? A kitesurf camp? Actually, the converted, lakefront Hotel Tilawa is all of the above, and living up to its legendary history among wind riders. The remodel is stunning, with polished-concrete floors, pastel paint jobs and high, slanted, dark-wood ceilings. There's a pool and Jacuzzi and the restaurant's pub-grub selections are scrawled on the chalkboard in true tavern style. Oh, and it brews three types of beer: a pale ale, a seasonal wheat beer and what they call a lemon-ginger-flavored shandy.

BRISAS DEL LAGO Soda **$$**
(2695-3363; mains US$6-11; P 🛜 👪) Simple Tico fare is done with panache at this dressed up *soda* (lunch counter). They marinate chicken breasts in their own BBQ sauce, skewer Thai-style shrimp, sauce teriyaki chicken, and the garlic fish is sensational. To get here head toward Tilarán, then make a left at the T-junction toward the community of San Luis. Continue for 800m.

TILARÁN
POP 8100

Near the southwestern end of Laguna de Arenal, the small town of Tilarán has a laid-back, middle-class charm – thanks to its long-running status as a regional ranching center. This tradition is honored on the last weekend in April with a rodeo that's popular with Tico visitors, and on

GIL GIUGLIO / ALAMY ©

June 13 with a *fiesta de toros* that's dedicated to patron San Antonio.

Sleeping & Eating

HOTEL CIELO AZUL Hotel $

(☎ 2695-4000; www.cieloazulresort.com; r US$20; P ❄ 🛜 🏊) Five hundred meters before town coming from Nuevo Arenal, this hillside property has eight recently redone rooms with new tile floors and bathroom tile. There's cable TV, the pool is lovely and it even has a spinning studio. This is Tilaran's best deal.

HOTEL TILARÁN Hotel $

(☎ 2695-5043; r with/without bathroom US$11/7; P) As cheap as they come, rooms are tiny and cleanish, but you will hear the caged bird sing. If you can get one of the rooms toward the back, this is a decent budget choice on the west side of Parque Central. Its cute, almost retro *soda* (mains US$3 to US$6) is on the streetfront.

HOTEL EL SUEÑO Hotel $

(☎ 2695-5347; s/d US$20/30; P) Near the bus terminal, this beautiful (in an aging, baroque sort of way) hotel has antique decorated rooms set around a cheerful atrium, but it's worth splurging for the balcony, where you can bask in the faded glory.

SODA Y RESTAURANTE EL NILO Soda $

(cnr Avenida 3 & Calle 1; empanadas US$1.50 meals US$6-8; ⏰ 7am-7pm) An oh-so-cute *soda* run by two ladies who fold the best chicken *empanadas* (turnovers) in town and craft delectable *casados* (cheap set meals), too. Meals are served on pressed tablecloths with local pottery mounted on the dining room walls.

❶ Getting There & Away

Tilarán is usually reached by a 24km paved road from the Interamericana at Cañas. The route on to Santa Elena and Monteverde is unpaved and rough, though ordinary cars can get through with care in the dry season.

Buses arrive and depart from the terminal, half a block west of Parque Central.

La Fortuna US$5, three hours, departs 10am, 2:30pm and 4:30pm.

Nuevo Arenal US$1, 1¼ hours, departs 5am, 6am, 8am, 9am, 10am, 11am, 1pm, 2:30pm and 3:30pm.

Puntarenas US$4, two hours, departs 6am and 1pm.

San José (Auto-Transportes Tilarán) US$7, four hours, departs 5am, 7am, 9:30am, 2pm and 5pm.

Santa Elena/Monteverde US$3, 2½ hours, departs once daily at 12:30pm.

MONTEVERDE & SANTA ELENA

Strung between two lovingly preserved cloud forests is this slim corridor of civilization, which consists of the Tico village of Santa Elena and the Quaker settlement of Monteverde. A 1983 feature article in *National Geographic* described this unique landscape and subsequently billed the area as the place to view one of Central America's most famous birds – the resplendent quetzal. Suddenly hordes of tourists armed with tripods and telephoto lenses started braving Monteverde's notoriously awful access roads, which came as a huge shock to the then-established Quaker community. In an effort to stem the tourist flow, local communities lobbied to stop developers from paving the roads. And it worked. Today the dirt roads leading to Monteverde and Santa Elena have effectively created a moat around this precious experiment in sustainable ecotourism.

The cloud forests near Monteverde and Santa Elena are one of Costa Rica's premier destinations for everyone from budget backpackers to well-heeled retirees. On a good day, Monteverde is a place where you can be inspired about the possibility of a world in which organic farming and alternative energy sources are the norm. On a bad day, Monteverde can feel like Disneyland in Birkenstocks and a zip-line harness.

By taking either of the Interamericana's first two turnoffs to the region, you'll first arrive in Santa Elena, a bustling community of budget hotels, restaurants and attractions. A road beginning at the northern point of the triangle leads to Juntas and Tilarán, with a turnoff to Reserva Santa Elena.

Sights & Activities

Ecotourism is a big business in Monteverde and Santa Elena, so it's unsurprising that there are a number of adventure-as-theme-park attractions scattered around both towns. And if there's a certain critter you're itching to see, there are plenty of places where your view won't be obscured by all those pesky trees.

EL JARDÍN DE LAS MARIPOSAS   Zoo
(Butterfly Garden; Map p136; ☎2645-5512; www.monteverdebutterflygarden.com; adult/student/children under 12 US$9/7/3; ⏱9:30am-4pm) One of the most interesting activities is visiting the butterfly garden where naturalist-led tours (in Spanish or English) begin with an enlightening discussion of butterfly life cycles and the butterfly's importance in nature. Visitors are taken into the greenhouses, where the butterflies are raised, and on into the screened garden, where hundreds of butterflies of many species are seen. The tour lasts about an hour.

RANARIO   Zoo
(Frog Pond; Map p136; ☎tel, info 2645-6320; ranariomv@racsa.co.cr; adult/student & child US$12/10, adult combo US$18; ⏱9am-8:30pm) Monteverde's cloud forest provides a heavenly habitat for amphibians, which, if you're lucky, you'll see in the park. But at the Ranario about 25 species of Costa Rica's colorful array of frogs and toads reside in transparent enclosures lining winding indoor-jungle paths. Sharp-eyed guides lead informative tours in English or Spanish, pointing out frogs, eggs and tadpoles with flashlights. Many resident amphibians are active by night, so it's best to visit during the evening. The adult combo ticket includes admission to the butterfly garden (above).

SERPENTARIO   Zoo
(Serpentarium; Map p136; ☎2645-6002; per person US$9; ⏱9am-8pm) Here you'll find about 40 species of snake, plus a fair number of frogs, lizards, turtles and other cold-blooded critters. Sometimes

Monteverde & Santa Elena

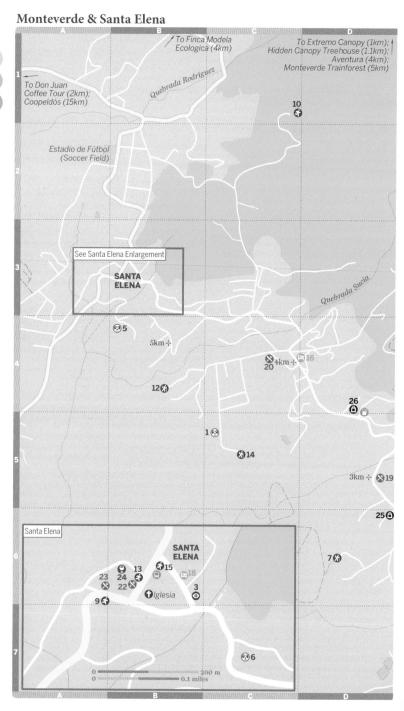

To Finca Modela
Ecologicà (4km)

To Extremo Canopy (1km);
Hidden Canopy Treehouse (1.1km);
Aventura (4km);
Monteverde Trainforest (5km)

Quebrada Rodríguez

To Don Juan
Coffee Tour (2km);
Coopeldós (15km)

10

Estadio de Fútbol
(Soccer Field)

See Santa Elena Enlargement

SANTA
ELENA

Quebrada Sucia

5

5km

20 4km 16

12

26

1

14

3km 19

25

Santa Elena

SANTA
ELENA

13

15

18

23
24

22

3

9

Iglesia

7

6

0 _____ 200 m
0 _____ 0.1 miles

136

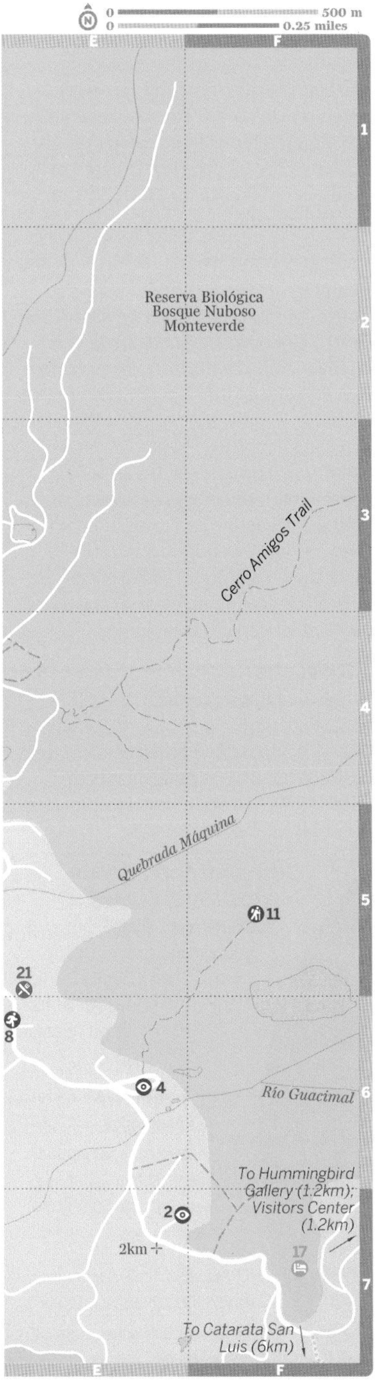
0 500 m
0 0.25 miles
Reserva Biológica Bosque Nuboso Monteverde
Cerro Amigos Trail
Quebrada Máquina
11
21
8
4
Río Guacimal
To Hummingbird Gallery (1.2km); Visitors Center (1.2km)
2
2km
17
To Catarata San Luis (6km)

Monteverde & Santa Elena

Sights

1 El Jardín de las Mariposas C5
2 Friends Meeting House E7
3 Jardín de Orquídeas B6
4 Monteverde Cheese Factory E6
5 Ranario B4
6 Serpentario C7

Activities, Courses & Tours

7 Bosque Eterno de los Niños D6
8 Café Monteverde E6
9 Desafío Adventure Company A6
10 Original Canopy Tour C1
11 Reserva Sendero Tranquilo F5
12 Santuario Ecológico B4
13 Selvatura B6
Sendero Bajo del Tigre (Jaguar Canyon Trail) .... (see 7)
14 Sendero Valle Escondido C5
15 SkyTram B6
SkyTrek .... (see 15)

Sleeping

16 El Establo Mountain Resort D4
17 Mariposa B&B F7
18 Pensión Santa Elena B6

Eating

19 Café Caburé D5
Musashi .... (see 15)
20 Sofia C4
21 Stella's Bakery E5
22 Tree House Restaurant & Café B6
23 Trio's A6

Drinking

24 Bar Amigos B6

Shopping

25 Alquima Artes D6
26 Luna Azul D4

Information

Paseo de Stella Visitors Center .... (see 19)

it's tough to find the slithering, venomous stars in their foliage-filled cages, but guides are available in Spanish or English for free tours.

JARDÍN DE ORQUÍDEAS Gardens

(Orchid Garden; Map p136; 2645-5308; www.monteverdeorchidgarden.com; adult/child under 12yr US$10/free; 8am-5pm) This sweet-smelling garden has shady trails winding past more than 400 types of orchid organized into taxonomic groups. Included with admission are guided tours in Spanish and English, on which you'll see such rarities as *Plztystele jungermannioides*, the world's smallest orchid, and several others marked for conservation by the Monteverde Orchid Investigation Project.

MONTEVERDE CHEESE FACTORY   Tour
(La Lechería; Map p136; ☏ 2645-5522; adult/child US$10/8; ☺ tours 9am & 2pm Mon-Sat, store 7:30am-5pm Mon-Sat, 7:30am-4pm Sun) Until the upswing in ecotourism, Monteverde's number-one employer was this cheese factory, also called La Lechería (the Dairy). Started in 1953 by Monteverde's original Quaker settlers, the factory produces everything from a creamy Gouda to a very nice sharp, white cheddar.

Coffee Plantations

Coffee-lovers will be excited to find some of the finest coffee in the world right here. Late April is the best time to see the fields in bloom, while the coffee harvest (done entirely by hand) takes place from December to February. Any time is a good time to see how your favorite beverage transforms from ruby-red berry to smooth black brew. Advance reservations are required for all tours, which you can book directly by phone or through many hotels. Most charge about US$30, including transportation.

CAFÉ MONTEVERDE   Tour
(Map p136; ☏ 2645-5901; www.monteverde-coffee.com; per person US$15; ☺ 7:30am-6pm) Run by Cooperative Santa Elena, this highly recommended tour takes visitors to coffee *fincas* that use entirely organic methods to grow the perfect coffee bean. You can help pick some beans, after which you'll be brought to the *beneficio* (coffee mill), where you can watch as the beans are washed and dried, roasted and then packed. Of course, you'll also get to taste the final product with a snack. The cafe offers free samples of six roasts, or buy some beans to take home.

COOPELDÓS   Tour
(☏ 2693-8441; www.coopeldos.com) This cooperative of 450 small and medium-sized organic coffee growers is Fairtrade-certified. One of its main clients is Starbucks. It's about halfway between Tilarán and Monteverde.

DON JUAN COFFEE TOUR   Tour
(☏ 2645-7100; www.donjuanc offeetour.com; adults/children 6-12 yrs/ children under 6 US$30/12/ free; ☺ 7am-4:30pm) Book this two-hour tour at its downtown shop near the SuperCompro.

EL TRAPICHE   Tour
(☏ 2645-5834; www.eltrapi chetour.com; per person $30; ☺ 10am & 3pm Mon-Sat, 3pm Sun) This traveller-recommended, family-run coffee plantation also grows sugarcane. Besides coffee,

Coffee picking
CHRISTOPHER BAKER / GETTY IMAGES ©

you can sample the area's other famous beverage, *saca de guaro*, a cane-based liquor.

Hiking

The best hikes are at the two cloud-forest reserves bookending the main road, Reserva Biológica Bosque Nuboso Monteverde and Reserva Santa Elena.

BOSQUE ETERNO DE LOS NIÑOS   Hiking

(Children's Eternal Forest; Map p136; ☎2645-5003; www.acmcr.org; adult/student day use US$8/5, guided night hike US$15/10, Estacion Biologica San Gerardo all-inclusive US$40; ☼7:30am-5:30pm) Funded by an international collective of school children, this enormous 220-sq-km reserve dwarfs both the Monteverde and Santa Elena reserves and is largely inaccessible – the children who paid the bills decided it was more important to provide a home for local wildlife than to develop a lucrative tourist infrastructure.

The effort has allowed for one fabulous trail that hooks into a system of unimproved trails. The 3.5km **Sendero Bajo del Tigre** (Jaguar Canyon Trail; Map p136) offers more open vistas than those in the cloud forest, so spotting birds tends to be easier.

Make reservations in advance for the popular two-hour night hikes, which set off at 5:30pm. The **Estación Biológica San Gerardo**, reachable from a rather gnarly 2½-hour trail from Reserva Santa Elena, is managed by Bosque Eterno de los Ninos.

SANTUARIO ECOLÓGICO   Hiking

(Ecological Sanctuary; Map p136; ☎2645-5869; adult/student/child US$10/8/6, guided night tour US$15/12/10; ☼7am-5:30pm, guided night tours 5:30-7:30pm) Offering hikes of varying lengths, Santuario Ecológico has four loop trails (the longest takes about 2½ hours at a slow pace) through private property comprising premontane and secondary forest, coffee and banana plantations, and past a couple of waterfalls and lookout points. Coatis, agoutis and sloths are seen on most days, and monkeys, porcupines and other animals are common. Bird-watching is also good.

Guided tours are available throughout the day, but you'll see even more animals on the guided night tours.

RESERVA SENDERO TRANQUILO   Hiking

(Tranquil Path Reserve; Map p136; ☎2645-5010; admission US$20; ☼tours 7:30am & 1pm) An 81-hectare private reserve, Reserva Sendero Tranquilo is located between the Reserva Biológica Bosque Nuboso Monteverde and the Río Guacimal. Trails here are narrow to allow for minimal environmental impact, and group size is capped at six people, which means you won't have to worry about chattering tourists scaring away all the animals. The trails pass through four distinct types of forest, including a previously destroyed area that's starting to bud again.

SENDERO VALLE ESCONDIDO   Hiking

(Hidden Valley Trail; Map p136; ☎2645-6601; day use US$5, night tour adult/child US$20/10; ☼7am-4pm) This trail begins behind the Pensión Monteverde Inn and slowly winds its way through a deep canyon into an 11-hectare reserve. In comparison with the more popular reserves, Valle Escondido is quiet during the day and relatively undertouristed, so it's a good trail for wildlife-watching. However, the reserve's two-hour guided night tour (at 5:30pm) is very popular, so it's best to make reservations in advance.

Canopy Tours

Santa Elena was the site of Costa Rica's first zip lines, and today 100 lines have sprung up around town. You won't be spotting any quetzals or coatis as you whoosh over the canopy, and questions remain over the ecological value of this type of pseudo-adventure tourism, but if you came to Costa Rica to fly, this is the place to do it.

Before you clip in, you're going to have to choose where, how fast and how high you will soar – this is more challenging than you'd think. Much like the rest of Costa Rica, Monteverde works on a commission-based system, so be skeptical of advice, and insist on choosing the tour that you want. We provide basic

Right: Reserva Biológica Bosque Nuboso Monteverde (p146);
Below: Nymphalid butterfly

(RIGHT) CHRISTER FREDRIKSSON / GETTY IMAGES ©; (BELOW) TOM BOYDEN / GETTY IMAGES ©

information on the five major players in town here, though it's good to talk to the friendly, unbiased staff at the Pensión Santa Elena for the full scoop.

AVENTURA Canopy Tour

(☎2645-6388; www.monteverdeadventure.com; per person US$45; ⏰7am-4pm) Aventura has 19 platforms that are spiced up with a Tarzan swing, a 15m rappel and a Superman zip line that makes you feel as if you really are flying. Aventura's cables and hammock bridge are laced through secondary forest only. It's about 3km north of Santa Elena on the road to the reserve, and transportation from your hotel is included in the price.

EXTREMO CANOPY Canopy Tour

(☎2645-6058; www.monteverdeextremo.com; adult/child US$40, Superman canopy ride US$5, Tarzan swing $35; ⏰8am-4pm) The newest player on the Monteverde canopy scene, this outfit runs small groups through secondary forest, and doesn't bother

with extraneous attractions. There's a Superman canopy ride, allowing you to fly Superman-style through the air, the highest and most adrenaline-addled Tarzan swing in the area, and a bungee jump. One way or another, you will scream.

ORIGINAL CANOPY TOUR Canopy Tour

(Map p136; ☎2645-5243; www.canopytour.com; adult/student/child US$45/35/25; ⏰7:30am-4pm) On the grounds of Cloud Forest Lodge, this is the fabled zip-line route that started this adventure–theme park trend. These lines aren't as elaborate as the others, but with 14 platforms, a rappel through the center of an old fig tree and 5km of private trails worth a wander afterward, you can enjoy a piece of history that's far more entertaining than most museums.

SELVATURA Canopy Tour

(Map p136; ☎2645-5929; www.selvatura.com; adult/child US$45/30; ⏰7:30am-4pm) One of the bigger games in town, Selvatura has 3km of cables, 18 platforms and one

Tarzan swing over a stretch of incredibly beautiful primary cloud forest. In addition to the cables it has a hummingbird garden, a butterfly garden and an amphibian and reptile exhibition. The office is across the street from the church in Santa Elena.

SKYTREK · Canopy Tour
(Map p136; ☎2645-5238; www.skyadventures. travel; adult/student/child US$83/66/53; ⏰7:30am-5pm) This seriously fast canopy tour consists of 11 platforms attached to cables that zoom over swatches of primary forest. We're talking serious speeds of up to 64km/h, which is probably why SkyTrek was the first canopy tour with a real brake system. The price includes admission to the SkyTram gondola and SkyWalk hanging bridges; cheaper packages are also available.

Hanging Bridges, Trams & Trains
OK, so you're too scared to zip through the canopy on a steel cable. Fear not: the makers of eco-fun have something special for you – hanging bridges and trams, the seemingly safer and slightly less expensive way to explore the tree tops.

Aventura, Selvatura and SkyWalk (owned by SkyTrek) have systems of hanging bridges across which you can traipse and live out Indiana Jones fantasies. There are subtle differences between all of them (some are fat, some are thin, some are bouncy, some are saggy), though the views of the canopy are good from all. They're all priced around US$30 for adults and US$20 for students and children. The two forest reserves also have rather impressive hanging bridges.

MONTEVERDE TRAINFOREST · Scenic Ride
(☎2645-5700; www.trainforest.com; adult/senior/student/child under 12yr US$50/40/35/free; ♿) Monteverde Trainforest is a miniature train system that travels 4 miles through the forest, penetrating one tunnel and crossing four bridges. The scenic railroad

141

offers amazing views of Monteverde and Arenal lake and volcano. This is a great option for families with young children, as kids under 12 ride free. It's located 5km north of downtown Santa Elena, on the road to Reserva Santa Elena.

SKYTRAM — Outdoors

(Map p136; 2645-5238; www.skyadventures. travel; SkyWalk & SkyTram adult/student/ children under 12 yrs US$55/44/29) Owned by SkyTrek, SkyTram is a wheelchair-accessible cable car that leads you on a gentle ride through the cloud forest; tickets can only be purchased in conjunction with SkyWalk or SkyTrek.

Horseback Riding

Until relatively recently this region was most easily traveled on horseback and, considering the roads around here, that's probably still true. Several operators offer the chance to test this theory with guided horseback rides ranging from two-hour tours to five-day adventures. Shorter trips generally run about US$15 per hour, while an overnight trek including meals and accommodations runs between US$150 and US$200.

DESAFÍO ADVENTURE COMPANY — Horse Riding

(Map p136; 2645-5874; www.monteverdetours. com) Does local treks for groups and individuals around town, day trips to Catarata San Luis (US$60 including admission, six hours) and several multiday rides. This established outfitter will arrange rides to La Fortuna ($85), usually on the Lake Trail. Located next door to Morpho's Restaurant.

SABINE'S SMILING HORSES — Horse Riding

(2645-6894, 8385-2424; www.horseback -riding-tour.com; waterfall tour US$50; depart 8am) Run by Sabine, who speaks English, French, Spanish and German, Smiling Horses offers a variety of treks including a popular waterfall tour (three hours). Her horses are in great condition.

 # Festivals & Events

The **Monteverde Music Festival** is held annually on variable dates from late January to early April. It has gained a well-deserved reputation as one of the top music festivals in Central America. Music is mainly classical, jazz and Latin, with an occasional experimental group to spice things up. Concerts are held on Thursday, Friday and Saturday, at different venues all over town and at the Monteverde Institute, which sponsors a few. Some performances are free, but most events ask US$5 to US$15 – proceeds go toward teaching music and the arts in local schools.

 # Sleeping

HIDDEN CANOPY TREEHOUSES — Resort $$$

(2645-5447; www.hiddencanopy.com; d garden rooms US$175-195, tree houses US$265-310, all incl breakfast & afternoon tea; P) This is the classiest spot in all of Monteverde. The American owner likes to call her unique boutique sleep 'glamping,' but only the glam fits, because this stylish spot is a long way from camping. Hidden within 13 acres of private rainforest are four stilted wood-and-glass tree houses, each with a unique floor plan, decor and name. All feature a treetop balcony, luxurious bedding, private bathroom, waterfall shower, custom-made furniture, paintings by local artists, plus high-end amenities such as minibar, coffeemaker, hair dryer, alarm clock and safe. The two-level Eden tree house has a fireplace, glass-enclosed Jacuzzi and canopied bed – perfect for honeymooners. The Neverland tree house sleeps four and overlooks its own koi pond and has 1½ baths. There are two less-expensive rooms in the main house, where breakfast and sunset teas (you may opt for bubbly) are held.

PENSIÓN SANTA ELENA — Hostel $

(Map p136; 2645-6240, 2645-5051; www. pensionsantaelena.com; camping per person

R H PRODUCTIONS / ALAMY ©

Don't Miss Friends Meeting House

In 1949 four Alabama Quakers (a pacifist religious group also known as the 'Society of Friends') were jailed for their refusal to be drafted into the Korean War. Since Quakers are obligated by their religion to be pacifists, the four men were eventually released from prison. However, in response to the incarceration, 44 Quakers from 11 Alabama families left the USA for the (much) greener pastures of Monteverde (Green Mountain). They chose this spot for two reasons – a few years prior, the Costa Rican government had abolished its military and the cool, mountain climate was ideal for grazing cattle. Ensconced in their isolated refuge they adopted a simple, trouble-free life of dairy farming and cheese production. In an effort to protect the watershed above its 15-sq-km plot in Monteverde, the Quaker community agreed to preserve the mountaintop cloud forests.

Quakerism began as a breakaway movement from the Anglican Church in the 1650s, founded by the young George Fox, who in his early 20s heard the voice of Christ, and claimed that direct experience with God was possible without having to go through the sacraments. Today, this belief is commonly described by Quakers as the 'God in everyone,' and the Monteverde community continues to lead a peaceful lifestyle in the Monteverde area and remain active in the local community.

The Society of Friends holds prayer meetings at the Friends Meeting House in Monteverde on Sunday at 10:30am and Wednesday at 9am. For more information, contact the Monteverde Friends School (www.mfschool.org).

NEED TO KNOW

Map p136; meetings 10:30am Sun, 9am Wed

US$4, dm/s/d US$7/25/30, d without bathroom US$16-20, cabinas US$35-50; P @ 🤶) This full-service hostel, located in central Santa Elena, is a perennial favorite. Each room is different, with something to suit every budget and group. The best rooms are in the new annex building, which features little touches like superior beds, stone showers and iPod docks in every room (the speakers are hidden in the ceiling). The charming Costa Rican staff is fully bilingual (Spanish and English), and they offer unbiased tourist information.

MARIPOSA B&B — Lodge $$

(Map p136; 🤶 2645-5013; vmfamilia@costarri cense.cr; s/d incl breakfast US$45/55; P 🤶) Just 1.5km from the Monteverde reserve, this friendly family-run place has quite nice rooms with terra-cotta floors and beamed ceilings, hot water, plush towels and a sweet Tico family to look after you. It's a great-value place, nestled into the forest with a little balcony for observing wildlife.

Eating

SOFIA — Restaurant $$

(Map p136; 🤶 2645-7017; mains US$12-16; 🕚 11:30am-9:30pm) Sofia has established itself as one of the best places in town with its Nuevo Latino cuisine – a modern fusion of traditional Latin American cooking styles. Think: sweet-and-sour fig roasted pork loin, plantain-crusted sea bass and shrimp with green mango curry. The ambience is flawless with pastel paintwork and potent cocktails to lighten the mood.

STELLA'S BAKERY — Bakery $

(Map p136; 🤶 2645-5560; mains US$2-6; 🕕 6am-10pm) Step into the terra-cotta entry way and browse temptations such as cinnamon rolls, cherry pie or the decadent frosted brownies. That spanakopita looks lovely too. It's all self-service, except for the wine.

CAFÉ CABURÉ — Cafe $$

(Map p136; 🤶 2645-5020; www.cabure.net; mains US$10-12; 🕘 9am-8pm Mon-Sat; 🤶) An Argentinean cafe set in the gorgeous Santa Fe style lodge above the bat cave in the Paseo de Stella visitors centre. It specializes in creative and delicious wraps, tortillas stuffed with chicken mole, chipotle-rubbed steak, curried potatoes and lemon shrimp. Its beef *empanadas* are fabulous, and it has magnificent gourmet truffles too! Seriously, the chocolate is high art.

MUSASHI — Japanese $$

(Map p136; 🤶 2645-7160; sushi US$5-8, rolls & mains US$5-18; 🕚 11am-11pm Tue-Sun) Crave good sushi in the Tico rainforest? Look no further than this tiny restaurant in the heart of Santa Elena. Jesus, the Venezuelan owner, is a classically trained sushi

Horseback riding, La Fortuna (p118)
JESUS OCHOA ©

chef, and his sushi boats are a good deal for groups. You'll also find other favorite Japanese dishes including teppanyaki, teriyaki and lunch bento box specials.

SABOR ESPAÑOL Spanish $$

(☎2645-5387; saborespanol@hotmail.com; mains US$6-15; ☺noon-9pm Tue-Su) One of the most authentic and lovely Spanish restaurants in Costa Rica specializes in paella, *papas bravas* (potatoes cooked in a spicy sauce), fresh fish, meats and chicken. Wash it down with some of the best sangria this side of the Atlantic. The ambience is rustic, intimate, super *tranquillo* and well worth the trip 2km north of downtown.

TREE HOUSE RESTAURANT & CAFÉ Cafe $$

(Map p136; ☎2645-5751; mains US$7-18; ☺11am-10pm; ☏) Built around a half-century-old *higuerón* (fig) tree, this hip cafe serves up everything from BLTs to pizza to grilled tenderloin to seafood specials. It's a lively space to have a bite, linger over wine and occasionally catch live music.

TRIO'S Restaurant $$

(Map p136; ☎2645-7254; mains US$7-17; ☺lunch & dinner) A touch of class in sweet Santa Elena, this rather Ikea-chic dining room behind SuperCompro is perched in the trees and the menu also aims high. At first blush you may be shocked at how un-*tipica* it is – coconut curry, pork ribs slathered in guava barbecue sauce, chicken breasts stuffed with figs and goat cheese – but dishes deliver big time.

🍷 Drinking & Entertainment

BAR AMIGOS Bar

(Map p136; ☎2645-5071; www.baramigos.com; ☺noon-3am) A disarming place because of its strange resemblance to one of those massive ski-lodge bars complete with picture windows overlooking the mountainside. But this is the one, consistent place in the area to let loose. There are DJs,

karaoke, all the sports from the US and a billiard room downstairs.

 Shopping

LUNA AZUL Jewelry

(Map p136; ☎2645-6638; lunaazulmonteverde@gmail.com; ☺9am-6pm Mon-Sat) A super-cute gallery with the best quality jewelry we saw in the entire area. It has soaps, some clothing racks, greeting cards, wood sculpture and macramé too, but its jewelry is the thing. Crafted from silver, shell, crystals and turquoise, the work is stylish and stunning.

HUMMINGBIRD GALLERY Handicrafts

(☎2645-5030; ☺8:30am-5pm) This gallery just outside Monteverde reserve has exceptionally beautiful nature photography, watercolors, art by the indigenous Chorotega and Boruca people and, best of all, feeders that constantly attract several species of hummingbird.

ALQUIMA ARTES Handicrafts

(Map p136; ☎2645-5847; www.alquimaartes.com; ☺9am-5pm) The work here is a tad more affordable than at some other places (check out the jewelry by Tarsicio Castillo from the Ecuadorian Andes), but this doesn't mean its collection of wood sculpture, paintings and prints by Costa Rican artists isn't astounding.

ℹ️ Getting There & Away

The government has been planning to build a series of bridges across the several rivers that feed Laguna de Arenal's southwestern shore for about 20 years. If completed, this would provide a road connection between Monteverde and La Fortuna, which would probably be the end of the eco-paradise formerly known as Monteverde. There are always a few scattered spots where some construction work is going on but, for the time being, they're not making too much progress.

Bus

All buses stop at the bus terminal (☎2645-5159; ☺5:45am-11am & 1:30am-5pm Mon-Fri, to 3pm Sat & Sun) in downtown Santa Elena and do not continue into Monteverde. You'll need to connect via taxi if that's where you plan to stay. On the trip in, keep an eye on your luggage, particularly on the San José–Puntarenas leg, as well as on the Monteverde–Tilarán run. Keep all bags at your feet and not in the overhead bin. Stories of theft and loss are common.

Reserva Monteverde US$1.20, 30 minutes, departs from front of Banco Nacional at 6:15am, 7:20am and 1:20pm, returning at 6:45am, 11:30am and 2pm.

Reserva Santa Elena US$2, 30 minutes, departs from front of Banco Nacional at 6:30am, 8:30am, 10:30am and 12:30pm, returning at 11am, 1pm and 4pm.

San José (TransMonteverde) US$5, 4½ hours, departs the Santa Elena bus station at 6:30am and 2:30pm.

Tilarán, with connection to La Fortuna US$3, seven hours, departs from the bus station at 6am. This is a long ride with a two-hour layover in Tilarán, so the jeep-boat-jeep option to La Fortuna is recommended.

There's no direct bus to Cañas. Most people take a bus to Juntas, then transfer from there to frequent Interamericana-route buses for Cañas, Liberia and beyond.

Horseback

There are a number of outfitters that offer transportation on horseback (per person US$65 to US$185, five to six hours) to La Fortuna, usually in combination with jeep rides. There are three main trails used: the Lake Trail (safe year-round), the Chiquito Trail (safe most of the year) and the gorgeous but infamous Castillo Trail (passable only in dry season by experienced riders). Stick to established, reputable tour companies, ask lots of questions and confirm the route before booking. According to sources, the best among the horseback outfitters is Desafio Adventure Company (p142).

Jeep-Boat-Jeep

The fastest route between Monteverde-Santa Elena and La Fortuna is a jeep-boat-jeep combo (around US$15 to US$25, three hours), which can be arranged through almost any hotel or tour operator in either town. A 4WD minivan takes you to Río Chiquito, meeting a boat that crosses Laguna de Arenal, where a van on the other side continues to La Fortuna. This is increasingly becoming the primary transportation between La Fortuna and Monteverde as it's incredibly scenic, reasonably priced and saves half a day of rough travel. Weirdly, there are no jeeps involved.

RESERVA BIOLÓGICA BOSQUE NUBOSO MONTEVERDE

This virginal **forest** (Monteverde Cloud Forest; 645 5122; www.cct.or.cr; adult/concession US$13/6.50; 7am-4pm; from Santa Elena) is dripping with mist, dangling with mossy vines, sprouting with ferns and bromeliads, gushing with creeks, and blooming with life in every direction. It is so moving that when Quaker settlers first arrived in the area, they agreed to preserve about a third of their property to protect this watershed. By 1972, however, encroaching squatters threatened its sustainability so the community joined forces with environmental organizations to purchase 328 hectares adjacent to the already-served area. It's one of Costa Rica's best natural attractions.

Note that some of the walking trails are very muddy, and even during the dry season (late December to early May) the cloud forest is rainy (hey, it's a rainforest, so quit complaining and bring rain gear, suitable boots and a smile). Many of the trails have been stabilized with concrete blocks or wooden boards and are easy to walk on, though unpaved trails deeper in the preserve turn sloppy during the rainy season.

Because of the fragile environment, the reserve allows a maximum of 160 people at any time. During the dry season this limit is almost always reached by 10am, which means you could spend the better part of a day waiting around for someone to leave. The best strategy is to get there before the gates open, or visit during the low season, usually May through June and September through November.

If you only have time to visit either the Monteverde or Santa Elena reserve, know that Monteverde gets nearly 10 times as many visitors, which means that the infrastructure is better and the trails are regularly maintained, though you'll

JUDY BELLAH ©

have to deal with much larger crowds. Also, most visitors come to Monteverde (and Santa Elena) expecting to see wildlife. However, both reserves cover large geographic areas which means that the animals have a lot of space to move around and away from annoying humans. The trees themselves are primitive and alone worth the price of admission.

 **Activities**

Wildlife-Watching

Monteverde is a bird-watching paradise and though the list of recorded species tops out at more than 400, the one most visitors want to see is the resplendent quetzal. The Maya bird of paradise is most often spotted during the March and April nesting season, though you may get lucky any time of year.

For those interested in spotting mammals, the cloud forest's limited visibility and abundance of higher primates (namely human beings) can make wildlife-watching quite difficult, though commonly sighted species

(especially in the backcountry) include coatis, howler monkeys, capuchins, sloths, agoutis and squirrels (as in 'real' squirrel, not the squirrel monkey).

Hiking

There are 13km of marked and maintained trails – a free map is provided with your entrance fee. The most popular of the nine trails, suitable for day hikes, make a rough triangle (El Triángulo) to the east of the reserve entrance. The triangle's sides are made up of the popular **Sendero Bosque Nuboso** (1.9km), an interpretive walk (booklet US$1 at gate) through the cloud forest that begins at the ranger station, and the 2km **El Camino**, a favorite of bird-watchers. The **Sendero Pantanoso** (1.6km) forms the far side of El Triángulo, traversing swamps, pine forests and the continental divide. Returning to the entrance, **Sendero Río** (2km) follows the Quebrada Cuecha past a few photogenic waterfalls.

Bisecting the triangle, the gorgeous **Chomogo Trail** (1.8km) lifts hikers to 1680m, the highest point in the triangle. Other little trails crisscross the region including the worthwhile **Sendero Brillante** (300m), with bird's-eye views of a miniature forest. However, keep in mind that despite valiant efforts to contain crowd sizes, these shorter trails are heavily trodden.

The trail to the **Mirador La Ventana** (elevation 1550m) is moderately steep and leads further afield to a wooden deck overlooking the continental divide. To the west, on clear days you can see the Golfo de Nicoya and the Pacific. To the east you can see the Penas Blanca's valley and the San Carlos plain. Even on wet, cloudy days it's magical. There's a 100m suspension bridge about 1km from the ranger station on Sendero Wilford Guindon, which rocks and sways with each step.

ℹ Information

The **visitors center** (☎ 2645-5122; www.cct. or.cr; park entry adult/student & child/child under 6yr US$17/9/free; ☉ 7am-4pm) is adjacent to the reserve gift shop, where you can buy trail guides, wildlife lists and maps. The shop also sells a variety of other souvenirs, and rents binoculars (US$10); you'll need to leave your passport. The annual rainfall here is about 3000mm, though parts of the reserve reportedly get twice as much. It's usually cool – high temperatures are around 18°C (65°F) – so wear appropriate clothing.

It's important to remember that the cloud forest is often cloudy (!) and can even be, gasp, rainy, and the vegetation is thick – this combination cuts down on sound as well as vision. Also remember that the main trails in this reserve are among the most trafficked in Costa Rica, so some readers have been disappointed with the lack of wildlife sightings. Hire a guide and you'll see more.

ℹ Getting There & Away

Public buses (US$1.20, 30 minutes) depart the Banco Nacional in Santa Elena at 6:15am, 7:20am and 1:20pm. Buses return from the reserve at 6:45am, 11:30am and 4pm. Taxis are also available for around US$9.

The 6km walk from Santa Elena is uphill, but lovely – look for paths that run parallel to the road. There are views all along the way, and

many visitors remark that some of the best bird-watching is on the final 2km of the road.

RESERVA SANTA ELENA

Though Monteverde gets all the attention, this exquisitely misty 310-hectare **reserve** (☎ 2645-5390, 2645-7107; www.reservasantae lena.org; adult/student US$14/7; ☉ 7am-4pm), just a fraction of the size of that other forest, has plenty to recommend it. You can practically hear the canopy, draped with epiphytes, breathing in humid exhales as water drops on to the leaf litter and mud underfoot. The odd call of the three-wattled bellbird or low crescendo of a howler monkey punctuates the higher-pitched bird chatter.

While Monteverde Crowd...er...Cloud Forest entertains almost 200,000 visitors annually, Santa Elena sees fewer than 20,000 tourists each year, which means its dewy trails through mysteriously veiled forest are usually far quieter. It's also much less developed; plus your entry fee is helping support another unique project.

The reserve is about 6km northeast of the village of Santa Elena. This cloud forest is slightly higher in elevation than Monteverde, and as some of the forest is secondary growth, there are sunnier places for spotting birds and other animals throughout. There's a stable population of monkeys and sloths, but unless you're a trained ecologist, the old-growth forest in Santa Elena will seem fairly similar in appearance to Monteverde, though the lack of cement blocks on the trails means that you'll have a much more authentic (note: muddy) trekking experience. Remember rule No 407 of cloud forests: it's often cloudy.

There's a simple restaurant, coffee shop and gift store, the proceeds of which go toward managing the reserve and local environmental programs.

LIBERIA

POP 63,000

The sunny, rural capital of Guanacaste has long served as a transportation hub connecting Costa Rica with Nicaragua, as well as being the standard-bearer of Costa Rica's *sabanero* (cowboy) culture.

Even today, a large part of the greater Liberia area is involved in ranching operations, but tourism is fast becoming a significant contributor to the economy. With an expanding international airport, Liberia is a safer and surprisingly chilled-out alternative Costa Rican gateway to San José, which means more travelers are spending a night or two in this small but sweet college town, knitted together by corrugated-tin fencing, mango trees and magnolias. And, though most of the historic buildings in the town center are a little rough around the edges, the 'white city' is a pleasant one. The streets in downtown Liberia are surprisingly well signed, a rarity in Costa Rica. Still, it's largely a launch pad for exploring Rincon de la Valle National Park and the beaches of the Península de Nicoya.

 Sights

Near the entrance of town, the statue of a steely-eyed *sabanero*, complete with an evocative poem by Rodolfo Salazar Solórzano, stands watch over the main street into town. The blocks around the intersection of Av Central and Calle Central contain several of Liberia's oldest houses, many dating back about 150 years.

AFRICA MÍA   Wildlife Reserve
(2666-1111; www.africamia.net; adult/child US$18/12, guided van tour US$30/24; 8am-6pm)
About 9km south of Liberia is a private wildlife reserve with free-roaming elephants, zebras, giraffes, ostriches and other animals. Splurge for the deluxe African Safari Wildlife Tour (adult/child US$65/55) in an open-top Hummer with a stop at a waterfall.

 **Sleeping**

BED & BREAKFAST EL PUNTO   Hotel $$
(Map p150; 2665-2986; www.elpuntohotel.com; cnr Interamericana & Av 4; d with/without airport pick up $97/80; P ❄ @ 🛜) This converted elementary school is now a chic loft hotel, and would definitely feel more at home in trendy Miami than in humble Guanacaste. The saturated tropical colors of the lofts manage to be understated and minimalist. All rooms have beautifully tiled bathroom, kitchenette, hammocks, free wi-fi and colorful modern art.

POSADA DE LA CALLE REAL   Hotel $$
(Map p150; 2666-0626; Cnr Calle Real & Av 4; r with bathroom US$60, without bathroom US$20-55; P ❄ 🛜 🛏) Set in a lovingly restored 1938 *posada* (guesthouse)this property has the most old-world class in Liberia. The two biggest and best rooms in the main house share a bath but have wood floors, soaring wood-paneled ceilings, cable TV and enough beds for a family of four. The attached restaurant

Green-crowned brilliant
PAUL SOUDERS / CORBIS ©

Liberia

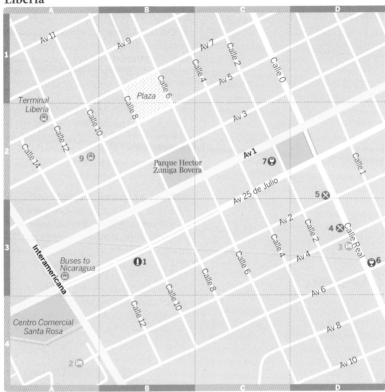

Liberia

⊙ **Sights**
1 Sabanero Statue B3

🛏 **Sleeping**
2 Bed & Breakfast El Punto A4
3 Posada de la Calle Real D3

🍽 **Eating**
4 Café Liberia D3
5 Copa de Oro D2

🍷 **Drinking**
6 Bar Kasa D3
7 Ciro's C2
8 Liberia Supremacy E1

ℹ **Transport**
9 Terminal Pulmitan A2

(open 11am to 11pm) serves pizzas and pastas (US$5 to US$16) on a patio overlooking a gorgeous backyard pool.

Eating

COPA DE ORO　　　　　Restaurant **$$**
(Map p150; ☎ 2666-0532; cnr Calle Central & Ave 2; mains US$5-16; ⊗ 11am-10pm Wed-Mon; 📶 ♿) Our favorite family restaurant is popular with locals and gringos alike. There's an extensive food and drink menu. The dish we loved best is the rice and seafood house specialty, *arroz copa de oro*, but its *casados* are excellent and it has a nice *ceviche* (seafood marinated in lemon or lime juice, garlic and seasonings) menu too.

original. It's not much, just a handful of tables, a simple bar and doors that roll open onto the sidewalk. But the sound system rocks and the locals bring the party.

LIBERIA SUPREMACY   Bar

(Map p150; Av 1 btwn Calles 5 & 7; ⊙4pm-late Tue-Sun) A bit of Jamaica bleeds over into Liberia at this popular reggae bar decorated with posters of Bob Marley and Che. There's a friendly vibe, cheap beer, an extensive Mexican *bocas* (appetizers) menu and the most uncomfortable bar stools ever crafted.

BAR KASA   Bar

(Map p150; Cnr Calle 0 & Av 6; ⊙7pm-1am) Liberia is something of a college town, and this new hot spot is where the hipsters like to bend their collective elbow, laugh, conspire, debate and flirt, most evenings.

ℹ Getting There & Away

Air

Since 1993 Aeropuerto Internacional Daniel Oduber Quirós (LIR), 12km west of Liberia, has served as the country's second international airport, providing easy access to beautiful beaches without the hassle of dealing with the bustle of San José. In January 2012 they unveiled a sleek new US$35 million terminal, which serves more destinations.

There are no car-rental desks at the airport; make reservations in advance, and your company will meet you at the airport with a car. There's a money-exchange, cafe, gift shops and a fantastic, inexpensive duty-free shop (it's tucked away and hard to find – keep looking). Taxis to Liberia cost US$20.

Bus

Buses arrive and depart from **Terminal Liberia** (Av 7 btwn Calles 12 & 14) and **Terminal Pulmitan** (Map p150; Av 5 btwn Calles 10 & 12). Routes, fares, journey times and departures are as follows:

Nicoya via Filadelfia & Santa Cruz US$2.25, 1½ hours, departs Terminal Liberia every 30 minutes from 3:30am to 9pm.

Playa Hermosa, **Playa Panamá** US$1.60, 1¼ hours, departs Terminal Liberia 4:30am, 4:40am, 4:50am, 7:30am, 11:30am, 1pm, 3:30pm and 5:30pm.

CAFÉ LIBERIA   Organic $

(Map p150; ☎2665-1660; www.cafeliberia.com; Calle 8 btwn Avs 2 & 4; dishes US$1-7; ⊙8am-7pm Mon-Fri, 10am-6pm Sat; ❷✷) This hip historic spot offers tasty breakfasts, organic juices, rich Costa Rican coffee, fresh sandwiches, salads and crepes, and lots of vegetarian items. Plus, there's free wi-fi, an art gallery and a yoga space (classes US$15) in the expansive courtyard. It's an upscale local and tourist scene.

⚇ Drinking

CIRO'S   Bar

(Map p150; Calle 2 btwn Av 0 & Av 1; ⊙11am-11pm) The newest and liveliest bar in Liberia belongs to this branch of the San José

BLICKWINKEL / ALAMY ©

Don't Miss **Catarata San Luis**

A popular (but strenuous) hike visits the Catarata San Luis, a gorgeous ribbon streaming in three tiers from the cloud forests into a series of swimming holes just screaming for a picnic. The distance from the parking area to the falls is only a few kilometers, but it's steeply graded downhill, and the rocky, muddy terrain can get very slick. It's important to go slow and turn back if it becomes too difficult. However, your efforts will be worth it as the waterfall is simply breathtaking. Alternatively, you may wish to join a guided hike to the falls, offered by the fantastic **Ecolodge San Luis** (☎ 2645-8049; www.ecolodgesanluis.com; bungalows s/d US$79/144, r US$102/192). Hikes must be reserved at least a day in advance. And be warned, you may never want to leave the lodge.

Drivers will need a 4WD to ford the little river and climb the muddy road out. You can park (US$6 per car) at a private farm, which is next to the trailhead. Several horseback-riding companies offer excursions to the falls (US$50 per person), but note that much of the road is now paved and this is hard on the horses' knees. A taxi from town to the falls will cost about U$15.

NEED TO KNOW
guided hike adult/child US$10/8.50

Playa Tamarindo US$2.75, 1½ to two hours, departs Terminal Liberia hourly between 3:50am and 6pm. Some buses take a longer route via Playa Flamingo.

San José US$6, four hours, 11 departures from Pulmitan from 4am to 8pm.

Car
Liberia lies on the Interamericana, 234km north of San José and 77km south of the Nicaraguan border post of Peñas Blancas. Highway 21, the main artery of the Península de Nicoya, begins in Liberia and heads southwest. A dirt road, passable to all cars in dry season (4WD is preferable), leads

25km from Barrio la Victoria to the Santa María entrance of Parque Nacional Rincón de la Vieja; the gravel road to the Las Pailas entrance begins from the Interamericana, 5km north of Liberia (4WD is recommended).

There are more than a dozen rental-car agencies in Liberia, based on Hwy 21 on either side of the airport (none have desks at the airport itself). Rates can vary and you'll get steep discounts for rentals of a month or more. Most companies can arrange pickup in Liberia and drop-off in San José, though they'll charge you extra. Some companies will drop off your car in town upon request.

VOLCÁN MIRAVALLES AREA

Volcán Miravalles (2028m) is the highest volcano in the Cordillera de Guanacaste, and although the main crater is dormant, the geothermal activity beneath the ground has led to its rapid development as a hot-springs destination.

Miravalles isn't a national park or refuge, but the volcano itself is afforded a modicum of protection by being within the Zona Protectora Miravalles. You can also take guided tours of the government-run Proyecto Geotérmico Miravalles, north of Fortuna, an ambitious project inaugurated in 1994 that uses geothermal energy to produce electricity. It produces about 18% of Costa Rica's electricity. But the geothermal energy most people come here to soak up comes in liquid form. The hot springs are north of the tiny village of Fortuna de Bagaces (not to be confused with La Fortuna de Arenal or Bagaces). The sleeping options in the area aren't fabulous, so we suggest basing yourself in Parque Nacional Volcán Tenorio and visiting the springs on a day trip, as the two mountains are linked by a rather glorious back road.

◎ Sights & Activities

TERMALES MIRAVALLES
Spring
(☎ 8357-8820, 8305-4072; adult/child US$4/3; ♿) For some local flavor, Termales Miravalles has two pools, a waterslide and lies along a thermal stream. The owners have set up a small restaurant and offer camping (US$6 per person) on the property. It's usually open on weekends year-round, and daily during high season. The access road is directly across from Yökö Hot Springs.

THERMO MANÍA
Spring
(☎ 2673-0233; www.thermomania.net; adult/child US$10/8; ⏰ 8am-10pm; ♿) The biggest complex in the area has some Disney–Flintstone queso (cheese) to it, but there are 11 thermal pools ranging from 36°C to 40°C, split into two areas. The upper pool complex is older, though it does have a swim-up bar and water slide. Much more tasteful are the five stone pools and sauna in the leafy lower sector. These are the best in the area, although all the pools could be a touch hotter. There's also a full spa and a busy restaurant-bar (mains US$4 to US$10). Guests who stay in the 26 log-cabin rooms (per person adult/child US$40/26) have free access to the pools during their stay. Families love it here.

EL GUAYACÁN
Spring
(☎ 2673-0349; www.termaleselguayacan.com; adult/child 3-10 yr US$7/5, fumaroles tour US$2; ♿) El Guayacán, whose hissing vents and mud pots (stay on the trail!) are on the family finca, lies just behind Thermo Manía. Seven thermal pools and one cold pool with a water slide are flanked by clean, simple cold-water cabinas (s/d US$30/60) brushed in loud colors. This unpretentious place has a mellow, family vibe to it. There's an onsite restaurant (mains US$4 to US$10) and it even has a hanging bridge in the nearby forest.

❶ Getting There & Away

Volcán Miravalles is 27km northeast of Bagaces and can be approached by a paved road that leads north of Bagaces through the communities of Salitral and Torno, where the road splits. From the left-hand fork, you'll reach Guayabo, with a few sodas and basic cabinas; to the right, you'll find Fortuna de Bagaces (so named as not to confuse it with La Fortuna, Bagaces overlap notwithstanding), with easier access to the hot springs. The road reconnects north of the two towns and continues toward Upala.

Buses (US$1.50, one hour) from Liberia to Guayabo or Aguas Claras (via Fortuna) depart at 6am, 9am, 11am and 2pm and pass by all the hot-spring entrances. Return buses to Liberia (via Guayabo) pass by the hot springs at about 2:30pm, 3:30pm and 4:30pm.

PARQUE NACIONAL RINCÓN DE LA VIEJA

Given its proximity to Liberia (really just a hop, skip and a few bumps away), this 141-sq-km national park feels refreshingly uncrowded and remote. Named after the active Volcán Rincón de la Vieja (1895m), the steamy main attraction, the park also covers several other peaks in the same volcanic range, including the highest, Volcán Santa María (1916m). The park exhales geothermal energy, which you can see for yourself in its multihued fumaroles, hot springs, bubbling and blooping ashy gray *pailas* (mud pots), and a young and feisty *volcancito* (small volcano). All of these can be visited on foot and horseback on well-maintained, but sometimes steep, trails.

The park was created in 1973 to protect a vital watershed that feeds 32 rivers and streams. Its relatively remote location means that wildlife, rare elsewhere, is out in force here, with the major volcanic crater a rather dramatic backdrop to the scene. Volcanic activity has occurred many times since the late 1960s, with the most recent eruption of steam and ash in 1997. At the moment, however, the volcano is gently active and does not present any danger – ask locally for the latest, as volcanoes do act up.

Elevations in the park range from less than 600m to 1916m, so visitors pass through a variety of habitats as they ascend the volcanoes, though the majority of the trees in the park are typical of those found in dry tropical forests throughout Guanacaste. Look out for the strangler fig, a parasitic species that covers the host tree with its own trunk and proceeds to strangle it by competing for water, light and nutrients. The host tree eventually dies and rots away, while the strangler fig survives as a hollow, tubular lattice.

Most visitors to the park are here for the hot springs, where you can soak to the sound of howler monkeys overhead. Many of the springs are reported to have therapeutic properties.

🏃 Activities

Hiking

A circular trail east of Las Pailas (about 3km in total) takes you past the boiling mud pools (Las Pailas), sulfurous fumaroles and a *volcancito*. About 350m west of the ranger station is the well-signed trail to Pozo Azul. Although the wooden

Boogie boarding
PHILIP AND KAREN SMITH / GETTY IMAGES ©

stairs are decrepit and being reclaimed by jungle, they lead to a marvelous river view and the stunning aquamarine swimming hole. Further away along the same trail are several waterfalls – the largest, Catarata La Cangreja, 5.1km west, is a classic, dropping 50m straight from a cliff into a small lagoon where you can swim. Dissolved copper salts give the falls a deep blue color. This trail winds through forest, past truly massive strangler figs, then on to open savanna spiked with yucca on the volcano's flanks, where you can enjoy views as far as the Palo Verde wetlands and the Pacific. The slightly smaller Cataratas Escondidas (Hidden Waterfalls) are 4.3km west on a different trail and a bit higher on the slope.

The longest and most adventurous hike in the area is the 16km round-trip trek to the summit of Rincón de la Vieja and Laguna de Jilgueros, which is reportedly where you may see tapirs – or more likely their footprints, if you are observant.

An easier option leads from the Santa María ranger station, 2.8km west through the 'enchanted forest' and past a waterfall to sulfurous hot springs.

Hot Springs & Spas

SIMBIOSIS SPA   Spa
(☏2666-8075; www.simbiosis-spa.com; admission US$15, massages & spa treatments US$30-75; ⊙9am-5:30pm) Under renovation when we visited and affiliated with Hacienda Guachipelín, this long-running spa should have reopened to the public by the time you read this. Expect volcanic mud baths, sauna, cold pool, showers and lounge chairs, all in a natural outdoor setting. You can also arrange massages and spa treatments on the spot, though it's recommended you reserve ahead.

Sleeping

BORINQUEN MOUNTAIN RESORT & SPA   Resort $$$
(☏2690-1900; www.borinquenresort.com; d incl breakfast US$185-365) If you want to splurge, wallow here. The most luxurious resort

If You Like…
Nature Reserves

If you like the Reserva Santa Elena, we think you'll like these other protected areas in northern Costa Rica.

1 PARQUE NACIONAL GUANACASTE
(www.acguanacaste.ac.cr; adult/child US$10/1) At one of the least visited parks in Costa Rica, the land transitions from dry tropical forest to humid cloud forest.

2 REFUGIO NACIONAL DE VIDA SILVESTRE CAÑO NEGRO
(admission US$6; ⊙8am-6pm) The lagoons of Caño Negro attract a wide variety of birds year-round.

3 ECOCENTRO DANAUS
(Ecological Center; Map p5; ☏2479-7019; www.ecocentrodanaus.com; admission with/without guide US$16/11, guided night tours US$35; ⊙8am-4pm Mon-Sat, 9am-3:30pm Sun) This small reserve has a well-developed trail system that's good for bird-watching, and spotting sloths, coatis and howler monkeys.

4 REFUGIO NACIONAL DE VIDA SILVESTRE BAHÍA JUNQUILLAL
(☏2666-5051; www.acguanacaste.ac.cr; adult/child 6-12/child under 5 US$13/5/free, camping per person US$2; ⊙8am-5pm) A small, peaceful protected site, this refuge has a beach backed by mangrove swamp and tropical dry forest.

in the area features plush, fully air-conditioned bungalows with private deck, minibar and satellite TV. The onsite hot springs, mud baths and natural saunas are beautifully laid out and surrounded by greenery, but a treatment (US$55 to US$200) at the unbelievably modern, elegant **Anáhuac Spa** (⊙10am-6pm) suspended over the river and steaming jungle, is the icing on this decadent mud pie.

ℹ Getting There & Away

The Las Pailas sector is accessible via a good 20km gravel road that begins at a signed turnoff from the Interamericana 5km north of Liberia;

a private road is needed to reach the park and costs US$1.50 per person. There's no public transportation, but any of the lodges can arrange transport from Liberia for around US$20 to US$30 per person each way (two or three people minimum). Alternately, you can hire a 4WD taxi from Liberia for about US$35 to Las Pailas, or US$65 to Santa María, each way.

PARQUE NACIONAL VOLCÁN TENORIO

They say when God finished painting the sky blue, he washed his paintbrushes in the Río Celeste. The heavenly blue river, waterfalls and lagoons of Parque Nacional Volcán Tenorio are among the most spectacular natural phenomena in Costa Rica, which is probably why the park is known to locals simply as Río Celeste.

Established in 1976, this magical 184-sq-km park remains one of the most secluded and least-visited parks in the country due to the dearth of public transportation and park infrastructure. As a result, it remains a blissfully pristine rainforest abundant with wildlife. Soaring 1916m above the cloud rainforest is the park's namesake, Volcán Tenorio, which actually consists of three peaked craters: Montezuma, Tenorio I (the tallest) and Tenorio II.

Your first stop will be the **Puesto El Pilón ranger station** (2200-0135; www.acarenaltempisque.org; adult/child under 12yr US$10/free; 8am-4pm, last entry at 2:30pm), which houses a small exhibit of photographs. Pick up a free English or Spanish hiking map.

◎ Sights & Activities

A well-signed trail begins at the ranger-station parking lot and winds 1.5km through the rainforest until you reach an intersection. Turn left and climb down a very steep and slippery staircase to the Catarata de Río Celeste, a milky-blue

waterfall that cascades 30m down the rocks into a fantastically aquamarine pool.

There are several more trails to explore on easy day hikes, including the one to the **Pozo Azul** (Blue Lagoon) and **Aguas Termales** (hot springs) to soak your weary muscles. This is the only place in the park where you're permitted to enter the water; bring your own towel and swimsuit. Plans for a circuit trail are afoot, but for now the trail ends here.

 ## Sleeping & Eating

CELESTE MOUNTAIN LODGE   Lodge **$$$**
(☎ 2278-6628; www.celestemountainlodge.com; s/d/tr incl all meals US$150/180/215 ; P) One of the most innovative and sustainable hotels we've ever seen, Celeste Mountain Lodge might be the perfect jungle lodge. The contemporary open-air hilltop lodge in the shadow of Volcán Tenorio is absolutely stunning. It was built in 2007 using ecofriendly materials such as recycled wood, plastic, old truck tires and coconut fiber. Lamps, sculptures and other decorative items are made of scrap metal. Hot water comes from solar power, and cooking gas is partially produced by kitchen waste. The 18 rooms are four-star stylish with colorful accents, concrete-tile floors and wooden shutters that open onto immobilizing volcano and jungle vistas. The property features a 2km interpretive hiking trail laid with geotextile (no more muddy shoes!), which makes for soundless hiking in one of Costa Rica's prime bird-watching zones. The price includes all meals at the amazing organic restaurant and service is simply outstanding. The lodge is located at the end of a 3.5km-long, rough (4WD required) access road that begins at the north end of Bijagua.

TENORIO LODGE   Lodge **$$$**
(☎ 8886-5382, 2466-8282; www.tenoriolodge. com; s/d incl breakfast US$115/125; P ❄ @ 🛜) Located on a lush hilltop with amazing views of Volcán Tenorio, Tenorio Lodge

has some of the most romantic and private accommodations around. There are eight roomy bungalows, each containing two orthopedic beds (one king and one queen), private bathroom with solar-heated water, panoramic windows and balcony with volcano views. The gorgeous lodge has a lovely restaurant featuring a daily changing dinner menu (but no lunch). On the 17-acre property you'll find two ponds, a heliconia garden and two hot tubs to enjoy after a long day of hiking. It's located 1km south of downtown Bijagua.

PARQUE NACIONAL SANTA ROSA

Among the oldest (established in 1971) and largest national parks in Costa Rica, this sprawling 386-sq-km national refuge on the Península Santa Elena protects the largest remaining stand of tropical dry forest in Central America, and some of the most important nesting sites of several species of sea turtle. However, the majority of travelers are here for one reason – the chance to surf the near-perfect beach break at Playa Naranjo, which is created by the legendary offshore monolith known as Witch's Rock (also known locally as Roca Bruja).

Santa Rosa is famous among Ticos as a symbol of historical pride. A foreign army has only invaded Costa Rica three times, and each time the attackers were defeated in Santa Rosa. The best known of these events was the Battle of Santa Rosa, which took place on March 20 1856, when the soon-to-be-self-declared president of Nicaragua, an American named William Walker, invaded Costa Rica. Walker was the head of a group of foreign pirates and adventurers known as the 'Filibusters' that had already seized Baja and southwest Nicaragua, and were attempting to gain control over all of Central America. In a brilliant display of military prowess, Costa Rican President Juan Rafael Mora Porras guessed Walker's intentions and managed to assemble a ragtag group of fighters that surrounded Walker's army in the main building of the old Hacienda Santa Rosa, known as La Casona. The battle was over in just 14 minutes, and Walker forever driven from Costa Rican soil.

 Sights

LA CASONA   Historic Building
(☺8am-11:30am & 1pm-4pm) The historic La Casona, the main building of the old Hacienda Santa Rosa, is near park headquarters in the Santa Rosa sector. Unfortunately, the original building was burnt to the ground by arsonists in May 2001, but was rebuilt in 2002 using historic photos and local timber. The boulder foundation is still authentic, and there are other 19th-century charms such as wagon wheels, a restored adobe kitchen and one prominently displayed yoke on the porch eaves, not to mention those fabulous old shade trees around the Casona corrals. Two hiking trails leave from behind the museum.

The battle of 1856 was fought around this building, and the military action, as well as the region's natural history, is described with wonderful new historical displays in English and Spanish detailing the old gold-rush route, William Walker's evil imperial plans, and the 20-day battle breakdown.

 **Activities**

Wildlife-Watching

The wildlife is both varied and prolific, especially during the dry season when animals congregate around the remaining water sources and the trees lose their leaves. More than 250 bird species have been recorded, including the raucous white-throated magpie jay, unmistakable with its long crest of manically curled feathers. The forests contain parrots and parakeets, trogons and tanagers, and as you head down to the coast, you will be rewarded by sightings of a variety of coastal birds.

Bats are also very common (about 50 or 60 different species have been identified in Santa Rosa), as are reptile species that include lizards, iguanas, snakes, crocodiles and four species of sea turtle. The olive

Detour: Llanos de Cortés Waterfall

If you have time to visit only one waterfall in Costa Rica, make it **Llanos de Cortés** (admission by donation; 8am-5pm). This beautiful hidden waterfall is located about 3km north of Bagaces; head north on the Interamericana, turn left on the dirt road after the Río Piedras bridge, then follow the bumpy road (4WD required) for about 1km, and turn right at the guarded gate where you'll make a donation (US$2 will do the job) in exchange for your admission. Proceeds help fund the local primary school. Continue down the dirt road about 300m to the parking area, then scramble down the short, steep trail to reach this spectacular 12m-high, 15m-wide waterfall, which you'll be able to hear from the parking lot. The falls drop into a tranquil pond with a white sandy beach that's perfect for swimming and sunbathing. Go 'backstage' and relax on the rocks behind the waterfall curtain, or shower beneath the lukewarm waters. The gated road is open 8am to 5pm daily. On weekends this is a popular Tico picnic spot, but on weekdays you'll often have the waterfall to yourself.

Apart from a portable toilet, there are no services here except for the occasional vendor selling fruit and cold coconut water in the parking area. Although the lot is guarded, don't leave valuables exposed in your car. If you don't have a car, any bus trawling this part of the Interamericana can drop you at the turnoff, but you'll have to hike from there to the falls.

ridley sea turtle is the most numerous, and during the July to December nesting season tens of thousands of turtles make their nests on Santa Rosa's beaches. The most popular beach is Playa Nancite, where, during September and October especially, it is possible to see as many as 8000 of these 40kg turtles on the beach at the same time. The turtles are disturbed by light, so flash photography and flashlights are not permitted. Avoid the nights around a full moon – they're too bright and turtles are less likely to show up. Playa Nancite is strictly protected and entry restricted, but permission may be obtained from **park headquarters** (2666-5051) to observe this spectacle; call ahead.

Surfing

The surfing at Playa Naranjo is truly world-class, especially near Witch's Rock, a beach break famous for its fast, hollow 3m rights (although there are also fun lefts when it isn't pumping). Beware of rocks near the river mouth, and be careful near the estuary as it's a rich feeding ground for crocodiles during the tide changes. Oh, and by the way, the beach is stunning, with a sweet rounded boulder-strewn point to the north and shark-fin headlands to the south. Even further south, Nicoya and Papagayo peninsular silhouettes reach out in a dramatic attempt to outdo each other.

The surfing is equally legendary at Ollie's Point off Playa Portero Grande, which has the best right in all of Costa Rica with a nice, long ride, especially with a south swell. The bottom here is a mix of sand and rocks, and the year-round offshore is perfect for tight turns and slow closes. Shortboarding is preferred by surfers at both spots.

Hiking

Near Hacienda Santa Rosa is El Sendero Indio Desnudo, an 800m trail with signs interpreting the ecological relationships among the animals, plants and weather patterns of Santa Rosa. The trail is named after the common tree, also called *gumbo limbo*, whose peeling orange-red bark can photosynthesize during the dry season, when the trees' leaves are lost (resembling a sunburned tourist...or 'naked Indian,' as the literal translation of the trail name implies). Also seen along the trail is the national tree of Costa Rica, the *guanacaste*. The province is named after this huge tree species, which is found along the Pacific coastal lowlands. You may also see birds, monkeys, snakes, iguanas, as well as petroglyphs (most likely pre-Columbian) etched into rocks along the trail.

Behind La Casona a short 330m trail leads up to the Monumento a Los Héroes and a lookout platform. There are also longer trails through the dry forest, including a gentle 4km hike to the Mirador, with spectacular views of Playa Naranjo. The main road is lined with short trails to small waterfalls and other photogenic natural wonders.

On the road to Playa Naranjo, and about 8km from shore, you'll pass a trailhead for the Mirador Valle Naranjo trail. It's a short 600m hump to a viewpoint with magical Naranjo vistas.

From the southern end of Playa Naranjo, there is also the 5km Sendero Carbonal trail that swings inland along the mangroves and past Laguna El Limbo where the crocs hang out; Sendero

Aceituno parallels Playa Naranjo for 13km and terminates near the estuary across from Witch's Rock.

Getting There & Away

The well-signed main park entrance can be reached by public transportation: take any bus between Liberia and the Nicaraguan border and ask the driver to let you off at the park entrance; rangers can help you catch a return bus. You can also arrange private transportation from the hotels in Liberia for about US$20 to US$30 per person round trip.

LA VIRGEN

Tucked into the densely jungled shores of the wild and scenic Río Sarapiquí, La Virgen was one of a number of small towns that prospered during the heyday of the banana trade. Although United Fruit has long since shipped out, the town remains dependent on their pineapple fields and they still lean on that river. For more than a decade, La Virgen was the premier kayaking and rafting destination in Costa Rica. Dedicated groups of hard-core paddlers spent happy weeks running the Río Sarapiquí. But a tremendous 2009 earthquake

La Casona (p158), Parque Nacional Santa Rosa

Hottest Spots for Thermal Pools & Mud Pots

Costa Rica's volcano-powered thermal pools and mud pots provide plenty of good, clean fun for beauty queens and would-be mud wrestlers alike.

On the slopes of Volcán Rincón de la Vieja, **Hot Springs Río Negro** (www. guachipelin.com; per person US$10, massage per hr US$75; ⊙9am-5pm) has several pools, in a transporting jungle setting.

While some hot spots around Arenal charge outrageous fees to soak in sparkly surrounds, **Eco Thermales Hot Springs** (Map p120; ☏2479-8484; adult/child US$34/29; ⊙10am-9pm; P⊞) maintains its sense of elegance by limiting guest numbers.

The pinnacle of luxurious dirt exists in the remote heights of Rincón de la Vieja at Borinquen Mountain Resort & Spa (p155), where, if mineral mud is not your thing, you can opt instead for a wine or chocolate skin treatment.

and landslide altered its course and flattened La Virgen's tourist economy. Some businesses folded, others relocated to La Fortuna. But independent kayakers are starting to come back and there are now three river outfitters offering exhilarating trips on Class II-IV waters. Although there are cheap digs in town, consider staying in one of the more luxurious lodges nearby.

 Sights

SERPENTARIO   Zoo
(☏2761-1059; adult/student & child US$8/6; ⊙9am-5pm) Get face-to-face with 50 different species of reptiles and amphibians, including a poison-dart frog, an anaconda and the star attraction, an 80kg Burmese python.

 **Activities**

The Río Sarapiquí isn't as wild as the white water on the Río Pacuare near Turrialba, though it will get your heart racing and the dense jungle that hugs the riverbank is lush and primitive. You can run the Sarapiquí year-round, but December offers the biggest water. The rest of the year, the river fluctuates with rainfall. The bottom line is, if it's been raining, the river will be at its best. Where

once there were nearly a dozen outfitters in La Virgen, now there are three. All offer roughly the same Class II-IV options at similar prices.

AVENTURAS DEL SARAPIQUI   Rafting
(☏2766-6768; www.sarapiqui.com; river trips US$55-80) Offers a variety of river trips.

HACIENDA POZO AZUL ADVENTURES   Adventure Sports
(☏2761-1360, in USA & Canada 877-810-6903; www.pozoazul.com; tours US$42-80, combo tours US$80-122; ⊞) Offers assorted river trips.

INFLATABLE DUCKIES   Kayaking
(☏8760-3787, 2761-0095; tours from US$65; ⊙departs 9:30am & 1:30pm) Offers beginners kayak instruction in inflatable kayaks, which allow for a fun paddle even when the river is low. Reserve ahead.

 Sleeping & Eating

HACIENDA POZO AZUL ADVENTURES   Bungalow $$
(☏2761-1360; www.haciendapozoazul.com; d luxury tent US$92; P@⊠⊠) Located near the south end of La Virgen, Pozo Azul features luxurious 'tent suites' scattered on the edge of the tree line, all on raised, polished-wood platforms and dressed with luxurious bedding and mosquito nets. At night the frogs and wildlife sing

161

you to sleep as raindrops patter on the canvas roof. Pozo Azul also boasts a restaurant-bar in town for lunch and dinner (mains US$6 to US$14), with a riverside veranda.

RESTAURANTE Y CABINAS
TÍA ROSITA Soda $

(☎ 2761-1125, 2761-1032; www.restaurante tiarosita.com; meals US$2-6; ☼breakfast, lunch & dinner; [P] 🛜) Tía Rosita is the most highly recommended *soda* in La Virgen, with excellent *casados* and Costa Rican–style *chiles rellenos* (stuffed fried peppers). The family also rents several *cabinas* (single/double US$10/15) with private hot shower, TV, fan and plenty of breathing space about 100m down the road. There's an onsite internet cafe (US$0.60 per hour).

Getting There & Away

La Virgen lies on Hwy 126, about 8km from San Miguel to the south, and 17km from Puerto Viejo de Sarapiquí to the northeast. Buses originating in either San José, San Miguel or Puerto Viejo de Sarapiquí make regular stops in La Virgen. If you're driving, the curvy road is paved between San José and Puerto Viejo de Sarapiquí, though irregular maintenance can make for a bumpy ride.

LA VIRGEN TO PUERTO VIEJO DE SARAPIQUí

This scenic stretch of Hwy 126 is home to a few lovely, popular ecolodges. However, if you're the kind of traveler that scrapes together a few hundred colones every morning to buy a loaf of bread from Palí supermarket, fear not, as these places do allow nonguests to see their unusual attractions and private trails for a small fee. Even better, arrange a homestay with the farming families in nearby Linda Vista through the **Chilamate Rainforest Eco Retreat** (☎ 2766-6949; www.chilamate rainforest.com; dm US$30, s/d incl breakfast US$76/96). Any bus between La Virgen and Puerto Viejo de Sarapiquí can drop you off at the entrances, while a taxi from La Virgen (or Puerto Viejo for Selva Verde) will cost from US$8 to US$10.

◉ Sights & Activities

TIRIMBINA
RAINFOREST CENTER Wildlife Reserve

(☎ 2761-1579; www.tirimbina.org) A working environmental research and education center, Tirimbina Rainforest Center also provides tours (US$22 to US$25) and accommodations (double including breakfast US$63) for visitors. The 345-hectare private reserve and the nearby Centro Neotrópico Sarapiquís are connected by two suspension bridges, 267m and 117m long. Halfway across, a spiral staircase drops to an island in the river. Tirimbina reserve has more than 9km of trails, some of which are paved or wood-blocked. There are also several guided tours on offer including bird-watching, frog and bat tours, night walks and a recommended chocolate tour, which lets you explore a working cacao plantation and learn about the harvesting, fermenting and drying processes. Child and student discounts are available. Tirimbina is about 2km north of La Virgen.

🛏 Sleeping & Eating

SARAPIQUÍS RAINFOREST
LODGE Lodge $$$

(☎ 2761-1004; www.sarapiquis.org; d US$117; [P] 😊 ❄ @) About 2km north of La Virgen, Sarapiquis Rainforest Lodge is a unique ecolodge run in conjunction with the Centro Neotropico Sarapiquis that aims to foster sustainable tourism by educating guests about environmental conservation and pre-Columbian culture. The complex consists of *palenque*-style, thatched-roof buildings modeled after a 15th-century pre-Columbian village, and contains a clutch of luxuriously appointed rooms with huge, solar-heated bathroom and private terrace.

It's worth stopping by just to visit the **Alma Ata Archaeological Park**, **Rainforest of Indigenous Cultures** and **Sarapiquís Gardens** (www.sarapiquis.org; self-guided adult/child 4-16 yr US$8/4, with guide US$15/8; ☼9am-5pm). The archaeological site is estimated to be around 600 years old, and is attributed to the Maleku.

Detour:
Parque Nacional Palo Verde

The 184-sq-km **Parque Nacional Palo Verde** (2524-0628; www.ots.ac.cr; adult/child under 12yr US$10/1; 8am-4pm) is a wetland sanctuary in Costa Rica's driest province. It lies on the northeastern bank of the mouth of Río Tempisque, and at the head of the Golfo de Nicoya. All of the major rivers in the region drain into this ancient intersection of two basins, which creates a mosaic of habitats, including mangrove swamps, marshes, savannas and forests. A number of low limestone hills provide lookout points over the park, and the park's shallow lagoons are focal points for wildlife.

Palo Verde has the greatest concentrations of waterfowl and shorebirds in Central America, and more than 300 different bird species have been recorded in the park. Bird-watchers come to see the large flocks of herons, storks (including the endangered jabirú), spoonbills, egrets, ibis, grebes and ducks. Forest birds, including scarlet macaws, great curassows, keel-billed toucans, and parrots are also common. Frequently sighted mammals include armadilloes, monkeys and peccaries, as well as the largest population of jaguarundi in Costa Rica. There are also numerous reptiles in the wetlands including crocodiles that are reportedly up to 5m in length.

The dry season, from December to March, is the best time to visit as flocks of birds tend to congregate in the remaining lakes and marshes and the trees lose their leaves, allowing for clearer viewing. However, the entire basin swelters during the dry season, so bring adequate sun protection. During the wet months, large portions of the area are flooded, and access may be limited.

Currently about 70 small stone sculptures marking a burial field are being excavated by Costa Rican archaeologists, who have revealed a number of petroglyphs and pieces of pottery. Although the site is modest, and definitely not comparable in size or scope to other Central American archaeological sites, it's one of the few places in Costa Rica where you can get a sense of its pre-Columbian history.

LA QUINTA DE SARAPIQUÍ LODGE
Lodge $$$

(2761-1052; www.laquintasarapiqui.com; d US$120; P) About 5km north of La Virgen, this pleasant family-run lodge is on the banks of the Río Sardinal, which branches off from the Sarapiquí. The lodge has covered paths through the landscaped garden connecting thatched-roof, hammock-strung rooms. All have a terrace, ceiling fan, natural wood vanities and private hot shower. You can also get meals in the open-air restaurant (mains US$9 to US$15).

Activities at the lodge include swimming in the pretty pool or river (there's a good swimming hole nearby), fishing, boat trips and bird-watching, and you can spend time in the large butterfly garden or hike the 30-minutes' worth of trails through secondary forest accessible from the hotel. There's also a full-service spa.

SELVA VERDE LODGE
Lodge $$$

(2761-1800, in USA & Canada 800-451-7111; www.selvaverde.com; s/d incl breakfast US$113/131, bungalow s/d US$130/160) In Chilamate, about 7km west of Puerto Viejo, this former *finca* is now an elegant lodge that protects over 500 acres of rainforest. Guests can choose to stay at the river lodge, which is elevated above the forest floor on wooden platforms, or in a private bungalow, quietly tucked away in the nearby trees. Wood-floored rooms have private hot shower, screened windows, in-room safe and, of course, your very own hammock.

163

There are three walking trails through the grounds and into the premontane tropical wet forest. The two self-guided trails take 45 minutes and two hours to complete respectively, but the longest trail leads into primary forest and must be guided. You can either get a trail map and/or hire a bilingual guide (US$15 per person) from the lodge. Even lodge guests must pay the premium to enjoy the primary forest. There's a medicinal and butterfly garden. Various boat tours on the Río Sarapiquí are also available, from rafting trips to guided canoe tours. Its Italian kitchen, **La Terazza** (mains US$7-9), has wood-fired pizza, chicken masala, veal, beef, fish and pasta dishes too.

PUERTO VIEJO DE SARAPIQUÍ & AROUND

At the scenic confluence of Ríos Puerto Viejo and Sarapiquí, Puerto Viejo de Sarapiquí was once the most important port in Costa Rica. Boats laden with fruit, coffee and other commercial exports plied the Sarapiquí as far as the Nicaraguan border, then turned east on the Río San Juan to the sea. Today it is simply a gritty palm-shaded market town. But there's grace here too, evidenced by the cute tiled benches and archways along the shopping district adjacent to the soccer field. Visitors can choose from any number of activities in the surrounding area, such as bird-watching, rafting, kayaking, boating and hiking. There is no dry season, but from late January to early May is the 'less wet' season. On the upside, when it rains here there are fewer mosquitoes.

 Activities

Taking the launch from Puerto Viejo to Trinidad, at the confluence of the Ríos Sarapiquí and San Juan, provides a rich opportunity to see crocodiles, sloths, birds, monkeys and iguanas sunning themselves on the muddy riverbanks or gathering in the trees. This river system is a historically important gateway from the Caribbean into the heart of Central America, and it's still off the beaten tourist track, revealing rainforest and ranches, wildlife and old war zones, deforested pasture land and protected areas.

🌿**LAGO JALAPA** Hiking, Canoeing
(☎ 8817-0452, 8317-2436; www.lagojalapa.com; per person US$20-45) The newest grassroots ecotourism effort in the area combines short hikes with an hour-long canoe trip on a lake about 8km from town. It even offers overnight kayaking and camping trips. The business gets excellent reviews from travelers but the administration is weak. Phones aren't

Witch's Rock, Playa Naranjo (p159)
NICK TURNER / ALAMY ©

always answered and prices can vary depending on the day, plus guides speak no English. Still, it is a local business and worth looking into because Lago Jalapa is a stunning lake in the Refugio de Vida Silvestre, surrounded by forest teeming with wildlife.

Sleeping & Eating

POSADA ANDREA CRISTINA B&B　　　　　Cabina $

(☏2766-6265; www.andreacristina.com; s/d incl breakfast US$32/52; P🛜) About 1km west of the center, this recommended B&B has eight quaint cabins in its garden, each with a colorful paint job, stone tile, high beamed ceilings, hot water and outdoor table and chairs. It's situated on the edge of the forest, so there are plenty of opportunities for bird-watching while you sit outside and eat breakfast.

HOTEL ARA AMBIGUA　　　　Hotel $$

(☏2766-7101; www.hotelaraambigua.com; d incl breakfast with/without air-con US$70/60; P❄@≋) About 1km west of Puerto Viejo near La Guaíra, this countryside retreat offers bright tiled rooms that are well equipped with private hot-water shower and cable TV. The real draws are the varied opportunities for wildlife-watching – you can see poison-dart frogs in the *ranario* (frog pond), caimans in the

small lake, and birds that come to feed near the onsite Restaurante La Casona.

🛈 Getting There & Away

Autotransportes Sarapiquí and **Empresarios Guapileños** run buses to San José (US$2.50; two hours) departing at 5am, 5:15am, 5:30am, 7am, 8am, 9:30am, 11am, 11:30am, 1:30pm, 3pm and 5:30pm.

SOUTH OF PUERTO VIEJO DE SARAPIQUÍ

Adventure-oriented tour groups make up the majority of guests at **Sueño Azul** (☏2764-1213; www.suenoazulresort.com; superior/junior ste US$124/143), a top-end adventure lodge upon a hill. It has an on-again off-again yoga-retreat program and the secluded bamboo yoga platform is lovely, but that's one small, ephemeral slice of its business. Its perch on the stunning confluence of the Ríos Sarapiquí and San Rafael, and vast property are the main draws. Here's a place with its own suspension bridge, canopy tour and waterfall. It has an enormous stable of gorgeous horses if you fancy a ride. There are hiking trails and hot tubs, a splashy pool, bar and a huge tiled patio replete with leather rockers. Rooms are huge with terra-cotta floors, log beds and river views, though some can smell musty.

Península de Nicoya

Península de Nicoya is an alluring place of magical beaches, turtles and good surf.
Archetypical tropical beaches edge this jungle-trimmed rich coast, whose shores have been imprinted on the memories of the millions of marine turtles who return to their birthplaces to nest. The travelers, too, descend on these beaches, seeking to witness such patterns of nature for themselves. And who can be blamed for wanting to play, beckoned by waves that never seem to close out, tropical forests teeming with wild things, the slow, sane pace of *la vida costarricense* (Costa Rican life) and what lies beyond that next turn down a potholed dirt road?

Humans, however, make more of an environmental impact than the leatherbacks do. Development is the name of the game at the moment, and Nicoya is the high-stakes playing field. The next moves will require a sustained effort to maintain the peninsula's intrinsic wildness, but we are betting on the Ticos and local expats to rise to the occasion.

Mal País (p199)

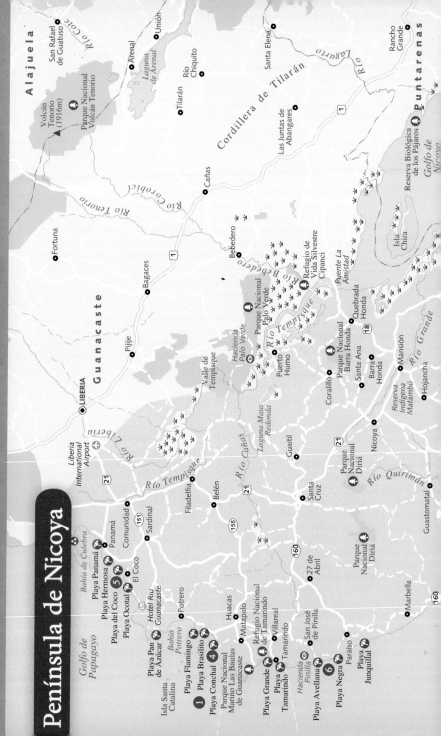

1 Surfing Península de
Nicoya

2 Montezuma

3 Playa Sámara

4 Playa Conchal

5 Playa del Coco

6 Playa Avellana & Playa
Negra

① Surfing Península de Nicoya

Península de Nicoya offers a great variety of surf spots, many of which break in front of lovely white-sand beaches and are aided by offshore winds. There are waves for beginners and intermediates, as well as plenty of waves for advanced surfers. In fact, nearly every beach along the north Pacific coast is surfable. Above and right: Surfers at Mal País

Need to Know

ACCESS Mal País and Tamarindo are served by bus; Playa Grande and Nosara are best reached by car **SURF REPORTS** Costa Rica Surf (www.crsurf. com) **For more see** p178

Surfing Península de Nicoya Don't Miss List

BY DEBBIE ZEC, PROFESSIONAL SURFER AND OPERATOR OF DOMINICAL SURF LESSONS

1 MAL PAÍS & SANTA TERESA

This long, sweeping stretch of coastline is one of the best places to surf along the peninsula. The waves are very consistent, and they have great shape during high and low tide. But there are some random rocks, so watch out! When you need a break from the crashing surf, the towns are full of hip restaurants and cafes.

2 PLAYA GRANDE

Famous for nesting sea turtles, this beach is also well known for the sheer number of waves that break along nearly 7km of coast. Tubes are easy to find here, so bring your board and get ready for some seriously hollow riding. In the evening, you can venture out onto the beach with the park rangers to witness newly hatched baby turtles scamper out to sea.

3 PLAYA TAMARINDO

The number one party destination in the Nicoya is this tourist town, which has a well developed infrastructure of resort hotels, sophisticated dining options and plenty of bars and dance clubs. The waves here are fairly tame, but they're great for beginners who need some time to practice standing up.

4 NOSARA AREA

Attracting both intermediate and advanced surfers, this collection of great wilderness beaches has simply amazing waves that are renowned for their beautiful shape and regular consistency. With so many different breaks to choose from, you could easily spend several days exploring the Nosara area without ever having to surf the same place twice.

Montezuma

One of Costa Rica's classic beach destinations, Montezuma (p194) is tucked away at Nicoya's southeastern end. Improved transportation links mean it's much easier to get here than it used to be, but that doesn't mean it's easy to leave. On the contrary, abandoned stretches of winding coastline invite long bouts of beachcombing, while calm Pacific waters provide refreshing respite from the tropical heat.

Playa Sámara

This up-and-coming beach destination (p192) really does seem to have it all. Families with little ones in tow positively rave about the spotless beach and tranquil town, while hipsters delight in the surprisingly sophisticated restaurants, cafes and bars. Given that it's far less high profile than Costa Rica's brasher beaches, you can't help but feel you're in on a secret that few other travelers know about.

Playa Conchal

Travelers from near and far flock to this lovely white-sand beach (p181), which boasts some of the Pacific's best snorkeling. Walking along the beach all day, you'll find increasingly wild and rugged shoreline. At night, a wash of colors light up the sky in an epic sunset. This is one of the most idyllic beaches in the region.

Playa del Coco

This rowdy little beach town (p178) has the deserved reputation of being one of Nicoya's biggest party destinations (though it generally takes second place to Tamarindo). Even if you're not a big boozer, you still might want to stop by – the waters offshore from Playa del Coco are home to some of the country's best scuba diving.

Playa Avellana & Playa Negra

Appearing in the silver-screen surf classic *Endless Summer II*, these adjacent beaches (p186) are thrashed on a daily basis by huge waves that are primarily the domain of intermediate and advanced surfers. If the gentle waves at Tamarindo start to get a little too easy, consider these challenging breaks just a bit further down the coast. Even if you don't surf at all, it's a great place to watch some of the best. Playa Negra

Península de Nicoya's Best...

Secret Spots

○ **Playa Conchal** (p181) A secret beach of crushed seashells best accessed by foot – this hidden gem is little like the crowded beaches elsewhere.

○ **Reserva Natural Absoluta Cabo Blanco** (p198) The country's first protected space helped give rise to the modern ecoboom.

○ **Montezuma Bike Tours** (p195) An excellent way to cruise the peninsula, this outfitter brings pedalers to a number of hidden spots.

Thrills

○ **Zip Lines** (p188) Get ready for the superman pose, with many chances to whiz through the jungle, including Miss Sky, where you fly from mountainside to mountainside.

○ **Off-Road Driving** If you have a 4WD and spare tire, head off-road for rewarding adventures.

○ **Surfing** (p181) Península de Nicoya is a surfing mecca. None surpass the righteous waves of Playa Grande.

○ **Diving & Snorkeling** (p178) The shops near Playa del Coco know the clearest spots on this stretch of coast.

Splurges

○ **Florblanca** (p200) Sets the standard for luxury in Mal País and Santa Teresa.

○ **El Jardín del Edén** (p185) A swim-up bar and private terraces make lasting memories.

○ **Sueño del Mar B&B** (p185) A secluded upmarket retreat that serves as a tranquil escape from nearby Tamarindo.

○ **Villa Deveena** (p189) It's the most talked about dinner spot in the Nosara area for good reason.

Eats

o **Koji's** (p201) This is home to the best sushi in the country, bar none.

o **La Luna** (p191) A trendy spot with great art, an excellent menu and tasty cocktails.

o **Playa de los Artistas** (p197) A romantic beachside eatery with local ingredients and artistic flourishes.

o **Cocolores** (p197) A romantic place with Tico-Mediteranean dishes that consistently impress.

ADVANCE PLANNING

o **Surfing school** Península de Nicoya is home to some serious surf, which means that you might want to practice elsewhere before showing up with board in hand.

o **Car Rental** While booking your car online ahead will save you money, check the fine print for compulsory insurance costs.

RESOURCES

o **Nicoya Peninsula Guide** (www.nicoyapeninsula. com)

o **Nosara Travel** (www. nosaratravel.com)

GETTING AROUND

o **Boat** Jacó, located along the central Pacific coast, is a quick boat ride away from Montezuma.

o **Bus** Intercity buses are frequent and cheap, which makes moving around a cinch.

o **Car** Península de Nicoya is one region in particular where a 4WD vehicle can come in handy.

o **Walk** From Playa Brasilito, you can easily walk to Playa Conchal.

BE FOREWARNED

o **Roads** If you're driving on unpaved roads during the rainy season, make sure you have a 4WD with high clearance, as well as a comprehensive insurance policy. Many roads will be impassable – always ask locally about conditions before setting out.

o **Riptides** Currents can get ferocious, even in shallow waters, so pay attention to local advisories. If you find yourself caught in a riptide, immediately call for help. It's important to relax, conserve your energy and not fight the current.

VITAL STATISTICS

o **Population** Nicoya 13,000; Santa Cruz 12,000

o **Best time to visit** December to March is bone-dry.

EMERGENCY NUMBERS

o **Emergency** 🔗911

o **Fire** 🔗118

o **Police** 🔗117

Left: Tropical cocktail
Above: Playa del Coco (p178)

Península de Nicoya Itineraries

A journey around Costa Rica's famous peninsula brings you to perfect beaches and iconic natural areas. You might not be alone, but these routes are well traveled for good reason: the landscape is stunning.

PLAYA GRANDE ②
PLAYA TAMARINDO ①
PLAYAS AVELLANA & NEGRA ③
NOSARA ④

PACIFIC OCEAN

Golfo de Nicoya

MAL PAÍS & SANTA TERESA ③ ① MONTEZUMA
RESERVA NATURAL ABSOLUTA CABO BLANCO ②

3 DAYS

PLAYA TAMARINDO TO NOSARA
Tamarindo & the Coast

Although most travelers who are focused on the Nicoya should probably book into the airport in Liberia instead, the romp through this lovely peninsula starts in the famed beach getaway of **(1) Playa Tamarindo**. You'll have no problem keeping busy in this cosmopolitan tourist enclave, which is home to a number of great surf schools and excellent restaurants. Here, active travelers have a burden of riches, with short side trips to ride zip lines, venture out into the sea on kayaks, or go hiking or surfing. Nature buffs can watch sea turtles nest on **(2) Playa Grande**, while surfers with a bit of experience under their belts can cut loose at **(3) Playas Avellana and Negra**. These beaches are buffered by mangroves and lush, gentle hillsides allowing plenty of space for all sorts of surfers and sunbathers to stretch out with a bit of privacy. When (or maybe if!) the options in the area are exhausted, follow the coast south to **(4) Nosara**, a quieter, more laid-back alternative to the coast's most famous tourist destinations. In Nosara, a creative, colorful enclave of surfers and expats surf, perfect their yoga poses and enjoy a welcoming slice of paradise where the ocean meets the forest.

5 DAYS

MONTEZUMA TO SANTA TERESA

The Far South Crawl

The southern tip of Península de Nicoya has a reputation for remoteness, but improved transport connections have made it possible to venture here and back in less than a week. Of course, once you set your eyes on the stunning wilderness, the beaches, and the overall lack of civilization, you might have second thoughts about heading anywhere else.

After arriving in the country, make for Jacó where you can catch a speedboat across the gulf to **(1) Montezuma** and begin your adventure. The ride is lovely (sometimes you can spot dolphins chasing the boat) and it saves you several long days of overland travel. With all this extra time added to your itinerary, you shouldn't feel guilty about winding down to a slow crawl. Of course, if you can manage to summon enough energy to leave the beach, there is some excellent hiking to be had just around the corner in the **(2) Reserva Natural Absoluta Cabo Blanco**, where white-sand beaches are home to a number of migratory seabirds. And, if you happen to have any extra steam you'd like to burn off, grab a board and hit the monumental surf at **(3) Mal País and Santa Teresa**.

Playa Guiones (p188)

Discover
Península de Nicoya

At a Glance

○ **Playa Tamarindo** (p183) Amazing beaches make this the country's popular place to surf and party.

○ **Mal País & Santa Teresa** (p199) Excellent surfing, boutiques and creative dining.

○ **Montezuma** (p194) Perfect white sand, yoga and a laid-back escape.

○ **Playa del Coco** Costa Rica's mass-market home for spring break hedonism.

PLAYA DEL COCO

Sport fishing is the engine that built this place, and you'll mingle with the American anglers at happy hour (it starts rather early here). That said, there is an actual Tico community here, and plenty of Tico tourists. And when you stroll along the grassy beachfront plaza at sunset and gaze upon that wide bay sheltered by long, rugged peninsular arms cradling a natural marina bobbing with motorboats and fishing *pangas* (small motorboats), all will be right in your world.

Activities

Diving & Snorkeling

DEEP BLUE DIVING ADVENTURES   Diving, Snorkeling
(☏2670-1004; www.deepblue-diving.com; 2 tanks US$79-110, PADI Open Water Course US$415) This outfitter runs two-tank local dives and trips further afield, which include equipment rental and snacks. It also rents bicycles for US$10 per day.

RICH COAST DIVING   Diving
(☏2670-0176, in USA & Canada 800-434-8464; www.richcoastdiving.com; 2 tanks per person US$100, Open Water Course US$450) On the main street, this Dutch-owned dive shop is the area's largest.

SUMMER SALT   Diving
(☏2670-0308; www.summer-salt.com; 2 tanks per person US$100-120) This friendly Swiss-run dive shop has professional, bilingual staff.

Palm trees on Playa Carrillo (p190)
HOLGER LEUE / GETTY IMAGES ©

Surfing

There's no surf in Playa del Coco, but the town is a jumping-off point for two legendary surf destinations: Witch's Rock and Ollie's Point, which are inside the Santa Rosa sector of the Area de Conservacion de Guanacaste. The best way to reach them is by boat, and several surf shops in Coco and Tamarindo are licensed to make the run.

Other Activities

Sportfishing, sailing, horseback riding and sea kayaking are other popular activities. Many places will rent sea kayaks, which are perfect for exploring the rocky headlands to the north and south of the beach.

BLUE MARLIN   Fishing
(☎8828-8250, 2670-0707; www.sportfishing
bluemarlin.com; up to 6 people US$350-
860; ⊙depart 6am) Offers high-quality sportfishing trips on either a 27' *panga* or a larger 42' boat. They cruise north of Coco and routinely hook mahi, mackerel, marlin, rooster fish and tuna.

PAPAGAYO GOLF & COUNTRY CLUB Golf
(☎2697-0169; www.papagayo-golf.com; 9/18
holes US$55/95, putting green US$6; ⊙6:30am-
5pm Tue-Sun) An 18-hole course located 10km southeast of Playa del Coco.

 Sleeping

HOTEL LA PUERTA DEL SOL   Hotel $$
(☎2670-0195; www.lapuertadelsolcostarica.
com; d incl breakfast US$80; P☀@🛜≋) A five-minute walk from town, this unpretentiously luxurious Mediterranean-inspired hotel has two large suites and eight huge pastel-color rooms with polished brick and concrete floors, each with its own private terrace. The well-manicured grounds have a glorious pool and a trellis-shaded gym.

HOTEL SAVANNAH   Hotel $$
(☎2670-0367; d US$50; P☀🛜≋) A quiet and relaxed inn with small, basic, but immaculate tiled rooms in a shady longhouse. It's on a quiet side road, with a swimming pool, communal kitchen, barbecue grills and pleasant garden.

VILLA DEL SOL B&B   Hotel $$
(☎2670-0085, in Canada 866-793-9523, in
USA 866-815-8902; www.villadelsol.com; r
US$70, studios US$90; P☀@🛜≋) This leafy, tranquil property, 1km north of the town center, has a good mix of spotless, well-furnished rooms and studio apartments. The hotel is about 100m from the beach, which isn't as crowded at this end. Reserve ahead.

CASA VISTA AZUL   Boutique Hotel $$$
(☎2670-0678; www.hotelvistaazul.com; r
incl breakfast US$90, apt per month US$500;
P☀≋) This stunning boutique hotel has seven rooms, and an apartment in a somewhat incomplete (and moderately depressing) McMansion subdivision, on a cliff high above the coast. All nests have air-con and bathroom, are flooded with light and have wide-open ocean views. There's also a breezy rooftop dining area, and the owner can help arrange tours. To get here, head west off the main road, just south of Flor de Itabo, and follow the signs.

 Eating & Drinking

LA VIDA LOCA   American $
(☎2670-0181; mains US$4-9; ⊙11am-11pm) Across a creaky wooden footbridge on the south end of the beach is where you'll find this popular gringo hangout. They specialize in US-style comfort food such as burgers, nachos, meat loaf, chili dogs, clam chowder and more. It's also the best bar in town, hosting a monthly live music show with buffet (US$20).

LAS OLAS   Seafood $$
(☎2670-2003; mains US$7-16; ⊙11am-10pm) Just north of the cramped commercial vortex on the main road, this is a dressed up seafood *soda* with tablecloths, bamboo design accents, and recommended fresh seafood in the kitchen. The lounge area is quite cool, featuring molded concrete booths and dripping candles, whirling fans and a gurgling fountain.

179

CONGO
Cafe $$

(2670-2135; mains US$6-8; ⊙8am-8pm Mon-Sat, 8am-6pm Sun; P 🛜 ✈) Part cafe, part funky retail boutique, the interior is groovy with arced booths, rattan sofas and a deconstructed wood and granite coffee bar. They serve all the espresso drinks and an array of sandwiches and salads.

RESTAURANTE DONDE CLAUDIO Y GLORIA
Seafood $$

(✆2670-0256; www.dondeclaudioygloria.com; mains US$7-30; ⊙7am-9pm Sun-Thu, 7am-10pm Fri & Sat) Founded by Playa del Coco pioneers Claudio and Gloria Rojas, this casual, beachfront seafood restaurant has been a local landmark since 1955. It's a must for seafood lovers, with such interesting dishes as spicy mahi in an almond, raisin and white-wine sauce. Be warned, service can be painfully slow, but the solid jazz soundtrack will keep you buoyant.

ⓘ Getting There & Away

Bus

All buses arrive and depart from the main terminal next to Immigration.

Filadelfia, for connection to Santa Cruz US$1; 45 minutes; departs 11:30am and 4:30pm.

Liberia US$1; one hour; departs seven times from 5:15am to 8pm.

San José (Pulmitan) US$8; five hours; departs 4am, 8am and 2pm.

PLAYA BRASILITO

Underrated Brasilito has an authentic pueblo feel. There's a town square, a beachfront soccer pitch, a pink-washed cobblestone *iglesia* and a friendly local Tico community. All of which makes up for the beach, which has its (much) betters on either side. Still, it's just a short stroll along the sea to sugary Conchal.

The owner of La Casita de Pescado offers the area's best horse tours. The nearest ATM is in Playa Flamingo.

🛌 Sleeping & Eating

HOTEL BRASILITO
Hotel $$

(✆2654-4237; www.brasilito.com; r with/without air-con US$49/25; P ❄ 🛜) On the beach side of the plaza, this recommended hotel offers simple, bright and clean rooms with

Fishing boats

wood floors and tiled baths. If it's available, splurge for the sea-view room. It has a private hammock-strung patio ideal for soaking up the sunset.

HOTEL Y RESTAURANTE NANY   Hotel **$$**
(📞 2654-4320; s/d US$50/60; 🅿️ ❄️ @ 🛜 🏊) Set back from the road and shrouded in mango and palm trees, this impressive Tico-run property offers large, good-value rooms painted in cheerful tropical colors. The rooms come with cable and air-con, and their pool is salinated, so no chlorine here.

LA CASITA DE PESCADO   Seafood **$$**
(📞 2654-5171; mains US$4-20; 🕙 9am-9pm) Set on either side of the sandy road to Conchal, this beachfront, Tico-owned fish house has cheap yet delicious seafood. The affable owner also offers horse tours (per person US$35) through area mountains to a secluded bay.

ℹ️ Getting There & Away

Buses to and from Playa Flamingo travel through Brasilito. There is a bus ticket office at the north end of Brasilito.

PLAYA CONCHAL

Just 1km south of Brasilito is Playa Conchal, one of the most beautiful beaches on the peninsula. The name comes from the billions of *conchas* (shells) that wash up on the beach, and are gradually crushed into coarse sand. The shallows drift from an intense turquoise to sea-foam green deeper out, a rarity on the Pacific coast. If you have snorkeling gear, this is the place to use it.

On weekends, the beach is often packed with locals, tourists and countless vendors, but on weekdays during low season, Playa Conchal can be pure paradise. The further south you stroll, the wider, sweeter and more spectacular the beach becomes.

The easiest way to reach Conchal is to simply walk 15 minutes down the beach from Playa Brasilito. You can also drive along the sandy beach road, though you'll be charged US$2 to park.

With 285 hectares of property, including an over-the-top, free-form pool and a championship golf course, the all-inclusive **Westin Resort & Spa** (📞 2654-3500; www.starwoodhotels.com; d all inclusive from US$812; 🅿️ ❄️ @ 🛜 🏊) really does have everything you could ever want and is the only hotel in Conchal.

PLAYA GRANDE

From Huacas, the southwesterly road leads to Playa Grande, a wide and gorgeous beach, famous among conservationists and surfers alike. By day, the offshore winds create steep and powerful waves, especially at high tide. By night, an ancient cycle continues to unfurl as leatherback sea turtles bearing clutches of eggs follow the ocean currents back to their birthplace. The name fits, as the beach runs from the Tamarindo estuary for three miles, around a dome rock – with tide pools and superb surf fishing – and onto equally grand Playa Ventanas. The water is exquisite, warm, clear and charged with dynamic energy. Even confident swimmers should obey those riptide signs, however. People have drowned here.

Since 1991 Playa Grande has been part of the Parque Nacional Marino Las Baulas De Guanacaste, which protects one of the most important leatherback nesting areas in the world. Add it all up and you have an epic beach town that attracted a growing expat community and lures return visitors who can't get enough Grande.

Surfing is most people's motivation for coming to Playa Grande, and it is indeed spectacular. If you get rolled too hard and need a doctor, find the **Playa Grande Clinic** (📞 2653-2767, 24 hr emergency 8827-7774) next to Kike's Place.

Sleeping & Eating

LA MAREJADA HOTEL   Boutique Hotel **$$**
(📞 2653-0594, in USA & Canada 800-559-3415; www.lamarejada.com; r incl breakfast US$70; ❄️ 🛜 🏊) Hidden behind a bamboo fence, this stylish boutique nest is the friendliest, most relaxing hotel in Playa Grande.

The eight elegantly understated rooms have stone tile floors, rattan and wooden furnishings, and queen beds. The lovely owners, Carli and Gail, are attentive to your every need, and after a day of surfing, treat yourself to an in-house massage (per hour US$60).

RIP JACK INN
Inn $$

(🖉 2653-0480; www.ripjackinn.com; d US$90; 🅿❄@☎) This comfy, convivial inn has a handful of clean, modern, artfully painted rooms, lovely floor lamps, and doublewide macramé hammocks on the front porch. They offer regular yoga classes (US$12, schedule varies by the season), and the upstairs open-air restaurant-bar features pork loin marinated in brown sugar and Worcestershire, mahi slathered in lime sauce, and flank steak dressed in whiskey and cream. Even the burger is masterful.

KIKE'S PLACE
Restaurant $

(🖉 2653-0834; www.kikesplacecr.com; mains US4-10; ⏱7am-midnight) On the road into town, take note of Kike's (pronounced 'kee-kays'), the friendly local bar and restaurant where you can shoot pool, grind *ceviche* and let your hair down. There are live bands on Saturday night, and they have a handful of basic affordable rooms from US$20.

ⓘ Getting There & Away

There are no buses to Playa Grande. You can drive to Huacas and then take the paved road to Matapalo, followed by a rough dirt road to Playa Grande.

PARQUE NACIONAL MARINO LAS BAULAS DE GUANACASTE

Playa Grande is considered one of the most important nesting sites in the world for the *baula* (leatherback turtle). In 1991 the entire beach and adjacent land (700 hectares), along with 220 sq km of ocean, was designated **Las Baulas National Marine Park** (🖉 2653-0470; admission incl tour US$25; ⏱8am-noon & 1-5pm, tours 6pm-2am). This government act followed a 15-year battle between conservationists and various parties including poachers, developers and tour operators.

The ecosystem is primarily composed of mangrove swamp, ideal for caiman and crocodile, as well as numerous bird species, including the beautiful roseate spoonbill. Other creatures to look for when visiting are howler monkey, raccoon, coati, otter and a variety of crab. But, as is to be expected, the main attraction is the nesting of the world's largest species of turtle, which can weigh in excess of 400kg. Nesting season is from October to March, and it's fairly common to see turtles lay their eggs here on any given night. Of course, it may not be a leatherback. Chances of seeing one of these giants hover are slim, while you are quite sure to see a green or black turtle nest.

During the day, the beach is free and open to all, which is a good thing as the breaks off Playa Grande are fast, steep and consistent. At night, however, it is only possible to visit the beach on a guided tour, to ensure that nesting cycles may continue unhindered.

 Activities

The park office (p182) is by the northern entrance to Playa Grande. Reservations for turtle-watching can be made up to seven days in advance, and they're highly recommended as there is limited space. You can show up without one, as there are frequent no-shows, though this is less likely on weekends and during the holiday season.

Many hotels and tourist agencies in Tamarindo can book tours that include transportation to and from Playa Grande, admission to the park and the guided tour. The whole package costs about US$45. If you don't have your own transportation, this is the best way to go.

The show kicks off anytime from 9pm to as late as 2am. You might only have to wait for 10 minutes before a turtle shows up, or you could be there for five hours. Bring a book or a deck of cards

Olive ridley sea turtle

SOLVIN ZANKL / NATURE PICTURE LIBRARY ©

for entertainment. It could be a very long night – but well worth it.

PLAYA TAMARINDO

Well, they don't call it Tamagringo for nothing. Tamarindo's perennial status as Costa Rica's top surf and party destination has made it the first and last stop for legions of tourists. It stands to reason, then, that this is the most developed beach on the peninsula with no shortage of hotels, bars and restaurants. Yet, despite its party-town reputation, Tamarindo is more than just drinking and surfing. It forms a part of the Parque Nacional Marino Las Baulas de Guanacaste, and the beach retains an allure for kids and adults alike. And Tamarindo's central location makes it a great base for exploring the northern peninsula.

 **Activities**

Diving

AGUA RICA DIVING CENTER   Diving
(Map p184; ☎ 2653-0094, 8888-0225; www.aguarica.net; two tanks US$100) Italian-owned Agua Rica Diving Center, the area's

scuba-diving expert, offers snorkeling and an assortment of dives in the Catalina Islands.

Mountain Biking

BLUE TRAILZ   Cycling
(Map p184; ☎ 2653-1705; www.bluetrailz.com; tours US$55-75; ☺ 7am-7pm Mon-Sat) The local expert on mountain biking, distance cycling, bike tours and repairs. They also rent beach cruisers (two hours US$10, all day US$20).

Sportfishing

There are more than 30 fishing outfitters offering a variety of tour packages. Prices vary wildly depending on boat size, but expect to pay at least US$250 for a half-day tour.

Surfing

Like a gift from the surf gods, Tamarindo is often at its best when neighboring Playa Grande is flat. The most popular wave is a medium-sized right that breaks directly in front of the Tamarindo Diria hotel. The waters here are full of virgin surfers learning to pop up.

183

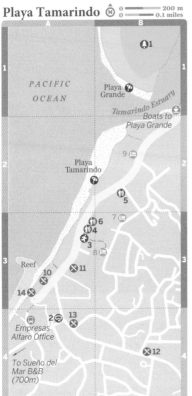

Playa Tamarindo

Playa Tamarindo 0 — 200 m / 0 — 0.1 miles

PACIFIC OCEAN

Playa Grande

Tamarindo Estuary
Boats to Playa Grande

Playa Tamarindo

Reef

Empresas Alfaro Office

To Sueño del Mar B&B (700m)

Playa Tamarindo

Sights
1 Parque Nacional Marino Las
 Baulas de Guanacaste B1

Activities, Courses & Tours
2 Agua Rica Diving Center A4
3 Blue Trailz A3
4 Iguana Surf A3
5 Kelly's Surf Shop B2
6 Matos Surf Shop A3

Sleeping
7 15 Love B3
 Cabinas Marielos .... (see 4)
8 El Jardín del Edén B3
9 Hotel La Laguna del Cocodrilo B2

Eating
10 Buon Apetito A3
11 El Casado del Carro A3
12 Gil's Place B4
13 Lazy Wave A4
14 Nogui's A3

Transport
 Sansa office .... (see 4)

 8am-6pm) Another solid surf shop across the street from the beach. They have lockers and rentals include rash guards.

KELLY'S SURF SHOP Surfing
(Map p184; ☏ 2653-1355; www.kellysurfshop. com; board rental per day/week US$15/90; ☺ 9am-6pm) One of the very best surf shops in the area, they have a terrific selection of newish boards that they rent by the day or week, and have premium boards that cost a bit more.

MATOS SURF SHOP Surfing
(Map p184; ☏ 2653-0845; www.matossurfshop. com; board rental from US$10, lessons US$35; ☺ lessons 9-11am & 2-4pm) The granddaddy of local surf shops is owned by a Uruguyan DJ-photo-entrepreneur. They offer lessons, and rent and sell boards at the cheapest rates in town.

IGUANA SURF Surfing
(Map p184; ☏ 2653-0613; www.iguanasurf. net; board rental US$20, private lessons US$45;

🛏 Sleeping

We constantly receive complaints about Tamarindo hotels, so choose wisely. Be mindful, most budget hotels have cold water only. Midrange options generally have hot-water bathrooms. The bulk of top-end hotels can arrange tours in the area, and accept credit cards. The rates given are high-season rates; low-season rates can be 25% to 40% lower.

CABINAS MARIELOS Cabina $$
(Map p184; ☏ 2653-0954, 2653-0141; www.cab inasmarieloscr.com; s/d US$40/55; P ❄) One of the best deals in town, this underrated property has a variety of cabinas to fit every budget. All have firm beds, colorful patios, slanted beamed ceilings, speckled tile floors, and share a communal kitchen.

HOTEL LA LAGUNA DEL COCODRILO
Hotel $$

(Map p184; ☎2653-0255; www.lalagunadelcocodrilo.com; d US$60-70, ste US$120; P❄🔧) A beachfront location blesses this charming French-owned hotel, with well-kept rooms overlooking either the shady grounds or the ocean and estuary. Adjacent to a crocodile-filled lagoon (hence the name), the hotel opens onto a rocky garden that rolls to the sand.

15 LOVE
B&B $$

(Map p184; ☎2653-0898; www.15lovebedandbreakfast.com; d incl breakfast US$95) A self-proclaimed contemporary B&B, this white-washed, concrete, mod villa with weathered louvered accents overlooks a plunge pool and two hard courts and is within earshot of the sea. Interiors are quite stylish with polished concrete floors, high ceilings, floating beds and designer light fixtures.

SUEÑO DEL MAR B&B
B&B $$$

(☎2653-0284; www.sueno-del-mar.com; d US$195, casitas US$220-240; P❄@🔧🐾) This exquisite bed and breakfast on Playa Langosta is set in a stunning faux-dobe Spanish-style *posada*. The six rooms have four-poster beds, artfully placed crafts and open-air garden showers, while the romantic honeymoon suite has a wrap-around window with sea views.

EL JARDÍN DEL EDÉN
Hotel $$$

(Map p184; ☎2653-0137; www.jardindeleden.com; standard/superior incl breakfast US$153/190; P❄@🔧🐾) On a hill overlooking Tamarindo, this luxurious French-run hotel has 36 exquisite rooms, each with a sitting area and private patio or balcony. There is a swim-up bar and gorgeous views from the pool deck.

🍴 Eating

BUON APETITO
Italian $

(Map p184; ☎2653-0598; mains US$6-10; ⏰8am-9pm) An authentic Italian deli with import-ed meats and cheeses piled and served on home-baked ciabatta by the endearing Italian *madre* at the counter. She also does pizza, pasta and, ahem, gelato. These are the best sandwiches in Tamarindo. Grab one and munch on the beach.

EL CASADO DEL CARRO
Costa Rican $

(Map p184; casados US$4-6; ⏰noon-2pm) Senora Rosaria has been delivering top quality meat and chicken *casados* (cheap set meal) from her late-model Toyota hatchback for nine years. Her devoted Tico following lines up daily at noon, and she generally sells out by 2pm. You'll get your meal in a Styrofoam platter (nobody's *perfecto*) and it will usually include yucca or plantains, rice, chicken or beef, and some tasty black beans. Get yours with a squeeze of chili.

GIL'S PLACE
Restaurant $

(Map p184; ☎2653-2641; dishes US$3-8; ⏰7:30am-8:30pm) A Tamarindo classic thanks to *grandisimo* burritos stuffed with chicken, beef or fish, beans, and cheese. And if you crave burritos for breakfast, it does those too.

NOGUI'S
Seafood $$

(Map p184; ☎2653-0029; mains US$8-22; ⏰11am-11pm) A fish shack with Mediterranean charm, this fabulously romantic, wooden and stained-glass, tin-roof gem on the beach flaunts local seafood. Make a dinner reservation, or get sloshed at the bar with the occasionally rowdy regulars.

❶ Getting There & Away

Air

The airstrip is 3km north of town; a hotel bus is usually on hand to pick up arriving passengers, or you can take a taxi. During high season, Sansa (Map p184; ☎2653-0012) has two daily flights to and from San José (each way US$111), while NatureAir (each way US$120) has three. All passengers must pay an additional US$3 departure tax.

Bus

Buses for San José depart from the Empresas Alfaro office behind the Babylon bar. Other buses depart across the street from Zullymar Hostel.

Liberia US$3, 2½ hours, departs 13 times per day from 4:30am to 6:30pm.

San José US$11, six hours, departs 5:30am and 2pm. Alternatively, take a bus to Liberia and change for frequent buses to the capital.

Santa Cruz US$2, 1½ hours, departs 6am, 9am, noon, 2pm, 3pm and 4pm.

Car & Taxi

By car from Liberia, take Hwy 21 to Belén, then Hwy 155 via Huacas to Tamarindo. If you're coming from the southern peninsula, drive just past Santa Cruz, turn left on the paved road to 27 de Abril, then northwest on a decent dirt road for 19km to Tamarindo. These routes are well signed. A taxi to or from Santa Cruz costs about US$30, and US$50 to or from Liberia.

PLAYAS AVELLANA & NEGRA

These popular surfing beaches were made famous in the surf classic *Endless Summer II*, and **Playa Avellana** is still an absolutely stunning, pristine sweep of pale golden sand. Backed by mangroves in the center and two gentle hillsides on either end, there's plenty of room for surfers and sunbathers to have an intimate experience even when there are lots of heads in town. The wave here is decent for beginners and intermediate surfers. **Little Hawaii** is the powerful and open-faced right featured in *Endless Summer II*, while **Beach Break** barrels at low tide. Still, advanced surfers get bored here.

 Sleeping & Eating

Playa Avellana

LAS AVELLANAS VILLAS Apartment $$
(☎ 8821-3681, 2652-9212; www.lasavellanas villas.com; s/d/tr/q US$55/65/75/85; P ❄ ⊚) Stunningly designed, these four *casitas* have polished concrete floors, a bedroom and living area linked by wooden bridges, open-air showers, and large windows looking out onto front and back terraces. They have full kitchens, and the grounds are just 300m from the beach at the northern end of Avellana.

Left: Playa Avellana (p186)
Below: School of fish off Isla del Caño (p255)
(LEFT) AARON MCCOY / GETTY IMAGES ©; (BELOW) JOHNNY HAGLUND / GETTY IMAGES ©

MAUNA LOA SURF RESORT
Bungalow $$

(☎ 2652-9012; www.hotelmaunaloa. com; d US$80; [P] [❄] [🌐] [🏊]) This hip and pleasant Italian-run spot is a great place for families, with a secure location that's a straight shot to the beach. Paths lead from the pool area through a well-tended garden to attractive pod-like bungalows with pastel-brushed walls, and swaying hammocks on their terrace. They offer discounts for stays of three nights or more.

CABINAS LAS OLAS
Bungalow $$

(☎ 2652-9315; www.cabinaslasolas.co.cr; d US$90; [P] [❄] [🌐] [🏊]) On the road from San José de Pinilla into Avellana, this pleasant hotel is set on spacious grounds only 200m from the beach. Ten airy, individual bungalows have shiny woodwork, stone detailing, hot-water showers and private decks. There's a restaurant (mains US$5 to US$30), and a specially built board-walk leads through the mangroves down to the beach.

LOLA'S ON THE BEACH
Cafe $$

(☎ 2652-9097; meals US$8-13; ⏰ 10am-5pm Tue-Sun) Lola's, a mod and hauntingly stylish beach cafe, is the place to hang out. Minimalist slanted wood chairs are planted in the sand beneath thatched umbrellas, and the tree stump bar over-looks a gorgeous open kitchen where the beachy cuisine includes an epic tuna *poke*, an overstuffed spicy grilled chicken pita, papaya salad and classic Dutch-style fries.

Playa Negra

CABINAS DEL MAR
Cabina $

(☎ 8829-0531, 2652-9279; d/tr US$20/30) Large, tiled-roof *cabinas* sleep up to three and have beamed ceilings, full kitchens, hammocks on the porch, a porchside grill, and are within earshot of the sea. The property is also home to the tastefully small scale Marvel Bikini Company. To get here take the left fork on your way to Playa Negra and follow the Marvel Bikini signs.

187

CAFÉ PLAYA NEGRA Hotel $$

(2653-4360, 8818-9092; www.cafeplaye negra.com; d with/without air-con incl breakfast US$65/55; P ❄ @ 🛜) These stylish, minimalist digs, upstairs from the cafe, have polished concrete floors and elevated beds dressed with colorful bedspreads. There's a groovy shared deck with plush lounges, and the downstairs cafe (mains US$7 to US$13) is open for breakfast, lunch and dinner (closing in between) and serves tasty Peruvianfusion fare. When the DJ rocks the spot it feels like an upscale island dance hall.

HOTEL PLAYA NEGRA Bungalow $$$

(2652-9134; www.playanegra.com; s/d/villas US$90/100/115-140; P ❄ 🛜) This sweet compound of thatched circular bungalows, slung with front porch hammocks is steps from a world-class reef break. Each cabin has a queen-sized bed, two single beds, and a bathroom with roomy hot-water showers. The newest and best bungalows are furthest from the beach. They host regular yoga classes in a beachside pavilion.

 Getting There & Away

The new daily bus to Playa Avellana departs Santa Cruz's Terminal Diria at 12:30pm (US$1.50, 1½ hours), passing by most of the hotels and restaurants of note. The bus to Santa Cruz departs at 5:30am.

Two daily buses to Playa Negra leave Santa Cruz at 6am and 8am; the bus for Santa Cruz departs at 1:30pm from the V on the main road (US$1.50, 1½ hours).

NOSARA AREA

A pocket of luxuriant vegetation backs the attractive beaches near the small Tico village of Nosara. The entire area is a magical destination as you can sometimes see parrots, toucans, armadillos and monkeys just a few meters from the beaches. The Nosara area is spread along the coast and a little inland (making a car a bit of a necessity). Log on to Nosara Travel's website (www.nosaratravel.com/map.html) for a handy map. North of the river is Playa Nosara, which is difficult to access and primarily used by fisher folk.

Further south is Playa Pelada, a small crescent-shaped beach with an impressive blowhole that sends water shooting through the air at high tide. The southernmost beach is Playa Guiones, a 7km stretch of sand that's one of the best surf spots on the central peninsula.

 **Activities**

MISS SKY Canopy Tour

(2682-0969; www.missskycanopytour.com; adult/child 5-12 US$65/45; ⊙office 7am-5pm) Miss Sky has brought a canopy tour to Nosara, with a total length of 11,000m above a pristine private reserve. The zip lines don't go from platform to platform, but from mountainside to mountainside, and have double cables for added safety. Your top speed will be about 45kph. Tours leave twice daily at 8am and 2pm.

PLAYA GUIONES Surfing

Check out Playa Guiones for the best beach break in the central Peninsula, especially when there is an offshore wind. Although the beach is usually full of surfers, there are fortunately plenty of take-off points.

STAND UP PADDLE NOSARA Kayaking

(2682-1418; www.theyogahousecostarica.com) Nosara's original SUP outfitter, located at Yoga House, runs tours, rentals and lessons, and offers a range of kayak trips through a third entity, Drifters Kayaking, which is the same company as the other two. Confused yet? Just call them. You'll have fun.

NOSARA YOGA INSTITUTE Yoga

(2682-0071, toll-free 866-439-4704; www. nosarayoga.com) In the hills near Playa Guiones is the famous Nosara Yoga Institute. Regular classes are open to the public, as well as workshops, retreats and instructor training courses.

YOGA HOUSE Yoga

(2682-1418, 2682-0289; www.theyogahouse costarica.com; per class US$10) An inviting, professional, nurturing yoga space tucked behind Cafe de Paris in the Guiones area,

COURTESY OF VILLA DEEVENA ©

Don't Miss **Villa Deevena**

Like a beautiful sunset or a Da Vinci painting, the French chef at this boutique, family-run villa property, off the main Negra drag, is spoken about in hushed tones by local *extranjeros* up and down the coast. And truth be told, the entire Balinese-themed property is worthy of praise, including those swish bungalows (double US$95) set around a gorgeous, glittering pool. But it's the food that's on another level. Think mahi baked with preserved lemon and rosemary, slow braised shortrib, duck confit, and lobster ravioli. Patrick Jamon, the former executive chef at LA's famed Regency Club where he cooked for Fortune 500 CEOs and a handful of presidents, even makes his own goat cheese from his herd in the hills.

NEED TO KNOW

📞2653-2328; www.villadeevena.com; mains US$18-28; ⏱restaurant 7am-9pm; P ❄ 🛜

---

they offer a Surfers Class at 12:30, geared to soothe and stretch the upper body, and a terrific, passive but still challenging Yin Yoga class that smooths out kinks in your faschia and demands surrender.

Turtle-Watching

Most hotels in the area can arrange guided tours to Refugio Nacional de Fauna Silvestre Ostional, where you can watch the mass arrivals of olive ridley turtles.

 Sleeping & Eating

Playa Guiones

CASA TUCAN   Hotel $$
(📞8611-7954; r US$75; P ❄ @ 🛜 🛉)
Charming, laid back and locally owned, sweet rooms have high beamed ceilings, new tasteful bathroom tiles, wood beds, minifridge, cable TV, an inviting pool and friendly restaurant bar. They even rent a

189

Detour:
Islita Area

The coast southeast of Playa Carrillo remains one of the peninsula's most isolated and wonderful stretches of coastline, mainly because it's largely inaccessible and lacking in accommodations. But if you're willing to tackle rugged roads or venture down the coastline in a sea kayak (or possibly on foot), you'll be rewarded with abandoned beaches backed by pristine wilderness and rugged hills.

There are a few small breaks in front of the Hotel Punta Islita, where you'll find a gorgeous cove punctuated with that evocative wave-thrashed boulder that is Punta Islita. At high tide the beach narrows, but at low tide it is wide and as romantic as those vistas from above. Another good beach and point break lies north of Punta Islita at **Playa Camaronal**, a charcoal gray stretch of sand strewn with driftwood and sheltered by two headlands. This beach also happens to be a protected nesting site for leatherback, olive ridley, hawksbill and black turtles, and is officially known as **Refugio Nacional de Vida Silvestre Camaronal** (⊘8am-6pm).

Also worth a visit is the small town of Islita, which is home to the **Museo Islita** (⊘8am-4pm Mon-Sat), an imaginative contemporary art house crusted with mosaic murals, and featuring carvings and paintings that adorn everything from houses to tree trunks. This project was organized by Hotel Punta Islita, which sells local art in its gift shop and invests proceeds in the community.

nice selection of boards on the cheap to guests (per day US$5 to US$10).

GILDED IGUANA　　　　　Hotel **$$**
(✆hotel 2682-0245, restaurant 2682-0259; www.thegildediguana.com; r US$50-75; P ✲ ⛱) Down the second access road to Guiones, this long-standing hotel for anglers and surfers has well-furnished, tiled rooms of varying sizes, with hot-water bathroom and refrigerator, that sleep three.

CAFÉ DE PARIS　　　　　Hotel **$$**
(✆2682-0087, 2682-1035; www.cafedeparis. net; d US$90; P ✲ @ ⛱ ⛱) This pleasant hotel is located at the corner of the main road and the first access road that leads to Playa Guiones. Splashy modern loft rooms are set in one shingled longhouse. Some have wood floors, others polished concrete, all have rain showers, molded concrete wash basins and ample style.

ROBIN'S　　　　　International **$**
(✆2682-0617; mains US$4-7 ; ⊘8am-5pm Mon-Sat, 10am-4pm Sun; ⛱ ⛱) Perfectly suited to the health-conscious yogis and surfers who live in and visit Nosara, Robin prepares salads, wraps and sandwiches on homemade, whole-wheat foccacia. She also has a worthy raw menu including 'living' pad thai and maki rolls.

BEACH DOG CAFÉ　　　　　Cafe **$**
(✆2682-1293; www.facebook.com/beach dogcafe; dishes US$6-9; ⊘8am-3pm daily, 8am-10pm Wed & Sat; P ⛱ ⛱) Just steps from the beach, this groovy cafe has tasty breakfasts (dig that banana bread French toast) and a lunch menu that includes quesadillas, a variety of sandwiches, and uber popular fish tacos.

MARLIN BILL'S　　　　　Seafood **$$$**
(✆2682-0548; www.facebook.com/pages/ Marlin-Bills-Restaurant/343540496705; meals US$11-25; ⊘11am-10 Mon-Sat) Across the main road from the Guiones swirl, this is your granddad's fish house, which makes it all the more satisfying. Grab lunch here (the menu is cheaper), though it's worth the coin anytime for a hearty filet of fresh

grilled tuna, prepared simply and perfectly, and a slab of creamy key lime pie.

Playa Pelada

REFUGIO DEL SOL Lodge $$
(☎ 8561-6211; www.refugiodelsol.com; s/d with kitchenette US$50/55, s/d without kitchenette US$35/45; P ❄ 🛜) This rustic lodge is decked out with ceramic tiled floors, beamed ceilings, artisanal crafts and wood furnishings, candles and lanterns, and other soulful touches that make it feel like home. Rooms open onto a wide L-shaped patio strung with hammocks, and the gorgeous young Italian couple who own it make tasty Italian food for guests every night.

ALMOST PARADISE Villa $
(☎ 2682-0172; www.almostparadise-costarica.com; dm/r $13/45) An aging, somewhat decrepit villa, with latter day charm. Though it is falling apart in a few places the all-wood rooms are airy and comfy with magnificent views. The restaurant is open for lunch and dinner and is worthy of a sunset beverage, for sure. Okay, so there is more than a hint of youth culture angst in this rusty old joint. But, hey, you're in a surf town. Goes with the territory.

LA LUNA International $$
(☎ 2682-0122; www.facebook.com/pages/LA-LUNA/187210908478; dishes US$6-24; ⏱ 8am-10pm) On the beach, to the right of Hotel Playas de Nosara, you'll find this impressive stone building that houses a trendy restaurant-bar and art gallery. The eclectic menu has Asian and Mediterranean flourishes, and the views (and cocktails) are intoxicating. Call ahead for reservations.

ⓘ Getting There & Away

Air

Both Sansa and NatureAir have one daily flight to and from San José for about US$111 to US$120 each way.

Bus

Local buses depart from the *pulpería* (corner grocery store) by the soccer field. Traroc buses depart for Nicoya (US$2, two hours) at 5am, 5:30am, 7am, noon and 3pm. There's no 5:30am bus on Sundays. Empresas Alfaro buses going to San José (US$9, five to six hours) depart from the pharmacy by the soccer field at 12:30pm.

Car

From Nicoya, a paved road leads toward Playa Sámara. About 5km before Sámara (signed), a windy, bumpy (and, in the dry season, dusty) dirt road leads to Nosara village (4WD recommended). Ask around before trying this in the rainy season, when Río Nosara becomes impassable.

Surfers hiking from Playa Tamarindo to Playa Avellana (p186)
AARON MCCOY / GETTY IMAGES ©

PLAYA SÁMARA

Is Sámara the black hole of happiness? That's what more than one expat has said after stopping here on vacation and never leaving. And perhaps it is more than the sum of its parts? Because on the surface it's just an easy-to-navigate beach town with barefoot, three-star appeal, and a crescent-shaped strip of pale-gray sand spanning two rocky headlands. Not spectacular, just safe, mellow, reasonably developed, easily navigable on foot and accessible by public transportation. The sea is also rather calm. Not surprisingly, you'll find it's popular with vacationing Tico and foreign families and backpackers, who enjoy Sámara's palpable ease and tranquility. But be careful, the longer you stay the less you'll want to leave.

If you've got some extra time and a 4WD, explore the hidden beaches north of Sámara such as Playa Barrigona, equally famous for its pristine beach as for its celebrity resident, Mel Gibson.

 ## Activities

WING NUTS Canopy Tour
(2656-0153; adult/child US$60/40) The local zip-line operator's 10 platforms are located on the eastern outskirts of town off the main paved road.

FLYING CROCODILE Scenic Flights
(2656-8048; www.flying-crocodile.com; flights 20/30/60-minutes US$110/150/230, lessons per hour US$200) Several kilometers west, in Playa Buenavista, the Flying Crocodile offers ultralight flights and lessons.

PURA VIDA DIVE CENTER Diving
(8523-0043; www.puravidadive.com; 2-tank dive incl equipment US$100) There are 25 dive sites within a 20-minute boat ride from Sámara, where you can see dozens of fish, blooming rock reefs, and, if you're lucky, hammerheads. The shop is located about 100m east of the main road.

 ## Sleeping

EL PEQUEÑO GECKO VERDE Bungalow $$
(2656-1176; www.gecko-verde.com; d from $90; P ❄ 🛜 ≋) A hidden slice of heaven, contemporary and beautifully decorated bungalows have beds dressed in plush linens, artisanal carvings on the walls, a private terrace with hammock and outdoor dining area. Onsite amenities include a saltwater swimming pool with waterfall, a lush garden and a fabulous open-air restaurant and bar. Behind the property, a 400m jungle trail and steep cement staircase lead to a secret beach that doesn't appear on any map – Playa Izquierda, a stunning cove

Playa Sámara
SIEPMANN / IMAGEBROKER ©

Detour:
Refugio Nacional de Fauna Silvestre Ostional

This 248-hectare coastal refuge extends from Punta India in the north to Playa Guiones in the south, and includes the beaches of Playa Nosara and Playa Ostional. It was created in 1992 to protect the *arribadas*, or mass nesting of the olive ridley sea turtles, which occurs from July to November with a peak from August to October. Along with Playa Nancite in Parque Nacional Santa Rosa, Ostional is one of two main nesting grounds for this turtle in Costa Rica.

The olive ridley is one of the smallest species of sea turtle, typically weighing around 45kg. Although they are endangered, there are a few beaches in the world where ridleys nest in large groups that can number in the thousands. Scientists believe that this behavior is an attempt to overwhelm predators.

Rocky Punta India at the northwestern end of the refuge has tide pools that abound with marine life, such as sea anemone, urchin and starfish. Along the beach, thousands of almost transparent ghost crabs go about their business, as do the bright-red Sally Lightfoot crabs. The vegetation behind the beach is sparse and consists mainly of deciduous trees, home to iguanas, crabs, howler monkeys, coatis and many birds. Near the southeastern edge of the refuge is a small mangrove swamp where there is good bird-watching.

backed by high cliffs with amazing sunset views.

TICO ADVENTURE LODGE
Lodge $$
(2656-0628; www.ticoadventurelodge.com; d US$50; P ❄ 🛜 🏊) The US owners are proud of the fact that they built this lodge without cutting down a single tree, and they have every reason to be – it's stunning. Nine double rooms with bathroom and wood accents aren't big or particularly bright, but they're surrounded by lush vegetation and old-growth trees. Cheaper weekly and monthly rates are available.

SAMARA INN
Inn $$
(2656-0482; www.hotelsamarainn.com; s/d US$55/80; P ❄ @ 🛜 🏊) A large, lovingly designed lodge with tiled rooms that are ... like glass ... ins, porcelain ... urniture. The ... operty is set ... nbroken views ... ast table.

SÁMARA TREE HOUSE INN
Bungalow $$$
(2656-0733; www.samaratreehouse.com; bungalows incl breakfast US$85-130; P ❄ @ 🛜 🏊) These five stilted tree houses for grown-ups are so appealing that you may extend your stay. Fully equipped kitchens have pots and pans hanging from driftwood racks, huge windows welcome light and breezes, and hammocks are hung underneath the raised bungalows. Even the bathroom tile is gorgeous.

 Eating

AHORA SI
Vegetarian $$
(2656-0741; sabinasalvatore@hotmail.com; mains US$5-11; P 🛜 🍴) A Venetian-owned vegetarian restaurant and all-natural cocktail bar, they do smoothies with coconut milk; gnocchi with nutmeg, sage and smoked cheese; soy burgers and yucca fries; wok stir fries; and thin-crust pizzas too. All served on a lovingly decorated tiled patio.

LO QUE HAY Restaurant $

(2656-0811; tacos US$2; meals from US$6; 7am-late) Brand new and already rocking, this beachside *taqueria* and pub strobes ball games on the big screen, offers four delectable taco fillings (fish, chicken, beef or pork), and mains such as blackened fish, slow-roasted pork and beef fajitas. The grilled avocados stuffed with *pico de gallo* are delicious, and the bar crowd sips into the wee small hours.

GUSTO Italian $$

(2656-2219; www.gustocostarica.com; dishes mains US$7-24) An Italian-fusion place with homemade pasta, three types of fish carpaccio, generous thai beef and tuna salads, and an assortment of meat, chicken and fish dishes, including a wasabi cream tuna, miso steak and spaghetti with lobster! It's located downtown.

Getting There & Away

The beach lies about 35km southwest of Nicoya on a paved road. No flights were operating out of the Samara airport (PLD) at research time.

Bus

Empresas Alfaro (7:30am-1pm, 1:30am-5pm) has a bus to San José (US$8, five hours) that departs at 4:30am and 8:30am. All buses depart from the main intersection just south of Entre Dos Aguas B&B. Buy your San José bus tickets at the Alfaro office behind Bazar d'Liss on the main intersection in town.

Traroc buses to Nicoya (US$2.50, two hours) depart hourly from 5:30am to 6:30pm from the *pulpería* by the soccer field; there's a more limited schedule on Sunday.

MONTEZUMA

Montezuma is an immediately endearing beach town that demands you abandon the car, stroll, swim and, if you are willing to stroll even further, surf. The warm and wild ocean, and that remnant, ever-audible jungle, has helped this rocky nook cultivate an inviting boho vibe. Typical tourist offerings, such as canopy tours, do a brisk trade here, but you'll also bump up against Montezuma's internationally inflected, artsy-rootsy beach culture in yoga

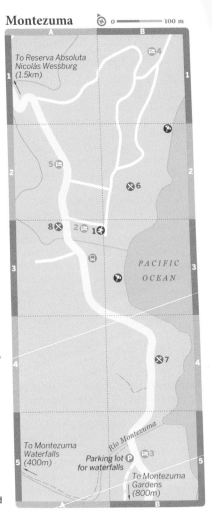

Montezuma

To Reserva Absoluta Nicolás Wessburg (1.5km)

To Montezuma Waterfalls (400km)

Río Montezuma

Parking lot for waterfalls

To Montezuma Gardens (800m)

PACIFIC OCEAN

Montezuma

Activities, Courses & Tours
1 Sun Trails A3

Sleeping
2 El Sano Banano A3
3 Hotel Amor de Mar .... F
4 Luz de Mono ....
5 Montezuma Pacific ....

Eating
6 Cocolores ....
7 Playa de los Artistas ....
8 Puggo's ....

classes, volunteer corps, festivals, veggie-friendly dining rooms, and neo-Rastas hawking uplifting herbs. No wonder locals lovingly call this town 'Montefuma.' It's not perfect. The lodging is particularly poor value, and the eateries can be that way too (though there are some absolute gems). But in this barefoot *pueblo* (small town), which unfurls along several kilometers of rugged coastline, you're never far from the rhythm and sound of the sea, and that is a beautiful thing.

 Sights & Activities

Picture-perfect white-sand beaches are strung along the coast, separated by small rocky headlands, offering great beachcombing and ideal tidepool contemplation. Unfortunately, there are strong rip tides, so inquire locally before going for a swim.

The beaches in front of the town are nice enough, but the best beach is just north of Cocolores, where the sand is powdery and sheltered from big swells. This is your glorious sun-soaked crash pad, and the further northeast you walk the more solitude you'll find. The water's shade of teal is immediately nourishing, the temperature is perfect and it's clean enough to attract wildlife. We saw two big rays at the water's surface. During low tide, the best snorkeling is at Playa Las Manchas, 1km west of downtown. Because of the town's carefree boho feel, topless and (sometimes) nude sunbathing have become de rigueur on some beaches. No one is likely to say anything if you choose to bare your wares, but keep in mind that many residents find it disrespectful.

MONTEZUMA BIKE TOURS   Cycling
(☎8871-1540; www.montezumabiketours.com; per person US$38-60) The Peninsula's top mountain-bike outfitter has a Montezuma address. Rides range in terrain and difficulty and last up to four hours, taking in hidden beaches, waterfalls and rugged mountains, and spanning from 8.7 miles

to 11.1 miles in length. They even offer a full moon ride.

MONTEZUMA GARDENS   Gardens
(☎2642-1317, 8888-4200; www.montezumagardens.com; adult/student/child US$8/6/4; ⌚8am-4pm) About 1km up the hill toward Cóbano, alongside the waterfall trail, you can take a tour through this lush *mariposario* (butterfly garden) and nursery where the mysterious metamorphoses occur. You'll learn about the life cycles and benefits of a dozen local species.

SUN TRAILS   Canopy Tour
(Map p194; ☎2642-0808; www.suntrailsadventures.com; US$40; ⌚office 8am-8pm) After you've flown down nine zip lines, this 2.5-hour canopy tour winds up with a hike down – rather than up – to the waterfalls; bring your swimsuit. Book at the Sun Trails office in town, where you'll also have internet access (per hour US$2).

RESERVA ABSOLUTA NICOLÁS WESSBURG   Hiking
Inland from Montezuma is a private conservation area that was the original site of Nicholas Olof Wessburg and Karen Mogensen's homestead. Although the reserve is closed to visitors, you can either hike or go horseback riding along its perimeter – tours can be arranged through operators in town or at the **Los Caballos Nature Lodge finca** (☎2642-0124; www.naturelodge.net; d incl breakfast US$70-100; P ❄ 🔊 ☲).

 Festivals & Events

FESTIVAL DE ARTE CHUNCHES DE MAR   Arts
(www.chunchesdemar.com) This arts festival brings together artists and musicians who camp on the beach for one month – note that exact dates change every year, but it is usually in January – and create art together from found objects.

MONTEZUMA INTERNATIONAL FILM FESTIVAL   Film
(www.montezumafilmfestival.com) Usually held in early November, this is a great excuse

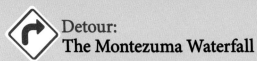

Detour: The Montezuma Waterfall

A 20-minute stroll south of Montezuma takes you to a set of three scenic waterfalls. The main attraction is to climb the second set of falls and jump in. Despite the warning sign, countless people do this every day, and about half a dozen people have died in the process.

The first waterfall has a good swimming hole, but it's shallow and rocky and not suitable for diving. From here, if you continue on the well-marked trail that leads around and up, you will come to a second set of falls. These are the ones that offer a good clean leap (from 10m up) into the deep water below. To reach the jumping point, continue to take the trail up the side of the hill until you reach the diving area. Do not attempt to scale the falls. The rocks are slippery and this is how almost all of the ill-fated jumpers have perished. From this point, the trail continues up the hill to the third and last set of falls. These are not safe for jumping. However, there is a rope swing that will drop you right over the deeper part of the swimming hole (just be sure to let go on the out-swing!). A lot of travelers enjoy the thrill, but indulge at your own risk.

To get there, follow the main Montezuma road south out of town and then take the trail to the right after Hotel La Cascada, past the bridge. You'll see a clearly marked parking area for visitors (US$2 per car), and the trailhead.

to celebrate the arts in Montezuma before high season kicks in.

Sleeping

HOTEL AMOR DE MAR B&B $$
(Map p194; 2642-0262; www.amordemar.com; d US$50-100, houses US$250; P 📶)
An absolutely lovable German-owned bed and breakfast with 11 unique rooms replete with exquisite touches like natural timber-framed mirrors, organic lanterns, and rocking chairs on a terrace laced with fishing netting and dotted with hundreds of potted plants. Then there's the palm-dappled lawn that rolls out to the tide pools and the Pacific beyond. In a town distinguished by overpriced, poor value lodging this place is the best there is.

EL SANO BANANO Boutique Hotel $$
(Map p194; 2642-0638; www.ylangylangbeachresort.com; d US$75; P 🌬@📶🏊) A well-run boutique hotel in the center of town. Although their many businesses take up an entire city block, they have just 12 prim and comfortable rooms. Although

the attached restaurant is way overpriced for simple dishes – 12 bucks for a *casado*. It's worth showing up in the evening when the restaurant shows nightly films for US$6 minimum consumption.

MONTEZUMA PACIFIC Guesthouse $$
(Map p194; 2642-0204; r US$45-65; P 🌬📶) A small, tucked away property worth considering, rooms in this older atrium-style guesthouse won't wow you, but the mosaic mix-match tile is cool and all rooms have air-con, mini fridge, cable TV and security boxes. Plus, the owner is a charming gentleman. More expensive rooms are larger and sleep three.

LUZ DE MONO Lodge $$
(Map p194; 2642-0090; www.luzdemono.com; r/ste incl breakfast US$60/80; P 📶🏊)
A stone lodge built into a lush inlet of remnant jungle, the upstairs rooms have high palm-beamed ceilings, wood furnishings, cable TV, and new tiles throughout, but the downstairs standard rooms aren't worth the cash. They don't have air-con but ceiling fans keep you cool, and there's a lovely pool area.

Eating

PLAYA DE LOS ARTISTAS
International $$

(Map p194; ☏2642-0920; www.playamontezuma.net/playadelosartistas.; mains US$9-13; ☉noon-9pm Mon-Sat) This artfully decorated beach spot is the most adored and romantic restaurant in town and one of the best on the peninsula. The international menu with heavy Mediterranean influences changes daily depending on locally available ingredients. We had a superb oven-roasted tuna shank smothered in olive oil, diced tomatoes and onions that was pink in the middle and perfectly crisp at the skin.

COCOLORES
Mediterranean $$

(Map p194; ☏2642-0348; mains US$9-22; ☉4:30am-9:30pm Tue-Sun) One of the best restaurants in Montezuma, beachside Cocolores has a pleasant, thatched-roof patio for candlelit dinners. The menu focuses on Tico-Mediterranean fusion. The curry and coconut shrimp with spicy mango chutney is divine as are the mahi mahi fajitas and their five flavors of spaghetti. It's not cheap but portions are ample. Don't miss it.

PUGGO'S
Middle Eastern $$

(Map p194; ☏2642-0308; mains US$7-20; ☉noon-11pm) A locally beloved restaurant decorated like a Bedouin tent that specializes in Middle Eastern cuisine including falafel, hummus, kebabs, and aromatic fish, which they dress in imported spices and herbs and roast whole. Cap it off with a strong cup of Turkish coffee.

ⓘ Getting There & Away

Boat
A fast passenger ferry connects Montezuma to Jacó in an hour. At US$40 or so, it's not cheap, but it'll save you a day's worth of travel. Boats depart at 9:30am daily and the price includes van transfer from the beach to the Jacó bus terminal. Book in advance from any tour operator. Dress appropriately; you will get wet.

Bus
Buses depart Montezuma from the sandy lot on the beach, across from the soccer field. Buy tickets directly from the driver. To get to Mal País and Santa Teresa, go to Cóbano and change buses.

Cabo Blanco via Cabuya US$1.50, 45 minutes, departs 8:15am and 4:30pm.

Waterfall near Montezuma

MARK NEWMAN / GETTY IMAGES ©

CHRISTER FREDRIKSSON / GETTY IMAGES ©

DISCOVER PENÍNSULA DE NICOYA   RESERVA NATURAL ABSOLUTA CABO BLANCO

Cóbano US$1, 30 minutes, departs every two hours from 8am to 8pm.

Paquera US$3, 1½ hours, departs 5:30am, 8am, 10am, noon, 2pm and 4pm.

San José US$14, six hours, departs 6:15am and 2pm.

Car & Taxi

During the rainy season the stretch of road between Cóbano and Montezuma is likely to require a 4WD. In the village itself, parking can be a problem, though it's easy enough to walk everywhere.

A 4WD taxi can take you to Mal País (US$70) or Cóbano (US$12).

Montezuma Expeditions (www.montezuma-expeditions.com) operates private shuttles to San José (US$45), La Fortuna (US$50), Tamarindo (US$45) and Sámara (US$45).

RESERVA NATURAL ABSOLUTA CABO BLANCO

Just 11km south of Montezuma is Costa Rica's oldest protected wilderness area. Cabo Blanco is comprised of 12 sq km of land and 17 sq km of surrounding ocean, and includes the entire southern tip of the Península de Nicoya. The moist micro-climate on the tip of the peninsula fosters the growth of evergreen forests, which are unique when compared with the dry tropical forests typical of Nicoya. The park also encompasses a number of pristine white-sand beaches and offshore islands that are favored nesting areas for various bird species.

The park was originally established by a Danish-Swedish couple, the late Karen Mogensen and Nicholas Olof Wessburg, who settled in Montezuma in the 1950s and were among the first conservationists in Costa Rica. The couple fought for increased conservation of ecologically rich areas, but, tragically, Olof was murdered in 1975 during a campaign in the Península de Osa. Karen continued their work until her death in 1994, and today they are buried in the Reserva Absoluta Nicolás Wessburg, which was the site of their original homestead.

Cabo Blanco is called an 'absolute' nature reserve because prior to the late 1980s visitors were not permitted. Even though the name hasn't changed, a limited number of trails have been opened to visitors, but the reserve remains closed on Monday and Tuesday to minimize environmental impact.

ⓘ Getting There & Away

Buses (US$1.50, 45 minutes) depart from the park entrance for Montezuma at 9am and 4pm. A taxi from Montezuma to the park costs about US$16.

During dry season, you can drive (4WD required) for 7km from Cabuya to Mal País via the stunningly scenic Star Mountain Rd.

MAL PAÍS & SANTA TERESA

Get ready for tasty waves, creative kitchens and babes in board shorts and bikinis, because the southwestern corner of Península de Nicoya has all that and more. Which is why it has become one of Costa Rica's most life-affirming destinations. Here, the sea is alive with wildlife and is almost perfect when it comes to shape, color and temperature. The hills are dotted with stylish boutique sleeps and sneaky good kitchens run by the occasional runaway top-shelf chef. Sure, there is a growing ribbon of mostly expat development on the coastline, but the hills are lush and that road is still rutted earth (even if it is intermittently sealed with aromatic vats of molasses). The entire area unfurls along one coastal road that rambles from Santa Teresa in the north through Playa El Carmen – the area's commercial heartbeat, terminating in the authentic Tico fishing hamlet of Mal País. The whole region is collectively known to Ticos as Mal País.

🤸 Activities

Surfing is the be-all-and-end-all for most visitors to Mal País, but the beautiful beach stretches north and south for kilometers on end, and many accommodations can arrange horseback-riding tours and fishing trips. Or find the fishing harbor in Mal País and arrange your own fishing tour. It does help to speak some Spanish, however.

♥ If You Like…
Parks & Reserves

If you like Reserva Natural Absoluta Cabo Blanco, we think you'll like these other parks and reserves on the Península de Nicoya:

1 PARQUE NACIONAL BARRA HONDA CAVERNS
(☎2659-1551, tour reservations 8662-4714; adult/child US$10/1; ⊙ trails 8am-4pm, caverns 8am-1pm) Best in the dry season, you can go spelunking in the limestone caves of this underground wonderland.

2 REFUGIO NACIONAL DE VIDA SILVESTRE CURÚ
(☎2641-0100; www.curuwildliferefuge.com; day fee adult/child 3-11/2 & under US$10/5/free; ⊙7am-3pm)

3 RESERVA BIOLÓGICA NOSARA
(☎2682-0035; www.lagarta.com; US$6, guided nature walks US$15) The private 35-hectare reserve behind the Lagarta Lodge has trails leading through a mangrove wetland down to the river and beach – a great spot for bird-watching.

Surfing

The following beaches are listed from north to south.

About 8km north of the Playa El Carmen intersection, **Playa Manzanillo** is a combination of sand and rock that's best surfed when the tide is rising and there's an offshore wind.

The most famous break in the area is at **Playa Santa Teresa**, and it's fast and powerful. This beach can be surfed at virtually any time of day, though be cautious as there are scattered rocks. To get here take the lane just north of La Lora Amarilla from the main road.

Playa El Carmen, down hill from the main intersection, is a good beach break that can also be surfed anytime. The beach is wide and sandy and curls into successive coves, so it makes good beach combing and swimming terrain too.

The entire area is saturated with surf shops, and competition has kept the prices low. This is a good place to pick

DISCOVER PENÍNSULA DE NICOYA MAL PAÍS & SANTA TERESA

up an inexpensive board, and you can probably get most of your money back if you sell it elsewhere.

Yoga

HORIZON YOGA HOTEL   Yoga
(☏2640-0524; www.horizon-yogahotel.com; per person US$10; ⊙classes 9am Mon-Sat, 11am Mon-Thu, 5pm Fri & Sun) Offers two classes daily in a serene environment overlooking the ocean.

 Sleeping & Eating

Santa Teresa
FLORBLANCA   Villas $$$
(☏2640-0232; www.florblanca.com; villas incl breakfast US$350-800; P ❄ @ ☈) Truly in a class of its own, these 11 romantic villas are scattered around three hectares of land next to a pristine white-sand beach.

Indoor-outdoor spaces are flooded with natural light and replete with design details, such as an open-air bathroom and sunken indoor-outdoor living area. Complimentary yoga and Pilates classes are offered, as are free use of bikes, surfboards and snorkeling equipment. Their sensational restaurant, Nectar (mains US$11 to US$24), is open to the public and is highly recommended for its innovative, seasonal, farm fresh Latin American cuisine. Children under 13 are not allowed.

CANAIMA CHILL HOUSE   Apartment $$
(☏8371-5680; www.hotel-canaima-chill-house. com; d US$60-100; P ☈ ☈) Spanish run, the 'rooms' are actually incredibly stylish bamboo loft apartments with kitchens, stone grotto showers, polished concrete floors and wide indoor-outdoor living rooms with a hanging bamboo bed outside and platform bed inside. Guests share the Jacuzzi and plunge pool off the sunken bean-bag lounge. It's set in the

hills, 500m from the main road, so you'll want to have wheels.

KOJI'S
Sushi $$

(☏ 2640-0815; dishes from US$5; ⏱ 5:30am-9:30pm Wed-Sun) Koji Hyodo's sushi shack in nearby Playa Hermosa is a twinkling beacon of fresh raw excellence. The atmosphere and service are superior, of course, but his food is a higher truth. The grilled octopus is only barely fired and sprinkled with sea salt. There's a sweet crunch to his lobster sashimi, sliced trace-paper thin and sprinkled with fresh ginger. Between bites sip one of two local microbrews on tap. There are generally bar seats available, but if you want a table, book ahead. They're located 2km north of Florblanca.

BRISAS DEL MAR
Seafood $$

(☏ 2640-0941; mains US$14-18; ⏱ 4-10pm Tue-Sun) Begin with a mango-passion fruit bellini on this gorgeous poolside dining patio at the otherwise non-descript Hotel Buenos Aires. The view is sensational and

the day's dishes are written in colorful hues on blackboards, emphasizing fresh seafood. Get yours cooked Moroccan style, tossed with linguini, blackened, sauced or curried. If you enjoy bold flavors you will love it here.

Playa El Carmen

FRANK'S PLACE
Hotel $$

(☏ 2640-0096, 2640-0155; www.franksplacecr. com; economy s/d US$25/40, standard s/d US$55/75, superior s/d US$65/95; P ✳ @ 🛜 ☎) Coming into town from Cóbano the first place you'll see is this historic surfer outpost, but Frank has grown up, and this is no longer the backpackers' paradise it once was. Standard tiled rooms have air-con and cable TV, economy rooms share baths. The free-form pool, whirlpool and restaurant are great places to hang out and get the latest surf report.

CASA AZUL
Hotel $$

(☏ 2640-0379; www.hotelcasaazul.com; s/d US$60/70, ste & casa US$125-350) 100m from the intersection and right on the

If You Like...
Restaurants

If you like the bold flavors and beautiful surroundings of restaurants such as Playa de los Artistas and Cocolores, try these other excellent dining options on the peninsula.

1 EL CASTILLO
(☎8893-9603; mains US$6-10; ⏰noon-midnight; P 🛜) This crenelated, stone wall, would-be surfside tourist magnet is brand new and rather cool, thanks to that fabulous old tree dangling with vines in the foreground. Tico-owned, they specialize in small plates with big flavors.

2 PAPAYA
(☎2640-0230; www.moanalodge.com; tapas US$6-9) The new, top-shelf tapas bar at Moana Lodge is on a stunning perch and has jaw-dropping views. The tasty tapas are crafted from local ingredients.

3 LAZY WAVE
(Map p184; ☎2653-0737; meals US$8-25; ⏰6-10pm Sat-Thu) Enjoy a glass of wine and Asian- and Euro-influenced *bocas* (appetizers) on the covered pavilion, where you can curl up amid pillows in cushy lounge chairs.

beach, this fabulous electric blue house looms over the garden, a pool and the waves just beyond. The downstairs rear room is the most economical. It isn't huge, but it's attractive with ceramic tile floors, wrought-iron bed and plenty of light. The secluded garden *casa* has a private patio with sea views, and sleeps three.

ARTEMIS CAFÉ　　Restaurant **$$**
(☎2640-0579; www.artemiscafe.com; mains US$7-14; ⏰7am-2:30am; 🛜) They have a menu to satisfy any homesick *extranjero*, with steak frites, oven-roasted turkey or pastrami sandwiches, cheese plates, and heaping Western breakfasts. There's also a groovy lounge scene at night with DJs

spinning cool tracks and occasional live music.

Mal País

MOANA LODGE　　Boutique Hotel **$$$**
(☎2640-0230; www.moanalodge.com; r US$100, stes US$225-260) A simply stunning boutique property etched into the wooded hillside above Mal País. Standard rooms are all-wood garden cottages, decked out with African art, and close to the pool and reception. The massive two-room, wood-sided junior suites are magnificent. Cantilevered so high they have 180-degree views of the coast, there are wood floors throughout, rain showers inside and outside, a wet bar, cable TV, wi-fi, and sliding glass door entry to both rooms revealing that mighty view. Their new, top-shelf tapas bar, Papaya (left), shares that stunning perch.

THE PLACE　　Bungalow **$$**
(☎2640-0001; www.theplacemalpais.com; d incl breakfast US$60, bungalows US$90-120; P ❄🛜🏊) This hipster euro-flavored spot feels like a dance party could break out at any moment, what with the electronica soundtrack and cushy blood-red lounges and day beds by the pool. It's absolutely worth it to splurge on the more expensive bungalows – each one is creatively decorated according to a different theme.

BLUE JAY LODGE　　Bungalow **$$**
(☎2640-0089; www.bluejaylodgecostarica.com; d incl breakfast US$58; P 🏊) These charming stilted bungalows are built along a forest-covered hillside, each with its own hot-water bathroom and a huge, screened-in veranda with hammocks. They sleep three, and though they're a bit on the rustic side, the luxury is in their spaciousness and openness to the dramatic surroundings. Book the Pizote bungalow if you can. The lodge is 200m from the beach.

Moana Lodge

DIDI / ALAMY ©

RESTAURANT

MARY International, Organic **$$**
(☎ 2640-0153; mains US$7-17; ⊙ 5:30am-10pm
Thu-Tue) Hidden in plain sight in Mal País
village, this charming restaurant with
polished concrete floor, wood oven, pool
table and chalkboard menu has a tremen-
dous reputation for delicious pizzas and
tasty menu staples like tacos and fresh
salads. But their specials are sensational.
Think: Thai lobster tails drizzled with
raw honey, a lamb *po'boy*, and seafood
chowder. Even dessert is fabulous. Their
secret? They use only fresh, organic in-
gredients from local farms and fishermen.

ℹ Getting There & Around

All buses begin and end at Ginger Café, 100m
south of Cuesta Arriba hostel; you can flag the bus
down anywhere along the road up to Frank's Place,
at which point buses turn left and head inland
toward Cóbano.

A new direct bus from Mal País to San José
via the Paquera ferry departs at 6am and 2pm
(US$13, six hours). Local buses to Cóbano (US$2,
45 minutes) depart at 7am, 11:30am, 2pm and
6:30pm.

Montezuma Expeditions (☎ 2642-
0919; www.montezumaexpeditions.com;
CentroComercial Playa El Carmen) organizes
shuttle-van transfers to San José, Tamarindo or
Sámara (US$45), plus La Fortuna and Monteverde
(US$50).

Central Pacific Coast

Beaches, rainforests and wildlife: this is Costa Rica in miniature. Stretching from the rough-and-ready port city of Puntarenas to the tiny town of Uvita on the shores of Bahía Drake, the central Pacific coast is brimming with killer surfing, a suite of excellent national parks that protect endangered animals, and kilometers of coastline where visitors spot migrating whales and pods of dolphins. With so much biodiversity packed into a small geographic area, it offers a taste of the whole country.

Given its proximity to San José and its well-developed system of paved roads, the region has traditionally served as a weekend getaway for everyone from sun-worshippers and sportfishers to tree huggers and outdoors enthusiasts. Foreign investment and expats alike have also flooded in, catapulting the central Pacific coast into the ranks of Costa Rica's wealthiest and most cosmopolitan regions.

Central Pacific coastline
CHRISTOPHER BAKER / GETTY IMAGES ©

Central Pacific Coast

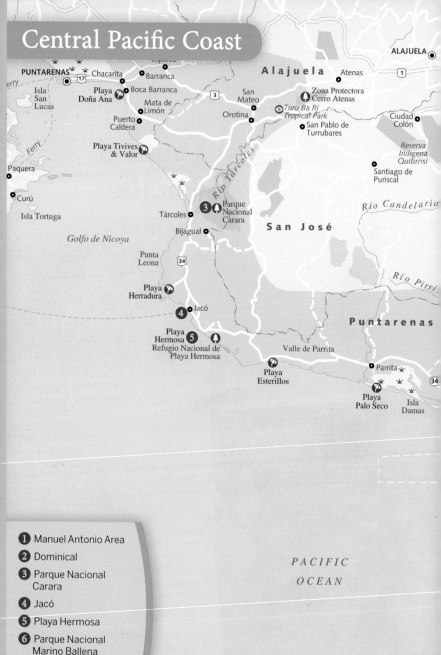

ALAJUELA

PUNTARENAS · Chacarita

Alajuela · Atenas

Isla San Lucas

Playa Doña Ana · Boca Barranca

Barranca

Mata de Limón

San Mateo

Puerto Caldera

Orotina

Turu Ba Ri Tropical Park

Zona Protectora Cerro Atenas

San Pablo de Turrubares

Ciudad Colón

Reserva Indígena Quitirrisí

Playa Tivives & Valor

Santiago de Puriscal

Paquera

Río Tárcoles

Curú

Isla Tortuga

Tárcoles

Río Candelaria

Parque Nacional Carara

San José

Golfo de Nicoya

Bijagual

Punta Leona

Río Pirrí

Playa Herradura

Puntarenas

Jacó

Playa Hermosa
Refugio Nacional de Playa Hermosa

Valle de Parrita

Parrita

Playa Esterillos

Playa Palo Seco

Isla Damas

Legend

1. Manuel Antonio Area
2. Dominical
3. Parque Nacional Carara
4. Jacó
5. Playa Hermosa
6. Parque Nacional Marino Ballena
7. Kayaking in Dominical and Uvita

PACIFIC OCEAN

N

0 ——— 40 km
0 ——— 20 miles

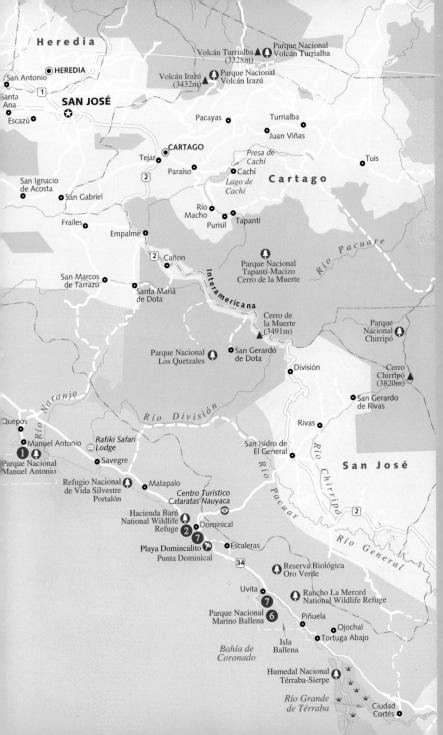

Central Pacific Coast Highlights

1 Manuel Antonio Area

Pristine beaches, luscious rainforests and an incredible variety of flora and fauna make it the complete nature experience. Where the jungle meets the ocean, you can follow well-designed trails in search of wildlife, lie on golden sands and swim in crystal-clear waters. Above and above right: Playa Manuel Antonio; Below right: Malachite butterfly

Need to Know

CROWDS Manuel Antonio is one of the country's busiest parks **ACCESS** Stay in Quepos or along the road connecting Quepos to Manuel Antonio **For more, see p225**

Manuel Antonio Area Don't Miss List

BY DENNYS QUIROS, ASSISTANT MANAGER OF THE HOTEL SÍ COMO NO

1 MANUEL ANTONIO BEACHES

The national park is home to a huge variety of wilderness beaches that start at the information center and stretch out along the coast of the peninsula. They're accessed by a network of trails that wrap around forests and hug the shoreline, providing ample opportunities for sunning, swimming and snorkeling. The beaches closest to the park entrance see the largest tourist crowds, though you can easily escape the masses by hiking a bit deeper in, and seeking out your own abandoned stretch of sand.

2 SANTA JUANA MOUNTAIN VILLAGE

If you're looking for an off-the-beaten-path experience in the Manuel Antonio area, consider a visit to the inland village of Santa Juana in the Fila Chonta mountain range. Here, the local villagers are embracing the concept of community-based ecotourism, and are experimenting with various initiatives aimed at achieving sustainable development through conservation. Independent excursions are possible if you have your own 4WD, though you can also book transportation and a bilingual guide.

3 FINCAS NATURALES

This private wildlife refuge features 1500m of trails, designed for all ages. The refuge is researching and developing ways to help protect and reproduce locally endangered species including orchids, bromeliads and amphibians. It is also home to Butterfly Botanical Gardens, an Aquatic Garden and the new Crocodile Lagoon exhibit. In-house naturalists regularly conduct guided tours in both Spanish and English.

4 WHITE-WATER RAFTING

For some memorable thrills and spills, consider taking a white-water rafting trip on the nearby Río Naranjo. Even if you're traveling as a family, there are a multitude of runs catering to all ages and skill levels.

Dominical

A legendary surf town, Dominical has been drawing in legions of boarders for decades. Even if you happen to be a self-professed newbie, Dominical still warrants a visit as the incredibly laid-back ambience of the beach is positively infectious. Don't be surprised if you get stuck here for much longer than you intended. Below and below right: Surfers at Dominical; Above right: Camping on the beach at Dominical

Need to Know

TOP SURVIVAL TIP The rip tides in Dominical can be deadly. Swim with caution
BEST PHOTO Grab a camera for watching the pros shred waves at sunset For more, see p231

2

Dominical Surf Scene Don't Miss List

BY CESAR VALVERDE, OWNER & SURF INSTRUCTOR, COSTA RICA SURF CAMP

1 DOMINICAL BEACH

Dominical is my favorite break in Costa Rica! You can't beat the waves and the community here. I love surfing in Dominical because of the great waves, great barrels and no crowds! There are waves of every size for every level of surfer. The waves are very consistent and we have waves all year round.

2 DOMINICALITO

This is a great beginner and intermediate beach. You can only surf here at high tide. The waves are a lot gentler and slower than Dominical, making is a great place for learning as well! It's about 2 km south of the town of Dominical and easy to get to by taxi or car.

3 PLAYA HERMOSA

The point is just a little south of Dominicalito and a point break. It breaks left and is about 300m long. This is a great wave when Dominical gets too big and closed out. It's a very fun wave!

4 TORTILLA FLATS

Right on the beach, this is a great place to go for a beer and to hang out. It is relaxed and there is always a crowd of locals and visitors. You can sit here and watch people surfing Dominical Beach. Plus, they always have a good time when there is live music!

5 MARACATU

For nightlife, I like Maracatu, a fun world-music bar that brings in a lot of people for its concerts. On Wednesday night it's Ladies Night too, which always brings a crowd. Even though Dominical is a small town, there is a lot to do!

Parque Nacional Carara

Lying at the intersection of Costa Rica's northern dry forests and southern rainforests, Carara (p218) exists as a unique transition zone. The species count here soars, though the undeniable star of the show is the scarlet macaw, a flaming-red bird with visually striking blu and yellow accents. *Birdlife in the wetlands of Parque Nacional Carara*

3

4 Jacó

The big city of the central Pacific coast, Jacó (p218) is loud and proud and unapologetic about it. Home to resident expats from around the world, Jacó has a cosmopolitan mix of restaurants, boutique hotels and a couple of large resort. The beach is shaped by decent novice-friendly surf, and there's a laundry list of activities for anyone who can't sit still.

Playa Hermosa

Something of a younger brother to Jacó, Playa Hermosa (p221) may lack size and sophistication, but it certainly holds its own when it comes to surf. For intermediate and experienced riders, Playa Hermosa offers some of the sickest waves in the Pacific, particularly in August when the annual surf competition is held.

5

6

Parque Nacional Marino Ballena

This off-the-beaten-path marine park (p237) lies at the extreme southern end of the central Pacific coast and has miles of empty, coconut-strewn beaches. Shaped like a giant whale's tale stretching out into the Pacific, Marino Ballena is a stunning slice of shore that harbors astonishing marine life including pods of dolphins and migrating whales. Uvita coastline (p235)

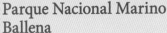

7

Kayaking in Dominical & Uvita

The coastal area between Dominical (p231) and Uvita (p235) has a great diversity of kayaking trips in a relatively small area. Here visitors navigate challenging ocean waves and lazy mangrove channels...sometimes both in the same afternoon. The wildlife-spotting is good, but the rare treat is a visit to local ocean caves, where you can break for a picnic of fresh local fruit. Kayaking through rainforest

The Central Pacific Coast's Best...

Wildlife

○ **Scarlet macaws** (p218) Catch a glimpse of red birds amid green trees in Parque Nacional Carara.

○ **Squirrel monkeys** (p227) Adorable little fur balls in Parque Nacional Manuel Antonio.

○ **Humpback whales** (p237) Migrating pods swim through Parque Nacional Marino Ballena.

○ **Tapir** (p230) Get off the tourist trail and onto the so-called 'Path of the Tapir' at the Hacienda Barú National Wildlife Refuge.

Activities

○ **Surfing** (p221) A string of surf towns, including Playa Hermosa, make this region ideal for thrashing some swells.

○ **Canopy tours** (p230) Zip-line your way through the lofty treetops along 'the Flight of the Toucan' at Hacienda Barú National Wildlife Refuge.

○ **Hiking** (p227) Navigate the easy trails of Parque Nacional Manuel Antonio to spot monkeys, macaws and lush tropical forests.

○ **Yoga** (p232) Get aligned with yoga and movement classes at Dominical's Bamboo Yoga Play.

Splurges

○ **Hotel Sí Como No** (p224) A family-friendly hotel with the government's highest rating for ecofriendliness.

○ **Arenas del Mar** (p224) This luxury ecoresort offers unmatched intimacy and excellent coast views.

○ **Docelunas** (p220) A teak-accented mountain retreat surrounded by virgin rainforest.

○ **Makanda by the Sea** (p224) With minimalist design and unmatched views, this tiny set of villas is a stunner.

Need to Know

Eats & Drinks

○ **Citrus** (p239) Mouth-watering Pan-Asian cuisine highlights the bounty of the Pacific Ocean.

○ **Agua Azul** (p224) Enjoy a two-handed hamburger while taking in a perfect view of the Pacific.

○ **El Avión** (p225) Savor an ice-cold beer in the shadow of a 1954 Fairchild C-123.

○ **Restaurante Exótica** (p239) French execution and cozy ambience make this Ojochal eatery a surprising delight.

ADVANCE PLANNING

○ **Surfing school** The Pacific coast is home to some serious surf, which means beginners will have to hunt out beach towns with easy beach breaks.

RESOURCES

○ **Queposlandia** (www.quepolandia.com)

GETTING AROUND

○ **Boat** The beach town of Montezuma on the tip of the Península de Nicoya is a quick boat ride away from Jacó.

○ **Bus** Intercity buses are frequent and cheap, which makes moving around a cinch.

○ **Car** The smoothly paved and well-signed coastal highway is conducive to self-driving.

○ **Walk** Parque Nacional Manuel Antonio has a range of hikes catering to both novices and seasoned trekkers.

BE FOREWARNED

○ **Prostitution** Jacó has a seedy underbelly at night, so be mindful of your surroundings and use discretion.

○ **Riptides** Currents here can be very strong, even in shallow waters. Ask locals for advice about when and where it's safe to swim. If you find yourself caught in a riptide, call for help. Conserve your energy and relax – don't try to fight the current.

VITAL STATISTICS

○ **Population** Puntarenas 10,400

○ **Best time to visit** Rains fall heavily from April to November, while December to March is comparatively dry.

EMERGENCY NUMBERS

○ **Emergency** ☏911

○ **Fire** ☏118

○ **Police** ☏117

Left: Scarlet macaw; **Above:** Parque Nacional Manuel Antonio (p227)

Central Pacific Coast Itineraries

A newly paved coastal road invites an ideal road trip into lesser developed areas that evoke the 'Old Costa Rica.' From a quick escape to a rambling escapade, the region holds all of Costa Rica's colorful charms.

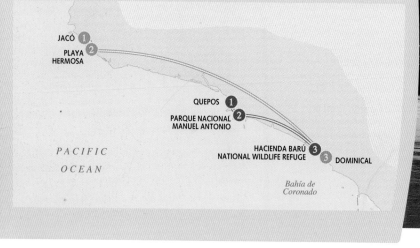

3 DAYS

QUEPOS TO HACIENDA BARÚ NATIONAL WILDLIFE REFUGE
Manuel Antonio & Beyond

It takes time to traverse the full length of the coast, though fortunately this itinerary will give you a quick but fulfilling taste of Pacific wonderment. You can do things easily with your own wheels or on public transportation, cruising the freshly paved Costanera Sur between tropical seas and forest-covered mountains.

Your first destination is none other than the authentic Tico town of **(1) Quepos**, which has tons of services for travelers, tour operators and a healthy nightlife. Friendly locals, a sparkling marina and inviting international restaurants make it a destination in its own right, but the

primary reason to visit is a jumping-off point for the **(2) Parque Nacional Manuel Antonio**. One of the country's top national parks, Manuel Antonio can be summed up with three words: beaches, rainforests and monkeys. The park has good hiking for families and some of the best swimming beaches in the Pacific. For more wildlife, take a guided hike through **(3) Hacienda Barú National Wildlife Refuge**, a small reserve that encompasses a range of tropical habitats and is part of a major biological corridor that protects a wide range of species.

5 DAYS

JACÓ TO DOMINICAL
Surfer's Paradise

If you're looking to burn off some adrenaline, the central Pacific is home to a string of spectacular beach towns with fairly consistent year-round surf. Don't fret if you're not an expert and don't have your own board; there are plenty of shops where you can get geared up and the surf schools are abundant. Surf's up – and even when it's not, there is still plenty of sun, sea and sand to enjoy. Also, the roads in this part of the country are good and don't require a 4WD.

With modest waves and a gentle beach break, **(1) Jacó** is a great place to get a longboard and practice standing up, balancing your weight and riding your first waves. Even if you don't succeed, you'll still enjoy your evenings in the unofficial party capital of the Pacific coast. More experienced surfers can test their skills a bit further south down the coast at **(2) Playa Hermosa**, where sharper curls and faster swells present a mighty challenge. Finally, sink into the laid-back charms of **(3) Dominical**, a true surfer's paradise and taste of the 'Old Costa Rica.' Along its unpaved main street are budget-friendly lodgings, surf shops and open-air eateries.

Horse riding at Parque Nacional Manuel Antonio (p227)
CHRISTER FREDRIKSSON / GETTY IMAGES ©

Discover Central Pacific Coast

At a Glance

○ **Jacó** The region's biggest town has a notorious party scene and great surf.

○ **Quepos** (p222) Gateway to the country's most popular national park, Manuel Antonio.

○ **Dominical** (p231) A more laid-back alternative to Nicoya for surfing and chilling out.

PARQUE NACIONAL CARARA

Straddling the transition between the dry forests of Costa Rica's northwest and the sodden rainforests of the southern Pacific lowlands, this national park is a biological melting pot of the two. Acacias intermingle with strangler figs, and cacti with deciduous kapok trees, creating heterogeneous habitats with a blend of wildlife to match. It's not the biggest, not the wildest and not the most beautiful, but the significance of this national park cannot be understated. Surrounded by a sea of cultivation and livestock, it is one of the few areas in the transition zone where wildlife finds sanctuary. The park can easily be explored in half a day's expedition.

Carara is also the famed home to one of Costa Rica's most charismatic bird species, the scarlet macaw. While catching a glimpse of this tropical wonder is a rare proposition in most of the country, macaw sightings are common at Carara. And, of course, there are more than 400 other avian species flitting around the canopy, as well as Costa Rica's largest crocodiles in the waterways – it's best to leave your swimming trunks at home!

Any bus traveling between Puntarenas and Jacó can leave you at the park entrance. If you're driving, the entrance to Carara is right on the Costanera and is clearly marked.

JACÓ

Few places in Costa Rica generate such divergent opinions and paradoxical realities as Jacó. Partying surfers, North American retirees and international developers laud

Jacó
FRANCK GUIZIOU / ALAMY ©

218

Jacó for its devil-may-care atmosphere, bustling streets and booming real-estate opportunities. Observant ecotourists, marginalized Ticos and loyalists of the 'old Costa Rica' absolutely despise the place for the *exact* same reasons.

While Jacó's ramshackle charm is not for everyone, the surfing is excellent, the restaurants and bars are cosmopolitan and the nightlife can be a throbbing, exciting adventure.

🤸 Activities

Surfing

Although the rainy season is considered best for Pacific Coast surfing, Jacó is blessed with consistent year-round breaks. If you're looking to rent a board for the day, shop around as the better places will rent you a board for US$15 to US$20 for 24 hours, while others will try to charge you a few dollars per hour. You'll find surf lessons all around town.

Other Activities

KAYAK JACÓ COSTA RICA OUTRIGGERS   Kayaking
(8869-7074, 2643-1233; www.kayakjaco. com; 2hr tour US$70) This reliable company facilitates kayaking and sea-canoeing trips that include snorkeling excursions to tropical islands, in a wide variety of customized day and multiday trips. This outfit does not have an office in Jacó – though you might see it set up in Playa Agujas 250m east of the beach. Still, it's best to either phone or email in advance.

HANGGLIDE COSTA RICA   Scenic Flights
(2643-4200; www.hangglidecr.com; from US$100) HangGlide Costa Rica will pick you up in Jacó and shuttle you to an airstrip south of Playa Hermosa where you can tandem-ride in a hang glider or fly in a three-seat ultralight plane. There's no office in town.

WATERFALLS CANOPY TOUR   Adventure Sports
(2632-3322; www.waterfallscanopy.com; tours from US$86) Because of its huge suite of

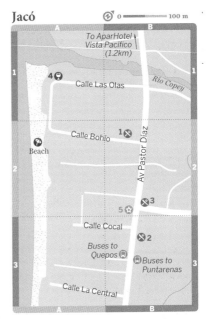

Jacó

🍴 Eating
1 Hotel Poseidon Restaurant.................B2
2 Lemon Zest B3
3 Los Amigos B2

🍹 Drinking
4 Clarita's Beach Hotel and
   Sports Bar and Grill.........................A1

🎭 Entertainment
5 Le Loft..B2

different packages (including nocturnal zip-line rides), this is the most highly recommended company.

🛏 Sleeping

SONIDOS DEL MAR   Guesthouse $$$
(2643-3912/24; www.sonidosdelmar.com; Calle Hidalgo; house US$250; P ❄ @ 🛜 🏊) Set within a mature garden at the bend of a river, 'Sounds of the Ocean' may be one of the most beautiful guesthouses in Costa Rica. Lauri, a skilled artist and collector, has

lovingly filled each room with original paintings, sculptures and indigenous crafts.

DOCELUNAS Boutique Hotel $$$

(☎2643-2277; www.docelunas.com; Costanera Sur; d/junior ste incl breakfast US$140/160; P🍴❄@🛜☈) Situated in the foothills across the highway, 'Twelve Moons' is a heavenly mountain retreat consisting of only 20 rooms sheltered in a pristine landscape of tropical rainforest. Each teak-accented room is intimately decorated with original artwork available for purchase, yoga classes are given daily and there's a free-form pool fed by a waterfall. To reach the hotel, make a left off the Costanera between the two entrances for Playa Jacó.

APARHOTEL VISTA PACÍFICO Apartment $$

(☎2643-3261; www.vistapacifico.com; d incl breakfast from US$68; P🍴@🛜☈) Located on the crest of a hill off Bullever, just outside Jacó, this Canadian-run hotel is an absolute gem that is worth seeking out. The views of the coastline from here are phenomenal, particularly at sunset when you'll have panoramic vistas of a fiery sky, and the mountaintop location also means that it's a few degrees cooler (and a whole lot quieter) than neighboring Jacó.

Eating

HOTEL POSEIDON RESTAURANT Seafood $$$

(Map p219; ☎2643-1642; Calle Bohío; mains US$10-30) This is one of the most sophisticated restaurants in town, and the specialty here is fresh seafood served up with Asian flare. Sauces are inventive, the staff professional and the atmosphere upscale yet relaxing. A good bet for top-quality food and refined European-style dining that consistently receives good marks from travelers.

LEMON ZEST Fusion $$$

(Map p219; ☎2643 2591; Av Pastor Díaz; mains US$15-20; ⏲5-10pm Mon-Sat; 🛜☈) Chef Richard Lemon (a former instructor at Le Cordon Bleu Miami) wins accolades for Jacó's most swish menu. The menu's roster of upscale standards, including shrimp and penne, seared duck in blackberry sauce and grilled tuna, are carried out with due sophistication in a dining room with soft light and modern paintings.

Playa Hermosa (p221)

LOS AMIGOS
Mexican $$

(Map p219; 2643-2961; cnr Av Pastor Díaz & Calle Pops; mains US$6-12; ⊙noon-11pm Sun-Thu, to 1am Fri & Sat; 🛜 👶) The English menu at Los Amigos announces a motley mix of Mexican and Thai food, lunch wraps and snacks that cater to North American tastes. Sounds like gringo central, right? Perhaps it is, but it fits perfectly in Jacó, and the pre-party atmosphere, wi-fi and cranked air-con feels just right.

Entertainment

LE LOFT
DJ

(Map p219; Av Pastor Díaz) The Loft is Jacó's sleekest nightlife offering and makes a good addition to the beach clubs and girly bars with some much needed urban sophistication. Live DJs spin essential mixes while glam-aspiring customers do their best to look beautiful and act fabulous. There's a calendar of special events and a balcony perch where travelers take in the action on the street below.

❶ Getting There & Away

Air

NatureAir (www.natureair.com) and **Alfa Romeo Aero Taxi** (www.alfaromeoair.com) offer charter flights. Prices are dependent on the number of passengers, so it's best to try to organize a larger group if you're considering this option.

Boat

The jet-boat transfer service that connects Jacó to Montezuma is, far and away, the most efficient to connect the central Pacific coast to the Península de Nicoya. The journey across the Golfo de Nicoya only takes about an hour (compared to about seven hours overland), though at US$40 it's definitely not cheap. Reservations are required and can be made at most tour operators in town.

Bus

Quepos US$1.75, 1½ hours, departs 6am, noon, 4:30pm and 6pm.

San José US$4, three hours, departs 5am, 7:30am, 11am, 3pm and 5pm.

Jacó for Kids

Jacó has long been on the radar screens of Tico families looking to swap the congestion of San José for the ocean breezes of the central Pacific Coast. Therefore, you'll find that your own children are very well cared for in Jacó, and there is enough on offer to keep even those with the shortest attention spans amused for days on end.

PLAYA HERMOSA

While newbies struggle to stand up on their boards in Jacó, a few kilometers south in Playa Hermosa seasoned veterans are thrashing their way across the faces of some truly monster waves. Regarded as one of the most consistent and powerful breaks in the whole country, Hermosa (Spanish for 'beautiful') serves up serious surf that commands the utmost respect. Still, even if you're not a pro, the vibe here is excellent, the surfers are chilled out and the beach lives up to its name.

Sleeping

TORTUGA DEL MAR
Lodge $$

(📞2643-7132; www.tortugadelmar.net; r US$75, studios from US$85; Ⓟ ❄ @ 🛜 ≋) Top-end accommodations with a recession-proof midrange price tag, this newish lodge is sheltered amid shady grounds, and is comprised of just a handful of rooms housed in a two-story building. Tropical modern is the style at hand, making excellent use of local hardwoods to construct lofty ceilings that catch every gust of the Pacific breezes.

BACKYARD HOTEL
Hotel $$$

(📞2643-7011; www.backyardhotel.com; r/ste from US$135/200; Ⓟ ❄ @ 🛜 ≋) The quality linens and mattresses here have substantially raised the bar for accommodations in Playa Hermosa. In addition, the proximity of the accompanying Backyard Bar makes this boutique hotel ideal if you want to be in the heart of the (admittedly limited) action – but maddening if you don't.

❶ Getting There & Away

Located only 5km south of Jacó, Playa Hermosa can be accessed by any bus heading south from Jacó.

QUEPOS

Located just 7km from the entrance to Manuel Antonio, the small, busy town of Quepos serves as the gateway to the national park, as well as a convenient port of call for travelers in need of goods and services. Although the Manuel Antonio area was rapidly and irreversibly transformed following the ecotourism boom, Quepos has largely retained an authentic Tico feel, particularly when you get out of the middle of town. Exuding an ineffable charm that is absent from so much of the central Pacific, Quepos still has glimmers of traditional Latin America, even while being a heavily traveled stop on the tourist-packed gringo trail.

Downtown Quepos is a small checkerboard of dusty streets that are lined with a mix of local- and tourist-oriented shops, businesses, markets, restaurants and cafes. The town loses its well-ordered shape as it expands outward, but southeast of the town center is the brand-new Pez Vela Marina, a shimmering jewel of architectural prowess that is bringing in more international yachters.

🤾 Activities

OCEANS UNLIMITED Diving, Snorkeling
(Map p228; ☎2777-3171, in USA 407-385-6598; www.scubadivingcostarica.com) This shop takes its diving very seriously, and runs most of its excursions out to Isla Larga and Isla del Caño, which is south in Bahia Drake (connected through a two-hour bus trip south).

BLUEFIN SPORTFISHING Fishing
(Map p228; ☎2777-1676, 2777-2222; www.blue finsportfishing.com) Across from the soccer field, this outfit does excellent fishing trips.

H2O ADVENTURES Adventure Tour
(Map p228; ☎2777-4092; www.riostropicales. com) The venerable Costa Rican rafting company Ríos Tropicales has an office in Quepos called h2o Adventures. Rates for Class III and IV rapids runs start at US$67 in low season and US$82 in summer.

🛏 Sleeping

HOTEL SIRENA Hotel $$
(Map p228; ☎2777-0572; www.lasirenahotel. com; s/d/tr incl breakfast US$60/75/85; P ❄ 🛜 ≋) This intimate boutique hotel is a welcome and warm addition to the Quepos

White-faced capuchin monkey
SHANNON NACE / GETTY IMAGES ©

scene, and is easily the best midrange option in town. Amid the bustle of Quepos' rough-and-ready street scene, the Sirena's whitewashed walls, soft pastel trims and aromatherapy offer a slice of breezy Mediterranean serenity.

LA FORESTA NATURE RESORT Ecolodge $$$
(☎2777-3130; www.laforestanatureresort.com; ste/bungalows/villas from US$118/146/280; P✶@☎) This resort hotel (formerly known as Rancho Grande), is located out of the action, on the road to the Quepos airport. Crisscrossed by hiking and horseback-riding trails, the property has a butterfly garden and a small zip line, making it good for families who need a lot of room to run around.

 Eating & Drinking

CEVICHERIA EL DORADO Ceviche $
(Map p228; ☎8942-2625; meals US$5; ⏱11am-9pm Mon-Sat) There's nothing to it – a tinny radio playing Costa Rican pop, a few well-worn stools and a couple of friendly ladies behind the counter – but locals seek out this tiny *ceviche* joint for amazing dishes of fresh affordable fish dressed in citrus and cilantro (coriander) and sided with a few cooked plantains. The selection changes with the seasonal catch, but the price always stays low.

CAFÉ MILAGRO Cafe $
(Map p228; meals US$5-8; ⏱6am-10pm Mon-Fri; 🛜) Serving some of the country's best cappuccino and espresso, this is a great place to perk up in the morning – try the *perezoso* (meaning 'lazy' or 'sloth'), which is a double espresso poured into a large cup of drip-filter coffee.

 Entertainment

REPUBLIK CLUB Club
(Map p228; cover charge for men US$3; ⏱6:30pm-2:30am) Republik hosts the most reliable party in central Quepos and has some kind of drink special nearly every night if you

---

Quepos for Children

The entire Quepos and Manuel Antonio area is one of Costa Rica's leading family-friendly destinations. With beaches and rainforest in close proximity – not to mention a healthy dose of charismatic wildlife – the region can enchant young minds regardless of their attention spans.

---

arrive before 10pm. (Of course the place is pretty lonely at that hour.) Later the volume gets loud, the drinks get more pricy and things tend to careen out of control.

ⓘ Getting There & Away

Air

Both NatureAir (Map p228; www.natureair.com) and Sansa (Map p228; www.sansa.com) service Quepos, which is the base town for accessing Manuel Antonio. Prices vary according to season and availability, though you can expect to pay a little less than US$75 for a flight from San José or Liberia.

Bus

Jacó US$1.50, 1½ hours, departs 4:30am, 7:30am, 10:30am and 3pm.

San Isidro de El General via Dominical US$4, three hours, departs 5:30am, 11:30am and 1:30pm.

San José (Transportes Morales) US$7 to US$8, four hours, departs 5am, 8am, 10am, noon, 2pm, 4pm and 7:30pm.

Uvita via Dominical US$8, 4½ hours, departs 10am and 7pm.

QUEPOS TO MANUEL ANTONIO

Sure, the park itself is a natural wonder, but the road to it is an overdeveloped mess. Still, it is home to some of Costa Rica's finest hotels and restaurants.

Sights & Activities

FINCAS NATURALES Farm
(Map p228; ☎2777-0850; www.wildliferefugecr.com; adult/child US$15/8; ⏰8am-4pm; 👪) Situated just across the road from Hotel Sí Como No, this private rainforest preserve and butterfly garden breeds about three dozen species of butterfly – a delicate population compared to the menagerie of lizards, reptiles and frogs that inspire gleefully grossed-out squeals from the little ones.

SERENITY SPA Spa
(Map p228; ☎2777-0777, ext 220; www.sicomono.com; Hotel Sí Como No) After a day's activities, you can relax at the Serenity Spa, a good place for couple's massages, sunburn-relief treatments, coconut body scrubs and tasty coffee.

AMIGOS DEL RÍO Rafting
(Map p228; ☎2777-1084; www.adventuremanuelantonio.com) Amigos del Río runs white-water rafting trips for all skill levels on the Ríos Savegre and Naranjo.

Sleeping

MAKANDA BY THE SEA Villas $$$
(Map p228; ☎2777-0442; www.makanda.com; studios/villas incl breakfast from US$265/400; P❄@📶🏊) Comprised of just six villas and five studios, Makanda has an unmatched air of intimacy and complete privacy. Villa 1 (the largest) will take your breath away – one entire wall is open to the rainforest and the ocean. The other villas and studios are air-conditioned and enclosed, though they draw upon the same minimalistic, Eastern-infused design schemes.

HOTEL COSTA VERDE Hotel $$$
(Map p228; ☎2777-0584; www.costaverde.com; efficiency/studios from US$115/149, Boeing 727 fuselage home US$500; P❄@📶🏊) This collection of rooms, studios and – believe it or not – a fully converted Boeing 727 fuselage occupies a lush, tropical setting that is frequented by regular troops of primate visitors. Efficiency units are attractively tiled, and face the encroaching forest, while slightly more expensive studios have full ocean views. But the real kicker here is the airplane–tree house hybrid, which gives new life to a previously decommissioned Boeing. When toucans flit by the cockpit, it's a bit surreal.

🍃 **HOTEL SÍ COMO NO** Hotel $$$
(Map p228; ☎2777-0777; www.sicomono.com; r US$230-290, ste US$305-340, child under 6yr free; P❄@📶🏊) This flawlessly designed hotel is an example of how to build a resort while maintaining environmental sensibility. Buildings are insulated for comfort and use energy-efficient air-con units; water is recycled into the landscape, and solar-heating panels are used to heat the water. No surprise here that the Sí Como No is one of only four hotels in the country to have been awarded five out of five leaves by the government-run Certified Sustainable Tourism campaign. The hotel is also packed full of family-friendly amenities.

🍃 **ARENAS DEL MAR** Boutique Hotel $$$
(Map p228; ☎2777-2777; www.arenasdelmar.com; r US$330-600; P❄@📶🏊) This visually arresting hotel and resort complex is consistently shortlisted among Costa Rica's finest upscale hotels. Despite the extent and breadth of the grounds, there are only 40 rooms, which ensures an unmatched degree of personal service and privacy. It has won numerous ecotourism awards since its inception and was designed to incorporate the beauty of the natural landscape. In short, the overall effect is breathtaking, especially when you're staring down the coastline from the lofty heights of your private open-air Jacuzzi.

Eating & Drinking

AGUA AZUL International $$
(Map p228; ☎2777-5280; meals US$7-18; ⏰11am-10pm Thu-Tue) Perched on the

Scarlet macaws

RALPH HOPKINS / GETTY IMAGES ©

2nd floor with uninterrupted ocean views, Agua Azul is a killer lunch spot on this stretch of road – perfect for early morning park visitors who are heading back to their hotel. The breezy, unpretentious open-air restaurant is renowned for its 'big ass burger.' But the burger is only the beginning of satisfying menu choices. Selections like the panko-crusted catch of the day or seared tuna on tequila lime cucumber salad are executed with artful precision.

EL AVIÓN Bar
(Map p228; 📞2777-3378; mains US$6-14; 📶🚼) This unforgettable airplane bar-restaurant was constructed from the body of a 1954 Fairchild C-123. It's a great spot for a beer, guacamole and a Pacific sunset, and in the evenings during the dry season there are regular live music performances.

KAPI KAPI RESTAURANT Fusion $$$
(Map p228; 📞2777-5049; meals US$15-40) Kapi Kapi, which is a traditional greeting of the indigenous Maleku people, welcomes diners with soft lights, earthy tones and soothing natural decor, which perfectly frame the dense forest lying just beyond

the perimeter. The menu is no less ambitious, spanning the globe from America to Asia, and making several pivotal stops along the way. Pan-Asian–style seafood is featured prominently on the menu.

ⓘ Getting There & Away

A good number of visitors who stay in this area arrive by private or rented car. The public bus from Quepos will let you off anywhere along the road.

PARQUE NACIONAL MANUEL ANTONIO & AROUND

As visitors find themselves along this small outcropping of land that juts out into the Pacific, the air becomes heavy with humidity, scented with thick vegetation and alive with the call of birds and monkeys, making it suddenly apparent that *this* is the tropics. The reason to come here is the stunning Parque Nacional Manual Antonio, one of the most picturesque bits of tropical coast in Costa Rica. If you get bored of cooing at the baby monkeys that scurry in the canopy and scanning for birds and sloths, the turquoise waves and perfect sand provide

225

COURTESY OF RAFIKI SAFARI LODGE ©

Don't Miss **Rafiki Safari Lodge**

Nestled into the rainforest, with a prime spot right next to the Río Savegre, the Rafiki Safari Lodge combines all the comforts of a hotel with the splendor of a jungle safari – all with a little bit of African flavor. The owners, who are from South Africa, have constructed nine luxury tents on stilts equipped with bathroom, hot water, private porch and electricity. All units are screened in, which allows you to see and hear the rainforest without actually having creepy-crawlies in your bed. There's a spring-fed pool with a waterslide and ample opportunity for horseback riding, bird-watching (more than 350 species have been identified), hiking and white-water rafting. And of course, South Africans are masters on the *braai* (BBQ), so you know that you'll eat well alongside other guests in the *rancho*-style restaurant.

The entrance to the lodge is located about 15km south of Quepos in the small town of Savegre. From here, a 4WD dirt road parallels the Río Savegre and leads 7km inland, past the towns of Silencio and Santo Domingo, to the lodge. However, if you don't have private transportation, the lodge can arrange all of your transfers with advance reservations.

NEED TO KNOW

☎ 2777-5327, 2777-2250; www.rafikisafari.com; s/d/ste incl all meals US$203/350/400, child under 5yr free; P @ 🛜 ☒

endless entertainment. However, there's no pretending that Manuel Antonio is anyone's secret – despite being the smallest of Costa Rica's national parks, it is also one of the most popular. Little Quepos, the once sleepy fishing and banana village on the park's perimeter, has rapidly ballooned with this tourism-based economy (although it is admirably clinging to its roots despite ongoing socioeconomic transformation), and the road leading from Quepos to the park is overdeveloped. However, the rainforested hills sweeping down to the sea and the blissful beaches make the park a stunning destination worthy of the tourist hype.

Parque Nacional Manuel Antonio

A place of swaying palms and playful monkeys, sparkling blue water and riotous tropical birds, **Parque Nacional Manuel Antonio** (*J* 2777-0644; park entrance US$10; ⏱7am-4pm Tue-Sun) embodies Costa Rica's postcard charms. It was declared a national park in 1972, preserving it (with just minutes to spare) from being bulldozed and razed to make room for a coastal development project. Although Manuel Antonio was enlarged to its present-day size of 16 sq km in 2000, it is still the country's smallest national park. Space remains a premium, and as this is one of Central America's top tourist destinations, you're going to have to break free from the camera-clicking tour groups and actively seek out your own idyllic spot of sand.

That said, Manuel Antonio is absolutely stunning, and on a good day, at the right time, it's easy to convince yourself that you've died and gone to a coconut-filled paradise. The park's clearly marked trail system winds through rainforest-backed tropical beaches and rocky headlands, and the views across the bay to the pristine outer islands are unforgettable. As if this wasn't enough, add a ubiquitous population of iguanas, howlers, capuchins, sloths and squirrel monkeys.

Gay Guide to Manuel Antonio

For jet-setting gay and lesbian travelers from the world over, Manuel Antonio has long been regarded as something of a dream destination. Homosexuality has been decriminalized in Costa Rica since the 1970s – a rarity in all-too-often machismo-fueled conservative Central America – and a well-established gay scene blossomed in Manuel Antonio soon after. Gay and lesbian travelers will find that it's unlike any other destination in the country.

During the daylight hours, the epicenter of gay Manuel Antonio is the famous La Playita, a beach with a long history of nude sunbathing for gay men. Alas, the days when you could sun in the buff are gone, but La Playita still is widely regarded as a playful pick-up scene for gay men on the prowl.

A significant number of hotels in the Manuel Antonio area advertise themselves as being gay-friendly and even the ones that don't are unlikely to discriminate. Of course, if you want to enjoy the freedom and peace of mind that comes with staying at exclusively gay accommodations, book a room at the gay-owned and operated **Hotel Villa Roca** (Map p228; www.villaroca.com; r incl breakfast from $350; P @ 🛜 ☒), a collection of brightly whitewashed rooms and apartments situated around a central pool and sundeck.

The Manuel Antonio area has always been proud to host one of the most sophisticated and cosmopolitan restaurant scenes on the central Pacific coast. While there are no exclusively gay restaurants and bars, there are a few with particularly good gay-oriented events. **Restaurante Barba Roja** (Map p228; *J* 2777-0331; meals US$7-20; ⏱4-10pm Mon, 10am-10pm Tue-Sun) is a reliably good restaurant with a good gay scene on Sunday nights and **Liquid** (Map p228; ⏱9pm-3am Tue & Thur-Sun), a nightclub near the bottom of the hill, is a good place for young gay guys to party.

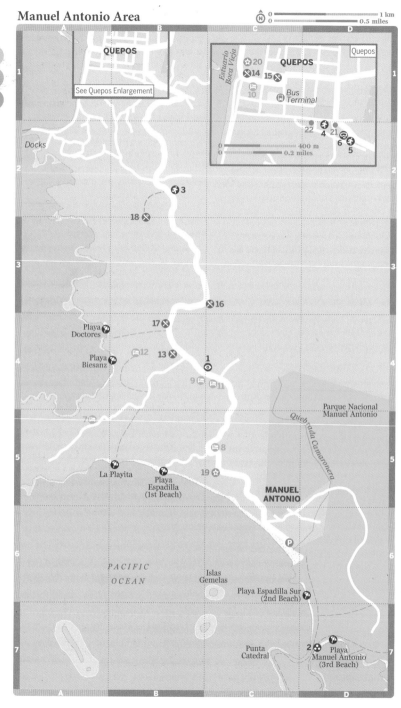

QUEPOS

See Quepos Enlargement

Quepos

Estuario Boca Vieja

QUEPOS

☆ 20
14 ✕ 15 ✕
10

Bus Terminal

22 4 21
6
5

Docks

3
18 ✕

16 ✕

17 Playa Doctores
12 13 ✕ 1
Playa Biesanz
9 11

7

8

La Playita 19 ☆
Playa Espadilla (1st Beach)

MANUEL ANTONIO

Parque Nacional Manuel Antonio

Quebrada Camaronera

P

PACIFIC OCEAN

Islas Gemelas

Playa Espadilla Sur (2nd Beach)

Punta Catedral

2 Playa Manuel Antonio (3rd Beach)

Manuel Antonio Area

◎ Sights
1 Fincas Naturales....................................C4
2 Turtle Trap D7

✈ Activities, Courses & Tours
3 Amigos del Río......................................B2
4 Bluefin Sportfishing............................D2
5 h2o Adventures D2
6 Oceans Unlimited D2
  Serenity Spa................................ (see 9)

⊜ Sleeping
7 Arenas del Mar.....................................A5
8 Hotel Costa Verde C5
9 Hotel Sí Como No B4
10 Hotel Sirena C1
11 Hotel Villa Roca..................................C4
12 Makanda by the Sea...........................B4

✷ Eating
13 Agua Azul B4
14 Café Milagro C1
15 Cevicheria El Dorado.........................C1
16 Kapi Kapi Restaurant C3
17 Restaurante Barba Roja.....................B4
18 Ronny's Place B2

❷ Drinking
  El Avión...................................... (see 11)

✺ Entertainment
19 Liquid Disco Lounge...........................C5
20 Republik Club......................................C1

❶ Transport
21 NatureAir...D2
22 Sansa..D2

◎ Sights & Activities

Hiking & Swimming

After the park entrance, it's about a 30-minute hike to **Playa Espadilla Sur** and **Playa Manuel Antonio**, the park's idyllic beaches, which is where most people spend a good part of their time in the park. There will be numerous guides leading clusters of groups along the flat hike, so if you join a tour, you can get a lesson on the many birds, sloths and monkeys along the way. Eventually the obvious, well-trodden trail veers right and through forest to an isthmus separating Playas Espadilla Sur and Manuel Antonio.

This is also where there's a park ranger station and information center (its hours are random, but we've yet to see it open, so be pleasantly surprised if it is staffed).

Geography fun fact: this isthmus is called a *tombolo* and was formed by the accumulation of sand between the mainland and the peninsula beyond, which was once an island. Along this bridge are the park's two amazing beaches, Playa Manuel Antonio, on the ocean side, and the slightly less-visited (though occasionally rough) Playa Espadilla Sur, which faces Manuel Antonio Village. With their turquoise waters, shaded hideouts and continual aerial show of brown pelicans, these beaches are dreamy.

At its end, the isthmus widens into a rocky peninsula, with a thick forest in the center. Several informal trails lead down the peninsula to near the center of it, the **Punta Catedral**. If you bushwhack your way through, there are good views of the Pacific Ocean and various rocky islets that are bird reserves and form part of the national park. Brown boobies and pelicans nest on these islands.

At the western end of Playa Manuel Antonio you can see a semicircle of rocks at low tide. Archaeologists believe these were arranged by pre-Columbian indigenous people to function as a **turtle trap (Map p228)** (turtles would swim in during high tide, but when they tried to swim out after the tide started receding, they'd be trapped by the wall). The beach itself is an attractive one of white sand and is popular for swimming. It's protected and safer than the Espadilla beaches.

Beyond Playa Manuel Antonio, if visitors return towards the trail from the entrance of the park, the trail divides and leads deeper into the park. The lower trail is steep and slippery during the wet months and leads to the quiet **Playa Puerto Escondido** and the upper trail climbs to a **lookout** on a bluff overlooking Puerto Escondido and Punta Serrucho beyond – a stunning vista.

Wildlife-Watching

Increased tourist traffic has taken its toll on the park's wildlife as animals are frequently driven away or – worse still – taught to scavenge for tourist handouts. To its credit, the park service has reacted by closing the park on Monday and limiting the number of visitors to 600 during the week and 800 on weekends and holidays.

Even though visitors are funneled along the main access road, you should have no problem seeing animals here, even as you line up at the gate. White-faced capuchins are very used to people, and normally troops feed and interact within a short distance of visitors; they can be encountered anywhere along the main access road and around Playa Manuel Antonio. You'll also see coatis, big lizards and lots of hummingbirds.

 Tours

Hiring a guide costs US$25 per person for a two-hour tour. The only guides allowed in the park are members of Aguila (a local association governed by the park service), who have official ID badges, and recognized guides from tour agencies or hotels. This is to prevent visitors from getting ripped off and to ensure a good-quality guide. Aguila guides are well trained and multilingual (French-, German- or English-speaking guides can be requested). Visitors report that hiring a guide virtually guarantees wildlife sightings.

 **Getting There & Away**

The entrance and exit to Parque Nacional Manuel Antonio lies in Manuel Antonio village.

HACIENDA BARÚ NATIONAL WILDLIFE REFUGE

Located on the Pacific coast 3km northeast of Dominical on the road to Quepos, this **wildlife refuge** (☎ 2787-0003; www.haciendabaru.com; admission US$6, each extra day US$2, guided tours US$20 to US$60) forms a key link in a major biological corridor called 'the Path of the Tapir.' It comprises more than 330 hectares of private and state-owned land that has been protected

Parque Nacional Manuel Antonio (p227)

from hunting since 1976. The range of tropical habitats that may be observed here include pristine beaches, riverbanks, mangrove estuaries, wetlands, selectively logged forests, secondary forests, primary forests, tree plantations and pastures.

This diversity of habitat plus its key position in the Path of the Tapir biological corridor accounts for the multitude of species that have been identified in Hacienda Barú. These include 351 birds, 69 mammals, 94 reptiles and amphibians, 87 butterflies and 158 species of trees, some of which are more than 8.5m in circumference. Ecological tourism provides this wildlife refuge with its only source of funds with which to maintain its protected status, so guests are assured that money spent here will be used to further the conservation of tropical rainforest.

There is an impressive number of **guided tours** (US$20-60) on offer. You can experience the rainforest canopy in three different ways – a platform 36m above the forest floor, tree climbing and a zip line called 'the Flight of the Toucan.' In addition to the canopy activities, Hacienda Barú offers bird-watching tours, hiking tours, and two overnight camping tours in both tropical rainforest and lowland beach habitats. Hacienda Barú's naturalist guides come from local communities and have lived near the rainforest all of their lives. Even if you don't stop here for the sights, the on-site store carries an excellent selection of specialist titles for bird-watchers.

For people who prefer to explore the refuge by themselves, there are 7km of well-kept and marked, self-guided trails, a bird-watching tower, 3km of pristine beach, an orchid garden and a butterfly garden.

The **Hacienda Barú Lodge** (d $65-75, extra person $10, child under 10yr free) consists of six clean two-bedroom cabins located 350m from Barú beach. The red-tile–roofed, open-air restaurant serves a variety of tasty Costa Rican dishes (restaurant meals US$6 to US$10).

The Quepos–Dominical–San Isidro de El General bus stops outside the hacienda entrance. The San Isidro de El General–Dominical–Uvita bus will drop you off at the Río Barú bridge, 2km from the hacienda office. A taxi from Dominical costs about US$5.

If you're driving, the El Ceibo gas station, 50m north of the Hacienda Barú Lodge, is the only one for a good distance in any direction. Groceries, fishing gear, tide tables and other useful sundries are available, and there are clean toilets.

DOMINICAL

Dominical hits a real sweet spot with the travelers who wander up and down its rough dirt road with a surfboard under arm, balancing the day's activities between the intense adrenaline rush of riding perfect waves and the lazy swing of a hammock. And although some may decry the large population of expats and gringos who have hunkered down here, proud residents are quick to point out that Dominical recalls the mythical 'old Costa Rica' – the days before the roads were all paved, and when the coast was dotted with lazy little towns that drew a motley crew of surfers, backpackers and affable do-nothings alike. Dominical has no significant cultural sights, no paved roads and no chain restaurants, and if you're not here to learn to surf or swing in a hammock it might not be the place for you.

But the overall picture is a bit more complex, especially since Dominical is starting to stretch its legs, seeking to attract more than the college-aged and shoestringer sets. The completion of the Costanera Sur, which runs right by town, is facilitating the spread of development further south along the coast. This has brought along with it an intense wave of foreign investment. At the time of writing they were building another, taller cell tower that promised – gasp! – reasonable internet connections and there were even rumors that they might pave the road. In the meantime, however, Dominical remains the sort of place where it's best to just slow down, unwind and take things as they come.

Learning to Surf in Dominical

Although Dominical attracts some serious surfers and the waves can be gnarly, the quality of surf instruction here is among the best and most affordable in the country. For beginners who need lots of time and attention, the two most important questions to ask are about the ratio of students to instructors and if rates include board rental. There are scores of shops and instructors who offer services with a wide range of quality; the following are highly recommended.

Costa Rica Surf Camp (☎ 8812-3625, 2787-0393; www.crsurfschool.com; Hotel Diu Wak; individual lessons from $40, all-inclusive packages per week from $1050) This fantastic, locally owned surf school prides itself on a 2:1 student-to-teacher ratio, teachers who have CPR and water-safety training and years of experience. The amiable owner, Cesar Valverde, runs a friendly, warm-hearted program.

Sunset Surf (www.sunsetsurfdominical.com) Operated by Dylan Park, who grew up surfing the waves of Hawaii and Costa Rica, Sunset offers a variety of packages (including one for women only). It has a 3:1 student-to-instructor ratio and Park is an excellent instructor.

The Costanera Sur bypasses the town entirely; the entrance to the village is immediately past the Río Barú bridge. There's a bone-rattling main road through the village, where many of the services are found, and a parallel road along the beach. For the most part, development remains low-key. The few roads around the village are still dusty and potholed, and forests – not fast-food outlets – front the majority of the beach.

 ## Festivals & Events

ENVISION ART, MUSIC & SACRED MOVEMENT FESTIVAL
Art, Music

(www.envisionfestival.com) This new event brings four days of alternative art, music, fire dancing, dreadlocks and DJs to sleepy Dominical in early March. Attendees set up camp in a field behind Bamboo Yoga Play.

 ## Activities

BAMBOO YOGA PLAY
Yoga

(☎ 2787-0229; www.bambooyogaplay.com) The salty old guard might roll their eyes at Bamboo Yoga Play – a studio which offers classes in yoga, dance and 'artful warrior coaching' – but the sessions offer a welcome new (new agey) addition to Dominical's surf-dominated offerings. Sofiah Thom, the primary teacher, leads the classes in honeyed tones and occasionally puts on spectacular fire-dancing shows. It has several tidy accommodations for people interested in yoga-intensive stays.

DOMINICAL SURF ADVENTURES
Rafting, Surfing

(☎ 2787-0431; www.dominicalsurfadventures. com; ☺ 8am-5pm Mon-Sat, 9am-3pm Sun) A bit of an adventurer's one-stop shop: visitors can book white-water trips, kayaking, snorkel and dive trips and surf lessons from this humble little desk on the main drag. Rafting trips start at US$80 (for runs on the Class II and III Guabo) and include a more gnarly run on the Río Coto Brus' Class IV rapids. Thankfully, there's no hustling sales pitch.

 ## Tours

Dominical has emerged as a jumping-off point for trips to Parque Nacional Marino Ballena and, further south, Parque

Nacional Corcovado. Get details at **Southern Expeditions** (☎2787-0100; www. southernexpeditionscr.com) at the entrance to the village. The staff can also organize trips to the Guaymí indigenous reserve near Boruca (inland), and all tours can be individually customized to meet your interests. Dominical Surf Adventures also has a suite of tours. Another excellent day trip is on offer from **Pineapple Kayak Tours** (☎2787-0302; www.pine applekayaktours.com), which runs a thrilling four-hour tour out to the beautiful Ventanas Caves.

Sleeping

In Town

POSADA DEL SOL   Hotel $
(☎2787-0082; d from US$25; P☎) There are only five rooms at this charming, secure, tidy little place, but if you score one, consider yourself lucky (no advance reservations are taken). Posada Del Sol hits the perfect price point and has basic comforts – hammocks outside each room, a sink to rinse out your salty suit and a clothesline to dry it. It's no place to party (it's a short stroll to the beach or to the bars in town) but the warm-hearted, watchful proprietor, Laticia, makes the place so inviting.

HOTEL DIUWAK   Hotel $$
(☎2787-0087; www.diuwak.com; r US$75-120, ste US$140-160; P✳@☎☎) This proper resort complex offers low-key luxury and is easily the most cushy place in town. The grounds surrounding the waterfall-fed pool are palm-fringed, which makes for relaxing days of idle laziness, and there are some great on-site amenities, including a

bar, restaurant, fitness center and health spa. Inquire about the size of the room as some are larger than others, and can easily accommodate you and a few of your friends.

Around Dominical

ALBERGUE ALMA DE HATILLO B&B   B&B $$
(☎8850-9034; www.cabinasalma.com; r US$65; P✳✳@☎☎) One of the most loved B&Bs on the entire Pacific coast, this hidden gem is a quiet base from which to explore the Dominical area, with immaculate cabins spread among several hectares of fruit trees. Guests rave about the organic produce on offer at the restaurant, and daily yoga classes. Alma de Hatillo is located about 6km north of town along the Constanera Sur.

HOTEL VILLAS RÍO MAR   Hotel $$
(☎787 0052; www.villasriomar.com; bungalows US$75-95, ste US$130-140; P✳@☎☎) Just beyond the edge of town, a sign points under the bridge to this property about 800m from the village. Here you'll

Eyelash palm pit viper
DOUGLAS STEAKLEY / GETTY IMAGES ©

Below: Collared aracari toucan;
Right: Parque Nacional Manuel Antonio (p227)

(BELOW) TOM BOYDEN / GETTY IMAGES ©; (RIGHT) CHRISTER FREDRIKSSON / GETTY IMAGES ©

find a few dozen polished-wood bungalows, each with a private hammock-strung terrace, as well as a handful of luxury suites that accommodate small groups. Río Mar also functions as a miniresort, offering a pool, Jacuzzi, tennis court, equipment rental, restaurant and bar.

CASCADAS FARALLAS Lodge **$$$**
(☎2787-8378; www.waterfallvillas.com; ste/villas from US$125/225; P ❄ @ ☰ ≋) Although it's a bit outside Dominical proper, this spiritual retreat is located beside a series of cascading waterfalls. Balinese-style suites and villas are decked out from floor to ceiling with Zen-inducing Asian art, and regular yoga and meditation sessions help guests seek peace and tranquility. To reach the property, take the San Isidro de El General fork (just north of the Dominical turnoff) for 3km, and look out for the Balinese dragon banners marking the entrance.

Eating & Drinking

SODA NANYOA Costa Rican **$**
(mains US$3-7) In a town that caters to gringo appetites with inflated price tags, Nanyoa is a gratifying find: an authentic, moderately priced, better-than-most Costa Rican *soda* (lunch counter). The big pinto breakfasts and fresh-squeezed juice are ideal after a morning session on the waves, and at night it lets patrons bring their own beer from the grocery across the street. All are enjoyed in a pleasant open-air dining area.

CHAPY'S HEALTHY SUBS & WRAPS Deli **$**
(☎2787-0283; meals US$5-10; ⏰9am-3pm Mon-Sat; 🥕 👪) With crunchy wraps and thick, grilled veg sandwiches stacked high on homemade focaccia, Chapy's is a vegetarian's dream come true. As healthy as they are delicious, the sandwiches can be dressed in spicy hummus and homemade

sauces. If you need a lunch to grab and go, this place has the best stuff in town.

CONFUSIONE Tapas $$$
(meals US$11-24; 3-11:30pm) Though the Italian-Latin fusion made this one of Dominical's top dining rooms (it's the only place in town with table linens *and* a full bar), it has recently overhauled the menu with an emphasis on small plates and tapas. You can stick to classics from the peninsula such as penne pasta and flatbread pizzas, stay local with freshly caught seafood and aged tenderloin, or strike a healthy balance – authentic gelato with tropical fruits. Of the small plates, the baby shrimp in brandy and cheese sauce is a rich and decadent delight.

 Getting There & Away

Bus
Buses pick up and drop off passengers along the main road in Dominical.

Quepos US$6, three hours, departs 7:30am, 8am, 10:30am, 1:45pm, 4pm and 5pm.

Uvita US$1.20, one hour, departs 4:30am, 10:30am, noon and 6:15pm.

UVITA
Just 17km south of Dominical, this little hamlet is really nothing more than a loose straggle of farms, houses and tiny shops, though it should give you a good idea of what the central Pacific coast looked like before the tourist boom. Uvita does, however, serve as the base for visits to Parque Nacional Marino Ballena, a pristine marine reserve famous for its migrating pods of humpback whales, in addition to its virtually abandoned wilderness beaches.

 Sights & Activities

Uvita is a perfect base for exploring Costanera Sur, which is home to some truly spectacular beaches that don't see anywhere near the number of tourists that

235

If You Like...
Watering Holes

If you like drinking an ice-cold Imperial during sunset, we think you'll like these watering holes with amazing Pacific views:

1 RONNY'S PLACE

(Map p228; ☑ 2777-5120; mains US$6-14; ☺ noon-10pm) Tucked away off the busy road to Manuel Antonio you'll find Ronny, offering excellent sangria and an insane view: two pristine bays and primitive jungle on all sides.

2 CLARITA'S BEACH HOTEL AND SPORTS BAR AND GRILL

(Map p219; western end of Blvr, Jacó) A mainstay of fishermen, surfers and expat beach bums, this place is excellent for a sundowner or three. It's best on Sunday, when a trio of local musicians sets up in the corner.

3 BACKYARD BAR

(☑ 2643-7011; Playa Hermosa; meals US$5-10; ☺ noon-late; ☎) As the town's de facto nightspot, the Backyard Bar occasionally hosts live music, and heavy pours at happy hour every night of the week. Plus, you're just steps to the beach.

4 HOTEL VILLA CALETAS

(☑ 2637-0505; www.hotelvillacaletas.com; ☎) The romantic, terraced cocktail lounge here is simply gorgeous, as are the expertly mixed drinks.

they should attract. Then again, perhaps this is a good thing as you'll have plenty of space to sprawl out and soak up the sun without having to worry about someone stealing your beach chair.

Sleeping & Eating

The main entrance to Uvita leads inland, east of the highway, where you'll find a number of eating and sleeping options. More guesthouses, *sodas* and local businesses are along the disorderly, bone-jarring dirt roads that surround the edges of the park.

BUNGALOWS BALLENA Bungalow $$
(☑ 2743-8543; www.bungalowsballena.com; apartments/bungalows US$115/230; P ☎ ☒) These fully outfitted apartments and stand-alone bungalows are an excellent midmarket option for families and large groups. All have kitchens, wi-fi and satellite television. The place is outfitted for kids – there's a playground and a big, welcoming pool in the shape of a whale's tail.

🍃 **FLUTTERBY HOUSE** Hostel $
(www.flutterbyhouse.com/; dm/tree house/d US$12/15/from 30; P @ ☎) Is it possible to fall in love at first sight with a hostel? If so, the ramshackle collection of colorful *Swiss Family Robinson*–style tree houses and dorms at Flutterby has us head over heels. Run by a pair of beaming Californian sisters, the hostel is friendly, fun and well situated within a short stroll of Marino Ballena's beaches. They rent boards and bikes, sell beer for a pittance, have a tidy, open-air communal kitchen and employ downright visionary sustainability practices. If it wasn't enough, the optional nightly dinner (with a pull of veggies from the local farmer's market or the onsite edible garden) is delicious. Follow the signs from the main highway; it's near the south entrance gate of the park.

FIVE SENSES Fusion $$
(☑ 8713-8767; meals US$8-20; ☺ Thu-Sun, with seasonal variations) Around the glow of a bonfire and breeze from the west, diners enjoy the newest fine-dining option on this stretch of coast. The menu is international fusion with a strong local bent – chili chicken, artful stir-fries, snapper in garlic sauce – and the vibe is relaxed and romantic.

Getting There & Away

Most buses depart from the two sheltered bus stops on the Costanera in the main village.

San Isidro de El General US$1.25, two hours, departs 6am and 2pm.

San José US$5, five hours, departs 5:15am and 2:15pm.

PARQUE NACIONAL MARINO BALLENA

This stunner of a **marine park (admission $10)** protects coral and rock reefs surrounding Isla Ballena. Despite its small size, the importance of this area cannot be overstated, especially since it protects migrating humpback whales, pods of dolphins and nesting sea turtles, not to mention colonies of seabirds and several terrestrial reptiles.

Although Ballena is essentially off the radar screens of most coastal travelers, this can be an extremely rewarding destination for beach-lovers and wildlife-watchers. The lack of tourist crowds means that you can enjoy a quiet day at the beach in near solitude – something that is not always possible in Costa Rica. And, with a little luck and a bit of patience, you just might catch a glimpse of a humpback breaching or a few dolphins gliding through the surf.

Activities

The beaches at Parque Nacional Marino Ballena are a stunning combination of golden sand and polished rock. All of them are virtually deserted and perfect for peaceful swimming and sunbathing. And the lack of visitors means you'll have a number of quiet opportunities for good bird-watching.

Water Sports

From the ranger station, you can walk out onto Punta Uvita and snorkel (at its best during low tide). Boats from Playa Bahía Uvita to Isla Ballena can be hired for up to US$45 per person for a two-hour snorkeling trip, although you are not allowed to stay overnight on the island.

If you're looking to get under the water, **Mystic Dive Center** (☎ 2788-8636; www.mysticdivecenter.com) is a PADI operation that offers scuba trips in the national park.

There is also some decent surfing near the river mouth at the southern end of Playa Colonia.

Surfing alongside the jungle

MICHAEL HANSON / GETTY IMAGES ©

Movies in the Jungle

Every Friday and Saturday night, a Minnesotan-born expat named Toby invites locals and travelers to watch his favorite flicks, high on the hillside in Escaleras – one of the most magical regular events on the entire Pacific coast. **Cinema Escaleras** (☎2787-8065; www.moviesinthejungle.com) is built on a hilltop with panoramic views of jungle-fronted coastline and features state-of-the-art projection equipment and surround sound. The film selection and programming choices are witty and fun, often including a short film, old news film or silent short before the featured presentation. Films are shown every Friday at 6pm, with a potluck dinner and breathtaking sunset preceding the screening at 5pm. Of course there's popcorn, too – from a 1950s air popper. To get to the cinema, follow the first entrance to Escaleras a few hundred meters up the mountain and look for a white house on the left-hand side (this is only advisable with a four-wheel drive). Note that a small donation is requested to pay for the projector bulbs. The films shown on Friday are in English; every other Saturday there are selected showings in Spanish.

Wildlife-Watching

Although the park gets few human visitors, the beaches are frequently visited by a number of different animal species, including nesting seabirds, bottle-nosed dolphins and a variety of lizards. And from May to November, with a peak in September and October, both olive ridley and hawksbill turtles bury their eggs in the sand nightly. However, the star attraction are the pods of humpback whales that pass through the national park from August to October and December to April.

Scientists are unsure as to why humpback whales migrate here, though it's possible that Costa Rican waters may be one of only a few places in the world where humpback whales mate. There are actually two different groups of humpbacks that pass through the park – whales seen in the fall migrate from California waters, while those seen in the spring originate from Antarctica.

ⓘ Getting There & Away

Parque Nacional Marino Ballena is best accessed from Uvita or Ojochal, either by private vehicle or a quick taxi ride; inquire at your accommodations for the latter.

OJOCHAL AREA

Beyond Uvita, the Costanera Sur follows the coast as far as Palmar, approximately 40km away. This route provides a coastal alternative to the Interamericana, as well as convenient access to points in the Península de Osa. En route, about 15km south of Uvita, you'll pass the tiny town of Ojochal, which is on the inland side of the highway.

Ojochal also serves as a convenient base for exploring nearby Parque Nacional Marino Ballena, and there are plenty of accommodations here to choose from. Unlike slowly growing places like Uvita or Dominical, Ojochal's tourism infrastructure has sprung up rapidly (even though the industry here is still small, there are loads of vacation rentals, menus in English and sundry gringo comforts), which is both a blessing and a curse.

Just north of Ojochal, about 14km south of Uvita, is the wilderness beach of Playa Tortuga, which is largely undiscovered and virtually undeveloped, but it's home to some occasional bouts of decent surf.

 # Sleeping

LOOKOUT AT PLAYA
TORTUGA
Boutique Hotel $$

(☎2786-5074; www.hotelcostarica.com; d US$78-99; P✳@☎❄) A signed turnoff on the eastern side of the road just after Km 175 leads to this beautiful hilltop sanctuary, where you'll find a dozen brightly painted rooms awash in calming pastels. The grounds are traversed by a series of paths overlooking the beaches below, but the highlight is the large deck in a tower above the pool. Here you can pursue some early morning bird-watching, or perhaps better yet, indulge in some late-afternoon slothful lounging.

HOTEL VILLAS GAIA
Cabina $$

(☎8382-8240; www.villasgaia.com; r from US$80; P@☎❄) Along the beach side of the road is this beautifully kept collection of shiny wooden cabins with shaded porches, set in tranquil forested grounds. There is also an excellent restaurant serving a wide variety of international standards, as well as a hilltop pool (excellent for kids) where you can swim a few laps while enjoying the panoramic view of Playa Tortuga. The beach itself is a pleasant 20-minute hike along a dirt path that winds down the hillside.

FINCA BAVARIA
Boutique Hotel $$

(☎8355-4465; www.finca-bavaria.de; s/d from US$64/74; P☎❄) This quaint German-run inn comprises a handful of pleasing rooms – some in their own stand-alone cottages – with wood accents, bamboo furniture and romantic mosquito net–draped beds. The lush grounds are lined with walkways and hemmed by forest, though take in sweeping views of the ocean from the hilltop pool. And of course, there's plenty of great German beer served by the stein. Look for the signed dirt road on the inland side of the road just beyond La Cusinga.

LA CUSINGA
Ecolodge $$$

(☎2770-2549; www.lacusingalodge.com; Finca Tres Hermanas; s/d US$124/156; P) About 5km south of Uvita, this beachside ecolodge is powered by the hydroelectric energy provided by a small stream, and centered on a working organic farm. It's a relaxing place to unplug – in place of televisions there are yoga classes. Accommodations are in natural-style wooden and stone rooms with terra-cotta tile floors and crisp white linens. Its location is excellent, with access to hiking, bird-watching, snorkeling and swimming in the national park.

 # Eating

CITRUS
International $$$

(☎2786-5175; meals US$10-30; ⊙11am-10pm Tue-Sat) With its fresh, bright, Moroccan-inspired flavors, Citrus is a standout, even among the excellent choices within strolling distance. Offering New World dishes that are heavily influenced by Southeast Asian and north African culinary traditions (fish with ginger and green onions, a spicy lamb burger, plus a killer flourless French chocolate cake), and benefiting from its candlelit riverside location, Citrus welcomes patrons with flair and bravado.

RESTAURANTE
EXÓTICA
International $$$

(☎2786-5050; dishes US$10-30; ⊙3-9pm Mon-Sat) While rural Ojochal isn't exactly a hot spot of cosmopolitan urbanity, this phenomenal gourmet restaurant certainly sets a high benchmark. The nouveau French dishes each emphasize a breadth of ingredients brought together in masterful combinations. With more than a decade in the business, yet only nine tables for diners to choose from, this is an intimate culinary experience that is certainly worth seeking out.

❶ Getting There & Away

Daily buses between Dominical and Palmar can drop you off near any of the places described here. However, given the infrequency of transportation links along this stretch of highway, it's recommended that you explore the area by private car.

Southern Costa Rica

Southern Costa Rica is wild, vast and largely unexplored.
It is cut through the middle by the jagged range of the Cordillera de Talamanca and buttressed by agricultural lowlands that produce edible exports. If you're over Costa Rica's well-oiled tourism machine or burned out by beaches, this region is rugged, undeveloped and frosted by high-altitude chill.

For thrill-seekers, southern Costa Rica packs a punch with the country's highest peak, Cerro Chirripó (3820m), and Central America's wildest swath of protected land, the incomprehensibly vast Parque Internacional La Amistad. And while Monteverde has the country's most iconic cloud forest, southern Costa Rica offers equally mystical environments, including the heavenly Cloudbridge Nature Preserve.

In a country where only distant echoes of pre-Columbian influence remain, this area is home to Costa Rica's visible indigenous presence. Large populations of Bribrí, Cabécar and Brunka live high in the mountains, clinging to traditions amid the changing tides of modernity.

Footbridge, Parque Nacional Chirripó (p271)
HANS ZAGLITSCH / IMAGEBROKER ©

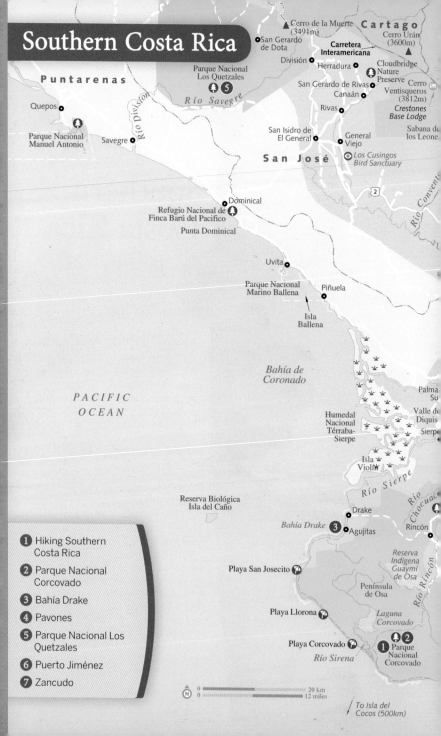

Southern Costa Rica

Puntarenas

Quepos

Parque Nacional
Manuel Antonio

Savegre

Río Division

Río Savegre

San Gerardo
de Dota

Parque Nacional
Los Quetzales **5**

Cerro de la Muerte
(3491m)

Cartago

Cerro Urán
(3600m)

**Carretera
Interamericana**

División

Herradura

Cloudbridge
Nature
Preserve

San Gerardo de Rivas

Canaán

Cerro
Ventisqueros
(3812m)

Rivas

*Crestones
Base Lodge*

San Isidro de
El General

General
Viejo

Sabana de
los Leone

San José

Los Cusingos
Bird Sanctuary

Río Convent

Dominical

Refugio Nacional de
Finca Barú del Pacifico

Punta Dominical

Uvita

Parque Nacional
Marino Ballena

Piñuela

Isla
Ballena

*Bahía de
Coronado*

PACIFIC
OCEAN

Palma
Su

Valle de
Diquis

Humedal
Nacional
Térraba-
Sierpe

Sierpe

Isla
Violín

Río Sierpe

*Río
Chocuac*

Reserva Biológica
Isla del Caño

Drake

Bahía Drake **3**

Agujitas

Rincón

Playa San Josecito **7**

*Reserva
Indígena
Guaymí
de Osa*

Península
de Osa

Río Rincón

Playa Llorona **7**

*Laguna
Corcovado*

Playa Corcovado **7**

Río Sirena

1 **2**
Parque
Nacional
Corcovado

Legend

1 Hiking Southern
Costa Rica

2 Parque Nacional
Corcovado

3 Bahía Drake

4 Pavones

5 Parque Nacional Los
Quetzales

6 Puerto Jiménez

7 Zancudo

0 — 20 km
0 — 12 miles

To Isla del
Cocos (500km)

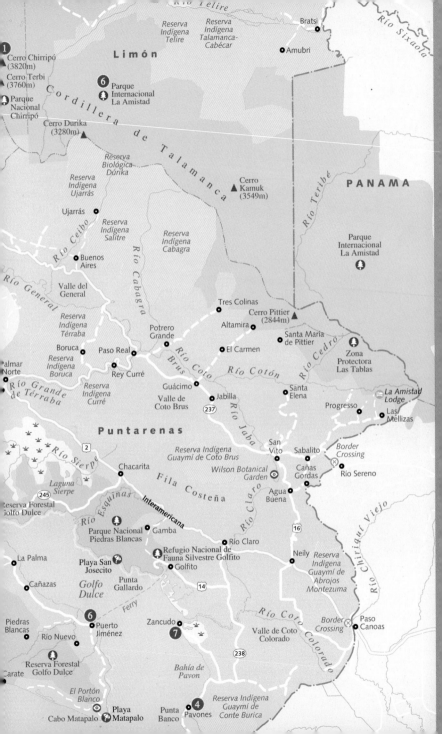

Southern Costa Rica Highlights

① Hiking Southern Costa Rica

Waking up atop Cerro Chirripó (p272) or in the rainforests of Corcovado (p263) allows you to journey beneath the first rays of the sun while the morning dew still clings to the vegetation. Trekking along remote trails through the wilds is an experience loaded with adventure and intensity.

Above and below right: Parque Nacional Chirripó; Above right: Crossing a river in Parque Nacional Corcovado

Need to Know

ADVANCE BOOKINGS Book ahead for dorm-style lodging in parks **HIKING TIP** Hiring a guide usually ensures seeing more many more animals **For further coverage, see p266**

Local Knowledge

Hiking Southern Costa Rica Don't Miss List

BY WALTER ODIO VICTORY, OWNER OF COSTA RICA TREKKING

1 PARQUE NACIONAL CHIRRIPÓ

Scaling Costa Rica's highest peak isn't a walk in the park. A minimum of two days is needed to climb from the ranger station in San Gerardo de Rivas to the summit and back. You'll get a few blisters and bruises, but the memories will last long after they heal.

2 BACKCOUNTRY CHIRRIPÓ

Hard-core adventurers should take an alternative route: the three-or four-day loop starting in Herradura with a day or two traversing cloud forest and *páramo* (highland habitat) on the slopes of Fila Urán. Hikers ascend Cerro Urán (3600m) before finally ascending Chirripó and descending through San Gerardo de Rivas.

3 SIRENA TO LA LEONA

In Parque Nacional Corcovado, the 16km hike from Sirena to La Leona follows the shoreline along deserted beaches, taking six or seven hours. You can camp at La Leona or hike the additional 3.5km to Carate, where you can stay in a lodge or catch a *colectivo* (shared taxi) to Puerto Jiménez.

4 SIRENA TO SAN PEDRILLO

At 23km, this is the longest trail in Corcovado, and not for the faint of heart. The majority is along the beach in loose sand and little shade – grueling, especially with a heavy pack. It's only open from December to April, since heavy rains can make the Río Sirena impassable.

5 SIRENA TO LOS PATOS

The expert-only route to Los Patos goes 18km through the heart of Corcovado, passing plenty of primary and secondary forest. The trail is relatively flat for the first 12km, but you must wade through two river tributaries before reaching the Laguna Corcovado. From there, the route undulates steeply, mostly uphill.

Parque Nacional Corcovado

Although Costa Rica is dotted with patches of rainforest, none are as exciting as Parque Nacional Corcovado, huge and wild, inviting rugged adventure. Trekking muddy trails through the wet, wild, fascinating park offers a view of the jungle filled with mind-blowing flora, exotic animals and empty beaches. Below: Banyan trees; Above right: Green iguana; Below right: Isla del Caño (p255)

Need to Know

GEAR Pick up thick-soled rubber boots from stores in Bahía Drake and Puerto Jiménez **ONLINE RESOURCE** www.corcovadoguide.com For further coverage, see p263

Around Parque Nacional Corcovado Don't Miss List

BY DIONISIO 'NITO' PANIAGUA, PARQUE NACIONAL CORCOVADO GUIDE

1 THREE-DAY TREK CORCOVADO

You have to spend one night at the Sirena ranger station. This is the best way to spot wildlife such as tapirs, wild pigs, bull sharks and crocodiles, among others, and also provides a good chance for catching a glimpse of pumas or ocelots. The ranger station is not a lodge but not as basic as travelers sometimes expect.

2 MATAPALO

Perfect place for a combination of beach, rainforest and waterfall. Here you can spot all four types of monkeys, sloths, coatis, agoutis, scarlet macaws and blue morpho butterflies. Matapalo is also good for seeing the poisonous dart frogs and giant trees of the rainforest. It is perfect for families and travelers who are short on time.

3 ISLA DEL CAÑO

There is access from Bahía Drake and the possibility of snorkeling and scuba diving. The visibility under water is great and lots of colorful fish can be spotted. It's a perfect day tour with the option to hike in the rainforest and spend some time on the beach.

4 KAYAKING IN THE GOLFO DULCE

On a marvelous three-hour kayaking trip in the mangroves around Puerto Jiménez you'll spot boas, white-faced capuchin monkeys, water birds and giant crabs. The return to Jiménez is along the Golfo Dulce and with some luck dolphins will accompany the kayaks.

Hiking Beyond Bahía Drake

Put your boots on and hoof it from Bahía Drake (p254) along the coast to Corcovado. You will find the country's wildest beaches, trails, lodges and campsites tucked away among thickly forested rocky points. It's a spectacular riot of wildlife as there are more monkeys, dolphins and waterfalls than people. Río Sierpe entering Bahía Drake

3

4

Pavones

You'll need to sacrifice a good chunk of your schedule to access this far-flung beach (p266). But it's worth the time and effort, especially if you take a crack at what is reportedly the longest left-hand surf break in the world. Even if you're not a hard-core surfer, this comparatively undeveloped corner makes for a quiet getaway.

Puerto Jiménez

5

The closest town of any real size to Parque Nacional Corcovado, 'Port Jim' (p258) is a great place to stock up on supplies and organize logistics before embarking on a trekking expedition. The town itself is loaded with character, with frequent wildlife encounters in proximity to diverse accommodations and eating options. Beachfront at Puerto Jiménez

NEIL MCALLISTER / ALAMY ©

SHANNON NACE / GETTY IMAGES ©

Parque Nacional Los Quetzales

6

Spread along both banks of the Río Savegre and one of Costa Rica's newest national parks (p274), this is the perfect spot to scan the trees for the brightly colored quetzal in a park of the same name. The mountain setting offers fresh air, cozy lodge stays and fresh trout from the rushing rivers near San Gerardo de Dota. Waterfall, Río Savegre

Zancudo

7

A low-key beach town (p266) that caters to do-it-yourself travelers, this is the blissfully lazy sort of place where you can explore things independently and at your own pace. Pacific waters gently lap the long sandy beaches, while nearby mangrove swamps have more intimidating adventures, offering close encounters with crocs and caimans. American crocodiles

Southern Costa Rica's Best...

Wildlife

∘ **Dolphins and whales** (p255) The waters of Bahía Drake are incredibly rich in marine life.

∘ **Tapirs** (p263) The largest land mammal in Costa Rica is found throughout Parque Nacional Corcovado.

∘ **Sloths and crocs** (p266) The mangrove swamps near Zancudo harbor all manner of creatures.

∘ **Macaws** (p263) Although macaws are common throughout Corcovado, you can also spot them hanging around town in Puerto Jiménez.

Splurges

∘ **Drake Bay Rainforest Chalet** (p255) A getaway in the middle of pristine rainforest.

∘ **Casa Botania** (p279) Intimate accommodations and exquisite meals.

∘ **Monte Azul: Boutique Hotel + Center for Art & Design** (p271) This luxury getaway is a masterful marriage of artistic and natural wonders.

∘ **Lookout Inn** (p263) Stay in a 'tiki hut,' a stunning A-frame jungle hideaway.

∘ **Dantica Lodge & Gallery** (p274) Elegant stone cabins high in the mountains.

Secret Spots

∘ **Reserva Indígena Boruca** (p275) Visitors are welcomed to this reserve to watch the unique festivals.

∘ **Parque Nacional Isla del Cocos** (p268) This island chain in the Pacific is a true Lost World.

∘ **Wilson Botanical Garden** (p278) This out-of-the-way mountain reserve is excellent for spotting a huge variety of birds.

∘ **Cloudbridge Nature Preserve** (p275) Scenic and quiet, most people skip the extensive network of trails here while rushing up Cerro Chirripó.

Ecohotels

○ **Lapa Ríos** (p262) A living classroom where sustainability meets ecoluxury.

○ **La Leona Eco-Lodge** (p262) A rustic beach chalet on the border of Parque Nacional Corcovado.

○ **Casa Mariposa** (p271) This homey, stone-built mountain hostel has a high standard of environmental stewardship.

○ **Las Caletas Lodge** (p258) Run by a Tico couple who are passionate about protecting the environment.

Need to Know

ADVANCE PLANNING

○ **Reservations** It's best to plan in advance if you want to sleep in Bahía Drake, trek across Parque Nacional Corcovado, explore Parque Internacional La Amistad or make the ascent of Cerro Chirripó.

○ **Gear** Last-minute supplies are available in Puerto Jiménez, but highly personalized items such as hiking boots are best brought from home.

RESOURCES

○ **Corcovado Guide** (www.corcovadoguide.com)

GETTING AROUND

○ **Air** Small planes and charters to Puerto Jiménez can save you lots of time-consuming overland travel.

○ **Car** Brave souls who want to take on an exploration of Osa with their own four wheels will absolutely need a 4WD vehicle. The roads here are extremely rough, even in the dry season.

○ **Boat** Lodges in Bahía Drake are accessed by boat from Sierpe.

○ **Bus** Large cities in southern Costa Rica are surprisingly well-served by public buses.

○ **Walk** Bring your hiking boots as the region is best explored on foot.

BE FOREWARNED

○ **Climate** Bring adequate clothing to climb Cerro Chirripó – it's cold and wet at high altitudes.

○ **Accommodation** The lodges around Bahía Drake are largely all-inclusive, due to the difficulty of getting supplies into the area by boat. For a more DIY experience, approach Corcovado from the Puerto Jiménez side.

VITAL STATISTICS

○ **Population** San Isidro de El General 45,000

○ **Best time to visit** During the rainy season (from mid-April through mid-December) the amount of precipitation is astounding. Even in the dry season (mid-December through mid-April) you can expect the occasional downfall.

EMERGENCY NUMBERS

○ **Emergency** ☏911

○ **Fire** ☏118

○ **Police** ☏117

Left: Two-toed sloth; **Above:** Bahiá Drake (p254)

Southern Costa Rica Itineraries

Much of southern Costa Rica is rough and rugged, and travel in the region is a slow-going, if thrilling adventure through mountains and jungles.

3 DAYS

SIERPE TO PARQUE NACIONAL CORCOVADO
Bahía Drake & Around

Southern Costa Rica is far from the main tourist circuit, but it is possible to dip in and out within a few days if you plan carefully. If this sounds like your cup of shade-grown coffee, focus on getting to one of the resorts lining Bahiá Drake. For the most part, accommodations options in this part of the country are fairly expensive, but bedding down in eco-paradise is worth the splurge.

First get to **(1) Sierpe** (those on a tight time schedule should fly here from San José). A boat will take you on a scenic ride through the sparkling-clear waters of **(2) Bahía Drake**. On the ride, you may even be chased by schools of dolphins. Upon arriving at your destination, expect to spend your entire stay swimming, hiking, boating and searching for all manner of wildlife. If you want to head a bit further down the coast, there are other excellent options spanning the stretch from **(3) Bahía Drake to Parque Nacional Corcovado**. This hike is tough (and the trail is closed and overgrown in the rainy season) but even venturing part of the way will reveal empty beaches and an amazing tropical shoreline.

Top Left: Park Nacional Corcovado (p263); **Top Right:** Cerro Chirippó (p271)

(TOP LEFT) BELE OLMEZ / IMAGEBROKER ©; (TOP RIGHT) CHRISTIAN KOBER / ALAMY ©

4
DAYS

SAN ISIDRO DE EL GENERAL TO PARQUE NACIONAL CHIRRIPÓ

Climbing Chirripó

One of the quintessential Costa Rican experiences is an ascent of Cerro Chirripó, the country's highest peak. From these lofty heights, you can enjoy panoramic views of both the Caribbean Sea and the Pacific Ocean – assuming, of course, that the weather holds. On that note, bring extra clothing as the weather up here is cold and wet, but the unpleasant climate is part of the exciting challenge.

(1) San Isidro de El General, the largest city in the southern zone, is the jumping-off point for this high-altitude adventure. The town is blissfully untouristed and its bars make for a fun night out. In the morning it's a quick skip and a jump (and a bus ride) away to the tiny town of **(2) San Gerardo de Rivas**, where you can finalize your reservations for the mountaintop hostel, carbo-load on *gallo pinto* (blended rice and beans) and get a good night's rest. Finally, start the ascent in the **(3) Parque Nacional Chirripó**. This hike to Costa Rica's highest point is a thrilling adventure.

Discover
Southern Costa Rica

At a Glance

- **Bahía Drake** Home to secluded, all-inclusive jungle lodges.

- **Puerto Jiménez** (p258) The main access point for the untouched rainforests of Parque Nacional Corcovado.

- **San Isidro de El General** (p269) The work-a-day hub of the region, between mountains and sea.

- **Cerro Chirripó** (p271) Costa Rica's highest mountain, excellent for hiking.

BAHÍA DRAKE

As one of Costa Rica's most isolated destinations, Bahía Drake is filled with tropical landscapes and abundant wildlife. In the rainforest canopy, howlers greet the rising sun with their haunting bellows, while pairs of macaws soar between the treetops, filling the air with their cacophonous squawking. Offshore in the bay itself, pods of migrating dolphins flit through turquoise waters. Bahía Drake is home to a number of stunning wilderness lodges, which all serve as ideal bases for exploring this veritable ecological gem.

 Activities

Swimming & Snorkeling

About 20km west of Agujitas, Isla del Caño is considered the best place for snorkeling in this area. Lodges offer day trips to the island (US$80 to US$100 per person), usually including the park fee, snorkeling equipment and lunch. The clarity of the water and the variety of the fish fluctuate according to water and weather conditions: it's worth inquiring before dishing out the cash for a tour.

There are other opportunities for snorkeling on the coast between Agujitas and Corcovado. **Playa San Josecito** (Map p256) attracts scores of colorful species, which hide out among the coral reef and rocks. Another recommended spot is **Playa Las Caletas** (Map p256), just in front of the Corcovado Adventures Tent Camp, and **Playa Cocalito** (p257), a small, pretty beach near Agujitas.

Puma
TOM BOYDEN / GETTY IMAGES ©

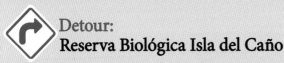

Detour:
Reserva Biológica Isla del Caño

Reserva Biológica Isla del Caño is a 326-hectare island that is among Bahía Drake's most popular destinations, not only for fish and marine mammals, but also for snorkelers, divers and biologists. It's the tip of numerous underwater rock formations, which is evident from the rocky cliffs along the coastline, some towering 70m over the ocean. This is not your stereotypical tropical island: the few white-sand beaches are small to start with, and they disappear to nothing when the tide comes in.

The submarine rock formations are among the island's main attractions, drawing divers to explore the underwater architecture. Snorkelers can investigate the coral and rock formations along the beach, right in front of the ranger station. The water is much clearer here than along the mainland coast, though rough seas can cloud visibility. Fifteen different species of coral have been recorded, as well as threatened animal species such as the Panulirus lobster and the giant conch. The sheer numbers of fish attract dolphins and whales, frequently spotted swimming in outer waters. Hammerhead sharks, manta rays and sea turtles also inhabit this area.

Hiking

All of the lodges offer tours to Parque Nacional Corcovado, usually a full-day trip to San Pedrillo ranger station (from US$85 to US$150 per person), including boat transportation, lunch and guided hikes.

The easiest and most obvious one is the long coastal trail that heads south out of Agujitas and continues about 10km to the border of the national park. Indeed, a determined hiker could make it all the way to San Pedrillo ranger station on foot but at the time of writing, rangers were strongly discouraging this route as it was overgrown.

Kayaking & Canoeing

The idyllic Río Agujitas attracts a huge variety of birdlife and lots of scaly reptiles. The river conveniently empties out into the bay, which is surrounded by hidden coves and sandy beaches ideal for exploring in a sea kayak. Most accommodations in the area have kayaks and canoes for rent for a small fee.

Dolphin- & Whale-Watching

Bahía Drake is rife with marine life, including more than 25 species of dolphin and whale that pass through on their migrations throughout the year. This area is uniquely suited for whale-watching: humpback whales come from both the northern and the southern hemispheres to calve, resulting in the longest humpback whale season in the world. Humpbacks can be spotted in Bahía Drake year-round (except May), but the best months to see whales are late July through early November.

Sleeping & Eating

This area is off the grid, so many places do not have electricity. Reservations are recommended in the dry season (mid-December to mid-April).

DRAKE BAY RAINFOREST CHALET Cabina $$$
(Map p256; ☎ 8382-1619; www.drakebayholiday. com; 3-/4-/5-/6-/7-day package per person from US$1150/1275/1400/1525/1650) Set on 18 hectares of pristine rainforest, this jungle getaway is a remote, romantic adventure. Huge French windows provide a panoramic view of the surrounding jungle, enjoyed from almost every room in the house.

255

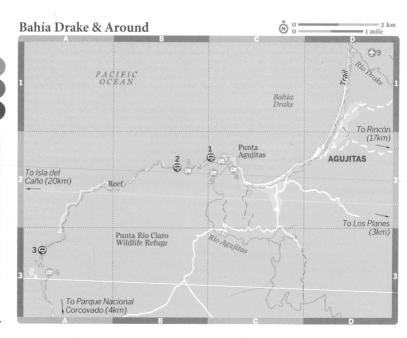

Bahía Drake & Around

⊕ Activities, Courses & Tours
1 Playa Cocalito	C2
2 Playa Las Caletas	B2
3 Playa San Josecito	A3

⊜ Sleeping
4 Aguila de Osa Inn	C2
5 Drake Bay Rainforest Chalet	C2
6 Guaria de Osa	A3
7 La Paloma Lodge	C2
8 Las Caletas Lodge	B2

ⓘ Transport
9 Drake Airstrip	D1

In an innovative twist on luxury, the Moroccan-themed kitchen is fully stocked for self-catering, though chef service is available for the culinarily impaired.

AGUILA DE OSA INN   Lodge $$$
(Map p256; ☎2296-2190; www.aguiladeosa.com; s/d 2-night package US$623/1048) On the east side of the Río Agujitas, this swanky lodge consists of roomy quarters with shining wood floors, cathedral ceilings and private decks overlooking the ocean. The vast centerpiece of the lodge, however, is the comfortable yet elegant open-air *rancho* (small houselike building), which serves signature cocktails and innovative snacks. Diving and sportfishing charters are available.

LA PALOMA LODGE   Lodge $$$
(Map p256; ☎2239-7502; www.lapalomalodge. com; 3-/4-/5-day package per person from US$1100/1245/1390; ☒) Perched on a lush hillside, this exquisite lodge provides guests with an incredible panorama of ocean and forest, all from the comfort of the sumptuous, stylish quarters. Rooms have shiny hardwood floors and queen-sized orthopedic beds, draped in mosquito netting, while shoulder-high walls in all the bathrooms offer rainforest views while you bathe.

ⓘ Getting There & Away

Air

Departing from San José, **NatureAir** (www. natureair.com) and **Sansa** (www.sansa.com) have daily flights to the **Drake airstrip** (Map p256), which is 2km north of Agujitas. Prices vary according to season, though you can expect to pay around US$130 to/from San José.

Alfa Romeo Aero Taxi (2735-5353; www.alfaromeoair.com) charters flights connecting Drake to Puerto Jiménez, Golfito, Carate and Sirena. One-way fares are typically less than US$100.

Most lodges provide transportation to/from the airport, which involves a jeep or a boat or both.

Boat

Unless you charter a flight, you'll arrive here by an exhilarating boat ride through mangrove channels and the ocean. It's one of the true thrills of visiting the area. All of the hotels offer boat transfers between Sierpe and Bahía Drake with prior arrangements. Most hotels in Drake have beach landings, so wear appropriate footwear.

BAHÍA DRAKE TO PARQUE NACIONAL CORCOVADO

This craggy stretch of coastline is home to sandy inlets that disappear at high tide, leaving only the rocky outposts and luxuriant rainforest. Virtually uninhabited and undeveloped beyond a few tourist lodges, the setting here is magnificent and wild. If you're looking to spend a bit more time along the shores of Bahía Drake before penetrating the depths of Parque Nacional Corcovado, consider a night or two in some of the country's most remote accommodations.

◉ Sights & Activities

A public trail follows the coastline for the entire spectacular stretch, and it's excellent for spotting wonderful wildlife. Among the multitude of animals you're likely to spot (and hear) are squawking scarlet macaws, hooting toucan and howler monkeys.

Scenic little inlets punctuate this entire route, each with a wild, windswept beach. Just west of Punta Agujitas, a short detour off the main trail leads to the picturesque **Playa Cocalito** (Map p256), a secluded cove perfect for sunning, swimming and body surfing. Further south, hikers will encounter the Río Claro as it empties out into the ocean, the 400-hectare Punta Río Claro Wildlife Refuge (formerly known as the Marenco Rainforest Reserve) and a

Diving off Isla del Caño (p255)

JOHNNY HAGLUND / GETTY IMAGES ©

number of waterfalls and empty beaches. Eventually, if the conditions are right and you have enough determination, you might even reach the border of Parque Nacional Corcovado, though this takes about four hours and is not for the faint at heart.

Sleeping

LAS CALETAS LODGE Lodge $$$
(Map p256; ☎ 8381-4052, 8326-1460; www.caletas.cr; r per person from US$70; @ 🛜)
This adorable little hotel is set on the picturesque beach of the same name and consists of five cozy wooden cabins that are awash with sweeping views. The Swiss-Tico owners are warm hosts who are passionate about environmental sustainability, and provide solar and hydroelectric power around the clock.

GUARIA DE OSA Lodge $$$
(Map p256; ☎ 2235-4313, in USA 510-235-4313; www.guariadeosa.com; per person US$100)
Cultivating a new-age ambience, this Asian-style retreat center offers yoga, tai chi and more typical rainforest activities. The lovely grounds include an ethnobotanical garden, which features exotic local species used for medicinal and other purposes. The architectural centerpiece is the Lapa Lapa Lounge, a spacious multistory pagoda, built entirely from reclaimed hardwood.

🛈 Getting There & Away

Boat

All of the hotels offer boat transfers between Sierpe and Bahía Drake with prior arrangements. If you haven't made advance arrangements with your lodge for a pickup, grab a private water taxi in Sierpe for a negotiable price.

SIERPE

This sleepy village on the Río Sierpe is the gateway to Bahía Drake, and if you've made a reservation with any of the jungle lodges further down the coast, you will be picked up here by boat.

🛈 Getting There & Away

Air

Scheduled flights and charters fly into Palmar Sur, 14km north of Sierpe.

Boat

If you are heading to Bahía Drake, your lodge will make arrangements for the boat transfer. If for some reason things go awry, there is no shortage of water taxis milling about, though you will have to negotiate to get a fair price.

PUERTO JIMÉNEZ

Full of ramshackle charms – a small airstrip, a fishing harbor, a few good *sodas* (cheap lunch counters) and a soccer field – Puerto Jiménez' dusty streets have a jungle frontier vibe. It's not unusual to spot scarlet macaws roosting on the soccer field, or white-faced capuchins swinging in the treetops adjacent to the main street.

It's not hard to understand why Puerto Jiménez is brimming with wildlife, mainly because the town lies on the edge of Parque Nacional Corcovado. As the preferred jumping-off point for travelers heading to the famed Sirena ranger station, the town is a great place to organize an expedition, stock up on supplies, eat a hot meal and get a good night's rest before hitting the trails.

Tours

OSA WILD Ecotour
(Map p259; www.osawildtravel.com; Rte 245, downtown Puerto Jimenez; ecotours day tours from US$17) Although it's a relatively young outfit, it's just what the area so desperately needed: a resource for travelers to connect with community-oriented initiatives that go to the heart of the real Osa through homestays, farm tours and sustainable local cultural exchanges. Of course it also offers the more typical stuff like kayaking tours and guided trips through Corcovado, but its focus on sustainability, environmental protection

Puerto Jiménez

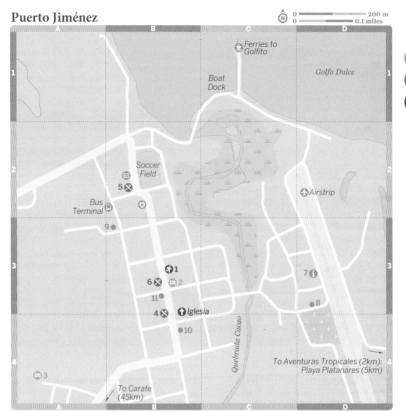

and community development leave it in a league of its own.

SURCOS TOURS Tour
(www.surcostours.com) A trio of excellent guides make Surcos the best company for tours into Osa that focus on wildlife and bird-watching. Arrangements for tours are made through its website.

AVENTURAS TROPICALES Adventure Tour
(2735-5195; www.aventurastropicales.com) A Tico-run operation that offers all sorts of tropical adventures. It's southeast of the center, on the way to Playa Platanares. Some of its most popular excursions include snorkeling and kayaking tours of the mangroves, which start at about $60 per person for half a day.

Puerto Jiménez

Activities, Courses & Tours
1 Osa Wild B3

Sleeping
2 Cabinas Marcelina..............................B3
3 Cacao Monkeys A4

Eating
4 Jade Luna..B3
5 Pizzamail.it...B2
6 Soda Veleria..B3

Information
7 Oficina de Área de
   Conservación Osa D3

Transport
8 Alfa Romeo Aero Taxi..........................D3
9 Colectivo Transportation...................B3
10 NatureAir..B4
11 Sansa...B3

 Sleeping & Eating

CACAO MONKEYS
Cabina $$

(Map p259; ☎2735-5248; www.cacaomonkeys.com; d incl breakfast US$60; **P** 🛜) On the fringes of downtown on a chocolate farm, this new joint has a set of five brightly painted wooden *cabinas* (cabins), each of a unique design, and an excellent riverside café (meals US$8). It's a good option for families as it is a bit out of the noise of town and there's loads of wildlife right out the door.

BLACK TURTLE LODGE
Cabina $$$

(☎2735-5005; www.blackturtlelodge.com; s/d from US$85/140; **P**) A peaceful yoga retreat along Playa Platanares, this ecolodge offers the choice of two-story cabinas, which have magnificent views over the treetops to the Golfo Dulce, and the less-spacious *cabinettas* (small cabins) nestled into the tropical garden below. All have bamboo furniture and hardwood floors, but the *cabinettas* share hot-water bathrooms.

CABINAS MARCELINA
Hotel $$

(Map p259; ☎2755-5286; Rte 245, Puerto Jimenez; d with/without air-con US$50/45; **P** ❄) Marcelina's place is a long-standing favorite among budget travelers looking for a peaceful night of sleep. The concrete building is painted salmon pink and is surrounded by blooming trees, lending it a homey atmosphere that invites good dreams. It's near the Catholic church in downtown Puerto Jiménez.

SODA VELERIA
Soda $

(Map p259; Rte 245, Puerto Jiménez; mains US$3-8) Clean, cute and smack-dab in the middle of town, this *soda* is a dream – the kind of place you know is good because the local government workers all pile in at lunch. The heaping *casados* (cheap set meals) change daily and are delivered with homemade tortillas and sided with fresh fruit.

PIZZAMAIL.IT
Pizzeria $$

(Map p259; pizzas US$9-18; ⏲4-10:30pm; 🛜) This place turns out thin-crust, wood-fired pieces of Italy in the middle of the

Left: Playa Las Caletas (p254); **Below:** Brown-throated sloth
(LEFT)TRAVELIB PRIME / ALAMY ©; (BELOW) ALFREDO MAIQUEZ / GETTY IMAGES ©

jungle. From its small patio diners can watch squawking macaws in the trees over the soccer pitch. *Bellissimo!*

JADE LUNA   Ice Cream **$**
(Map p259; ⏱10am-5pm) With boutiquey, inventive flavors like dark chocolate, bacon and key lime, Jade Luna might seem a bit out of place in Port Jim, but the locally sourced, organic flavors are heaven after a sweaty hike in the park. Look for the stand along main street.

🛈 Getting There & Around

Air

NatureAir (Map p259; www.natureair.com) and **Sansa (Map p259; www.sansa.com)** have daily flights to/from San José; one-way flights are approximately US$130.

Alfa Romeo Aero Taxi (Map p259; ☎8835-3325, 2735-5178; www.alfaromeoair.com) has light aircraft (three and five passengers) for charter flights to Golfito, Carate, Drake, Sirena, Palmar Sur, Quepos and Limón. Prices are dependent on the number of passengers, so it's best to try to organize a larger group if you're considering this option. Sometimes, if there's already a trip planned into the park, this can be as low as US$60 per person.

Bus & Taxi

Most buses arrive at the peach-color terminal on the west side of town.

San Isidro de El General US$7, five hours, departs 1pm.

San José via San Isidro de El General (Autotransportes Blanco Lobo) US$12, eight hours, departs 5am and 11am.

Colectivo Transportation (Map p259; ☎8837-3120, 8832-8680; Soda Deya) runs to Carate (three hours, US$10) on the southern tip of the national park. Departures leave Soda Deya at 6am and 1:30pm, returning at 8:30am and 4pm.

4WD taxis usually charge up to US$80 for the ride to Carate, up to US$100 for the overland trek to Drake.

CABO MATAPALO & CARATE

Cabo Matapalo is along the rough road between Puerto Jiménez and Carate and home to a number of plush jungle lodges. As for Carate, if you make it all the way here, congratulations. A bone-rattling 45km south of Puerto Jiménez, this is where the dirt road rounds the peninsula and comes to an abrupt dead end. Carate is nothing to see by itself, but it is the southwestern gateway for anyone hiking into Sirena ranger station in Parque Nacional Corcovado.

A handful of recommended wilderness lodges in the area make a good night's rest for travelers heading to or from Corcovado.

Sleeping

LAPA RÍOS Lodge $$$
(☎ 2735-5130; www.laparios.com; road to Carate, Km 17; s/d US$470/720; P ☎) A few hundred meters beyond El Portón Blanco along the road to Carate, this top-notch all-inclusive wilderness resort combines the right amount of luxury with a rustic, tropical ambience. Scattered over the site are 16 spacious, thatched bungalows, all decked out with queen-sized beds, bamboo furniture, garden showers and private decks with panoramic views. If you need substantial proof that ecotourism can be a profitable and successful vehicle for ensuring wilderness preservation and empowering local communities with increased economic opportunities, look no further.

RANCHOS ALMENDROS Cabina $$$
(Kapu's Place; ☎ 2735-5531; http://home.earth link.net/~kapu/; r per person from US$$100; P) This is the end of the line on Cabo Matapalo, where the road stops pretending and turns into a sandy beach path. The property includes three cozy *cabañas* (cabins) that are equipped with solar power, large screened windows, full kitchens and garden showers. As per the name, 'Almond Tree Ranch' is part of an ongoing project dedicated to the reforestation of Indian almond trees to create habitat for the endangered scarlet macaw.

🌿 LA LEONA ECO-LODGE Ecolodge $$$
(☎ 2735-5704; www.laleonaecolodge. com; s/d from US$95/180; P ☎) On the edge of Parque Nacional Corcovado 2km west of the *pulpería* (corner store), this friendly lodge offers all of the thrills of camping, without the hassles. Sixteen comfy forest-green tents are nestled between the palm trees, with decks facing the beach. All are fully screened and comfortably furnished; solar power provides electricity in the restaurant. Behind the accommodations,

Cabo Matapalo
TRAVELIB PRIME / ALAMY ©

30 hectares of virgin rainforest property offer opportunities for waterfall hiking, horseback riding and wildlife-watching.

LOOKOUT INN
Hut $$$

(☎ 2735-5431; www.lookout-inn.com; r per person from US$115; **P @ ☎**) A deep wilderness retreat, Lookout Inn has comfortable quarters with mural-painted walls, hardwood floors, beautifully carved doors and unbeatable views. Accommodations are in 'tiki huts' – open-air, A-frame huts accessible only by a wooden walkway winding through the giant joba trees (prime bird-watching territory). Behind the inn, 360 steps – known as the 'Stairway to Heaven' – lead straight up the side of the mountain to four observation platforms and a waterfall trail. And here's an interesting twist: if you don't spot a scarlet macaw during your stay, your lodging is free!

PARQUE NACIONAL CORCOVADO

Famously labeled by National Geographic as 'the most biologically intense place on earth,' this national park is the last great original tract of tropical rainforest in Pacific Central America. The bastion of biological diversity is home to Costa Rica's largest population of scarlet macaws, as well as countless other endangered species, including Baird's tapir, the giant anteater and the world's largest bird of prey, the harpy eagle. Corcovado's amazing biodiversity has long attracted a devoted stream of visitors who descend from Bahía Drake and Puerto Jiménez to explore the remote location and spy on a wide array of wildlife.

 **Activities**

Wildlife-Watching

The best wildlife-watching in Corcovado is at Sirena, but the coastal trails have two advantages: they are more open, and the constant crashing of waves covers the sound of noisy walkers. White-faced capuchins, red-tailed squirrels, collared peccaries, white-nosed coatis and northern tamandua are regularly seen on both of the following trails.

On the less-traveled San Pedrillo–Sirena trail, **Playa Llorona** is a popular nesting spot for marine turtles, including leatherback, olive ridley and green turtles. Nesting turtles attract ocelots, jaguars and other predators, though they are hard to spot. While planning to make this hike, inquire with rangers as this trail can be closed seasonally when it gets overgrown.

Both coastal trails – the San Pedrillo–Sirena trail and the Carate–Sirena trail – produce an endless pageant of birds. Pairs of scarlet macaws are guaranteed, as the tropical almond trees lining the coast are a favorite food. The sections along the beach shelter mangrove black hawk by the dozens and numerous waterbird species.

For wildlife-watchers frustrated at the difficulty of seeing rainforest mammals, a stay at Sirena ranger station is a must. Baird's tapirs are practically assured – that is a statement that can be made at few other places in the world. This endangered and distant relative of the rhinoceros is frequently spotted grazing along the airstrip after dusk.

Corcovado is the only national park in Costa Rica with all four of the country's primate species. Spider monkey, mantled howler and white-faced capuchin can be encountered anywhere, while the Los Patos–Sirena trail is best for the fourth and most endangered species, the Central American squirrel monkey. Sirena also has fair chances for the extremely hard-to-find silky anteater, a nocturnal animal that frequents the beachside forests between the Río Claro and the station.

Hiking

Paths are primitive and the hiking is hot, humid and insect-ridden, but the challenge of the trek and the interaction with wildlife at Corcovado are thrilling. Hiring a local guide – to help spot wildlife and avoid getting lost – is highly recommended. Otherwise, travel in a small group. Carry plenty of food, water and insect

263

repellent. And always verify your route with the rangers before you depart.

The most popular route traverses the park from Los Patos to Sirena, then exits the park at La Leona (or vice versa). This allows hikers to begin and end their journey in or near Puerto Jiménez, offering easy access to La Leona and Los Patos. The trek between Sirena and San Pedrillo is difficult, both physically and logistically.

Hiking is best in the dry season (from December to April), when there is still regular rain but all of the trails are open. It's still muddy, but you won't sink quite as deep.

🛏 Sleeping & Eating

Simple dormitory lodging (US$15) and meals are available at Sirena station only. Here, you'll find a vinyl mattress and simple bunk beds. We've had reports that this station had a bed-bug problem, so camping (US$4) on one of the platforms is recommended. The station serves excellent meals (breakfast is US$20, dinner is US$25). Other than that, food

and cooking fuel have to be packed in, so reserve as far in advance as possible through the Oficina de Área de Conservación Osa in Puerto Jiménez.

ℹ Information

Information and maps are available at the **Oficina de Área de Conservación Osa** (Osa Conservation Area Headquarters; Map p259 ☎2735-5580; park fee per person per day US$10; ⏱8am-noon & 1-4pm Mon-Fri) in Puerto Jiménez. Contact this office to make reservations for lodging and meals at all of the ranger stations and to pay your park fee. Be sure to make these arrangements a few days in advance as facilities are limited, and they do fill up on occasion in the dry season. Always check with rangers before setting out about trail conditions and possible closures (especially during the wettest months, from June to December).

ℹ Getting There & Away

From Carate

In the southeast, the closest point of access is Carate, from where La Leona station is a one-hour, 3.5km hike west along the beach.

Carate is accessible from Puerto Jiménez via a poorly maintained, 45km dirt road. This journey

Boat tour, Bahía Drake (p254)

CHRISTER FREDRIKSSON / GETTY IMAGES ©

is an adventure in itself, and often allows for some good wildlife-spotting along the way. A 4WD *colectivo* travels this route twice daily for US$10. Otherwise you can hire a 4WD taxi; prices depend on the size of your party and the season. If you have your own car, the *pulpería* in Carate is a safe place to park for a few days.

From Bahía Drake

From Bahía Drake, you can walk the coastal trail that leads to San Pedrillo station (about four hours from Agujitas), or any lodge can drop you here as a part of their regular tours to Corcovado. Alternatively, you can consider heading inland to the Los Planes station, though this is a longer, more heavily forested route. The route from San Pedrillo to Sirena is tough going - if it is open at all. During the time of writing, just after the rainy season, the trail was overgrown and closed, though rangers expect it to reopen in the dry season.

You can also charter a boat to San Pedrillo (US$80 to US$125) or Sirena (US$135 to US$180). If you have a car, most hotels and lodges along Bahía Drake can watch over it for you for a few dollars a day.

GOLFITO

A rough-and-ready little city with a long and sordid history, Golfito is a ramshackle port that stretches out along the Golfo Dulce. The town was built on bananas – the United Fruit Company moved its regional headquarters here in the '30s. In the 1980s declining markets, rising taxes, worker unrest and banana diseases forced the company's departure.

In an attempt to boost the region's economy, the federal government built a duty-free facility, the so-called Zona Americana, in Golfito. This surreal shopping center attracts Ticos from around the country, who descend on the otherwise dying town for 24-hour shopping sprees. And as charmless as it is by day, by night the place is home to surly ex-military men, boozy yachters, prostitutes and goons.

Still, as the largest town in Golfo Dulce, Golfito is a transportation hub for hikers heading to Corcovado, surfers heading to Pavones and sportfishers.

Sleeping & Eating

CASA ROLAND MARINA RESORT
Resort $$$

(☎2775-0180; www.casarolandgolfito.com; d from US$192; P ❄ @ ☎ ☀) A brand-new construction in the Zona Americana, the Casa Roland is now Golfito's most swish hotel, and primarily caters to duty-free shoppers looking for an amenity-laden base. You can expect to find all the usual top-end standards, including a swimming pool, restaurants and bars, tennis courts and a health spa, as well as a few extras such as a movie theatre and a casino. Rooms themselves lack the character typically found at this price range, but they're by far the most comfortable in town.

HOTEL SIERRA
Resort & Casino $$

(☎2775-0336, 2775-0666; www.hotelsierra.com; s/d/tr $68/80/92) Appropriate to its location in the Zona Americana, this place feels like a US-style motor lodge, though its sterility shouldn't deter you from staying here. Far removed from the grit and grime of Golfito, the Hotel Sierra is a mini-island where you can pass the night in relative ease, especially since there is a good restaurant and a small casino onsite.

RESTAURANTE BUENOS DÍAS
Breakfast $$

(meals US$5-10; ☺6am-10pm; P) Rare is the visitor who passes through Golfito without stopping at this cheerful spot opposite the Muellecito. Brightly colored booths, bilingual menus and super-convenient location ensure a constant stream of guests – whether for an early breakfast, a typical Tico *casado* or a good old-fashioned burger.

 Drinking

8° LATITUDE
Bar $

(meals US$6-12) Northwest of the soccer field, this popular expat bar is frequented by Americans who divide their time between sportfishing and boozy gossip.

If You Like...
National Parks

If you like Parque Nacional Corcovado, we think you'll like these other national parks in southern Costa Rica:

1 HUMEDAL NACIONAL TÉRRABA-SIERPE
Approximately 330 sq km of protected mangrove wetlands that harbor numerous species of aquatic birds.

2 REFUGIO NACIONAL DE FAUNA SILVESTRE GOLFITO
(☑ MINAE Office in Golfito 2775 2620; park fee US$10)
This tiny 28-sq-km reserve surrounding the town of Golfito is home to rare cycads (living plant fossils).

3 RESERVA BIOLÓGICA DÚRIKA
This private reserve within Parque Internacional La Amistad (p281) is home to an independent, sustainable community committed to conservation.

ⓘ Getting There & Away

Air

The airport is 4km north of the town center near the duty-free zone. NatureAir (www.natureair. com) and Sansa (www.sansa.com) have daily flights to/from San José. One-way tickets are approximately US$100.

Bus

Pavones US$5, three hours, departs 10am and 3pm. This service may be affected by road and weather conditions, especially in the rainy season.

San José via San Isidro de El General (Tracopa) US$11, seven hours, departs from the terminal near Muelle Bananero at 5am and 1:30pm.

Zancudo US$5, three hours, departs 1:30pm.

ZANCUDO & PAVONES

Occupying a slender finger of land that juts into the Golfo Dulce, the tiny village of Zancudo is about as laid-back a beach destination as you'll find in Costa Rica.

On the west side of town, gentle, warm Pacific waters lap onto black sands, and seeing more than a handful of people on the beach means it's crowded. On the east side, a tangle of mangrove swamps attracts birds, crocodiles and plenty of fish, which in turn attract fishers hoping to reel them in. Unlike nearby Pavones, an emerging surf destination, Zancudo is content to remain a far-flung village in a far-flung corner of Costa Rica.

Pavones, on the other hand, has been well known among surfers for a generation since it boasts one of the longest left-hand breaks known to man. The town itself is a bit of a ramshackle collection of *cabinas* and *sodas*. It is connected to its bustling sister-village Zancudo via a set of rough roads and wild beaches.

Activities

The main activities at Zancudo and Pavones are undoubtedly swinging on hammocks, strolling on the beach and swimming in the aqua-blue waters of the Golfo Dulce. Here, the surf is gentle, and at night the water sometimes sparkles with bioluminescence – tiny phosphorescent marine plants and plankton that light up if you sweep a hand through the water. The effect is like underwater fireflies.

The mangrove swamps around Zancudo offer plenty of opportunities for exploration: birdlife is prolific, while other animals such as crocodiles, caiman, monkeys and sloths are also frequently spotted. The boat ride from Golfito gives a glimpse of these waters, but you can also paddle them yourself: rent kayaks from any of the accommodations listings in town.

In Pavones surfing is the draw – when the surf's up, this tiny beach town attracts hordes of international elite, usually between April and October. However, because Pavones is inside Golfo Dulce, it can go for weeks without seeing any waves. Pavones has become legendary among surfers for its long left. When Pavones has nothing head south to Punta Banco, a reef break with decent rights and lefts.

Sleeping & Eating

COLOSO DEL MAR   Cabina $
(www.coloso-del-mar.com; d with/without view US$45/40; P 🛜) Rocky, a lazy, lovable dog, pads around the grounds of this, our favorite beachfront property in Zancudo. It's the little things that make Coloso stand out – matching sheets, shiny hardwood floors and coffeemakers. Of course, it also has an ideal location just steps from the surf.

OCEANO   Cabina $$
(📞 2776-0921; http://bestcostaricavacations. com; r US$79; P) With its back to the beach, this friendly little Canadian-run inn has just two rooms, both spacious and airy with wood-beamed ceilings, tile bathrooms and quaint details such as throw pillows and folk art. The open-air restaurant is also inviting for dinner or drinks, especially if the sea has been kind to the local fishermen.

EL COQUITO   Costa Rican $
(meals US$7-8; ⏱7am-8pm Sun-Wed, later Thu-Sat) Bright, cheerful and right in the middle of Zancudo's main drag, this *soda* is a charmer. It offers a filling US$7 *casado* of fresh fish, rice and fruit, and the *licuado* (smoothies) are magically refreshing after the long, dusty ride into town. On weekends the adjoining space transforms into a nightclub, with booming music and dancing.

🛈 Getting There & Away

Bus

A bus to Neily leaves from the *pulpería* near the dock at 5:30am (US$5, three hours). The bus for Golfito (US$5) leaves at 5am for the three-hour trip, with a ferry transfer at the Río Coto Colorado. Service is erratic in the wet season, so inquire before setting out.

For Pavones, most bus connections go through Zancudo. You can also arrive via 4WD taxi from Golfito for about US$65.

Aerial view over Parque Nacional Corcovado (p263)

Detour:
Parque Nacional Piedras Blancas

Formerly known as Parque Nacional Esquinas, this national park was established in 1992 as an extension of Parque Nacional Corcovado. Piedras Blancas has 120 sq km of undisturbed tropical primary rainforest, as well as 20 sq km of secondary forests, pasture land and coastal cliffs and beaches.

As one of the last remaining stretches of lowland rainforest on the Pacific, Piedras Blancas is also home to a vast array of flora and fauna. According to a study conducted at the biological station at Gamba, the biodiversity of trees in Piedras Blancas is the densest in all of Costa Rica, even surpassing Corcovado.

Car

It's possible to drive to Zancudo by taking the road south of Río Claro for about 10km. Turn left at the Rodeo Bar and follow the signs across the newly constructed bridge. From there, you'll see signs for Pavones, or take 30km of poorly maintained dirt road to Zancudo. In the rainy season you'll want a 4WD.

PARQUE NACIONAL ISLA DEL COCOS

Even though it's a tiny speck of green amid the endless Pacific, the Isla del Cocos looms large in the imagination of the adventurer: jagged mountains and tales of treasure, a pristine and isolated ecosystem filled with wildlife and some of the world's best diving. Remember the opening shot of *Jurassic Park,* where the helicopter sweeps over a tropical island? That was here.

Isla del Cocos is around 500km southwest of the mainland in the middle of the eastern Pacific. As it's the most far-flung corner of Costa Rica, you'll have to pay through the nose to get here, though few other destinations in the country are as wildly exotic and visually arresting.

As beautiful as the island may be, its terrestrial environs pale in comparison to what lies beneath. Named by PADI as one of the world's top 10 dive spots, the surrounding waters of Isla del Cocos harbor abundant pelagics including one of the largest known schools of hammerhead sharks in the world.

Since the island remains largely uninhabited and is closed to overnight visitors, visits require either a private yacht or, more realistically, a liveaboard dive vessel. While nondivers are certainly welcome to make the trip, it pays to have some significant underwater experience in your logbook – sites around Isla del Cocos are as challenging as they are breathtaking.

Activities

Diving

The diving is excellent, and is regarded by most as the main attraction of the island. But strong oceanic currents can lead to treacherous underwater conditions, and Isla del Cocos can only be recommended to intermediate and advanced divers with sufficient experience.

Wildlife-Watching

Because of its remote location, Isla del Cocos is the most pristine national park in the country and one of Costa Rica's great wildlife destinations. Since the island was never linked to the Americas during its comparatively short geological history, Cocos is home to a very large number of rare endemic species.

Tours

UNDERSEA HUNTER   Diving
(☎2228-6613, in USA 800-203-2120; www.
underseahunter.com) Offers 10-/12-day land
and sea expeditions with room for 14 to 18
people from US$5045 per person.

OKEANOS AGGRESSOR   Diving
(☎in USA 866-653-2667; www.aggressor.
com) Offers eight-/10-day land and
sea expeditions with room for 22 from
US$3335/3735 per person.

❶ Getting There & Away

With advance reservations, both of the tour
companies listed earlier will arrange transfers
from either San José or Liberia to Puntarenas,
which is the embarkation/disembarkation point
for the tour.

SAN ISIDRO DE EL GENERAL

With a population of only 45,000, San
Isidro de El General is little more than
a sprawling, utilitarian town at the
crossroads between some of Costa Rica's
prime destinations. Still, the strolling
lovers and teenage troublemakers give
the town square some charm, as does its
unexpectedly lively bar scene.

'El General' is the region's largest
population center and major
transportation hub. If you're traveling to
the southern Pacific beaches or Chirripó,
a brief stop is inevitable.

Sleeping & Eating

Options in San Isidro proper serve as one-
night crash pads of varying levels of style
and sophistication, while options outside
the town generally have more character
and warrant a longer stay.

TALARI MOUNTAIN LODGE   Lodge $$
(☎2771-0341; www.talari.co.cr; Rivas; s/d
US$49/72; P🛜🏊) This secluded moun-
tain lodge exudes an incredible amount

of charm, as do the Dutch-Tica couple
who run the place. Accommodations are
in simple wooden cabins on the edge of
the forest. To get here, drive 7km south of
San Isidro on the road from San Gerardo
de Rivas.

**THUNDERBIRD HOTEL &
CASINO**   Hotel $$
(Map p269; ☎2770-6230; www.tbrcr.com/hotel
costarica; cnr Av 3 & Calle 4; standard/luxury r
US$40/60; P❄@🛜) 'Executive Elegance'
is the boast of this upscale business hotel
(which used to be the Hotel Diamante
Real). After a series of upgrades it's surprisingly swish. The quarters are brightly
painted and fitted with shiny black-
lacquer furniture. There's a small casino
downstairs where you can drink for free
while feeding the slots.

KAFE DE LA CASA   Cafe $
(Map p269; Av 3 btwn Calles 2 & 4; meals US$6-13;
⏱7am-8pm) Set in an old Tico house, this
bohemian cafe features eclectic artwork,
an open kitchen and breezy garden seating. The menu has excellent breakfasts,

San Isidro de El General

RALPH HOPKINS / GETTY IMAGES ©

light lunches, gourmet dinners and plenty of coffee drinks.

ⓘ Getting There & Away

Bus

San José US$4.25, three hours, departs 7:30am, 8am, 9:30am, 10:30am, 11am, 1:30pm, 4pm, 5:45pm and 7:30pm.

Dominical US$3.70, 2½ hours, departs 7:30am, 9am and 5:30pm.

Palmar Norte/Puerto Jiménez US$6, five hours, departs 6:30am and 3pm.

Quepos US$4, three hours, departs 7am and 1:30pm

Uvita US$1.60, 1½ hours, departs 8:30am, 4pm

Taxi

A 4WD taxi to San Gerardo de Rivas will cost between US$25 and US$30. To arrange one, it is best to inquire through your accommodations.

SAN GERARDO DE RIVAS

If you have plans to climb Chirripó, you're in the right place – the tiny, tranquil town of San Gerardo de Rivas is at the doorstep of the national park. This is a place to get supplies, a good night's rest and a hot shower before embarking on the trek.

Although hikers are keen to press on to Parque Nacional Chirripó as quickly as possible, the logistics of getting up the mountain and the infrequent bus schedule will almost certainly mean that it is necessary to stay overnight in San Gerardo either before the hike, the night after or both. Luckily, the boulder-strewn Río Chirripó and bird-filled alpine scenery make it a beautiful place to linger.

🏃 Activities

COCOLISOS TRUCHERO   Fishing
(☎ 2742-5023; ⊙ arrive before 4pm; 🚻) If you're hanging out the day before or after a trip into the park, a perfect afternoon can be made out of sitting by the trout pools and taking in the celebrated orchid collection. Naturally, the fish is the best part; matronly Garita puts together a homemade feast of trout and home-cooked sides for US$5.

Sleeping & Eating

Most options are situated along the narrow road parallel to the river. The majority rent equipment (sleeping bags, air mattresses, cooking stoves etc), though supplies are limited and quality varies.

CASA MARIPOSA Hostel **$**

(2742-5037; www.hotelcasamariposa.net; dm/s/d US$13/17/32; **P @**) Just a short walk from the entrance of the park, this adorable lodge is built into the side of the mountain and has a warm, glowing atmosphere. Traveler-oriented details – warm clothes to borrow for the hike, laundry service, assistance with booking Chirripó lodge – make it ideal. There's a tidy kitchen, a hammock-slung lookout on the roof and a stone soaking tub. There's only space for 15 guests, so advance booking is recommended.

MONTE AZUL: BOUTIQUE HOTEL + CENTER FOR ART & DESIGN Boutique Hotel **$$$**

(2742-5222; www.monteazulcr.com; Rivas; r from US$259; **P ☎**) Exposed beams and brightly colored furniture, fine linens and bold art – the luxurious and elegant Monte Azul single-handedly boosts the quality of accommodations within a stone's throw of Chirripó. Set on a private 125-hectare reserve, the luxury riverfront suites have tasteful contemporary art, small kitchens, luxury mattresses and linens, and custom-designed furniture. It's a class act from start to finish.

RÍO CHIRRIPÓ RETREAT Hotel **$$**

(2742-5109; www.riochirripo.com; Canaán; r per person incl 3 meals from US$120; **P @ ☎ ☎**) About 1.5km below the ranger station, in Canaán, this upscale lodge is centered on both a beautiful yoga studio overlooking the river, and a vast open-air, Santa Fe–style communal area. You can hear the rush of the river from eight secluded cabins, where woven blankets and stenciled walls evoke the southwest USA.

 # Information

The Chirripó ranger station (Sinac; 2200-5348; ☉6:30am-noon & 1-4:30pm) is about 1km below the soccer field on the road from San Isidro. Stop by early to check for availability at Crestones Base Lodge (p273), and to confirm and pay fees before setting out. The Base Lodge holds 10 first-come, first-served beds, which can only be reserved the day prior to arrival.

Getting There & Away

Arriving via public transportation requires a connection through San Isidro. Buses to San Isidro depart from the soccer field at 5:15am, 11:30am and 4pm (US$1.60, 1½ to two hours). Any of the hotels can call a taxi for you.

Driving from San Isidro, head south on the Interamericana and cross Río San Isidro south of town. About 500m further on, cross the unsigned Río Jilguero and take the first, steep turn up to the left, about 300m beyond the Jilguero. Note that this turnoff is not marked.

PARQUE NACIONAL CHIRRIPÓ

Costa Rica's highest peak, **Cerro Chirripó**, rising 3820m above sea level, is the focus of popular **Parque Nacional Chirripó** (200 5348; park fee for 2 days US$15, each additional day US$15; , 4WD recommended). Of course, while Chirripó is the highest and most famous summit in Costa Rica, it is not the only one: two other peaks inside the park top 3800m, and most of the park's 502 sq km lies above 2000m.

Like a tiny chunk of the South American Andes, Parque Nacional Chirripó's rocky high-altitude features are an entirely unexpected respite from the heat and humidity of the rainforest (it's downright cold at night). Above 3400m, the landscape is *páramo*, which is mostly scrubby trees and grasslands, and supports a unique spectrum of highland wildlife. Rocky outposts punctuate the otherwise barren hills, and feed a series of glacial lakes that earned the park its iconic name: Chirripó means 'eternal waters.'

The only way up to Chirripó is by foot. Although the trekking routes are long and challenging, watching the sunrise from such lofty heights, literally above the clouds, is an undeniable highlight of Costa Rica. You will have to be prepared for the cold – and at times wet – slog to the top, though your efforts will be rewarded with some of the most sweeping vistas that Costa Rica can offer. The vast majority of travelers visit Chirripó over three days: one to get to San Gerardo de Rivas to secure permits, one to hike to the Crestones Base Lodge and one to summit the peak and return back to San Gerardo.

There are alternate and more extensive routes to get to the top, including a departure from the tiny village of Herradura. Spending a bit more time in the area will give you the chance to see other spectacular peaks, including Fila Urán.

The dry season (from late December to April) is the most popular time to visit Chirripó. February and March are the driest months, though it may still rain. The park is closed in May. The maps available at the ranger station are serviceable for the major trails.

Activities

Climbing Chirripó

The park entrance is at San Gerardo de Rivas, which lies 1350m above sea level; from here the summit is 2.5km straight up! A well-marked 16km trail leads all the way to the top and no technical climbing is required. It would be nearly impossible to get lost.

The amount of time it takes to get up varies greatly – it can take as little as five and as many as 14 hours to cover the 10km from the trailhead to the hostel, depending on how fit you are: the recommended departure time is 5am or 6am. The trailhead lies 50m beyond Albergue Urán in San Gerardo de Rivas (about 4km from the ranger station). The main gate is open from 4am to 10am to allow climbers to enter; no one is allowed to begin the ascent after 10am (although it is unlikely that a fast-moving latecomer would be turned away). Inside the park the trail is clearly signed at every kilometer. Reaching the hostel is the hardest part. From there the hike to the summit is about 5km on relatively flatter terrain (although the last 100m is very steep): allow at least two hours if you are fit, but carry a warm jacket, rain gear, water, snacks and a flashlight just in case. From the summit on a clear day, the vista stretches to both the Caribbean Sea and the Pacific Ocean.

Wildlife-Watching

The varying altitude means an amazing diversity of fauna in Parque

Collared peccaries
TOM BOYDEN / GETTY IMAGES ©

Nacional Chirripó. Particularly famous for its extensive birdlife, the national park is home to several endangered species, including the harpy eagle (the largest, most powerful raptor in the Americas) and the resplendent quetzal (especially visible between March and May).

In addition to the prolific birdlife, the park is home to some unusual high-altitude reptiles, such as the green spiny lizard and the highland alligator lizard. Mammals include puma, Baird's tapirs, spider monkeys, capuchins and – at higher elevations – Dice's rabbits and the coyotes that feed on them.

 Sleeping & Eating

Since no camping is allowed in the park, the only accommodations in Parque Nacional Chirripó are at **Crestones Base Lodge** (Centro Ambientalista el Parámo; dm US$10), which houses up to 60 people in dorm-style bunks that have serviceable vinyl-coated matresses. The basic stone building has a solar panel that provides electric light for limited hours and spo-radic heat for showers. Amazingly, it also has wi-fi. All crude comforts – sleeping bags, cooking stoves, blankets and the like – should be rented in San Gerardo de Rivas, where they're ubiquitous.

The lodge reserves 10 spaces per night for travelers who show up in San Gerardo and are ready to hike on the following day. This is far and away the more practical option for most travelers. Even though there is no certainty that there will be space available on the days you wish to hike, local lodge owners say that showing up immediately when the ranger station opens is almost guaranteed to work.

❶ Information

It is essential that you stop at the Chirripó ranger station (Sinac; ☎2200-5348; ⏰6:30am-noon & 1-4:30pm) at least one day before you intend to climb Chirripó so that you can get a space at the mountaintop hostel and pay your park entry fee (US$15 for two days, plus US$15 for each additional day).

Day Hiking Chirripó

Although it might be possible to leave San Gerardo de Rivas, summit Chirripó and return to town in a single day, don't do it. It would be an utterly exhausting slog for even the most fit hikers, and nearly guarantees returning in the dark over the muddiest parts of the trail. If you don't have the time, consider a long day hike in the Cloudbridge Nature Preserve.

❶ Getting There & Around

Buses depart for Parque Nacional Chirripó from San Gerardo de Rivas (US$1.60, 1½ hours) from the local terminal on Av 6 at 9:30am, 2pm and 6:45pm.

SAN GERARDO DE DOTA

San Gerardo de Dota is unlike any other place in Costa Rica – a bucolic mountain town run through by a clear, rushing river and surrounded by forested hills that more resemble the alps than the tropics. It's set deep within a mountain valley; the air is crisp and fresh, and chilly at night, and orchard-lined Savegre basin hosts high-altitude species that draw bird-watchers from around the world. The elusive and resplendent quetzal is such a celebrity in these parts that in 2005 the national government demarcated a national park in its honor.

Visiting the national park is largely a self-organized, DIY affair since it has no permanent infrastructure, but the town of San Gerardo provides easy access to the trailheads and offers a wide assortment of tourist lodges. In stunning contrast to Costa Rica's famous tropical regions, San Gerardo de Dota is a charmer, well worth seeking out for a quiet couple of days of fresh mountain air.

Activities

Sportfishing

The trout-fishing in the Río Savegre is excellent: May and June is the time for fly-fishing and December to March for lure-fishing. A number of trout farms surround the village as well.

Bird-Watching & Hiking

The best place to go bird-watching and hiking in the area is Parque Nacional Los Quetzales. Unfortunately there are no information facilities for tourists in the park, so inquire at the lodges in San Gerardo before you set out. You can hire local guides through the hotels. Travelers who wish to do extensive hiking in the area are advised to collect maps before they arrive.

Sleeping & Eating

Note that many of the lodges offer dinner with their accommodation and have access to the Parque Nacional Los Quetzales.

DANTICA LODGE & GALLERY Lodge $$$
(✆8352-2761; www.dantica.com; r/ste from US$142/180; P✻@🛜) Definitely the most elegant place in San Gerardo, if not the whole southern zone, this upscale lodge consists of lovely natural wood and stone cabins and beautiful Colombian artwork. The modern comforts – leather sofas, plasma TVs, Jacuzzis and track lighting – are nice, but the stunning vistas over the cloud forest are the biggest appeal. Romantic breakfasts are served on guests' private terraces. A nature reserve complete with private trails is just steps away, as well as a spa where you can pamper yourself after hiking.

SAVEGRE HOTEL DE MONTAÑA Lodge $$$
(✆2740-1028; www.savegre.co.cr; s/d/ste incl 3 meals US$125/179/254; P@🛜) Set on a 160-hectare orchard and reserve, this famous lodge has been owned and operated by the Chacón family since 1957. It's now something of a Costa Rican institution, especially among bird-watchers keen to catch a glimpse of the quetzal. The edges of the grounds are lined with avocado trees, the favorite perch of the bird of paradise. The suites are gorgeous: wrought-iron chandeliers hang from the high wooden ceilings, while rich wooden furniture surrounds a stone fireplace. It also has a roster of professional guides and an onsite spa.

KAHAWA CAFÉ & RESTAURANTE Cafe $
(✆2740-1051) With an ideal riverside location, brightly polished wood tables and sparkling fish tanks filled with trout, this is an excellent little place to grab a bite after hiking in the park. There's a small boutique onsite.

Getting There & Away

The turnoff to San Gerardo de Dota is near Km 80 on the Interamericana. From here, the dirt road descends 8km to the village. The road is very, very steep: take it slowly if you're driving an ordinary car. The buses between San José and San Isidro de El General can drop you at the turnoff.

PARQUE NACIONAL LOS QUETZALES

Formerly known as Reserva Los Santos, Parque Nacional Los Quetzales officially became a national park in 2005. Spread along both banks of the Río Savegre, at an altitude of 2000m to 3000m, Los Quetzales covers 50 sq km of rainforest and cloud forest lying along the slopes of the Cordillera de Talamanca.

The lifeblood of the park is the Río Savegre, which starts high up on the Cerro de la Muerte and feeds several mountain streams and glacial lakes before pouring into the Pacific near the town of Savegre. Although relatively small, this region is remarkably diverse – the Savegre watershed contains approximately 20% of the registered bird species in Costa Rica.

True to the park's new name, the resplendent quetzal is here, along with the trogon, hummingbird and sooty

MICHAEL HANSON / ALAMY ©

Don't Miss Cloudbridge Nature Preserve

About 2km past the trailhead to Cerro Chirripó you will find the entrance to the mystical, magical Cloudbridge Nature Preserve. Covering 182 hectares on the side of Cerro Chirripó, this private reserve is an ongoing reforestation and preservation project spearheaded by New Yorkers Ian and Genevieve Giddy. A network of trails traverses the property, which is easy to explore independently. Even if you don't get far past the entrance, you'll find two waterfalls, including the magnificent Catarata Pacifica.

NEED TO KNOW

☏ in USA 212-362-9391; www.cloudbridge.org; admission by donation; ☺ sunrise-sunset

robin. Avians aside, the park is home to endangered species including jaguars, Baird's tapirs and squirrel monkeys. The park is also home to premontane forests, the second-most endangered life zone in Costa Rica.

The park has no facilities for tourists aside from a small **ranger station** (☏ 2200-5354; admission US$10; ☺ 8am-4pm), which collects fees. From here, a modest network of bird-watching trails radiates into the forest. All the lodges around San Gerardo de Dota organize hiking and bird-watching tours.

The park is bordered by the Interamericana; the entrance is just past

Km 76. Any bus along this route can drop you off at the ranger station, though most people arrive in a private car or coach.

RESERVA INDÍGENA BORUCA

The picturesque valley of the Río Grande de Térraba cradles several mostly indigenous villages that comprise the reserve of Brunka (Boruca) peoples. At first glance it is difficult to differentiate these towns from typical Tico villages, aside from a few artisans selling their handiwork. In fact, these towns hardly cater to the tourist

DISCOVER SOUTHERN COSTA RICA RESERVA INDÍGENA BORUCA

trade, which is one of the main reasons why traditional Brunka life has been able to continue without much distraction.

Be sensitive when visiting these communities – dress modestly, avoid taking photographs of people without asking permission, and respect the fact that these living communities are struggling to maintain traditional culture amid a changing world.

Tours to Boruca, which include homestays, hikes to waterfalls, handicraft demonstrations and storytelling, can be arranged through Galería Namu (p70) in San José. Note that transportation is not included.

 Festivals & Events

FIESTA DE LOS DIABLITOS   Cultural
A three-day Brunka event that symbolizes the struggle between the Spanish and the indigenous population. Sometimes called the Danza de los Diablitos, or 'dance of the little devils,' the culmination of the festival is a choreographed battle between the opposing sides. Villagers wearing wooden devil masks and burlap costumes play the role of the natives in their fight against the Spanish conquerors. The Spaniards, represented by a man in a bull costume, get whipped by branches and lose the battle. (There's a lot of homemade corn-based alcohol involved.) This festival is held in Boruca from December 31 to January 2 and in Curré from February 5 to 8.

🔒 **Shopping**

The Brunka are celebrated craftspeople and their traditional art plays a leading role in the survival of their culture. While most people make their living from agriculture, some indigenous people have begun producing fine handicrafts for

tourists. The tribe is most famous for its ornate masks, carved from balsa or cedar, and sometimes colored with natural dyes and acrylics. Brunka women also use pre-Columbian backstrap looms to weave colorful, natural cotton bags, place mats and other textiles. These crafts are not widely available elsewhere in the country.

ⓘ Getting There & Away

Drivers will find a better road that leaves the Interamericana about 3km south of Rey Curré – look for the sign. In total, it's about 8km to Boruca from Rey Curré, though the going is slow, and a 4WD is recommended.

SAN VITO

Although the Italian immigrants who founded little San Vito in the 1850s are long gone, this hillside village proudly bears traces of their legacy in linguistic, cultural and culinary echos. As such, the town serves as a base for travelers in need of a steaming plate of pasta and a good night's sleep before descending into the deep wilderness.

The proximity of the town to the Reserva Indígena Guaymí de Coto Brus means that indigenous peoples pass through this region (Guaymí enclaves move back and forth undisturbed across the border with Panama). You might spot women in traditional clothing – long, solid-colored *pollera* dresses trimmed in contrasting hues – riding the bus or strolling the streets.

Tucked in between the Cordillera de Talamanca and the Fila Costeña, the Valle de Coto Brus offers some glorious geography, featuring the green, rolling hills of the coffee plantations backed by striking mountain facades, towering as much as 3350m above. The principal road leaves the Interamericana at Paso Real (near Rey Curré) and follows the Río Jaba to San Vito, then continues south to rejoin the Interamericana at Neily. This winding mountain road (paved, but poorly maintained) offers spectacular scenery and a thrilling ride.

CINDY MILLER HOPKINS / ALAMY ©

Don't Miss **Wilson Botanical Garden**

Wilson Botanical Garden lies about 6km south of San Vito. Covering 12 hectares and surrounded by 254 hectares of natural forest, this world-class garden was established by Robert and Catherine Wilson in 1963 and thereafter became internationally known for its collection. Today the well-maintained garden holds more than 1000 genera of plants from about 200 families and plays a scientific role as a research center.

The gardens are well laid out, many of the plants are labeled and a trail map is available for self-guided walks, featuring exotic species such as orchids, bromeliads, palms and medicinal plants. The many ornamental varieties are beautiful, but the tours explain that they are useful too (eg the delicate cycad, used by Cabécar and Bribrí people as a treatment for snakebites). The gardens are very popular among bird-watchers, who may see scarlet-thighed dacni, silver-throated tanager, violaceous trogons, blue-headed parrots, violet sabre-wing hummingbirds and turquoise cotingas.

If you want to stay overnight at the botanical gardens, make your reservations well in advance: facilities are often filled with researchers and students. Accommodations are in comfortable cabins in the midst of the gorgeous grounds. The rooms are simple, but they each have a balcony with an amazing view of the surrounding flora. Rates include entry to the gardens.

Buses between San Vito and Neily pass the entrance to the gardens. Take the bus that goes through Agua Buena, as buses that go through Cañas Gordas do not stop here. A taxi from San Vito to the gardens costs up to US$5.

NEED TO KNOW

📞2773-4004; www.esintro.co.cr; Las Cruces Biological Station; admission US$8, guided tours half-/full-day US$18/24; ⏰7am-5pm Mon-Fri, 8am-5pm Sat & Sun

◉ Sights

About 3km south of town, **Finca Cántaros** (☏2773-3760; www.fincacantaros.com; admission $4, campsites per person $8; ⊙9:30am-5pm Tue-Sun; 👪) is a recreation center, campground and reforestation project. The 10 hectares of grounds – which used to be coffee plantations and pasture land – are now a lovely park with garden trails, picnic areas and a dramatic lookout over the city. The reception is housed in a pretty, well-maintained cabin that contains a small but carefully chosen selection of local and national crafts. You can take a self-guided hike to Laguna Zoncho and picnic at one of the small shelters, which is a good perch for watching rare birds and has a nice view of the surrounding hills.

🛏 Sleeping & Eating

In addition to the following accommodations options, camping is available at Finca Cántaros.

CASA BOTANIA　　　B&B $$
(☏2773-4217; www.casabotania.com; d from US$55; ❄🛜) This, the freshest B&B in the region, is exquisitely run by a Belgian-Tico couple and located 5km south of town on the road between the Wilson Botanical Garden and San Vito. It hits every note with pitch-perfect elegance, from the modern, brightly adorned rooms, to the library of bird-watching guides, to the gourmet meals, which are served on a polished deck overlooking the steaming foliage of the valley below. If you don't stay, book a dinner reservation; the three-

course, locally sourced, ever-changing menu of smart European-touched Costa Rican fare wins raves.

HOTEL EL CEIBO　　　Hotel $$
(☏2773-3025; s/d from US$36/52; P❄🛜) The best option in town – though fairly subdued by any account – is El Ceibo, conveniently located about 100m west of the main intersection, in a private, secure cul-de-sac. Here you can sleep easy in simple but functional rooms (some with balconies that have forest views, all with fans and nice little touches, like reading lamps) and dig into some authentic Italian pastas and wines in the sky-lit dining room.

CABINAS RINO　　　Hotel $
(☏2773-3071; s/d from US$12/20; P🛜) This 2nd-floor hotel is located above a block of shops on the main road, though it's fairly well insulated from the street noise below. Basic rooms with whitewashed walls are reasonably clean and comfortable, and staff are polite and courteous.

Resplendent quetzal, female
SIEPMANN / IMAGEBROKER ©

PHILIP & KAREN SMITH / GETTY IMAGES ©

PIZZERÍA RESTAURANTE
LILLIANA   Pizzeria $

(www.ilprosciuttolerici.com; pizzas US$4-9;
⊙10:30am-10pm) This great spot for Italian
fare offers more than a dozen different
kinds of pizza, all of which are made from
scratch with authentic flavors. The lovely
mountain views and old-world environs
make this a pleasant place to spend an
afternoon.

ℹ Information

If you're planning on heading to Parque
Internacional La Amistad, San Vito is home to the
Minae parks office (☎2773-3955; Calle 2 btwn
Avs 4 & 6; ⊙9am-4pm), which can help you get
your bearings before heading to the national park.

ℹ Getting There & Away

Air

Alfa Romeo Aero Taxi (www.alfaromeoair.com)
offers charter flights to San Vito from Puerto
Jiménez and Golfito; prices vary according to the
number of people and season. The airstrip is 1km
east of town.

Bus

The main Tracopa bus terminal (☎2773-3410) is
at the northern end of the main street.

San Isidro US$4.24, three hours, departs
6:45am and 1:30pm

San José US$9 seven hours, departs 5am,
7:30am, 10am and 3pm

A local bus terminal at the northwest end of town
runs buses to Neily and other destinations.

Neily US$0.65, 30 minutes, departs 5:30am,
7am, 7:30am, 9am, 11am, noon, 2pm and 5pm

Río Sereno US$1.60, 1½ hours, departs 7am,
10am, 1pm and 4pm

Car

The drive north from Neily is a scenic one, with
superb views of the lowlands dropping away as
the road winds up the hillside. The paved road is
steep, narrow and full of hairpin turns. You can
also get to San Vito from San Isidro via the Valle
de Coto Brus – an incredibly scenic and less-used
route with fantastic views of the Cordillera de
Talamanca to the north and the lower Fila Costeña
to the south.

PARQUE INTERNACIONAL LA AMISTAD

The 4070-sq-km Parque Internacional La Amistad was established jointly in 1988 by Panama and Costa Rica – hence its Spanish name, La Amistad (Friendship). It is by far the largest protected area in Costa Rica, and stands as a testament to the possibilities of international cooperation in the name of environmental conservation. In 1990 La Amistad was declared a Unesco World Heritage Site, and later became part of the greater Mesoamerican Biological Corridor, which protects a great variety of endangered habitats. Although most of the park's area is high up in the Talamanca and remains virtually inaccessible, there is no shortage of hiking and camping opportunities available for intrepid travelers at lower altitudes.

Sleeping

Asoprola (2743-1184; www.actuarcostarica. com) runs a small, simple lodge and can make arrangements for lodging in local homes in the village of Altamira for a resonable fee (usually US$10 to US$15 per person). For an intimate look at the lives of people living on the fringes of the rainforest, there is no better way than to arrange a homestay.

❶ Getting There & Away

If you have a tight schedule, a 4WD drive and steely nerves are required to get around this area – the buses are unreliable, and the roads are terrible.

Caribbean Coast

With fewer tourists and rough charms, the Caribbean coast moves to a distinct rhythm.
While the sunny climate and easy accessibility of the Pacific have paved the way (literally) for development on that rich coast, the Caribbean side has languished in comparison. The same rain-drenched malarial wildness that thwarted the first 16th-century Spaniards has isolated this region for centuries. Thus, its culture – influenced by indigenous peoples and West Indian immigrants – blended slowly and organically and is distinctly different from the rest of Costa Rica. It still takes a little more effort to travel here to see the nesting turtles of Tortuguero, raft the Río Pacuare or dive the reefs of Manzanillo. But its unique flavor is well worth a taste: in the *rondón* (spicy seafood gumbo) or the refreshment of a cold Imperial sipped on an uncrowded stretch of black-sand beach. Costa Rica, Caribbean-style, embodies *pura vida* (pure life).

Carnival band, Puerto Limón (p294)

283

Caribbean Coast

1 Manzanillo
2 Parque Nacional Tortuguero
3 Puerto Viejo de Talamanca
4 Salsa Brava
5 Cahuita
6 Rainforest Aerial Tram

20 miles
40 km

N

CARIBBEAN

SEA

San Juan de Nicaragua (Greytown)

NICARAGUA

Río San Juan

Barra del Colorado

Río Colorado

Heredia

Río Chirripó

Refugio Nacional de Vida Silvestre Barra del Colorado

Intercoastal Waterway

Llanura de Tortuguero

Tortuguero

Cuatro Esquinas Ranger Station

Parque Nacional Tortuguero

Canales de Tortuguero

Parque Nacional Tortuguero

Jalova Station

La Pavona

247

Cariari

Río Tortuguero

Limón

Santa Rosa

Río Suerte

Río Chirripó

Río Frío

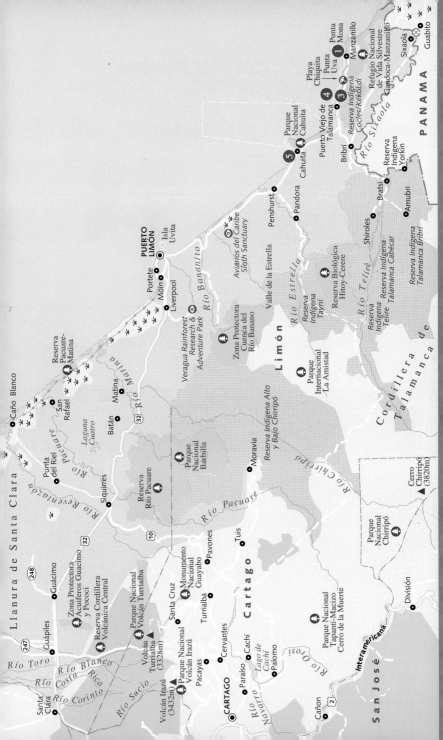

Caribbean Coast Highlights

① Manzanillo

This community, surrounded by reef and rainforest, has the most positive vibe of any in the region. Here grows a beautiful tolerance – no matter where you're from, you can make friends immediately. Everything's within walking, swimming or paddling distance. The town lives up to its slogan: in Manzanillo the least you can get is the best.

Above: Playa Manzanillo; Above right: Manzanillo; Below right: Bottlenose dolphins

Need to Know

SURVIVAL Apply sunblock religiously when snorkeling **SEA-CREATURE CHECKLIST** Dolphins; leatherback, green, hawksbill and loggerhead turtles **For more, see p315**

Manzanillo Don't Miss List

BY SHAWN LARKIN, CO-OWNER/
MANAGER OF COSTA CETACEA

1 JOURNEY TO PUNTA MONA

One of the best adventures in the Manzanillo area involves following the coastal trail to Punta Mona in the Refugio Nacional de Vida Silvestre Gandoca-Manzanillo. On land, seeing the incredible range of biomes will put your legs to the test, or you can rent a kayak and follow the winding coastline.

2 DOLPHIN-WATCHING

Several species of dolphin call the Caribbean Sea home, though the most widely known is the Atlantic bottlenose. Their playful and dramatic antics are a highlight of the shallow seas near Manzanillo. Although Costa Rican law prohibits swimming with dolphins, with a knowledgeable local guide you can get up close and personal, watching these amazing creatures from a safe distance.

3 CORAL REEFS

Directly in front of town are coral reef formations that are as unique as their evocative names: Sugar, Bloody, Jimmy and Wash a Woman. The easiest way to explore the underwater world is to don a mask, fins and snorkel, and spend a while cruising above the reef and occasionally diving down for a closer look.

4 SCUBA DIVING

In addition to the nearby outlying reefs, there are some further-flung dive spots that harbor astonishing varieties of marine life. Even though there are many other more spectacular dive sites in Central American and the Caribbean, it can be a blast. From spiny lobsters hiding in the rocks to enormous pilot whales, the Caribbean Sea is a never-ending showcase of some of the planet's weirdest and most wonderful wildlife.

Parque Nacional Tortuguero

Shattering stereotypes of idyllic Caribbean landscapes, this national park (p302) is rugged and untamed. Navigation through Tortuguero's largely impenetrable jungles and expansive marshlands consists of canoeing down narrow waterways and imagining yourself as a Victorian-era jungle explorer. Your reward? Phenomenal wildlife-watching, with nesting sea turtles bounding troops of monkeys and a few more dangling serpents than you'd care to spot.

Puerto Viejo de Talamanca

This is without a doubt the cultural heart of the Caribbean coast. A loud and proud bastion of Rastafarianism, Puerto Viejo (p311) lures in countless visitors with the promise of Jamaican-influenced music and munchies. When you're not either jamming to reggae beats or stuffing your face full of jerk chicken, you can simply kick back on a blissful stretch of sand while sipping fresh coconut milk.

Salsa Brava

4

A gnarly break just off the coast of Puerto Viejo de Talamanca, Salsa Brava (meaning 'spicy sauce') serves up massive waves onto the sharp, shallow reef. This truly legendary wave (p316) has been chewing up and spitting out surfers for generations – it's the biggest and baddest break in Costa Rica. Salsa Brava is a tricky ride, but it's a rush (and most definitely not for beginners).

JESÚS OCHOA ©

5

Cahuita

This Afro-Caribbean beach town isn't nearly as developed as Puerto Viejo de Talamanca, though that's exactly the way the local residents like it. Indeed, Cahuita (p305) offers a measure of salt-of-the-earth authenticity that is missing from its brasher neighbor, not to mention that it's also the jumping-off point for a stunning national park of the same name. Keel-billed toucan

6

Rainforest Aerial Tram

If you truly want to appreciate the scale of the rainforests lining the Caribbean coast, there is no better place than the Rainforest Aerial Tram (p300), which allows you to glide through it in silence. Something of a glorified ski lift (minus the snow, of course), this tram carries you up into the canopy in search of lofty vegetation and high-flying avians.

The Caribbean Coast's Best...

Journeys

○ **Parque Nacional Tortuguero** (p304) Boating through remote backwaters is arguably the best journey in the Caribbean.

○ **Puerto Viejo de Talamanca** (p311) Departing Puerto Viejo and cycling down the coast lets you slow down the pace and enjoy the journey.

○ **Rainforest Aerial Tram** (p300) A true journey up into the clouds.

Splurges

○ **Tortuga Lodge & Gardens** (p299) Take a break from the paddling by exploring acres of private gardens.

○ **Cashew Hill Jungle Cottages** (p314) A secluded spot set far back from the Puerto Viejo scene.

○ **Congo Bongo** (p315) Bed down in the middle of a reclaimed cacao plantation.

○ **Magellan Inn** (p308) This small inn has loads of intimacy (only six rooms!) and lovely private terraces.

Vistas

○ **Parque Nacional Tortuguero** (p302) Panoramic views of incredible nature surround your tiny canoe.

○ **Parque Nacional Cahuita** (p309) Watching the sunrise over Caribbean shores is a spiritual moment.

○ **Salsa Brava** (p311) Even if you don't have the experience to ride this wave, watching others tackle the 'spicy sauce' is memorable.

○ **Refugio Nacional de Vida Silvestre Gandoca-Manzanillo** (p317) Make the thrilling hike out to Punta Uva for sweeping ocean views.

Eats

- **Cha Cha Cha** (p308) Take in a dinner of world cuisine on the veranda at this sophisticated charmer.

- **Stashu's con Fusion** (p314) Tuck into a heady fusion of Caribbean, Indian, Mexican and Thai flavors.

- **Selvin's Restaurant** (p315) The chicken caribeño is a perfect blend of Caribbean flavors.

- **La Pecora Nera** (p315) Candlelight and Italian dishes make this a romantic, upscale treat.

Need to Know

ADVANCE PLANNING

- **Surfing school** The Caribbean coast is home to some serious surf, which means you might want to practice elsewhere before showing up with board in hand.

- **Visiting Parque Nacional Tortuguero** This remote park is hard to visit on a whim and best approached with a good transportation plan.

RESOURCES

- **Tortuguero Information** (www.tortugueroinfo.com)

- **Puerto Limón Guide** (www.puertolimon.net)

GETTING AROUND

- **Bicycle** From Puerto Viejo de Talamanca to Manzanillo, this is the best way to travel.

- **Boat** The only way to access Parque Nacional Tortuguero – other than flying in, of course.

- **Bus** The Caribbean coast is well serviced by buses, alleviating the need for a rental car.

- **Walk** Any of the region's beaches invite long sessions of beachcombing.

BE FOREWARNED

- **Crime** Puerto Limón (like many places on the Caribbean) has a few rough corners, so keep your wits about you if you're transiting this gritty city.

- **Riptides** Currents here can be very strong, so check with locals before swimming. If you get caught in a riptide, immediately call for help. It's important not to panic – relax and conserve your energy.

VITAL STATISTICS

- **Population** Puerto Limón 58,500

- **Best time to visit** It rains throughout the year, though precipitation tends to be lighter in February and March, as well as in September and October.

EMERGENCY NUMBERS

- **Emergency** ☎911

- **Fire** ☎118

- **Police** ☎117

Left: Bare-throated tiger heron; **Above:** Canoeing, Parque Nacional Tortuguero (p302)

(LEFT) STEPHEN SAKS / GETTY IMAGES ©;
(ABOVE) JOHN BORTHWICK / GETTY IMAGES ©

Caribbean Coast Itineraries

While most visitors head directly for Pacific waves, the Caribbean allows for an entirely different cultural perspective. The highlights are strung out along calm waters, making for a lazy, relaxing coastal trip.

TORTUGUERO

PARQUE NACIONAL TORTUGUERO

CARIBBEAN SEA

MOÍN   PUERTO LIMÓN

MANZANILLO

PUERTO VIEJO DE TALAMANCA

REFUGIO NACIONAL DE VIDA SILVESTRE GANDOCA-MANZANILLO

PANAMA

3 DAYS

PUERTO VIEJO DE TALAMANCA TO THE PANAMA BORDER

Puerto Viejo & Around

If you can only spare a few days on the Caribbean coast, your first port of call should be none other than **(1) Puerto Viejo de Talamanca**. The region's most developed beach town will not only give you a good taste of Afro-Caribbean culture, but it also serves as a convenient jumping-off point for nearby attractions and has a rollicking party scene. It's easy to get here from San José; a direct bus takes only a few hours' travel time. After arriving, stow your belongings and make straight for the beach. Serious surfers should consider testing their mettle at the infamous Salsa Brava, while less-experienced riders can head next door to

the less-intense breaks of Playa Cocles. In the evening you'll find the Caribbean groove as you dine on some of the country's best cuisine and relax to the rhythm of reggae beats.

If you have extra energy to burn off, rent a bike and head along the 13km road past gorgeous palm-lined beaches to the idyllic community of **(2) Manzanillo**, for some snorkeling, diving or kayaking. Finally, end this dreamy trip by hiking and searching for animals in the **(3) Refugio Nacional de Vida Silvestre Gandoca-Manzanillo**, which stretches all the way to the Panamanian border.

PUERTO LIMÓN TO PARQUE NACIONAL TORTUGUERO
Exploring Tortuguero

4 DAYS

If you've got a bit more time – and a serious adventurous streak – you might want to consider forgoing Caribbean comforts and tackling the region's wildest national park. From spying on sea turtles to canoeing past caimans and crocodiles, Tortuguero is rightfully regarded as the Amazon in miniature and a must-see for die-hard naturalists.

Although you're unlikely to want to stay too long, start in the port city of **(1) Puerto Limón**, where you can take in the sights of the Caribbean's largest city before heading to the docks in nearby **(2) Moín** for the real start of your journey. By boat, you'll travel the canal-lined coast to the remote village of **(3) Tortuguero**. Although the strong Afro-Caribbean roots and hordes of sea turtles make it a destination in its own right, your journey continues into the jungles and mangroves of the surrounding **(4) Parque Nacional Tortuguero**. A true wilderness that is prime for excellent viewing of nesting sea turtles, frogs and amphibians galore. This area is a world away from the airbrushed beach towns further down the coast.

Playa Manzanillo (p315)
CHRISTOPHER BAKER / GETTY IMAGES ©

Discover
Caribbean Coast

At a Glance

○ **Puerto Limón** The slightly seedy big city on the coast.

○ **Tortuguero Village** (p296) In the heart of the Caribbean's wildlife wonderland.

○ **Puerto Viejo de Talamanca** (p311) The thriving cultural capital of the Caribbean with lots of Rastas.

○ **Manzanillo** (p315) A little southern Caribbean village off the beaten track.

PUERTO LIMÓN

POP 58,500

The biggest city on Costa Rica's Caribbean coast, the birthplace of United Fruit and capital of Limón Province, this hard-working port city sits removed from the rest of the country. Cruise ships deposit passengers between October and May.

A general lack of political and financial support from the federal government means that Limón is not a city that has aged gracefully. With a grid of dilapidated buildings and high crime rates, the city is of little interest to anyone except the most adventurous urban explorers.

 Sights

PARQUE VARGAS   Park

(Map p295) The city's waterfront centerpiece won't win best in show, but its decrepit bandstand, paths and greenery, shaded by palms and facing the docks, are surprisingly appealing.

 Tours

TORTUGUERO WILDLIFE TOURS   Boat Tour

(☎ 2798-7027, 2758-2534; www.tortu guero-wildlife.com) This agency, run by the personable William Guerrero, organizes a variety of area tours.

 Festivals & Events

FESTIVAL FLORES DE LA DIÁSPORA AFRICANA   Cultural

(Late August) A celebration of Afro-Caribbean culture. While it is centered

Carnival costume, Puerto Limón
IAN CUMMING / AURORA PHOTOS ©

Puerto Limón

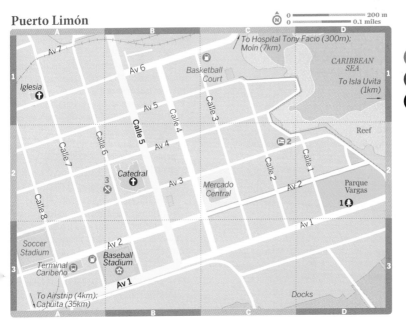

on Puerto Limón, the festival sponsors events showcasing African heritage throughout the province and San José.

DÍA DE LA RAZA Cultural
(Columbus Day; October 12) Columbus' historic landing on Isla Uvita has traditionally inspired a small carnival, with street parades, live music and dancing. During this time, book hotels in advance.

 Sleeping & Eating

PARK HOTEL Hotel $$
(Map p295; ☏2798-0555; www.parkhotel limon.com; Av 3 btwn Calles 1 & 2; s/d standard US$52/72, superior US$58/82, deluxe US$70/98; P ⊖ ❄ @) Downtown Limón's most attractive hotel has 32 rooms in a peach-colored building that faces the ocean. Tiled rooms are tidy and sport clean bathrooms with hot water. Superior rooms have ocean views while the deluxe ones come with private balconies. The hotel also houses the swankiest restaurant in the town center. Credit cards accepted.

Puerto Limón

◎ **Sights**
1 Parque Vargas D2

🛏 **Sleeping**
2 Park Hotel C2

🍴 **Eating**
3 Caribbean Kalisi Coffee Shop.............B2

**CARIBBEAN KALISI
COFFEE SHOP** Caribbean $
(Map p295; ☏2758-3249; Calle 6 btwn Avs 3 & 4; mains from US$5; ⏱7:30am-7:30pm Mon-Fri, 8am-7:30pm Sat, 8am-5pm Sun) Step up to the cafeteria-style counter at this friendly family spot and cobble together a plate of coconut rice, red beans and whatever's cooking that day – typically a wide variety of fabulous Caribbean meat and veggie dishes.

ℹ Getting There & Away

Buses to and from San José, Moín, Guápiles and Siquirres arrive at **Terminal Caribeño** (Av 2 btwn Calles 7 & 8) on the west side of the baseball stadium.

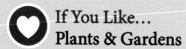

If You Like...
Plants & Gardens

If you like exploring the medicinal and nutritional plants of the region so abundant in Parque Nacional Tortuguero, we think you'll like these other places along the coast:

1 JARDÍN BOTÁNICO LAS CUSINGAS
(☎2382-5805; guided tour US$6; ⏱by appointment) This well-kept garden has more than 80 varieties of medicinal plants.

2 ECOFINCA ANDAR
(☎2272-1024; www.andarcr.org; 1-day admission US$14, per person homestay incl meals US$17) North of Guápiles, 3km northeast of the village of Santa Rosa, is this ecological farm, an impressive educational facility that shows how plants are cultivated for medicinal purposes and used as sources of renewable energy.

3 ATEC
(Asociación Talamanqueña de Ecoturismo y Conservación; Map p312; ☎2750-0191, 2750-0398; www.ateccr.org; ⏱8am-9pm) This community organization, based in Puerto Viejo, offers a variety of tours into the refuge and focuses on traditional uses of plants.

Moín, for boats to Tortuguero (Tracasa) US$0.60, 20 minutes, departs hourly 5:30am to 6:30pm.

San José (Autotransportes Caribeños) US$5.50, three hours, departs almost hourly 5am to 7pm.

MOÍN

This is Puerto Limón's main transportation dock, where you can catch a boat to Parismina or Tortuguero.

🛈 Getting There & Away

The journey by boat to Tortuguero can take anywhere from three to five hours, depending on how often the boat stops to observe wildlife (many tours also stop for lunch). Indeed, it is worth taking your time. As you wind your way through

these jungle canals, you are likely to spot howler monkeys, crocodiles, two- and three-toed sloths and an amazing array of wading birds, including roseate spoonbills.

The route is most often used by tourist boats, which means that if the canal becomes blocked by water hyacinths or logjams, the route might be closed altogether. Schedules exist in theory only and they change frequently depending on demand.

Asociación de Boteros de los Canales de Tortuguero (Abacat; ☎8360-7325) Regular service to Tortuguero.

Caribbean Tropical Tours (☎8371-2323, 2798-7027; wguerrerotuca@hotmail.com) Run by master sloth-spotter William Guerrero and his wife; ideal for leisurely rides to Tortuguero with plenty of pit stops to see wildlife.

Moín–Parismina–Tortuguero Water Taxi (☎2709-8005; 1 way US$35) Reservations essential, especially for stops in Parismina.

Tropical Wind (☎8313-7164, 8327-0317, 2798-6059) Almost-daily shuttles between Tortuguero and Moín in high season.

Viajes Bananero (☎8833-1066, in San José 2222-8973) Regular (though not daily) trips between Moín and Tortuguero.

CARIARI
POP 14,100

Due north of Guápiles, Cariari is a blue-collar, rough-around-the-edges banana town. Most travelers make their way quickly through here, en route to Tortuguero. If that's you, Cariari is your last opportunity to get cash.

🛈 Getting There & Away

Buses to San José (US$3) depart from Estación Nueva at 5:30am, 6:30am, 7:30am, 8:30am, 11:30am, 1pm, 3pm and 5:30pm.

TORTUGUERO VILLAGE

Located within the confines of Parque Nacional Tortuguero, accessible only by air or water, this bustling little village with strong Afro-Caribbean roots is best known for attracting hordes of sea turtles (the name Tortuguero means 'turtle place') – and the hordes of tourists who

Around Tortuguero

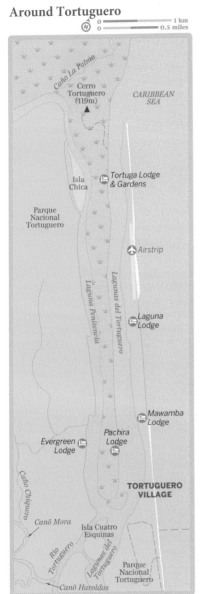

the sea, caravans of families and adventure travelers arrive to go on jungle hikes and to canoe the area's lush canals.

 Sights & Activities

CARIBBEAN CONSERVATION CORPORATION   Wildlife Reserve
(CCC; ☎ 2709-8091, in USA 800-678-7853; www.cccturtle.org; admission US$1; ⊙ 10am-noon & 2-5pm Mon-Sat, 2-5pm Sun) About 200m north of Tortuguero village, the CCC operates a research station that has a small visitor center and museum. Exhibits focus on all things turtle-related, including a video about the history of local turtle conservation.

CANADIAN ORGANIZATION FOR TROPICAL EDUCATION & RAINFOREST CONSERVATION   Wildlife Reserve
(Coterc; ☎ 2709-8052, in Canada 905-831-8809; www.coterc.org; admission free) This not-for-profit organization operates the Estación Biológica Caño Palma, 7km north of Tortuguero village. This small biological research station houses a diminutive museum that contains, among other things, an impressive collection of skulls. From here, a network of trails wind through the surrounding rainforest. Coterc is surrounded on three sides by water, so you'll have to hire a boat to get here.

◎ Activities

Boating & Canoeing

Signs all over Tortuguero advertise boat tours and boats for hire. This is obviously the best way to explore the surrounding waterways. See the list of recommended companies and guides in the Tours section following. Our advice: for optimum wildlife-spotting, forego the motors (the noise scares off wildlife) and opt for a guided tour by canoe.

Numerous area businesses rent kayaks and canoes; inquire locally.

want to see them. While the peak turtle season is in July and August, the park and village have begun to attract travelers year-round. Even in October, when the turtles have pretty much returned to

Hiking

A number of trails extend from the village into the national park and around Coterc. Enquire at the agencies listed in Tours below for guided tours. Note: night hiking in the national park is not allowed.

Tours

Guides have posted signs all over town advertising their services for canal tours and turtle walks. The **Tortuguero Info Center** (2709-8055; tortuguero_info@racsa.co.cr) can provide information. Going rates are about US$20 per person for a two-hour turtle tour, and US$15 for a two-hour hiking or boat excursion.

BARBARA HARTUNG　　　Boat Tour
(8842-6561, 2709-8004; www.tinamontours.de) Trained zoologist offers hiking, canoe, cultural and turtle tours in German, English, French or Spanish.

CASTOR HUNTER THOMAS　　Boat Tour
(8870-8634; castorhunter.blogspot.com; Soda Doña María) Excellent local guide who has led hikes, turtle tours and canoe tours for over 20 years.

DARYL LOTH　　　Boat Tour
(2709-8011, 8833-0827; safari@racsa.co.cr) Canadian-born naturalist (formerly of Coterc) offers supersilent electric motorboat trips, turtle tours and guided hikes.

CHICO　　　Boat Tour
(2709-8033; Cabinas Miss Miriam) His hiking and canoe tours receive rave reviews.

 Sleeping

Tortuguero Village

There is a wide range of budget and midrange options here. Lodgings in the northern half of town are quieter.

CASA MARBELLA　　　B&B $$
(8833-0827, 2709-8011; casamarbella.tripod.com; s US$35-60, d US$40-65, extra person US$10, all incl breakfast; @ 🛜) Owned by naturalist Daryl Loth, this charming B&B manages to be wonderfully serene while also being in the middle of it all. Ten simple whitewashed rooms have good light-

Boat tour, Tortuguero Village (p296)

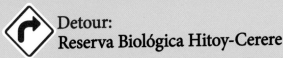

Detour:
Reserva Biológica Hitoy-Cerere

One of the most rugged and rarely visited reserves in the country, **Hitoy-Cerere** (2795-3170; admission US$6; 8am-4pm) is only about 60km south of Puerto Limón. The 99-sq-km reserve sits on the edge of the Cordillera de Talamanca, and is characterized by varying altitudes, evergreen forests and rushing rivers. This may be one of the wettest reserves in the parks system, inundated with 4000mm to 6000mm of rain annually.

Naturally, wildlife is abundant. The most commonly sighted mammals include gray four-eyed opossums, tayras (a type of weasel), and howler and capuchin monkeys. There are plenty of ornithological delights as well (with more than 230 avian species), including keel-billed toucans, spectacled owls and the green kingfisher. And, you can hardly miss the Montezuma oropendola, whose massive nests dangle from the trees like twiggy pendulums. The moisture, in the meantime, keeps the place hopping with various species of poison-dart frog.

The reserve is surrounded by some of the country's most remote indigenous reserves, which you can visit with a local guide.

Although there is a ranger station at the reserve entrance with bathrooms, there are no other facilities nearby. A 9km trail leads south to a waterfall, but it is steep, slippery and poorly maintained. Jungle boots are recommended.

ing and ceiling fans, as well as superclean bathrooms. Hearty breakfasts (think fresh pancakes with tropical fruit) are served on a lovely canal-side deck. It's opposite the Catholic church.

HOTEL MISS JUNIE
Cabina $$
(2709-8102; www.iguanaverdetours.com; s/d standard US$45/50, superior US$55/60, all incl breakfast) Miss Junie's place is set on wide grounds, shaded by palm trees and strewn with hammocks and wooden armchairs. Spotless, wood-paneled rooms in a nicely kept tropical plantation–style building are tastefully decorated with wood accents and bright bedspreads. Upstairs rooms share a breezy balcony overlooking the canal. Credit cards accepted. It's at the northern end of the main road.

North of the Village

Most of the lodges north of the village cater to high-end travelers on package deals, though most will accept walk-ins (er, boat-ins) if they aren't full. Rates include all meals and are based on double occupancy; credit cards are mostly accepted.

RANA ROJA
Lodge $$
(8824-5758, 2709-8260; www.tortuguero ranaroja.com; per person US$60;) This Tico-run spot offers one of the best-value options in the area. Small, earth-colored cabins – all with private terraces and rockers – are connected by elevated walkways. The units are immaculate, with tile floors, hot showers and awesome jungle views. Free kayaks are available onsite and guests can make use of the turtle-shaped swimming pool at the neighboring Evergreen Lodge, just a couple of meters away.

TORTUGA LODGE & GARDENS
Lodge $$$
(2257-0766, 2521-6099; www.costaricaexpedi tions.com/tortuga-lodge; 2-night package per adult/child US$528/304;) Tortuguero's most elegant lodge, operated by Costa Rica Expeditions, is set amid 20 hectares of private gardens. Here you'll find a serene environment, as well as 27 demure rooms that channel a 19th-century safari vibe. The grounds come equipped with private trails, a pool and a bar-restaurant – both riverside.

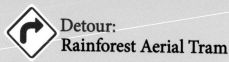

Detour:
Rainforest Aerial Tram

The brainchild of biologist Don Perry, a pioneer of rainforest canopy research, the **Rainforest Aerial Tram** (2257-5961; www.rainforestrams.com; adult/student & child US$55/28, full-day tour with lunch & guided hike US$99/56;) carries visitors to the heights of the forest canopy in a gondola. The 2.6km ride takes 40 minutes each way, affording unusual plant-spotting and bird-watching opportunities. The fee includes a knowledgeable guide, which is helpful since the dense vegetation can make observing animals difficult. A variety of other tours, as well as zip lining, are also available. Book online or in its San José **office** (2257-5961; reservations. cr@rainforestadventure.com; Av 7 btwn Calles 5 & 7; 9am-5pm Mon-Fri).

PACHIRA LODGE Lodge $$$
(2256-6340, 2257-2242; www.pachira lodge.com; 2-night package per adult/child US$289/100;) A sprawling compound set on 5 hectares of land, this 88-room hotel is a popular family spot, with pristine, brightly painted clapboard bungalows and rooms that sleep up to four. (There are even cribs and children's beds.) All have private terraces, mini-fridge and safe – and there's a turtle-shaped pool, in addition to the region's only zip line (US$30).

MAWAMBA LODGE Lodge $$$
(2709-8181; www.mawamba.com; 2-night package per adult US$285, adult/child superior US$423/212;) With pool tables, foosball, a mosaic swimming pool, and butterfly and frog gardens, this is one of the most tricked-out lodges around. Rooms are simple, wood-paneled affairs with firm beds, good fans and roomy bathrooms with hot water. All are fronted by wide verandas with hammocks and rocking chairs. Packages include several tours.

LAGUNA LODGE Lodge $$$
(2272-4943, 2709-8082; www.lagunatortugue ro.com; 2-night package per person from US$250;) This expansive lodge, liberally decorated with gorgeous mosaic art and trim, has 110 graceful rooms with high ceilings and wide decks lined with Sarchí-made leather rocking chairs. It also has a restaurant, two bars (canal-side and poolside), a massage room, soccer pitch and a Gaudí-esque reception area.

 Eating

One of Tortuguero's unsung pleasures is the cuisine: the homey restaurants lure you in from the rain with steaming platters of Caribbean-style food.

WILD GINGER Fusion $$
(mains US$10-30; noon-9pm) This new beachfront standout is a fantastic addition to village dining options. Well-balanced fusion cuisine utilizes fresh ingredients and includes filet mignon with tamarind sauce and spaghetti carbonara. Leave room for dessert. It's 150m north of the elementary school.

MISS JUNIE'S Caribbean $$
(2709-8029; mains US$9-14; 7-9am, 11:30am-2:30pm & 6-9pm) Tortuguero's best-known restaurant grew from a personal kitchen to a full-blown restaurant and lodge. Local specialties on the menu include chicken, fish, and whole lobster cooked in flavorful Caribbean sauces, with coconut rice and beans. It's at the northern end of the main road.

SUPER MORPHO Self-Catering
(6:30am-9pm Mon-Sat, 8am-8pm Sun) Self-caterers can pick up basic groceries at the Super Morpho *pulpería* (corner store).

ⓘ Getting There & Away

Bus & Boat

Tortuguero is accessible by boat from Cariari or Moín.

Getting to Tortuguero is not difficult; there are a number of companies that offer bus-boat transport service from Cariari to Tortuguero (via La Pavona) several times a day. But competition among rival transport agencies is fierce, and some will say anything to get your fare – including telling you that they're the only transport option in town. Don't believe the hype. During the peak of the turtle-nesting season, we recommend purchasing your tickets at least one day in advance.

FROM SAN JOSÉ

Take the 6:10am, 9am or 10:30am bus to Cariari (three hours) from San José's Gran Terminal del Caribe. In Cariari, you will arrive at a bus station at the south end of town (known as the estación nueva – new station). From here, walk or take a taxi 500m north to the estación vieja (old station) or Terminal Caribeño.

PUBLIC TRANSPORTATION FROM CARIARI

The cheapest option is by public transportation on **Clic Clic** (☏ 8844-0463, 2709-8155) or **Coopetraca** (☏ 2767-7137, 2767-7590), both of which charge US$5 per person for bus-boat service from the estación vieja all the way to Tortuguero. For these two options, the bus service will be the same, but the boat service will be different. Bring colones, as they may not accept US dollars. Buses depart Cariari at 6am, 9am, 11:30am and 3pm.

If you choose Clic Clic, buy only the bus ticket to La Pavona (US$2); if you choose Coopetraca, you'll buy the combined bus-boat ticket (US$5) up front. After a ride through banana plantations, you will arrive at the Río Suerte, where a number of boat companies will be waiting at the dock. If you're riding with Clic Clic, you will pay the remainder of your fare (US$3) to the boatman. Boats depart daily at 7:30am, 1pm and 4:30pm.

Private Transportation from Cariari

For a more expensive private service, there is **Viajes Bananero** (☏ 2709-8005; per person one-way US$35), which has an office inside the San José bus terminal in Cariari. Buy your boat ticket here (US$10). From this same point, you will then take a bus (US$1.20) to its proprietary boat dock. Bus departure times are at 11:30am and 2pm. If you are traveling in a group, Bananero can arrange custom pick-ups. For private service, you will need to reserve ahead.

Private Transportation from Moín

Moín–Tortuguero is primarily a tourist route – and while boats ply these canals frequently, there isn't a scheduled service. **Tropical Wind** (☏ 8313-7164, 8327-0317, 2798-6059; per person one way US$30) and Viajes Bananero are two Tortuguero-based agencies that make the run regularly; both of these can stop in Parismina (one way US$25).

Rainforest Aerial Tram
SIEPMANN / IMAGEBROKER ©

Likewise, you can always call the companies operating out of Puerto Limón, since they frequently have boats in the area. Note: it may take 24 to 48 hours to secure transport – especially in the low season.

PARQUE NACIONAL TORTUGUERO

'Humid' is the driest word that could truthfully be used to describe Tortuguero, a 311-sq-km coastal park that serves as the most important breeding ground of the green sea turtle. With an annual rainfall of up to 6000mm in the northern part of the park, it is one of the wettest areas in the country. In addition, the protected area extends into the Caribbean Sea, covering about 5200 sq km of marine habitat. In other words, plan on spending quality time in a boat.

The famed **Canales de Tortuguero** are the introduction to this park. A north–south waterway created to connect a series of lagoons and meandering rivers in 1974, this engineering marvel allowed inland navigation between Limón and coastal villages in something sturdier than a dugout canoe. Regular flights service the village of Tortuguero – but if you fly, you'll be missing half the fun. The leisurely taxi-boat ride, through banana plantations and wild jungle, is equal parts recreation and transportation.

Most visitors come to watch sea turtles lay eggs on the area's wild beaches. The area attracts four of the world's eight species of sea turtle, making it a crucial habitat for these massive reptiles. It will come as little surprise, then, that these hatching grounds gave birth to the sea turtle–conservation movement. The Caribbean Conservation Corporation, the first program of its kind in the world, has continuously monitored turtle populations here since 1955. Today green sea turtles are increasing in numbers along this coast, but the leatherback, hawksbill and loggerhead are in decline.

The area, however, is more than just turtles: Tortuguero teems with wildlife. You'll find sloths and howler monkeys in the treetops, tiny frogs and green iguanas scurrying among buttress roots, and mighty tarpon and endangered manatee swimming in the waters.

Activities

Turtle-Watching

Most female turtles share a nesting instinct that drives them to return to the beach of their birth, or natal beach, in order to lay their eggs. (Only the leatherback returns to a more general region, instead of a specific beach.) During their lifetimes, they will usually nest every two to three years and, depending on the species, may come ashore to lay eggs 10 times in one season. Often,

Yellow-crowned night heron
SHANNON NACE / GETTY IMAGES ©

Detour:
Parque Nacional Braulio Carrillo

Enter this under-explored national park and you will have an idea of what Costa Rica looked like prior to the 1950s, when 75% of the country's surface area was still covered in forest: steep hills cloaked in impossibly tall trees are interrupted only by cascading rivers and canyons. It has an extraordinary biodiversity due to the range of altitudes, from steamy 2906m cloud forest alongside Volcán Barva to lush, humid lowlands on the Caribbean slope. Its most incredible feature, however, is that this massive park (the size of Rhode Island) is only 30 minutes north of San José.

Founded in the 1970s, Braulio Carrillo's creation was the result of a unique compromise between conservationists and developers. At the time, the government had announced a plan to build a new highway that would connect the capital to Puerto Limón. Back then San José's only link to its most important port was via a crumbling railway or a slow rural road through Cartago and Turrialba. The only feasible route for the new thoroughfare was along a low pass between the Barva and Irazú volcanoes – an area covered in primary forest. Conservationists were deeply worried about putting a road (and any attendant development) in an area that served as San José's watershed. So a plan was hatched: the road would be built, but the 400 sq km of land to either side of it would be set aside as a national park. Thus, in 1978, Parque Nacional Braulio Carrillo was born.

a turtle's ability to successfully reproduce depends on the ecological health of this original habitat.

To lay her eggs, the female turtle digs a perfect cylindrical cavity in the sand using her flippers, and then lays 80 to 120 eggs. She diligently covers the nest with sand to protect the eggs, and she may even create a false nest in another location in an attempt to confuse predators. She then makes her way back to sea – after which the eggs are on their own. Incubation ranges from 45 to 70 days, after which hatchlings – no bigger than the size of your palm – break out of their shells using a caruncle, or temporary tooth. They crawl to the ocean in small groups, moving as quickly as possible to avoid dehydration and predators. Once they reach the surf, they must swim for at least 24 hours to get to deeper water, away from land-based predators.

Because of the sensitive nature of the habitat and the critically endangered status of some species, tours of this activity are highly regulated. By law, tours can only take place between 8am and midnight. Some guides will offer tours after midnight; these are illegal.

Visitors should wear closed-toe shoes and rain gear. Tours cost US$20 (a flat rate established by the village). Nesting season runs from March to October, with July and August being prime time.

Other Wildlife-Watching

More than 300 bird species, both resident and migratory, have been recorded in Tortuguero – a bird-watchers' paradise. Due to the wet habitat, the park is especially rich in waders, including egrets, jacanas, 14 different types of heron, as well as species such as kingfishers, toucans and the great curassow (a type of jungle peacock known locally as the *pavón*). The great green macaw is a highlight, most common from December to April, when the almond trees are fruiting. In September and October look for flocks of migratory species such as eastern kingbird, barn swallows and purple martins.

The Caribbean Conservation Corporation conducts a biannual monitoring program, in which scientists take inventory of local and migratory species.

Certain species of mammals are particularly evident in Tortuguero, especially mantled howler monkeys, the Central American spider monkey and white-faced capuchin. With good binoculars and a guide, you can usually see both two- and three-toed sloths. In addition, normally shy neotropical river otters are reasonably habituated to boats.

Boating

Four aquatic trails wind their way through Parque Nacional Tortuguero, inviting waterborne exploration. **Río Tortuguero** acts as the entrance way to the network of trails. This wide, beautiful river is often covered with water lilies and frequented by aquatic birds such as herons, kingfishers and anhinga – the latter of which is known as the snakebird for the way its slim, winding neck pokes out of the water when it swims.

Caño Chiquero and **Canõ Mora** are two narrower waterways with good wildlife-spotting opportunities. According to park regulation, only kayaks, canoes and silent electric boats are allowed in these areas (a rule that is constantly violated by many area tour companies and lodges). Caño Chiquero is thick with vegetation, especially red guácimo trees and epiphytes. Black turtles and green iguana like to hang out here. Caño Mora is about 3km long but only 10m wide, so it feels like it's straight out of *The Jungle Book*. **Caño Harold** is actually an artificially constructed canal, but that doesn't stop the creatures – such as Jesus Christ lizards and caiman – from inhabiting its tranquil waters.

Canoe rental and boat tours are available in Tortuguero village.

Hiking

Behind Cuatro Esquinas station, **El Gavilán Land Trail** is the only public trail through the park that is on solid ground. Visitors can hike the muddy, 2km

Left: Bungalow, Puerto Viejo de Talamanca (p311); **Below:** Howler monkeys
(LEFT) CHRISTER FREDRIKSSON / GETTY IMAGES © (BELOW) CHRISTER FREDRIKSSON / GETTY IMAGES ©

out-and-back trail that traverses the tropical humid forest and follows a stretch of beach. Green parrots and several species of monkeys are commonly sighted here. The short trail is well marked. Rubber boots are required (for rent at hotels and near the park entrance).

ℹ Information

Park headquarters is at **Cuatro Esquinas** (📞2709-8086; admission US$10; ⏰5:30am-6pm with breaks for breakfast & lunch), just south of Tortuguero village. This is an unusually helpful ranger station, with maps, information and access to a 2km-loop nature trail. Wear boots: it's muddy, even in the dry season.

Jalova Station (⏰6am-6pm) is on the canal at the south entrance to the national park, accessible from Parismina by boat. Tour boats from Moín often stop here for a picnic; you will find a short nature trail, bathroom, drinking water and rudimentary camping facilities that may or may not be open (and may or may not be flooded).

ℹ Getting There & Away

The park is a short walk from the village of Tortuguero (the most common entry point) and also accessible by boat from Parismina.

CAHUITA
POP 600

Even as tourism has mushroomed on Costa Rica's southern coast, Cahuita has managed to hold onto its laid-back Caribbean vibe. The roads are made of dirt, many of the older houses rest on stilts and chatty neighbors still converse in Mekatelyu. A graceful black-sand beach and a chilled-out demeanor hint at a not-so-distant past, when the area was little more than just a string of cacao farms.

Cahuita proudly claims the area's first permanent Afro-Caribbean settler – a turtle fisherman named William Smith, who moved his family to Punta Cahuita in 1828. Now his descendants, along

Cahuita

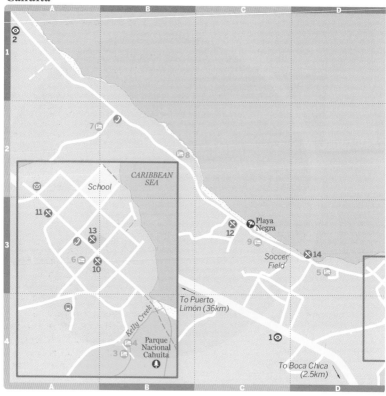

Cahuita

◎ **Sights**
1 Mariposario de Cahuita.........................C4
2 Tree of Life A1

🛏 **Sleeping**
3 Alby Lodge B4
4 Bungalows Aché B4
5 El Encanto B&B.......................................D3
6 Hotel La Casa de las Flores.................A3
7 Magellan Inn...A2
8 Piscina Natural.......................................B2
9 Playa Negra Guesthouse C3

✕ **Eating**
10 Cafe Chocolatte 100%
       Natural..A3
11 Cha Cha Cha A3
12 Chao's Paradise....................................C3
13 Restaurant La Fé A3
14 Sobre Las Olas D3

with those of so many other West Indian immigrants, run the backyard eateries and brightly painted bungalows that hug this idyllic stretch of coast.

Situated on a pleasant point, the town itself has a waterfront, but no beach. For that, most folks make the jaunt to Playa Negra or into neighboring Parque Nacional Cahuita.

◎ Sights

MARIPOSARIO DE CAHUITA Gardens
(Map p306; ☎2755-0361; admission US$10; ⊗8:30am-3:30pm Mon-Fri, to noon Sat; ⊕) Stroll around the fountain-filled grounds of this butterfly farm and admire the local residents, including many friendly cater-pillars. Descriptions are posted in several

wood cabins have bright red-and-white linens and come stocked with a lockbox, minifridge, kettle and private decks with hammocks.

ALBY LODGE
Bungalow $$

(Map p306; 2755-0031; www.albylodge. com; d/tr/q US$50/55/60; P 🛜) This fine German-run lodge on the edge of the park has spacious landscaped grounds that attract howler monkeys and birds. Four raised bungalows are spread out, allowing for plenty of privacy. High ceilings, mosquito nets and driftwood details make for pleasant jungle decor. A common *rancho* (thatched gazebo) has excellent communal kitchen facilities.

HOTEL LA CASA DE LAS FLORES
Hotel $$

(Map p306; 2755-0326; www.lacasadelasflore shotel.com; d incl breakfast US$80, additional person US$15; P ✳ 🛜) This bright Italian-owned spot has 10 large, sleek contemporary rooms (one of which is wheelchair-accessible) equipped with spacious bathrooms, cable TV and efficient air-con. The close proximity to Coco's, however, puts you within thumping distance of the bar's well-endowed speakers. Credit cards accepted.

Playa Negra

PLAYA NEGRA GUESTHOUSE
Bungalow $$

(Map p306; 2755-0127; www.playanegra. cr; d US$60-75, cottage US$95-140; P 🛜 🏊) This beautiful Caribbean-style plantation house, with several freestanding storybook cottages (equipped with full kitchens), is meticulously decorated and maintained. Guest rooms are painted sherbety colors and feature charming tropical accents, such as colorful mosaics in the bathrooms and cozy wicker lounge chairs on the private decks. Every unit has a minifridge and coffeemaker; there is a barbecue and honor bar, plus a lovely free-form pool is set into a well-manicured garden dotted with fan palms. A winner all around. Credit cards accepted. Find it 200m west of the soccer field.

languages; guided tours are available. It's located just off of Hwy 36.

Sleeping

There are two general areas to stay in Cahuita: the town center (which can be a little noisy), or north of town along Playa Negra.

Center

BUNGALOWS ACHÉ
Bungalow $$

(Map p306; 2755-0119; www.bungalowsache. com; bungalows US$40-50; P 🛜) In Nigeria, Aché means 'Amen,' and you'll likely say the same thing when you see these spotless octagonal bungalows nestled into a delightful garden bordering the national park. The three charming, polished-

PISCINA NATURAL
Cabina **$$**

(Map p306; 2755-0146; piscinanaturalcr. hotels.officelive.com; d/tr US$40/50; P) This gem of a spot lies about 1km northwest of the soccer field along the main road. Run by inimitable Cahuita native Walter, it's a self-proclaimed 'Caribbean Paradise,' and rightfully so. Painted cement rooms are comfortable and come equipped with bathrooms. What makes this chilled-out little place so special are the lush grounds and the natural pool amid the rocks. There is a huge shared kitchen and an outdoor lounge studded with intriguing driftwood sculptures.

MAGELLAN INN
Inn **$$$**

(Map p306; 2755-0035; www.magellaninn. com; d with fan/air-con US$85/108, d deluxe US$130, all incl breakfast; P ✳ 🖥 ☲) An elegant little oasis in a very peaceful location, this very comfortable inn has six spacious rooms with rustic wood furnishings, firm mattresses and private terraces with hammocks. It also has a refined, open-air bar that overlooks a beautifully landscaped garden and pool. It's located along the road that branches off toward the Hotel Suizo Loco Lodge.

EL ENCANTO B&B
B&B **$$**

(Map p306; 2755-0113; www.elencantoca huita.com; s/d/studio/ste/house US$65/75/95/125/220, all incl breakfast; P 🖥 ☲) This charming French-owned B&B, only about 200m west of downtown Cahuita, is set into lovingly landscaped grounds that are dotted with easy chairs and hammocks. Demure bungalows have high ceilings, tile floors and firm beds draped in colorful textiles. The studio and the beach house both have fully equipped kitchens. Credit cards accepted.

 Eating

Center

CHA CHA CHA
International **$$**

(Map p306; 8394-4153; mains US$9-20; ⏱ noon-10pm Tue-Sun; 🍴) In a corner veranda of an old house, this attractive expat favorite is adorned with the chef's artwork and offers sophisticated world cuisine. Exquisite sauces star in dishes from filet mignon with wild mushrooms and truffle oil to mussels in Dijon sauce. Plenty of vegetarian options feature as well. Evocatively named cocktails, like the Dulce Amor (Sweet Love), made with star fruit and *guaro* (a local firewater made with sugarcane), are highly worthwhile, as are the decadent desserts.

RESTAURANT LA FÉ
Seafood **$$**

(Map p306; dishes US$7-30; ⏱ 7am-11pm) Chef and owner Walter, a Cahuita native, serves up tall tales and tasty meals at this reasonably priced spot. There's a laundry list of Tico and Caribbean items, but the main draw is anything doused

Villager in Cahuita (p305)
CHRISTER FREDRIKSSON / GETTY IMAGES ©

in the restaurant's spicy-delicious coconut sauce.

CAFE CHOCOLATTE 100% NATURAL
International **$**

(Map p306; dishes US$3-11; ⏰6:30am-2pm Mon-Fri) There's no better place in Cahuita to greet the morning with a coffee or unwind in the afternoon with a refreshing *jugo* (juice). Hearty sandwiches on homemade whole-grain bread are perfect for beach picnics in the national park.

Playa Negra

SOBRE LAS OLAS   Seafood **$$**

(Map p306; ☎2755-0109; pastas US$11-13, mains US$11-25; ⏰noon-10pm Wed-Mon; 🐟) Cahuita's top option for waterfront dining (an ideal spot for a date) is only a 300m walk out of town. It is owned by a lively Tico-Italian couple who serve a variety of Mediterranean-influenced specialties.

CHAO'S PARADISE   Caribbean **$$**

(Map p306; ☎2755-0480; seafood mains US$7-15; ⏰11am-11pm) Follow the wafting smell of garlic and simmering sauces to this highly recommended Playa Negra outpost that serves fresh catches cooked up in spicy 'Chao' sauce. The open-air restaurant-bar has a pool table and live music some nights.

ℹ️ Getting There & Away

All public buses arrive and depart at the bus terminal, 200m southwest of Parque Central.

Bribrí/Sixaola US$3.50, two hours, departs hourly from 6am to 7pm.

Puerto Limón (Autotransportes Mepe) US$5.10, 1½ hours, departs 6am, 9:30am, 10:45am, 1:45pm and 6:15pm. (These times are approximate because these buses originate in Manzanillo. Get there early just in case.)

Puerto Viejo de Talamanca US$1.25, 30 minutes to one hour, departs 6:15am, 6:45am, 11:15am, 3:45pm and 6:45pm.

San José (Autotransportes Mepe) US$8.25, four hours, departs 7am, 8am, 9:30am, 11:30am and 4:30pm.

♥ If You Like... Parks, Reserves & Wildlife

If you like Parque Nacional Tortuguero, we think you'll like these other parks, reserves and wildlife along and near the Caribbean coast:

1 VERAGUA RAINFOREST RESEARCH & ADVENTURE PARK

(☎2296-5056; www.veraguarainforest.com; adult with/without zip-line tour US$89/55, child with/without zip-line tour US$65/45; 🚼) In Las Brisas de Veragua, you'll find an aerial tram, a reptile vivarium, an insectarium, and hummingbird and butterfly gardens.

2 TREE OF LIFE

(Map p306; ☎8610-0490, 2755-0014; www.treeoflifecostarica.com; adult/child US$12/6, guided tour US$15; ⏰9am-3pm Nov–mid-Apr, daily tour 11am Jul-Aug, closed mid-Apr–Jun & Sep-Oct) This wildlife center and botanical garden 2km west of Cahuita on the Playa Negra road rescues and rehabilitates animals, while also promoting conservation through education.

3 JAGUAR CENTRO DE RESCATE

(☎2750-0710; www.jaguarrescue.com; admission US$15; ⏰tours 9:30am & 11:30am Mon-Sat) Named in honor of its original resident, this wildlife rescue center in Playa Chiquita now focuses mostly on sloths and monkeys. Founded by Spanish zoologist Encar and her partner Sandro, an Italian herpetologist, the center rehabilitates orphaned, injured and rescued animals for reintroduction into the wild.

ℹ️ Getting Around

The best way to get around Cahuita – especially if you're staying out along Playa Negra – is by bicycle. In town, rent bikes at Mister Big J's. At Playa Negra, bikes are available at Centro Turístico Brigitte for similar prices.

PARQUE NACIONAL CAHUITA

This small park – just 10 sq km – is one of the more frequently visited national parks in Costa Rica. The reasons are simple: the nearby town of Cahuita provides

GIL GIUGLIO / ALAMY ©

Don't Miss Cacao Trails

Visit this exquisite new botanical garden and outdoor museum, where educational tours demonstrate the various uses of medicinal plants and the workings of a cacao plantation (plus you can see and sample the final product), with plenty of opportunities for wildlife sightings along the way.

An additional expedition allows further exploration by kayak. It's midway between Cahuita and Puerto Viejo; any bus between the two can drop you at the entrance. This is a great outing for kids.

NEED TO KNOW

☏ 8812 7460; www.cacaotrails.com; guided tour US$25; ⊙ 8am-5pm

attractive accommodations and easy access; more importantly, the white-sand beaches, coral reef and coastal rainforest are bursting with wildlife.

Declared a national park in 1978, Cahuita is typical of the entire coast (very humid), which results in dense tropical foliage, as well as coconut palms and sea grapes. The area includes the swampy **Punta Cahuita**, which juts into the sea between two stretches of sandy beach. Often flooded, the point is covered with cativo and mango trees and is a popular hangout spot for birds such as green ibis, yellow-crowned night herons, boat-billed herons and the rare green-and-rufous kingfishers.

Red land and fiddler crabs live along the beaches, attracting mammals such as crab-eating raccoons and white-nosed coatis. White-faced capuchins, southern opossums and three-toed sloths also live in the area. The mammal you are most likely to see (and hear) is the mantled howler monkey, which makes its presence known. The coral reef represents another rich ecosystem that abounds with life.

Activities

Hiking

An easily navigable 8km **coastal trail** leads through the jungle from Kelly Creek to Puerto Vargas. At times the trail follows the beach; at other times hikers are 100m or so away from the sand. The trail continues around Punta Cahuita to the long stretch of Playa Vargas. It ends at the southern tip of the reef, where it meets up with a road leading to the Puerto Vargas ranger station.

Swimming

Almost immediately upon entering the park, you'll see the 2km-long **Playa Blanca** stretching along a gently curving bay to the east. The first 500m of beach may be unsafe for swimming, but beyond that, waves are generally gentle. (Look for green flags marking safe swimming spots.) The rocky Punta Cahuita headland separates this beach from the next one, **Playa Vargas**.

Snorkeling

Parque Nacional Cahuita contains one of the last living coral reefs in Costa Rica. While the reef represents some of the area's best snorkeling, it has incurred damage over the years from earthquakes and tourism-related activities. In an attempt to protect the reef from further damage, snorkeling is only permitted with a licensed guide. The going rate for one person is about US$30.

You'll find that conditions vary greatly, depending on the weather and other factors. In general, the drier months in the highlands (from February to April) are best for snorkeling on the coast, as less runoff results in less silt in the sea. Conditions are often cloudy at other times.

 Eating

BOCA CHICA　　　　Costa Rican **$**
(☎2755-0415; meals US$7-20; ⏱9am-6pm)
After the long, hot hike through the jungle, you may think you are hallucinating when you see Boca Chica, a small, whitewashed

family recreation center, at the end of the road. It's not a mirage, just a well-placed bar and eatery, run by a charming Italian owner, offering cold *jugos*, homemade pasta, and Tico and Caribbean specialties.

ℹ **Getting There & Away**

The Kelly Creek ranger station (☎2755-0461; admission by donation; ⏱6am-5pm) is convenient to the town of Cahuita, while 1km down Hwy 36 takes you to the well-signed Puerto Vargas ranger station (☎2755-0302; admission US$10; ⏱8am-4pm Mon-Fri, 7am-5pm Sat & Sun).

PUERTO VIEJO DE TALAMANCA

There was a time when the only travelers to the little seaside settlement once known as Old Harbor were intrepid surfers who padded around the quiet, dusty streets, board under arm, on their way to surf Salsa Brava. That, certainly, is no longer the case. This burgeoning party town is bustling with tourist activity: street vendors ply Rasta trinkets and Bob Marley T-shirts, stylish eateries serve global fusion everything and intentionally rustic bamboo bars pump dancehall and reggaetón. The scene can get downright hedonistic, attracting dedicated revelers who arrive to marinate in ganja and *guaro*.

Despite that reputation, Puerto Viejo nonetheless manages to hold on to an easy charm. Nearby, you'll find rainforest fruit farms set to a soundtrack of cackling birds and croaking frogs, and wide-open beaches where the daily itinerary revolves around surfing and snoozing.

 **Activities**

Surfing

Breaking on the reef that hugs the village is the famed **Salsa Brava**, a shallow break that is also one of the country's most infamous waves. It's a tricky ride – if you lose it, the waves will plow you straight into the reef – and definitely not for beginners. Salsa Brava offers both rights and lefts,

Puerto Viejo de Talamanca

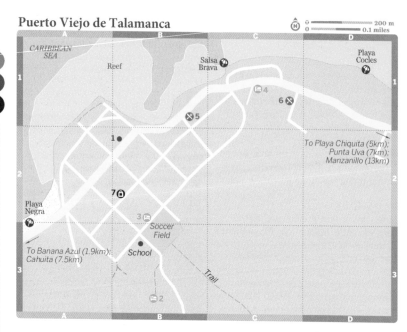

Puerto Viejo de Talamanca

◉ Sights
1 ATEC...B2

🛏 Sleeping
2 Cashew Hill Jungle Cottages..............B3
3 Hotel Pura Vida..................................B2
4 Lotus Garden C1

✗ Eating
5 Koki Beach B1
6 Stashu's con Fusion C1

🛍 Shopping
7 Lulu Berlu Gallery B2

although the right is usually faster. For more information see p316.

For a softer landing, try the beach break at **Playa Cocles** – where the waves are almost as impressive and the landing far less damaging. Cocles is about 2km east of town. Conditions are usually best early in the day, before the wind picks up.

Swimming

The entire southern Caribbean coast – from Cahuita all the way south to Punta Mona – is lined with unbelievably beautiful beaches. Just northwest of town, **Playa Negra** offers the area's safest swimming.

Snorkeling

The waters from Cahuita to Manzanillo are protected by Costa Rica's only two living reef systems, which form a naturally protected sanctuary, home to some 35 species of coral and 400 species of fish, not to mention dolphins, sharks and, occasionally, whales. Generally, underwater visibility is best when the sea is calm.

Just south of **Punta Uva**, in front of the Arrecife restaurant, is a decent spot for snorkeling, when conditions are calm. The reef at **Manzanillo** is also easily accessible. Most of the dive companies offer snorkeling trips for about US$35 to US$55 per person.

Diving

Divers in the southern Caribbean will discover upward of 20 dive sites, from the coral gardens in shallow waters to deeper sites with amazing underwater vertical walls. Literally hundreds of species of fish swim around here, including angelfish, parrotfish, triggerfish, shark and different species of jack and snapper.

Hiking

The immediate vicinity of Puerto Viejo is not prime hiking territory: the proximity of the Parque Nacional Cahuita and the Refugio Nacional de Vida Silvestre Gandoca-Manzanillo means that most trekkers will head to these protected areas to look for toucans and sloths.

Sleeping

BANANA AZUL Lodge **$$**

(☏2750-2035; www.bananaazul.com; s/d from US$74/79, d ste US$149, all incl breakfast; P🛜🏊) Removed from town, this wonderful hotel sits at the edge of a blissfully tranquil black-sand beach. Rooms are all done up in the finest jungle chic: shining wooden floors, white linens, mosquito nets and private decks with views – as well as graceful touches such as bromeliads in the showers. An onsite restaurant-bar serves meals and sensational cocktails. Bikes, body boards and snorkeling gear are available for rent, and beach access is steps away. No children under 16; credit cards accepted.

HOTEL PURA VIDA Hotel **$**

(Map p312; ☏2750-0002; www.hotel-puravida.com; s/d/tr US$28/32/42, without bathroom US$34/38/48; P🛜) Though this place has budget prices, the atmosphere and amenities are solidly midrange. Ten breezy, immaculate rooms, clad in polished wood, bright linens and ceramic tile floors make up this homey Chilean-German run inn on a quiet street near the soccer field. Alongside a lovingly

tended garden, you'll find a serene lounge with easy chairs and hammocks. A great spot for couples; credit cards accepted.

LOTUS GARDEN Hotel **$$**

(Map p312; ☏2750-0232; www.lotusgardencr.com; d US$65-90; P❄🛜🏊) Infusing a little Kyoto into Puerto Viejo, the nine large, stone-lined suites at this inn come with king-sized four-poster beds, cable TV, air-con, lockbox, Jacuzzi tubs, gobs of Asian textiles and Japanese names such as 'Shogun.' Several smaller doubles have simple decor and ceiling fans. To complete the mood, there's the recommended Lotus Garden Restaurant.

SAMASATI RETREAT CENTER Hut, Bungalow **$$**

(☏2750-0315, in USA 800-563-9643; www.samasati.com; per person guesthouse/bungalow incl 3 meals from US$85/135; P) Set on a hillside 8km west of Puerto Viejo, this attractive yoga retreat center has sweeping views of the coast as well as nine wooden bungalows with wraparound screened windows and a guesthouse stocked with single beds

FRANCK GUIZIOU / ALAMY ©

Don't Miss Aviarios del Caribe Sloth Sanctuary

About 10km northwest of Cahuita, this wildlife sanctuary sits on an 88-hectare property bordering the Río Estrella. Here, proprietors Luis Arroyo and Judy Avery help injured and orphaned sloths – providing travelers with an opportunity to see these unique animals up close. (Irrefutable fact: there is nothing cuter than a baby sloth.) Though many of the rehabilitated sloths remain on the grounds (animals orphaned at a very young age don't have the skills to return to the wild), Luis and Judy have been successful at releasing more than 80 of them back into area forests.

Volunteer opportunities may be available; however, at the time of writing, the sanctuary was overwhelmed with volunteers (a response to viral videos introducing the internet to the aforementioned cuteness of baby sloths). Check the website for updates.

NEED TO KNOW

2750-0775; www.slothsanctuary.com; tour adult/child US$25/15; 8am-5pm

---

(for solo travelers on a budget). Meals are vegetarian, with an organic focus (including organic chocolate cake) and are served buffet-style on a terrace with views.

CASHEW HILL JUNGLE COTTAGES
Bungalow $$$

(Map p312; 2750-0256, 2750-0001; www.cashewhilllodge.co.cr; cottages US$90-150; P 🛜 🐾) Set on a lush hillside studded with pre-Columbian style statuary, the seven cottages at this lovely jungle spot are bright,

colorful and comfortable. The wood houses are painted in vivid shades and come with full kitchens, loft-style sleeping areas and charming rustic touches such as shell-encrusted sinks.

 Eating

STASHU'S CON FUSION
Fusion $$

(Map p312; 2750-0530; meals US$7-18; 5-10pm Thu-Tue; 🍴) This romantic candlelit patio cafe serves up creative fusion cuisine that combines elements of Caribbean, Indian, Mexican and Thai cooking. Steamed spicy mussels in red-curry sauce and tandoori chicken in coconut are just a couple of standouts. Excellent vegetarian and vegan items round out the menu. Owner and chef Stash Golas is an artist inside the kitchen and out. Do not miss.

SELVIN'S RESTAURANT Caribbean $$
(☎2750-0664; mains US$7-15; ⊗8am-8pm Wed-Sun) Selvin is a member of the extensive Brown family, noted for their charm, and his place is considered one of the region's best, specializing in shrimp, lobster, a terrific *rondón* (seafood gumbo) and a succulent chicken *caribeño* (chicken stewed in a spicy Caribbean sauce).

LA PECORA NERA Italian $$$
(☎2750-0490; mains US$11-30; ⊗5pm-late Tue-Sun; 🍴) If you splurge for a single fancy meal during your trip, do it here. A lovely, candlelit patio off the main road is home to this romantic eatery run by Tuscan-born Ilario Giannoni. It serves deftly prepared Italian seafood and pasta dishes, as well as unusual offerings like the delicate *carpaccio di carambola:* transparent slices of star fruit topped with shrimp, tomatoes and balsamic vinaigrette. There is an extensive wine list (from US$16 a bottle), but you can't go wrong with the well-chosen and relatively inexpensive house wines. The restaurant has also branched out to a more casual spot next door, **Gatta Ci Cova** (sandwiches US$6-11, mains US$8-11; ⊗noon-10pm Tue-Sun; 🍴), where you can grab panini and drinks.

KOKI BEACH Latin American $$$
(Map p312; ☎2275-0902; www.kokibeach.com; meals US$11-26; ⊗2pm-midnight Wed-Sun; 🛜) Reminiscent of Miami Beach, this sleek spot cranks reggae-lite and sports colorful Adirondack chairs that face the ocean from an elevated wooden platform on the east end of town. There's a decent selection of Peruvian-inflected *ceviches* (seafood marinated in lemon or lime juice, garlic and seasonings), meat and seafood dishes, but slim pickings for vegetarians.

🛍 Shopping

Makeshift stalls clutter the main road, selling knickknacks and Rasta-colored accoutrements.

LULU BERLU GALLERY Arts & Crafts
(Map p312; ☎2750-0394; ⊗9am-9pm) Lulu Berlu Gallery carries folk art, one-of-a-kind clothing and mosaic mirrors, among many other locally made items.

🛈 Getting There & Away

Buses connect to the following locations:
Bribrí/Sixaola US$2.90, 30/90 minutes, departs roughly every hour from 6:30am to 7:30pm.

Cahuita/Puerto Limón US$3.20, 30/90 minutes, departs roughly every hour from 5:30am to 7:30pm.

Manzanillo US$0.85, 30 minutes, departs 6:45am, 7:15am, 11:45am, 4:15pm and 7:15pm.

San José US$9.50, five hours, departs 9am, 11am and 4pm.

MANZANILLO

The chill village of Manzanillo has long been off the beaten track, even since the paved road arrived in 2003. This little town remains a vibrant outpost of Afro-Caribbean culture and has also remained pristine, thanks to the 1985 establishment of the Refugio Nacional de Vida Silvestre Gandoca-Manzanillo, which includes the village and imposes strict regulations on regional development.

Activities are of a simple nature: hiking, snorkeling and kayaking are king. (As elsewhere, ask about riptides before heading out.) Other than that, you may find the occasional party at the locally renowned Maxi's bar and restaurant at the end of the road, which is the end of the line (where buses arrive).

🛏 Sleeping & Eating

CONGO BONGO Bungalow $$$
(☎2759-9016; www.congo-bongo.com; d/tr/q US$145/170/195, per week US$870/1020/1170;

JAN CSERNOCH / ALAMY ©

Don't Miss Surfing Salsa Brava

The biggest break in Costa Rica, for expert surfers only and dangerous even then, Salsa Brava is named for the heaping helping of 'sauce' it serves up on the sharp, shallow reef, continually collecting its debt of fun in broken skin, boards and bones.

One take-off point: newbies waiting around to catch the popular North Peak should keep in mind that there are plenty of people in this town who gave up perks like mom's cooking and Walmart just to surf this wave regularly. Don't get in their way. In a sense, it was the Salsa Brava that swept Puerto Viejo into the limelight it enjoys today.

NEED TO KNOW

Conditions are usually best from December to March, and early in the day before the wind picks up.

P) On the road to Punta Uva, you'll find six charming wooden cottages set in a reclaimed cacao plantation (now dense forest). They offer fully equipped kitchens and plenty of living space, including open-air terraces and strategically placed hammocks that are perfect for spying on the wildlife. A network of trails leads through the 6 hectares of grounds to the beautiful beach.

CABINAS BUCUS   Cabina $
(☎2759-9143; www.costa-rica-manzanillo. com; s/d/tr US$25/35/45; P ☎) Four tidy, brightly painted tiled rooms in a two-storey mustard-yellow structure have mosquito nets and private bathrooms, all sharing a small kitchen. Find it just beyond Cabinas Manzanillo. Omar, one of the co-owners, is one of Manzanillo's top guides.

MAXI'S RESTAURANT Caribbean $$
(mains US$5-42, lobster from US$18; ⏲6am-close; ♪) Manzanillo's most famous restaurant attracts travelers from all over for large platters of tender, grilled seafood, whole red snappers (*pargo rojo*), steaks and Caribbean-style lobsters (expensive and not necessarily worth it). Despite the tourist traffic, it's still a wonderful seaside setting for a meal and a beer. And the bar can get hopping on weekends, with live music and DJs.

ℹ Information

Casa de Guías (☎2759-9064) Opposite the Ministry of Environment and Energy (Minae) office on the way into town, this small operation provides information on local guides.

ℹ Getting There & Away

Buses from Puerto Viejo to Manzanillo (US$0.85, 30 minutes) depart at 6:45am, 7:15am, 11:45am, 4:15pm and 7:15pm. They return to Puerto Viejo at 5am, 7am, 8:30am, 12:45pm and 5:15pm. These buses all continue to Puerto Limón (US$3.20, 2½ hours) for onward transfers.

REFUGIO NACIONAL DE VIDA SILVESTRE GANDOCA-MANZANILLO

This little-explored refuge, – called Regama for short – protects nearly 70% of the southern Caribbean coast, extending from Manzanillo all the way to the Panamanian border. It encompasses 50 sq km of land plus 44 sq km of marine environment. The peaceful, pristine stretch of sandy white beach is one of the area's main attractions. It's the center of village life in Manzanillo, and stretches for miles in either direction – from Punta Uva to Punta Mona in the east. Offshore, a 5-sq-km coral reef is a teeming habitat for lobster, sea fan and long-spined urchin.

Other than the village itself, and the surrounding farmland areas (grandfathered in when the park was created in 1985), the wildlife refuge is composed largely of rainforest. Cativo trees form the canopy, while there are many heliconia in the undergrowth. A huge 400-hectare swamp – known as **Pantano Punta Mona** – provides a haven for waterfowl, as well as the country's most extensive collection of holillo palms and sajo trees. Beyond Punta Mona, protecting a natural oyster bank, is the only red mangrove swamp in Caribbean Costa Rica. In the nearby Río Gandoca estuary there is a spawning ground for Atlantic tarpon, and caiman and manatee have been sighted.

The variety of vegetation and the remote location of the refuge attract many tropical birds; sightings of the rare harpy eagle have been recorded here. Other birds to look out for include the red-lored parrot, the red-capped manikin and the chestnut-mandibled toucan, among hundreds of others. The area is also known for incredible raptor migrations, with more than a million birds flying overhead during autumn.

Costa Rica
In Focus

Costa Rica Today   p320
Get up to speed with this quick look into Costa Rica's major issues of the day.

History   p322
Browse colorful historical discourses on the country's indigenous communities, banana barons and colonial past.

Family Travel   p332
This covers all the bases for having a safe, exciting tropical adventure with little explorers.

Costa Rica Outdoors   p335
Surfing, hiking, white-water rafting and zipping through the trees: a suite of outdoor thrills are on offer.

Tico Way of Life   p340
This primer on *pura vida* (pure life) helps get you acquainted with Costa Rica's most valuable treasure: its people.

Costa Rica Landscapes   p343
Learn about the volcanic mountains, dense rainforests and endless beaches that make up Costa Rica's treasured landscape.

Wildlife Guide   p348
Squawking macaws, curious monkeys and lazy lizards are around every corner of a trip through Costa Rica.

Shopping   p353
Your guide on the best mementos to take home from your trip to paradise.

Green violetear
PHOTOGRAPHER: JUDY BELLAH ©

Costa Rica Today

Plaza de la Cultura (p63), San José.

> Tourism now outpaces both agriculture and industry for the biggest slice of the economy.

belief systems
(% of population)

76	14	1	6	3
Roman Catholic	Evangelical	Jehovah's Witnesses	None	Other

if Costa Rica were 100 people

94 would be white & mestizo
3 would be black
1 would be Chinese
1 would be Amerindian
1 would be other

population per sq km

COSTA RICA   UNITED STATES   CANADA

 ≈ 2 people

Weathering the Economic Storm

Despite the economic tumult that has rocked the world since 2008, Costa Rica's economy has remained remarkably stable thanks to consistently growing returns on tourism. Tourism now outpaces both agriculture and industry for the biggest slice of the economy.

Increased legal and illegal immigration from Nicaragua has started to put a strain on the economic system. Half a million Nicaraguans live in Costa Rica and serve as an important source of mostly unskilled labor, but some believe they threaten to overwhelm the welfare state. Although approximately 21% of the populace lives below the poverty line – up 5% since 2008 – beggars are few and far between, and you won't see the street kids you see in other Latin American capitals.

The country's political stability continues to attract foreign investors. In recent years, while American investment has been

JEFF GREENBERG / ALAMY ©

gled most colorfully in frozen sharks, surfboards and containers of wigs.

With drug cartels moving in to control the northbound flow of cocaine, Costa Rica's proudly peaceful society is challenged by criminal forces that have long plagued Central America. Mexico's Sinaloa cartel has been in Costa Rica for years, but the presence of new rivals threatens a battlefield for violent regional drug wars. Most drugs are seized on the Interamericana and in the Pacific (in fact the Puntarenas bay is a graveyard of Coast Guard–seized ships), but relatively unguarded borders and no standing army makes the nation an ideal trafficking hub.

While Ticos (inhabitants of Costa Rica) grapple with the darkening storm, travelers will find the drug trade remains largely invisible aside from a few more police checkpoints along the highways. Still, the Costa Rican government's increased attention to the drug problem makes it all the more foolish for visitors to investigate illicit nightlife options.

Faux Pas

Don't be put off if your local host views an appointment as more of a ballpark suggestion for when to meet. Give or take 30 minutes for information meetings.

It isn't appropriate for women to bathe topless in public areas and it can be offensive to your hosts. The first warning from police may be gentle, but the second can result in a ticket.

It is worth remembering that Costa Rica is also part of the Americas, so when a Tico asks someone from the States about their origin it's good form to be specific: 'Los Estados Unidos' or 'USA'.

checkered, China has become Costa Rica's most promising international economic partner. China has made a number of large investments in the country's infrastructure in recent years, including a $1.7 billion investment in 2012 to modernize an oil refinery on the Caribbean and the shiny new Estadio Nacional de Costa Rica, the nation's largest sporting venue, which was completed in 2011.

Nacrotrafficking

Security Minister Janina Del Vecchio's report from April 2012 was bleak: the violent drug trade of Costa Rica's neighbors had finally crossed its borders. Once merely a bridge for the flow of drugs between South and North America, Costa Rica is rapidly becoming a storage and trading center for cartels. Between 2009 and 2012 authorities seized more than 90 tons of cocaine that had been smug-

Basílica de Nuestra Señora de Los Ángeles (p96), Cartago

JESÚS OCHOA ©

Although humans have inhabited Central America for at least 10,000 years and some 400,000 people were in today's Costa Rica before Europeans arrived, much of our knowledge of these pre-Columbian cultures has been lost to natural disasters and the brutalities of the Spanish colonization.

Heirs of Columbus

On his fourth and final voyage to the New World in 1502, Christopher Columbus was forced to drop anchor near present-day Puerto Limón after a hurricane damaged his ship. While waiting for repairs, Columbus ventured into the verdant terrain and exchanged gifts with hospitable and welcoming chieftains. He returned from this encounter, claiming to have seen 'more gold in two days than in four years in Española.' Columbus dubbed the stretch of

11,000 BC
The first humans occupy Costa Rica and populations flourish due to the rich land and marine resources along both coastlines.

shoreline from Honduras to Panama Veraguas, but it was excited descriptions of *la costa rica* (the rich coast) by subsequent explorers that gave the country its lasting name.

To the great disappointment of Columbus' conquistador heirs, the region was not abundant with gold and the locals were considerably less than affable. Spain's first colony in present-day Panama was abruptly abandoned when tropical disease and warring tribes decimated its ranks. Successive expeditions launched from the Caribbean coast also failed, as pestilent swamps, oppressive jungles and volcanoes made Columbus' paradise seem more like a tropical hell.

Fast Fact

In the 1940s children in Costa Rica learned to read with a text that stated 'Coffee is good for me. I drink coffee every morning.'

New World Order

It was not until the 1560s that a Spanish colony was firmly established in Costa Rica. Hoping to cultivate the rich volcanic soil of the Central Valley, the Spanish founded the village of Cartago on the banks of the Río Reventazón. Although the fledgling colony was extremely isolated, it survived under the leadership of its first governor, Juan Vásquez de Coronado. Preferring diplomacy over firearms to counter indigenous resistance, Coronado used Cartago as a base to survey the lands south to Panama and west to the Pacific, and secured deed and title to make the loose network of native tribes and their surrounding lands into a unified colony.

Though Coronado was later lost at sea in a shipwreck, his legacy endured: Costa Rica was an officially recognized province of El Virreinato de Nueva España (Viceroyalty of New Spain), which was the name given to the viceroy-ruled territories of the Spanish empire in North America, Central America, the Caribbean and Asia. Coronado's long-lasting legacy as the father of Costa Rica's political elite was also something that lasted generations. In the 1970s his family tree included some 29 heads of state and more than two hundred members of parliament.

For roughly three centuries the Captaincy General of Guatemala (also known as the Kingdom of Guatemala), which extended from modern-day Texas to Panama, with the exception of Belize, was a loosely administered colony in the vast Spanish empire. Since the political-military headquarters of the kingdom were in Guatemala, Costa Rica became a minor provincial outpost that had little, if any, strategic significance or exploitable riches. Additionally, Costa Rica's relatively small indigenous population played a role in limiting the development of the country during this period. With fewer

1000 BC
The Huetar power base in the Central Valley is solidified around Guayabo, continuously inhabited until its mysterious abandonment in 1400.

100 BC
Costa Rica becomes part of an extensive trade network for gold and other goods extending from present-day Mexico to the Andean empires.

AD 800
Indigenous production of granite spheres begins in the Diquis region, but archaeologists remain divided as to their function and significance.

323

indigenous workers to be used in forced labor, Spanish and European settlers had to work much of the difficult terrain on their own, and weren't able to establish the kind of large haciendas that existed elsewhere in Central America and Mexico.

The Fall of an Empire

On October 27 1807, the Treaty of Fontainebleau, which defined the occupation of Portugal, was signed between Spain and France. Under the guise of reinforcing the Franco-Spanish army occupying Portugal, Napoleon moved tens of thousands of troops into Spain. In an act of military genius, Napoleon ordered his troops to abandon the ruse and seize key Spanish fortifications. Without firing a single shot, Napoleon's troops captured Barcelona after convincing the city to open its gates for a convoy of wounded soldiers. Although Napoleon's invasion by stealth was successful, the resulting Peninsular War was a horrific campaign of guerrilla combat that crippled both countries. As a result of the conflict, as well as the subsequent power vacuum and internal turmoil, Spain lost nearly all of its colonial possessions in the first third of the 19th century.

In 1821 the Americas wriggled free of Spain's imperial grip following Mexico's declaration of independence for itself and the whole of Central America. Of course, the Central American provinces weren't too keen on having another foreign power reign over them and subsequently declared independence from Mexico. However, all these events hardly disturbed Costa Rica; it learned of its liberation a month after the fact.

The newly liberated colonies pondered their fates: to stay together in a United States of Central America or to go their separate national ways. At first they came up with something in between, namely the Central American Federation (CAF), though it could neither field an army nor collect taxes. Accustomed to being at the center of things due to its size, wealth and long-standing strategic advantages as a hub of trade and military power, Guatemala attempted to dominate the CAF, alienating smaller colonies and hastening its demise.

Meanwhile, an independent Costa Rica was taking shape under Juan Mora Fernández, first head of state (1824–33). He tended toward nation-building and organized new towns, built roads, published a newspaper and coined a currency. His wife even partook in the effort by designing the country's flag.

Life returned to normal, unlike in the rest of the region where postindependence civil wars raged on. In 1824 the Nicoya-Guanacaste Province seceded from Nicaragua and joined its more easygoing southern neighbor, defining the territorial borders. In 1852 Costa Rica received its first diplomatic emissaries from the USA and Great Britain.

Coffee Rica

In the 19th century the riches Costa Rica had long promised were uncovered when it was realized that the soil and climate of the Central Valley highlands were ideal for

1522
Spanish settlement develops though it will be decades before the colonists get a sturdy foothold on the land.

1540
The Kingdom of Guatemala is established. It covers much of Central America, including present-day Costa Rica.

1563
The first permanent Spanish colonial settlement in Costa Rica is established by Juan Vásquez de Coronado in Cartago.

coffee cultivation. Costa Rica led Central America in introducing the caffeinated bean, which transformed the impoverished country into the wealthiest in the region.

When an export market was discovered, the government actively promoted coffee to farmers by providing free saplings. At first Costa Rican producers exported their crops to nearby South Americans, who processed the beans and re-exported the product to Europe. By the 1840s, however, local merchants had already built up domestic capacity and learned to scope out their own overseas markets. Their big break came when they persuaded the captain of the HMS *Monarch* to transport several hundred sacks of Costa Rican coffee to London, percolating the beginning of a beautiful friendship.

The Costa Rican coffee boom was on. The drink's quick fix made it popular among working-class consumers in the industrializing Northern Hemisphere. The aroma of riches lured a wave of enterprising German immigrants to Costa Rica, enhancing technical and financial skills in the business sector. By century's end more than one-third of the Central Valley was dedicated to coffee cultivation, and coffee accounted for more than 90% of all exports and 80% of foreign-currency earnings.

Coffee wealth became a power resource in politics. Costa Rica's traditional aristocratic families were at the forefront of the enterprise. At midcentury three-quarters of the coffee barons were descended from just two colonial families. The country's leading coffee exporter at this time was President Juan Rafael Mora Porras (1849–59), whose lineage went back to the colony's founder, Juan Vásquez de Coronado.

The Best...
Places to Feel History

1 Guayabo (p102)

2 San José (p62)

3 Cartago (p97)

4 Alajuela (p88)

5 Heredia (p93)

Banana Empire

The coffee trade unintentionally gave rise to Costa Rica's next export boom – bananas. Getting coffee out to world markets necessitated a rail link from the central highlands to the coast, a costly and difficult proposition, but well worth it considering the potential for exporting the lucrative beans to North America. Limón's deep harbor made an ideal port but inland was dense jungle and insect-infested swamps, which prompted the government to contract the task to Minor Keith, nephew of a North American railroad tycoon.

The project was a disaster. Malaria and accidents churned through workers as Tico recruits gave way to US convicts and Chinese indentured servants, who were

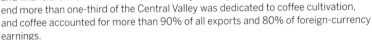

1737
San José is established as the future capital, sparking a rivalry with Cartago that leads to civil war. Central Post Office, San José

1821
Following a unanimous declaration by Mexico on behalf of all of Central America, Costa Rica gains independence from Spain.

JOHN BORTHWICK / GETTY IMAGES ©

Pre-Columbian Costa Rica

The early inhabitants of Costa Rica were part of an extensive trading zone that extended as far south as Peru and as far north as Mexico. The region hosted roughly 20 small tribes, organized into chiefdoms, indicating a permanent *cacique* (leader), who sat atop a hierarchical society that included shamans, warriors, toilers and slaves.

Adept at seafaring, the Carib dominated the Atlantic coastal lowlands, and served as a conduit of trade with the South American mainland. In the northwest, several tribes were connected to the great Mesoamerican cultures. Aztec religious practices and Maya jade and craftsmanship are in evidence in the Península de Nicoya, while Costa Rican quetzal feathers and golden trinkets have turned up in Mexico. In the southwest, three chiefdoms showed the influence of Andean indigenous cultures, including the cultivation of coca leaves for medicine and yucca and sweet potatoes in their diets – all of which were staples of the Andean societies.

There is also evidence that the language of the Central Valley, Huetar, was known by Costa Rica's indigenous groups, which may be an indication of their power and influence. The Central Valley is home to the only major archaeological site uncovered in Costa Rica, namely Guayabo. Thought to be an ancient ceremonial center, Guayabo once featured paved streets, an aqueduct and decorative gold. Here, archaeologists uncovered exquisite gold ornaments and unusual life-size stone statues of human figures, as well as distinctive types of pottery and *metates* (stone platforms that were used for grinding corn). For travelers interested in Costa Rica's pre-Columbian history, it is far and away the most significant site in the country. Today the site consists of little more than ancient hewed rock and stone, though Guayabo continues to stand as a testament to a once-great civilization of the New World.

in turn replaced by freed Jamaican slaves. Some 4000 men, including three of Keith's brothers, died in the process of laying the first 40km of track. To entice Keith to continue, the government turned over 3200 sq km of land along the route and provided a 99-year lease to run the railroad. In 1890 – nearly 20 years after the plan had been approved – the line was finally completed and running at a loss.

Keith had begun to grow banana plants along the tracks as a cheap food source for the workers. Desperate to recoup his investment, he shipped some bananas to New Orleans in the hope of starting a side venture. He struck gold, or rather yellow. Consumers went crazy for the elongated finger fruit. By the early 20th century,

April 1823
Liberal San José becomes the Costa Rican capital after intense skirmishes with the conservative residents of Cartago.

December 1823
The Monroe Doctrine declares the intentions of the USA to be the dominant imperial power in the Western Hemisphere.

1824
The Nicoya-Guanacaste region votes to secede from Nicaragua and become a part of Costa Rica.

bananas surpassed coffee as Costa Rica's most lucrative export and the country became the world's leading banana exporter. Unlike in the coffee industry, however, the profits were exported to the USA.

Costa Rica was transformed by the rise of Keith's banana empire. His first venture, the Tropical Trading and Transport Company, made him among the richest and most powerful men in the country. When he joined forces with another North American importer to found the infamous United Fruit Company, Keith's side business in bananas became the largest employer in Central America. To the , it was known as *el pulpo* (the octopus), as its tentacles stretched across the region, becoming entangled with the local economy and politics. United Fruit soon owned huge swaths of lush lowlands, much of the transportation and communication infrastructure and bunches of bureaucrats. The company sparked a wave of migrant laborers from Jamaica, changing the country's ethnic makeup and provoking interracial tensions.

If travelers look close enough today, the remains of the United Fruit Company are still all over the country, including rusting railroad tracks near Puntarenas and along the Pacific coast, and the historic buildings that housed the company headquarters in Golfito.

Coffee plantation, Parque Nacional Volcán Poás (p90)
PHOTOGRAPHER: CHRISTER FREDRIKSSON / GETTY IMAGES ©

1856

USA expansionist aims are dampened by Costa Rica, which defeats William Walker's army at the Battle of Santa Rosa.

1889

Costa Rica's first democratic elections are held, though unfortunately blacks and women are prohibited by law to vote.

1890

Construction of the railroad between San José and Puerto Limón is completed despite years of hardship and countless deaths.

Birth of a Nation

The inequality of the early 20th century led to the rise of José Figueres Ferrer, a self-described farmer-philosopher and the father of Costa Rica's unarmed democracy. The son of Catalan immigrant coffee planters, Figueres excelled in school and went to MIT, in Boston, to study engineering. Upon returning to Costa Rica to set up his own coffee plantation, he organized the hundreds of laborers on his farm into a utopian socialist community and appropriately named the property La Luz Sin Fin (The Struggle Without End).

In the 1940s Figueres became involved in national politics as an outspoken critic of President Rafael Ángel Calderón Guardia. In the midst of a radio interview in which he badmouthed the president, police broke into the studio and arrested Figueres. He was accused of having fascist sympathies and banished to Mexico. While in exile he formed the Caribbean League, a collection of students and democratic agitators from all over Central America, who pledged to bring down the region's military dictators. When he returned to Costa Rica, the now 700-man-strong Caribbean League went with him and helped protest against the powers that be.

Anastasio Somoza monument, San José (p62)
PHOTOGRAPHER: OLIVER GERHARD / IMAGEBROKER ©

1914

Costa Rica is given an economic boost following the opening of the Panama Canal, forged by 75,000 laborers.

1919

Dictator Federico Tinoco Granados is ousted in an episode of brief violence in an otherwise peaceful political history.

1940

Rafael Ángel Calderón Guardia is elected president and enacts minimum-wage laws and an eight-hour day.

When government troops descended on the farm with the intention of arresting Figueres and disarming the Caribbean League, it touched off a civil war. Figueres emerged victorious from the brief conflict and seized the opportunity to put into place his vision of Costa Rican social democracy. After dissolving the country's military, Figueres quoted HG Wells: 'The future of mankind cannot include the armed forces.'

As head of a temporary junta government, Figueres enacted nearly 1000 decrees. He taxed the wealthy, nationalized the banks and built a modern welfare state. His 1949 constitution granted full citizenship and voting rights to women, blacks, indigenous groups and Chinese minorities. Today Figueres' revolutionary regime is regarded as the foundation for Costa Rica's unarmed democracy.

The American Empire

Throughout the 1970s and '80s, the USA played the role of watchful big brother in Latin America, challenging the sovereignty of smaller nations. Big sticks, gunboats and dollar diplomacy were instruments of a United States policy to curtail socialist politics, especially the military oligarchies of Guatemala, El Salvador and Nicaragua.

In 1979 the rebellious Sandinistas toppled the American-backed Somoza dictatorship in Nicaragua. Alarmed by the Sandinistas' Soviet and Cuban ties, anticommunist President Ronald Reagan decided to intervene in the 1980s. The Cold War arrived in the hot tropics.

The organizational details of the counterrevolution were delegated to Oliver North, a lieutenant colonel working out of the White House basement. North's can-do creativity helped to prop up the famed Contra rebels to resist the Sandinistas in Nicaragua. While both sides invoked the rhetoric of freedom and democracy, the war was really a turf battle between left-wing and right-wing forces.

Under intense US pressure, Costa Rica was reluctantly dragged in. The Contras set up camp in northern Costa Rica, from where they staged guerrilla raids. Not-so-clandestine CIA operatives and US military advisers were dispatched to assist the effort and there were multiple allegations in Costa Rican and American media that Costa Rican authorities were bribed to keep quiet. A secret jungle airstrip was built near the border to fly in weapons and supplies. To raise cash for the rebels, North allegedly used his covert supply network to traffic illegal narcotics through the region.

The Best... Historic Buildings

1 Basílica de Nuestra Señora de los Ángeles (p96)

2 Teatro Nacional (p63)

3 La Casona (p158)

4 Iglesia de la Inmaculada Concepción (p93)

5 Iglesia San Bartolomé, Barva (p95)

1948

Conservative and liberal forces clash, resulting in a six-week civil war that leaves 2000 Costa Ricans dead.

1949

A new constitution abolishes the army and grants women and blacks the right to vote.

1963

Reserva Natural Absoluta Cabo Blanco becomes Costa Rica's first federally protected conservation area.

The Best... Colonial Parks & Plazas

1 Plaza de la Cultura (p63)

2 Parque Morazán (p63)

3 Plaza de la Basílica, Cartago (p97)

4 Parque Central (p88)

Although North vehemently denied the US government had ever helped the Nicaraguan resistance with 'running drugs,' a congressional investigation found that North and other senior officials helped create a network that attracted drug traffickers and then turned a blind eye to reports of narcotic trafficking.

The war polarized Costa Rica. Conservatives wanted to re-establish the military and join the anticommunist crusade, but more than 20,000 demonstrators marched through San José in a demonstration for peace. The debate climaxed in the 1986 presidential election, which went to Oscar Arias Sánchez, an intellectual reformer in the mold of Figueres.

Once in office, Arias affirmed his commitment to a negotiated resolution and reasserted Costa Rican national independence. He vowed to uphold his country's pledge of neutrality and to vanquish the Contras from the territory, which prompted the US ambassador to suddenly quit his post. In a public ceremony, Costa Rican school children planted trees on top of the CIA's secret airfield. Arias became the driving force in uniting Central America around a peace plan, which ended the Nicaraguan war and earned him the Nobel Peace Prize in 1987.

In 2006 Arias once again returned to the presidential office, winning the popular election by a 1.2% margin, and subsequently ratifying the controversial Central American Free Trade Agreement (Cafta).

Costa Rica Tomorrow

In the presidential elections of February 2010, Costa Rica elected Oscar Arias Sánchez' former Vice President Laura Chinchilla, who won just under 47% of the vote. Chinchilla campaigned on similar economic platforms as her political mentor, namely on the platforms of promoting free trade and further increasing access to US markets. However, critics argue that these aims do not protect small farmers and domestic industries.

Unlike Arias, Chinchilla is a staunch social conservative who is diametrically opposed to legalized abortion, same-sex marriage and emergency contraception in the so-called 'morning-after pill'. In a striking departure from her political mentor, she has pledged to fight against proposed legislation that would strip Costa Rica of its official Roman Catholic designation and establish a secular state.

1987

President Oscar Arias Sánchez wins the Nobel Peace Prize for his work on the Central American peace accords.

2000

The population tops four million, though the number may be far greater due to illegal settlements on the fringes of the capital.

2007

A national referendum passes Cafta; opinion is divided as to whether opening up trade with the USA will be beneficial.

Aside from relatively conservative social issues, Chinchilla's appointment has been marked by stern anticrime legislation in response to Costa Rica's growing security and safety issues related to the violent Central American drug trade. She has also targeted climate change as a major platform of her presidency and taken a notable expansion of pro-free-trade policies, which have resulted in closer economic ties with emerging Asian and South American countries.

Costa Rica will most likely continue its reign as the global pioneer in sustainable development, providing a model in which economic and environmental interests are complementary. But it is not without some contention. Conservation and ecotourism are administered by two powerful bureaucracies – the Ministry of Environment & Energy (Minae) and the Costa Rica Tourism Board (ICT) – which frequently clash. There is also a widening gap between the motives of the San José–based eco-elite and the concerns of rural residents, who still use the land to survive.

2010
Costa Rica elects its first woman president, National Liberation Party candidate Laura Chinchilla.

AFP/GETTY IMAGES ©

2011
Central American drug wars encroach on the borders. Costa Rica is listed among the USA's list of major drug-trafficking centers.

Family Travel

Applying mud masks, Liberia (p148)

PHILIP & KAREN SMITH / GETTY IMAGES ©

Costa Rica is a kid-friendly country, especially since Ticos (Costa Ricans) themselves tend to be extremely family oriented and will go out of their way to lavish attention on children. In fact, Costa Rica is arguably the most accessible family destination in Latin America, so check your worries and concerns along with the baggage and get ready for what may be the best family vacation you've ever taken.

Where to Go

Although you will have to take certain precautions to ensure the health and safety of little ones, Costa Rica's safety standards are more similar to those in North America and Europe than they are to other countries in Central America.

Families could go just about anywhere in Costa Rica and be perfectly happy. Even San José has a few sights for children, but it's best to get out of the cities and towns and into the countryside or along the coastlines.

Snorkeling on the Caribbean coast, taking a surfing road trip along the central Pacific coast, and spotting monkeys and tropical birds in Manuel Antonio National Park are highlights they'll never forget. Families who want to maximize their time should look into the Península de Nicoya and central Pacific coast, as these regions are packed with activites, natural highlights and excellent infrastructure.

What to Eat

Costa Rican cuisine is simple and hearty, if somewhat bland (beans, rice and grilled chicken or steak are omnipresent). The ubiquity of these dishes might be a bit dull for adults with adventurous appetites, but it makes it easier to cater to finicky young eaters. Special kids' meals are not normally offered in restaurants, though some fancy lodges prepare them. However, most local eateries will accommodate two children splitting a meal or can produce child-size portions on request.

If you're traveling with an infant, stock up on milk formula and baby food before heading to remote areas, and always carry snacks for long drives in remote areas – sometimes there are no places to stop for a bite.

Tired of juice and water? Here are some local drinks that your kids are sure to love: *batidos* (fresh fruit shakes), either *al agua* (made with water) or *con leche* (with milk); coconut milk (sipped through a straw straight from the cracked-open coconut); and *horchata* (cinnamon-spiked rice milk).

And don't worry too much – generally speaking, tap water and ice cubes in Costa Rica are safe for foreigners to consume.

Can You Drink the Water?

Yes. Yes. Yes. The tap water is perfectly safe to drink in Costa Rica. You can drink from the tap in all but the most remote regions of the country's wilderness areas.

Where to Stay

When it comes to accommodation in Costa Rica, families have a lot to choose from. From plush jungle ecolodges to beachside tents, you can find the type of accommodation your family needs at most tourist destinations. There are many rooms to accommodate families on a tight budget, and most midrange and top-end hotels have reduced rates for children under 12, provided the child shares a room with parents. Top-end hotels will provide cribs and usually have activities for children, as well as swimming pools and play areas. Throughout this book, we have marked particularly family-friendly accommodation with this symbol: 🚼.

Need to Know

- o **Breastfeeding** OK in public
- o **Change facilities** In upmarket hotels and resorts
- o **Cots** In upmarket hotels and resorts (best to book in advance)
- o **Health** Food-borne and infectious diseases are of very minor concern
- o **High chairs** In most tourist-friendly restaurants
- o **Nappies (diapers)** Widely available
- o **Strollers** Available, but best to bring your own
- o **Transport** Consider private shuttles or rental car

The Best...
Places for Kids

1 Monteverde & Santa Elena (p135)

2 Parque Nacional Manuel Antonio (p227)

3 Parque Nacional Tortuguero (p302)

4 Playa Sámara (p192)

5 Volcán Arenal (p125)

Anything Else?

Here are some additional tips and resources:

● Children under the age of 12 get a 25% discount on internal air travel, while children under two fly free (provided they sit on an adult's lap).

● If you're traveling with an infant, bring disposable nappies (diapers), baby creams or toiletries, baby aspirin and a thermometer from home, or stock up in San José. Supplies may be difficult to find in rural areas, though cloth nappies are more widespread.

● Strollers may help you get around high-end resorts, but are challenging anywhere else in the country. Few national parks are set up to accommodate them, so consider investing in a quality hiking baby harness if you plan to spend much time in the parks.

● Young kids won't have a problem with the paths in most of Costa Rica's national parks, which are easy, short and well marked. Notable exceptions are Parque Nacional Corcovado, Parque Nacional Chirripó and Parque Nacional Amistad, which are more challenging to navigate.

● Although many surf schools allow for very young students, kids under 10 will likely have to take the class with a parent or guardian.

Costa Rica Outdoors

Canopy tour (p139), Santa Elena

PAUL KENNEDY / GETTY IMAGES ©

What truly distinguishes Costa Rica is the diversity and accessibility of the outdoors. While hard-core enthusiasts can seek out complete solitude in absolute wilderness, families and novices are equally well catered for. From jungle trekking and beachcombing to surfing and whitewater rafting, Costa Rica has most definitely got whatever activity you're looking for.

Canopy Tours

Costa Rica's lofty tally of national parks and reserves provides an incredible stage for lovers of the outdoors. Natural spaces are so entwined with Costa Rica's ecofriendly image that it's difficult to envisage the country without them. For the vast majority of travelers, Costa Rica equals rainforest, and you're certain to encounter charismatic wildlife, including primates, birds and butterflies galore. As you'll quickly discover, no two rainforests are created equal, providing a constantly shifting palette of nature.

Life in the rainforest takes place at canopy level. But with trees extending 30m to 60m in height, the average human has a hard time getting a look at what's going on up there. Indeed, it was only a matter of time before someone in Costa Rica invented the canopy tour.

Some companies have built elevated walkways through the trees that allow visitors to stroll through. SkyTrek (p141), in Monteverde, and Rainmaker Aerial Walkway, near Quepos, are two of the most established operations in the country.

For adrenaline seekers, consider zipping from tree to tree while harnessed into a sophisticated cable-suspension system. With a total length of 11,000m connecting no fewer than 21 platforms, Miss Sky (p188), in the Nosara area, is the longest canopy tour in the world, stretching from mountainside to mountainside and finishing on the top floor of a disco-bar.

Major tourist centers, such as Monteverde and Santa Elena and La Fortuna, offer the largest number of canopy-tour operators.

You can also take a ski-lift-style ride through the treetops; the Rainforest Aerial Tram (p300) is near the Caribbean coast, while the smaller Monteverde Trainforest (p142) is in Monteverde.

Hiking

Whether you're interested in taking a walk in the park or embarking on a rugged mountaineering circuit, the hiking opportunities around Costa Rica are seemingly

The Best... Hikes

1 Reserva Santa Elena (p139)

2 Reserva Biológica Bosque Nuboso Monteverde (p146)

3 Parque Nacional Corcovado (p263)

4 Cerro Chirripó (p271)

5 Parque Internacional La Amistad (p281)

CHRISTER FREDRIKSSON / GETTY IMAGES ©

Parque Nacional Manuel Antonio (p227)

endless. Nearly every visitor to the country will have a hike or trek on their agenda – whether they know it before they arrive or not. With its extensive mountains, canyons, dense jungles, cloud forests and two coastlines, Costa Rica is one of Central America's best and most varied hiking destinations.

These hikes come in an enormous spectrum of difficulty. At tourist-packed destinations such as Monteverde and Santa Elena, trails are clearly marked and even lined with cement blocks in parts. This is very appealing if you're traveling with little ones, or if you're lacking navigational prowess. For long-distance hiking, there are lots more options in the remote corners of the country.

Opportunities for moderate hiking are also available in most parks and reserves, particularly once you leave the well-beaten tourist path. As this is Costa Rica you can, for the most part, still rely on signs and maps for orientation, though it helps to have a bit of experience under your belt. Good hiking shoes, plenty of water and confidence in your abilities will enable you to combine several shorter day hikes into a lengthier expedition. Tourist information centers at park entrances are great resources for planning out your intended route.

If you're properly equipped with camping essentials (tent, sleeping bag, air mattress etc), the country's longer and more arduous multiday treks are at your disposal. Costa Rica's top challenges are scaling Cerro Chirripó, traversing Parque Nacional Corcovado and penetrating deep into the heart of Parque Internacional La Amistad. While all three endeavors can be undertaken either solo or with trusted companions, local guides provide an extra measure of safety and can help in identifying flora and fauna.

The Best... Wicked Surf

1 Parque Nacional Santa Rosa (p159)

2 Puerto Viejo de Talamanca (p311)

3 Mal País & Santa Teresa (p199)

4 Dominical (p231)

5 Playa Tamarindo (p183)

6 Jacó (p218)

IN FOCUS COSTA RICA OUTDOORS

Surfing

Point and beach breaks, lefts and rights, reefs and river mouths, warm water and year-round waves make Costa Rica a favorite surfing destination. For the most part, the Pacific coast has bigger swells and better waves during the latter part of the rainy season, but the Caribbean cooks from November to May. Basically, there is a wave somewhere waiting to be surfed at any time of the year.

For the uninitiated, lessons are available at almost all of the major surfing destinations – especially popular towns include Jacó, Dominical and Tamarindo on the Pacific coast. For our money, the best-value schools and lessons in the country are in Dominical. Surfing definitely has a steep learning curve, and can be potentially dangerous if the currents are strong. With that said, the sport is accessible to children and novices, though it's always best to inquire locally about conditions before you paddle out. Having trouble standing up? Here is a tip: long boards readily maintain their stability, even in heavy crashing surf.

Throughout Costa Rica, waves are big (though not Hawaii-big), and many offer hollow and fast rides that are perfect for intermediates. As a bonus, Costa Rica is one of the few places on the planet where you can surf two different oceans in the same day. Advanced surfers with plenty of experience under their belts can tackle some of the sport's most famous waves. The top ones include: world-famous Ollie's Point and Witch's Rock, off the coast of Parque Nacional Santa Rosa; Mal País and Santa Teresa, with a groovy scene to match the powerful waves; Playa Hermosa, the bigger, faster curls of which attract a more determined (and experienced) crew of wave-chasers; Pavones, a legendary long left across the sweet waters of the Golfo Dulce; and the infamous Salsa Brava in Puerto Viejo de Talamanca, which is for experts only.

White-Water Rafting & Kayaking

Since the birth of the ecotourism-based economy in the mid-1980s, white-water rafting has emerged as one of Costa Rica's top-billed outdoor pursuits. Ranging from family-friendly Class II swells to borderline unnavigable Class V rapids, Costa Rica's rivers offer highly varied white-water experiences.

First-time runners are catered for year-round, while seasoned enthusiasts arrive en masse during the wildest months from June to October. There is also much regional variation, with gentler rivers located near Manuel Antonio along the central Pacific coast, and truly world-class runs along the Pacuare and Reventazón rivers in the Central Valley. Since all white-water rafting in Costa Rica requires the presence of a certified guide, you will need to book trips through a reputable tour agency.

River kayaking is not as popular as rafting, though it has its share of loyal fans. The tiny village of La Virgen in the northern lowlands is the unofficial kayaking capital of Costa Rica, and the best spot to hook up with other like-minded lovers of the sport. The Río Sarapiquí has an impressive variety of runs that cater to all ages and skill levels.

With 1228km of coastline, two gulfs and plentiful mangrove estuaries, Costa Rica is ideal for sea kayaking. This is a great way for paddlers to access remote areas and catch rare glimpses of birds and wildlife. Difficulty of access varies considerably and is largely dependent on tides and currents.

Diving & Snorkeling

The good news is that Costa Rica offers body-temperature water with few humans and abundant marine life. The bad news is that the visibility is low because of silt and plankton, and soft corals and sponges are dominant. If you are looking for turquoise waters and plenty of hard coral, head for Belize and Honduras.

However, those who do venture underwater will find massive schools of fish and larger marine animals such as turtles, sharks, dolphins and whales. It's also worth pointing out that there are few places in the world where you can dive in the Caribbean and the Pacific on the same day, albeit with a good amount of effort and some advanced planning.

The Caribbean Sea is better for novice divers and snorkelers, with the beach towns of Manzanillo and Cahuita particularly well suited to youngsters. Puerto Viejo lays claim to a few decent sites that can be explored on a discovery dive. Along the Pacific, Playa del Coco and Isla del Caño up the ante slightly, offering a variety of beginner- and intermediate-level sites.

Isla del Cocos is the exception to the rule – this remote island in the deep Pacific is regarded by veteran divers as one of the best dive spots in the world. In order to

The Best... Rafting & Kayaking

1 Turrialba (p100)

2 La Virgen (p160)

3 Quepos and Manuel Antonio (p223)

4 Parque Nacional Tortuguero (p304)

5 Bahía Drake (p254)

catch a glimpse of the underwater world of Cocos, you'll need to visit on a liveaboard, and have some serious experience in your logbook.

Wildlife- & Bird-Watching

Costa Rica's biodiversity is legendary, so it should come as no surprise that the country offers unparalleled opportunities for watching birds and wildlife. As a bonus, people of all ages are already familiar with Costa Rica's most famous, commonly spotted, animals. You'll instantly recognize monkeys bounding through the treetops, sloths clinging to branches and toucans gliding beneath the canopy. Young children, even if they've been to the zoo dozens of times, typically enjoy the thrill of spotting creatures in the wild.

For the slightly older, keeping checklists is a fun way to add an educational element to your travels. Want to move beyond the novice level? Check out your local bookstore prior to landing in Costa Rica to pick up wildlife and bird guides – look for ones with color plates that make positive identification a cinch.

A quality pair of binoculars is highly recommended and can make the difference between far-off movement and a face-to-face encounter. A spotting scope is essential for expert bird-watchers, and multipark itineraries will allow you to quickly add dozens of new species to your all-time list. Finally, it's worth pointing out that Costa Rica is brimming with wildlife at every turn, so always keep your eyes peeled and your ears pricked – you never know what's waiting for you just ahead!

The Best...
Wildlife-Watching

1 Parque Nacional Corcovado (p263)

2 Parque Nacional Santa Rosa (p158)

3 Parque Nacional Tortuguero (p302)

4 Refugio Nacional de Vida Silvestre Caño Negro (p121)

5 Monteverde and Santa Elena (p135)

Tico Way of Life

Drinking coconut milk, Parque Nacional Corcovado (p263)

'Pura vida' (pure life) is more than just a slogan that rolls off the Tico tongue and emblazons souvenirs; uttered in a laid-back tone, the phrase is a mantra for the Costa Rican way of life. Perhaps the essence of the pure life is something better lived than explained, but hearing it again and again across this beautiful country as a greeting, farewell or acknowledgement of thanks makes it evident that the concept is deep within the DNA of this country.

Lifestyle

The living seems particularly pure when Costa Rica is compared with its Central American neighbors such as Nicaragua and Honduras; there's little poverty, illiteracy or political tumult here, the country is crowded with ecological jewels and has high standards of living. And though the Ticos (Costa Rican people) are justifiably proud, a compliment to the country is likely to be met simply with a warm smile and an enigmatic two-word reply: *pura vida*.

With long life expectancy, a relatively sturdy economy and the lack of war, Costa Ricans live fairly rich and comfortable lives for the most part, even by North American standards. As in many places in Latin America, the family unit remains the nucleus of life in Costa Rica.

Families socialize together and extended families often live near each other. When it's time to party it's also largely a family affair. Celebrations, vacations and weddings are a social outlet for rich and poor alike, and those with relatives in positions of power – nominal or otherwise – don't hesitate to turn to them for support.

Life expectancy in Costa Rica is almost the same as in the USA. A comprehensive socialized health-care system and proper sanitation account for these positive statistics, as does a generally low-stress lifestyle, the tropical weather and a healthy and varied diet.

Economy

Even despite the economic tumult that has rocked the world since 2008, Costa Rica's economy has remained remarkably stable thanks to consistently growing returns on tourism, a sector that outpaces agriculture and industry for the biggest slice of the economy. If you're concerned about the availability of an English menu, take note: North Americans account for nearly half of the 2.2 million annual tourists.

Poverty levels have been in check for more than 20 years thanks to strong welfare programs. Although approximately 21% of the populace lives below the poverty line (up 5% since 2008), beggars are few and far between, and you won't see the street kids you would in other Latin American capitals.

For more about Costa Rica's economy, see the Costa Rica Today chapter.

The Best... Cultural Hot Spots

1 Teatro Nacional (p70), San José

2 Museo de Jade (p66), San José

3 Museo de Arte y Diseño Contemporáneo (p66), San José

4 Jazz Café (p74), San José

5 Monteverde and Santa Elena (p135)

IN FOCUS TICO WAY OF LIFE

Population

In the 1940s Costa Rica was overwhelmingly an agricultural society, with the majority of the population employed by coffee and banana plantations. These days the service sector employs more than half of the labor force, while industry (especially agro-industry) employs another one-fifth.

Most inhabitants are *mestizos,* having a mix of Spanish and indigenous and/or African roots, though the vast majority of Ticos consider themselves to be white. Although it's difficult to offer a precise explanation for this cultural phenomenon, it is partly due to the fact that Costa Rica's indigenous populations were virtually wiped out by the Spanish conquistadors. As a result, most Costa Ricans trace their ancestry back to the European continent and take considerable pride in their Spanish heritage.

Indigenous Costa Ricans, Chinese immigrants and black Costa Ricans together make up only 5% of the population. In recent years North American and European immigration has greatly increased, and it is estimated that roughly 50,000 expats from these two regions presently live in the country.

Literature

Costa Rica has a relatively young literary history and few works of Costa Rican writers or novelists are available in translation. Carlos Luis Fallas (1909–66) is widely known for *Mamita Yunai* (1940), an influential novel that took the banana companies to task

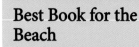

Best Book for the Beach

If you're looking for a bit of beach reading, pick up *Costa Rica: A Traveler's Literary Companion,* edited by Barbara Ras. This fine collection of 26 short stories by modern Costa Rican writers offers a valuable glimpse of society from Ticos (Costa Ricans) themselves.

for their labor practices, and he remains very popular among the Latin American left.

Carmen Naranjo (1928–) is one of the few contemporary Costa Rican writers to receive international acclaim. Her collection of short stories, *There Never Was a Once Upon a Time,* is widely available in English. Another important figure is José León Sánchez (1930–), an internationally renowned memoirist of Huetar descent. After being convicted for stealing from the famous Basílica de Nuestra Señora de Los Angeles in Cartago, he authored one of the continent's most poignant books: *La isla de los hombres solos* (God Was Looking the Other Way).

Visual Arts

The visual arts in Costa Rica first took on a national character in the 1920s, when Teodorico Quirós, Fausto Pacheco and their contemporaries began painting landscapes that differed from European styles and depicted distinctly Costa Rican scenes.

The contemporary scene is varied, making it difficult to define a unique Tico style. Look out for the magical realism of Isidro Con Wong, and surreal paintings and primitive engravings from Francisco Amighetti. The Museo de Arte y Diseño Contemporáneo in San José is the top place to see modern work.

Music & Dance

Although there are Latin American musical hotbeds of more renown, Costa Rica's central geographical location and colonial history have resulted in a varied music culture.

San José features a regular lineup of domestic and international rock, folk and hip-hop artists, but you'll find that regional sounds also survive, each with its own special rhythm, instruments and style. The Península de Nicoya has a rich musical history, most of it made with guitars, maracas and marimbas (wooden percussion instruments similar to a xylophone), and the traditional sound on the Caribbean coast is calypso, which has roots in Afro-Caribbean culture.

Popular dance music includes salsa, merengue, bolero and *cumbia* (Colombian dance tunes). Guanacaste is the birthplace of many traditional dances, most of which depict courtship rituals between country folk. The most famous dance is the *punto guanacasteco.* What keeps it lively is the *bomba,* a funny (and usually racy) rhymed verse, shouted out by male dancers during the musical interlude.

Costa Rica Landscapes

Parque Nacional Corcovado (p263)

RALPH HOPKINS / GETTY IMAGES ©

Despite its diminutive size (at 51,000 sq km it's slightly smaller than the USA's West Virginia), Costa Rica's land is an explosion of vivid contrasts and violent contradictions. On one coast are the breezy skies and big waves of the Pacific. Only 119km away lie the muggy and languid shores of the Caribbean. In between there are several active volcanoes, alpine peaks and crisp high-elevation forest. Few places on Earth can compare with this little country's spectacular interaction of natural, geological and climatic forces.

The Pacific Coast

Start by twisting and turning around the endless gulfs, sandy peninsulas and deserted bays of Costa Rica's 1016km-long Pacific coast. Rugged, rocky headlands give way to classic white- and black-sand beaches bedecked with palms. Strong tidal action creates an excellent habitat for waterbirds, a dramatic crash of waves and some exquisite surfing.

Two major peninsulas hook out into the Pacific along this coast: Nicoya in the north and Osa in the south. The two could hardly be more different. Nicoya is one of the driest places in the country and holds some of Costa Rica's most developed tourist infrastructure; Osa is wet and rugged, run through by wild, seasonal rivers and rough dirt roads that are always under threat from the creeping jungle.

Six Ways to Save the Rainforest

Although talk about 'Saving the Rainforest' has provided a common slogan for bumper stickers and T-shirts for the better part of two decades, much of the hype does little to address the core issues. To help minimize the negative impact on the rainforest, travelers to this part of the world can bear in mind a few simple measures to *actually* make a difference.

○ **Plant a tree** At **Selva Bananito Lodge** (☏ 8375-4419, 2253 8118; www.selvabananito. com; 3-day package US$432) on the Caribbean coast, visitors can help to reforest a former banana plantation.

○ **Drink the water** There's no point in buying bottled water in Costa Rica, where it is perfectly safe to drink from the tap. A refillable water bottle is one little step that can make a big difference to waste reduction.

○ **Drink organic, shade-grown coffee** Organic coffee-growing avoids the use of chemical pesticides and fertilizers, minimizing their environmental impact and ensuring the survival of old-growth forests.

○ **Say no to beef** The number-one reason for forest clearing in Central America is to feed cows, mostly for export. Consider grass-fed beef, which is better for health and better for the environment.

○ **Green impact** Money talks, especially when it's in the hands of sustainable tour operators such as Osa Wild (p258), **Fundación Corcovado** (www. corcovadofoundation.org) or **ASCONA** (www.asconacr.org), which are all community-led grassroots organizations dedicated to preserving one of Costa Rica's last true frontiers, Parque Nacional Corcovado.

○ **Bring it home** Sustainability practices that protect Costa Rica are just as urgent at home. Take the inspiration to protect the rainforest home with you.

Just inland from the coast, the Pacific lowlands are a narrow strip of land backed by mountains. This area is equally dynamic, ranging from dry deciduous forests to misty, mysterious tropical rainforests.

Central Costa Rica

Just inland from the Pacific coast ascends the jagged spine of the country: the majestic Cordillera Central in the north and the rugged, largely unexplored Cordillera de Talamanca in the south. Continually being revised by earthquakes and volcanic activity, these mountains are part of the majestic Sierra Madre chain that runs north through Mexico.

A land of active volcanoes, clear trout-filled streams and ethereal cloud forest, these ranges generally follow a northwest to southeast line, with the highest and most dramatic peaks in the south near the Panamanian border. The highest in the country is the rugged, windswept 3820m peak of Cerro Chirripó.

In the midst of this powerful landscape, surrounded on all sides by mountains, are the highlands of Meseta Central – the Central Valley. This fertile central plain, some 1000m above sea level, is the agricultural heart of the nation and enjoys abundant rainfall and mild temperatures. It includes San José and is home to more than half the country's population.

The Caribbean Coast

Cross the mountains and drop down the eastern slope and you'll reach the elegant line of the Caribbean coast – a long, straight 212km along low plains, brackish lagoons and waterlogged forests.

A lack of strong tides allows plants to grow right over the water's edge along coastal sloughs, creating walls of green vegetation. Broad, humid plains that scarcely rise above sea level and murky waters characterize much of this region. As if taking cues from the slow-paced Caribbean-influenced culture, the rivers that rush out of the central mountain take on a languid pace here as they curve toward the sea.

Compared with the smoothly paved roads and popular beaches of the Pacific coast, much of the land here is still inaccessible except by boat or plane. The best access points for travelers is the Parque Nacional Tortuguero, which allows intimate visits to this little-discovered border between land and sea.

The Best...
Ecolodges

1 **Celeste Mountain Lodge** (p157)

2 **Hotel Sí Como No** (p224)

3 **Arenal Observatory Lodge** (p128)

4 **Lapa Ríos** (p262)

National Parks & Protected Areas

The vibrancy of its natural resources has made Costa Rica something of a comeback kid: the deforestation here in the early 1990s was among the worst in Latin America. Today the country is a global leader in tropical conservation. Now in charge of an exemplar system of well-managed and accessible parks, Costa Rica is among the best places in the world to experience rainforest habitats. Ready for a tour?

The national-park system began in the 1960s and has since been expanded into a National Conservation Areas System with an astounding 186 protected areas, including 32 national parks, eight biological reserves, 13 forest reserves and 51 wildlife refuges. At least 10% of the land is strictly protected and another 17% is included in various multiple-use preserves. The most amazing number might be the smallest of all: Costa Rica's parks are safe haven to approximately 5% of the world's wildlife species.

Travelers may be surprised to learn that, in addition to the system of national preserves, there are hundreds of small, privately owned lodges, reserves and haciendas (estates) set up to protect the land. These are well worth visiting. Many are owned by longtime Costa Rican expats who decided that this country was the last stop down their journey along the 'gringo trail' in the 1970s and '80s. The abundance of foreign-owned protected areas is a bit of a contentious issue with Ticos (Costa Ricans). Although these are largely nonprofit organizations with keen interests in conservation, they are private and often cost money to enter.

Most national parks can be entered without permits, though a few limit the number they admit on a daily basis and others require advance reservations for accommodation within the park's boundaries (Parque Nacionals Chirripó, Corcovado and La Amistad). The average entrance fee to most parks is US$10 per day for foreigners, plus additional fees for overnight camping where permitted.

Most parks in the country have a ranger station of some kind and, though these are largely administrative offices with few formal services for travelers, it is worth dropping in if you plan to deeply explore the park. The *guardeparques* (park rangers) know the parks inside and out and can offer tips on trail conditions, good camping spots and places to see wildlife. Naturally, these conversations will be most helpful if you speak Spanish.

With Costa Rican parks contributing significantly to national and local economies through the huge influx of tourist money, there is little question that the country's healthy natural environment is important to its citizens. In general, support for land preservation remains high because it provides income and jobs to so many people, plus important opportunities for scientific investigation.

Geology

If the proximity to all this wildly diverse beauty makes Costa Rica feel like the crossroads between worlds, that's because it is. As part of the thin strip of land that separates two continents with vastly different wildlife and topographical characteristics and sitting in between the world's two largest oceans, it's little wonder that Costa Rica boasts such a colorful collision of climates, landscapes and wildlife.

Costa Rica's geological history began when the Cocos Plate, a tectonic plate that lies below the Pacific, crashed headlong into the Caribbean Plate, which is off the isthmus' east coast. At a rate of about 10cm every year, it might seem slow by human standards but the collision was a violent wreck by geological standards, creating the area's 'subduction zone' that is rife with geological drama. The plates continue to collide, with the Cocos Plate pushing the Caribbean Plate toward the heavens and making the area prone to earthquakes and ongoing volcanic activity (Arenal, one of the world's most active volcanoes, is in Costa Rica's north).

But despite all the violence underfoot, these forces have blessed this country with some of the world's most beautiful and diverse tropical landscapes.

Plants

Simply put, Costa Rica's floral biodiversity is mind-blowing – close to 12,000 species of vascular plants have been described in Costa Rica, and the list gets more and more crowded each year. Orchids alone account for about 1400 species.

Costa Rica's Easter Blossom

Among Costa Rica's 1400 species of orchid, the *guaria morada (Guarianthe skinneri)* is celebrated with special reverence. Blooming around the time of Lent and Easter, this gorgeous orchid with dense clusters of lavender-rose flowers is prominently displayed on altars and in homes and churches everywhere in Central America. In the old days these flowers grew liberally on the walls and roofs of old houses and courtyards, where they added a special charm. However, this ancient custom fell by the wayside and they are no longer a common sight. In honor of its links to history and tradition, the orchid was chosen as Costa Rica's national flower in 1937. Unfortunately, the plant's amazing popularity has resulted in wild populations being harvested without restraint, and an alarm was raised in 2004 that it could become extinct in the wild without immediate action. Hopefully, the orchid's numbers will begin to increase again, because although it is easy to grow commercially, no quantity of orchids in a greenhouse can replace the flowers found in the wild forests of Costa Rica.

The diversity of habitats created when this many species mix is a wonder to behold; one day you're canoeing in a muggy mangrove swamp, and the next you're squinting through bone-chilling fog to see orchids in a montane cloud forest. Jump on a bus and after a short ride you'll be fighting your way through the vines of a tropical rainforest. Sure, everyone loves Costa Rica's celebrated beaches, but travelers would be remiss to visit the country without seeing some of its most distinctive plant communities, including rainforests, mangrove swamps, cloud forests and dry forests.

Experiencing a tropical forest for the first time can be a bit of a surprise for visitors from North America or Europe, who are used to temperate forests with little variety. Such regions are either dominated by conifers, or have endless tracts of oaks, beech and birch. Tropical forests, on the other hand, have a staggering number of species – in Costa Rica, for example, almost 2000 tree species have been recorded. If you stand in one spot and look around, you'll see scores of different plants, and if you walk several hundred meters you're likely to find even more.

Playa Jacó (p218)

Collared redstart

Nowhere else are so many types of habitat squeezed into such a tiny area. In Costa Rica species from different continents have been mingling for millennia. Costa Rica tops the list of countries for number of species per 10,000 sq km, at 615 species. To compare, wildlife-rich Rwanda has 596 and the comparatively impoverished USA has 104 species per 10,000 sq km. This fact alone (not to mention the ease of travel and friendly residents) makes Costa Rica the world's premier destination for nature lovers.

Birds

Bird-watchers delight: Costa Rica's amazing biodiversity includes approximately 850 species of birds, including six endemics. The country holds a greater variety of birds than Europe, North America or Australia.

Of the 16 parrot species in Costa Rica, none is as spectacular as the scarlet macaw. Unmistakable for its large size, bright-red body, blue-and-yellow wings, long red tail and white face, it's common in Parque Nacional Carara (p218) and the Península de Osa. Macaws have long, monogamous relationships and can live 50 years.

The quetzal, Central America's most dazzling bird, has great cultural importance and was of great ceremonial significance to the Aztecs and the Maya. Look for its bright-blue mohawk, red breast and long green tail at high elevations and near Parque Nacional

Los Quetzales (p274). Quetzals love to feed on young avocados, which they swallow whole and later spit out the seed.

With their dark bodies, yellow chests and brilliant beaks, toucans are classic rainforest birds; six species are found in Costa Rica. Huge bills and vibrant plumage make the chestnut-mandibled toucan and the keel-billed toucan hard to miss, and they are common across the country. Listen for the keel-billed's song: a repetitious 'carrrick!' at dusk.

The descriptively named roseate spoonbill has a white head and a distinctive spoon-shaped bill, and feeds by touch, swinging its open bill back and forth underwater. It's the only pink bird in Costa Rica and is common around the Península de Nicoya and along Pacific lowlands.

The little blue-gray tanager is always seen in pairs and is the ubiquitous songbird of tropical woodlands and gardens. There are 42 species of tanager in the country – many are brightly colored and all have bodies that are about the size of an adult's fist. Look for them everywhere except at high elevation. Their common name in Costa Rica is *viuda*, meaning 'widow'.

The distinctive black frigatebird, with its inflatable red throat pouch, is large, elegant and streamlined. It makes an acrobatic living by aerial piracy, harassing smaller birds into dropping their catch, then swooping in to steal their meal midair. They are common along both coasts, where they can be seen circling above the water.

More than 50 species of hummingbird have been recorded – and most live at high elevations. The largest is the violet sabrewing, with a striking violet head and body with dark-green wings.

The Best... Bird-Watching Spots

1 Parque Nacional Carara (p218)

2 Wilson Botanical Garden (p278)

3 Parque Nacional Corcovado (p263)

4 Parque Nacional Los Quetzales (p274)

Land Mammals

A wild selection of land mammals inhabit Costa Rica's multitudinous biomes, but the rainforest has the stars: fierce predators, crafty prey and more than a few playful primates.

Costa Rica is home to the brown-throated three-toed sloth and Hoffman's two-toed sloth. Both are 50cm to 75cm in length, have stumpy tails, and tend to hang motionless from branches or slowly progress upside down along a branch toward leaves, their primary food. Look for them in Parque Nacional Manuel Antonio (p227).

The spider monkey is named for its long, thin legs, arms and tail, which enable it to pursue an arboreal existence in forests near Monteverde. It swings from arm to arm through the canopy and can hang supported just by its prehensile tail.

The king of Costa Rica's big cats, the jaguar, is extremely rare, shy and well camouflaged, so the chance of seeing one is virtually nonexistent (the best chance is in Parque Nacional Corcovado; see p263). They have large territories, however, so you may see their prints or droppings, or even hear their roars – a sound more like a series of deep coughs.

The loud vocalizations of a male mantled howler monkey can carry for more than 1km even in dense rainforest and will echo through many of the nation's national parks including Parque Nacional Corcovado, Parque Nacional Santa Rosa and Reserva

Biológica Bosque Nuboso Monteverde. This crescendo of noise is one of the most characteristic and memorable of all rainforest sounds.

The small and inquisitive white-faced capuchin monkey has a prehensile tail that is typically carried with the tip coiled. This species is likely to steal your lunch near the Volcán Arenal or Parque Nacional Manuel Antonio. Capuchins occasionally descend to the ground for food and count corn and even oysters as part of their diet.

The diminutive squirrel monkey travels in small to medium-sized groups during the day, squealing or chirping noisily and leaping and crashing through vegetation in search of insects and fruit. It lives only along the Pacific and is common in Parque Nacional Manuel Antonio and the Península de Nicoya.

The white-nosed coati is a frequently seen member of the raccoon family, but is brownish, longer and slimmer than a common raccoon. Its most distinctive feature is a long, mobile, upturned whitish snout with which it snuffles around in search of food.

Other mammals you might encounter in the remote forests include the bristly, stinky little white-lipped peccary and collared peccary and Baird's tapir, a large pudgy, piglike browsing animal.

Marine Mammals

Costa Rica has one of the most biologically diverse marine ecosystems in the world and an astounding variety of marine animals. Deepwater upwellings are constant year-round, making these waters extremely productive and creating ideal viewing conditions at any season.

The smallest of Costa Rica's sea turtles, the little olive ridley, is easy to love – it has a heart-shaped shell. It nests during the rainy season, and between September and October arrives in huge numbers at Refugio Nacional de Fauna Silvestre Ostional beach in the Guanacaste province. This species is legendary for its synchronized nesting – 200,000 emerge from the sea during a short period of a few days.

Migrating whales, which arrive from both the Northern and Southern Hemispheres, include orca, blue and sperm whales, and several species of relatively unknown beaked whales. Humpback whales are commonly spotted along the Pacific coast by tour boats. The best place to see them is in Bahía Drake.

Costa Rica's Most Venomous Critters

Note that bites from any of these are exceptionally rare and nonlethal.

○ **Bark scorpion** A jab from this common brown variety is painful but not lethal.

○ **Vampire bat** After anticoagulant saliva inhibits blood clotting, these bats lick up their dinner.

○ **Roadguarders** A bite from this large brown snake of the northwest can cause vomiting, headache and bleeding, but won't kill.

○ **Yellow-bellied sea snake** Though no deaths have been recorded, a bite from this bicolored sea snake attacks the nervous system.

○ **Tarantula hawk** This wasp packs a wallop that kills tarantulas, though it only stings humans when provoked.

The massive 360kg leatherback sea turtle is much, much bigger than the olive ridley, and distinguished by its soft, leathery carapace with seven ridges. It nests on the Pacific beaches of the Osa and Nicoya peninsulas. Sadly, many die each year from eating plastic bags, which they mistake for jellyfish, a key part of their diet.

Divers are relatively likely to encounter the whale shark, the world's biggest fish, in the waters off Reserva Biológica Isla del Caño (p255), the Golfo Dulce or Isla del Cocos. While these creatures can certainly post some impressive stats (some reach 6m long and over 2 tonne, adult males have been known to live 70 years), the majestic whale sharks are not dangerous for divers.

With wings that can reach 7m, the elegant manta ray is common in the warm Pacific waters and can be seen when diving off the coast of Guanacaste and around Catalina island. Sometimes you don't have to don a wet suit to see them either – fortunate visitors might glimpse one jumping from the waves in what is thought to be a sign of play.

Bottle-nosed dolphins are year-round residents in Costa Rica and also quite common. These charismatic cetaceans are among the most intelligent animals on the planet, and have been observed exhibiting complex sociocultural behaviors. Keep a lookout for them on the boat ride to Bahía Drake; they sometimes chase water taxis across the bay.

Reptiles & Amphibians

More than half of the 220 species of reptiles in Costa Rica are snakes, though only a couple could be deadly – and then only without treatment. Of the 160 species of amphibians, frogs and toads garner the most attention as early-warning indicators of climate change.

The stocky green iguana is regularly encountered draping its 2m-long body across a branch over water. Despite their enormous bulk, iguanas are vegetarians, and prefer to eat young shoots and leaves. You'll see them just about everywhere in Costa Rica.

Red-eyed tree frog

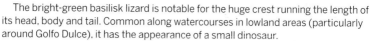

The bright-green basilisk lizard is notable for the huge crest running the length of its head, body and tail. Common along watercourses in lowland areas (particularly around Golfo Dulce), it has the appearance of a small dinosaur.

The poison-dart frog has skin glands exuding toxins that can cause paralysis and death in animals. Indigenous populations traditionally used them as a poison for the tips of hunting arrows.

With a shimmering blue throat and sharp, featherlike black-spotted green scales, the green spiny lizard is a common reptile in the driest parts of the country. It's often seen lazing on fenceposts or exposed tree branches on the Península de Nicoya.

The unofficial symbol of Costa Rica, the red-eyed tree frog has red eyes, a green body, yellow and blue side stripes and orange feet. Despite this vibrant coloration, it's well camouflaged in the rainforest and rather difficult to spot. This species is widespread, apart from on the Península de Nicoya, which is too dry.

The crocodile is an ancient species that has changed little over millions of years. The best place to spot them is on the central Pacific coast.

Shopping

Fabric on sale in Parque Nacional Manuel Antonio (p225)

LEE FOSTER ©

Costa Rica is certainly a memorable destination itself, but a few carefully selected souvenirs can help make the memories last. There is excellent shopping to be had around the country, with items ranging from shade-grown coffee and locally brewed liqueurs to artisan-crafted woodworks and indigenous handicrafts. You'll want to arrive with a bit of extra room in your suitcase so that you can bring home a few pieces of Tico (Costa Rican) culture.

Take Home a Taste

The most popular gifts to take home are culinary souvenirs: woven bags of rich, deep-roasted coffee, Café Rica liqueur and chocolate-covered espresso beans. Another simple way to bring a dash of Costa Rica home is with a bottle of Salsa Lizano, the ubiquitous condiment of the country, which can be added to breakfast dishes and meats.

Tico tipples are also easy to pack in a suitcase. Costa Rica has several brands of internationally recognized rum that can be enjoyed either on ice or artfully mixed with a splash of soda and lime. Guaro, the local firewater, may not win awards for precision crafting, but it's guaranteed to help get the good times rolling. And of course, it's nearly requisite to pick up an Imperial T-shirt, a symbol of Costa Rica's most celebrated brew.

Hardwoods

The tiny town of Sarchí in the Central Valley is famous for producing *carretas,* the elaborate, colorfully painted oxcarts that are the unofficial souvenir of Costa Rica – as well as a symbol of the Costa Rican worker.

In Sarchí these come ready for the road (oxen sold separately) or in scaled-down versions (ready to display in gardens or used as minibars). But the town produces plenty of other curios as well: leather-and-wood furniture (including incredible rocking chairs that collapse for shipping), wooden tableware and an infinite array of trinkets emblazoned with the colorful mandala design popularized by *carretas.*

Tropical-hardwood items include plates, goblets, jewelry boxes and a variety of carvings and ornaments. The most exquisite woodwork is available at Biesanz Woodworks in the San José suburb of Escazú. All of the wood here is grown on farms for the express purpose of resale.

Arts & Crafts

Art galleries throughout Costa Rica are geared primarily toward tourists and specialize in 'tropical art' (for lack of an official description) – brightly colored, whimsical folk paintings depicting flora and fauna. The mountaintop getaway towns of Monteverde and Santa Elena are chock-full of cutesy, cool galleries and tourist shops where you can quickly survey the artistic scene.

Although they're not particularly common, Costa Rica also offers a number of indigenous crafts for those willing to seek them out: intricately carved and painted masks, handwoven bags and linens. The best place to shop for these items is at Galería Namu in San José, which cuts out the middle man and deals directly with the various indigenous craft-production centers.

The Best...
Places to
Shop

1 Sarchí (p91)

2 Monteverde and Santa Elena (p145)

3 Mercado Central (p70), San José

4 Biesanz Woodworks (p75), Escazú

5 Galería Namu (p70), San José

Survival Guide

DIRECTORY	356
Accommodations	356
Business Hours	357
Climate	357
Customs Regulations	358
Discount Cards	358
Electricity	358
Food	358
Gay & Lesbian Travelers	359

Health	360
Internet Access	362
Legal Matters	362
Money	363
Safe Travel	363
Telephone	364
Time	365
Tourist Information	365
Travelers with Disabilities	365

Visas	365
Women Travelers	365

TRANSPORT	366
Getting There & Away	366
Getting Around	366

LANGUAGE	372

Children in Cahuita (p305)
PHOTOGRAPHER: CHRISTOPHER BAKER / GETTY IMAGES ©

A-Z

Directory

Accommodations

o Rates provided are for the high or dry season, generally December to April. Many lodges lower their prices during the low or rainy season, from May to November. Keep in mind that prices change quickly in Costa Rica, so it's best to see the given prices as approximations. Expect to pay a premium during Christmas, New Year and Easter week (Semana Santa).

o Prices are inclusive of tax and given in US dollars, which is the preferred currency for listing rates in Costa Rica. However, colones are accepted everywhere, and will usually be exchanged at current rates without an additional fee.

Book Your Stay Online

For more accommodations reviews by Lonely Planet authors, check out http://hotels. lonelyplanet.com. You'll find independent reviews, as well as recommendations on the best places to stay. Best of all, you can book online.

o A sales and tourism tax of 16.3% is added to all room fees. Paying with a credit card often incurs additional fees. This book has attempted to include taxes in the prices listed throughout.

o Many hotels charge per person, rather than per room – read rates carefully.

o The term *cabina* (cabin) is a catch-all for Costa Rican hotels that can define a wide range of prices and amenities – from very rustic to very expensive.

RATES

BUDGET

o Budget accommodations in the most popular regions of the country are competitive and need to be booked well in advance during the high season.

o At the top end of the budget scale, rooms will frequently include a fan and bathroom with hot water.

o Hot water in showers is often supplied by electric showerheads, which will dispense hot water if the pressure is kept low.

o Wireless internet is increasingly available at budget accommodations, particularly in popular tourist destinations.

Price Ranges

The following price ranges refer to a standard double room with bathroom in high season. Unless otherwise stated, a combined sales and tourism tax of 16.3% is included in the price.
$ less than US$40
$$ US$40–US$100
$$$ more than US$100

MIDRANGE

o Midrange rooms will be more comfortable than budget options, and will generally include a bathroom with gas-heated hot water, a choice between fans and air-con, and cable or satellite TV.

o Most midrange hotels have wireless internet, though often it is limited to the area near reception or the office.

o Many midrange places offer tour services, and many will have an on-site restaurant or bar and a swimming pool.

o Many hotels in this price range offer kitchenettes or even full kitchens.

TOP END

o This price bracket includes many ecolodges, all-inclusive resorts, business and chain hotels, in addition to a strong network of intimate boutique hotels, remote jungle camps and upmarket B&Bs.

o Top-end places in Costa Rica adhere to the same standards of quality and service as similarly priced accommodations in North America and Europe.

○ Staff will likely speak English.

○ Many lodgings include amenities such as hot-water bath tubs, private decks, satellite TV and air-con as well as concierge, tour and spa services.

APARTMENTS & VILLAS

A number of networks of rental apartments, like Airbnb and **Vacation Rentals By Owner** (www.vrbo.com), are peer reviewed and cover a spectrum of prices, sophistication and amenities. They are throughout the country.

B&BS

Almost unknown in the country prior to the ecotourism boom, the B&B phenomenon has swept through Costa Rica in the past two decades, primarily fueled by the increasing number of resident European and North American expats. Generally speaking, B&Bs in Costa Rica tend to be midrange to top-end affairs. While some B&Bs are reviewed in this guide, you can also find this type of accommodations listed in the *Tico Times* and on the following websites:

Airbnb Costa Rica
(www.airbnb.com/costa-rica)

BedandBreakfast.com
(www.bedandbreakfast.com/costa-rica.html)

Costa Rica Innkeepers Association
(www.costaricainnkeepers.com)

HOTELS

It is always advisable to ask to see a room (and a bathroom) before committing to a stay, especially in budget lodgings. Rooms within a single hotel can vary greatly.

Business Hours

Unless otherwise stated, count on sights and activities to be open daily.

○ **Banks** Hours are variable, but most are open at least from 9am to 3pm Monday to Friday.

○ **Government offices** Generally open 8am to 5pm Monday to Friday, but often closed between 11:30am and 1:30pm.

○ **Restaurants** Usually open from 7am and serve dinner until 9pm daily, though upscale places may open only for dinner. In remote areas, even the small *sodas* (inexpensive eateries) might open only at specific meal times.

○ **Shops** Most are open from 8am to 6pm Monday to Saturday.

Climate

Costa Rica's diverse landscapes and geographical

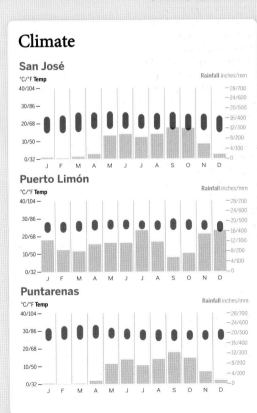

position create a number of varied climates in close proximity to each other. The highlands are cold, the cloud forest is misty and cool and San José and the Central Valley get an 'eternal spring.' Both the Pacific and Caribbean coasts are pretty much sweltering year-round, though rainier from May to November.

Customs Regulations

o All travelers over the age of 18 are allowed to enter the country with 5L of wine or spirits and 500g of processed tobacco (400 cigarettes or 50 cigars).

o Camera gear, binoculars, and camping, snorkeling and other sporting equipment are readily allowed into the country.

o Dogs and cats are permitted entry providing they have obtained both general-health and rabies-vaccination certificates.

o Pornography and illicit drugs are prohibited.

Discount Cards

Costa Rica Card (www. costaricacard.org; individual/ couple/family US$30/40/60) offers hotels and restaurant discounts through affiliated networks. They must be picked up once you're in the country and used with photo ID.

Electricity

120V/60Hz

120V/60Hz

Food

o Traditional Costa Rican staples, for the most part, are very basic, somewhat bland and frequently described as comfort food. The diet consists largely of rice and beans.

o Food is not heavily spiced, unless you're having traditional Caribbean-style cuisine.

o Along the coast seafood is plentiful. Fish is often fried, but may also be grilled or blackened.

o Tourist districts offer a wide selection of international food.

o Tap water is generally safe to drink in Costa Rica.

VEGANS & VEGETARIANS

o Menus always have rice and beans, making Costa Rica a relatively comfortable place for vegetarians to travel.

o Vegetarian-friendly restaurants in this guide will be marked by this symbol: 🌱

o Most restaurants will make veggie *casados* (cheap set meals) on request, which usually include rice and beans, cabbage salad and one or two selections of variously prepared vegetables or legumes.

o A number of specialty vegetarian restaurants or restaurants with a veggie menu

Price Ranges

The following price ranges refer to a standard meal. Prices at small *sodas* (lunch counters)will be the most economical, and will always be posted in colones. Unless otherwise stated, tax is included in the price.

$ less than US$9
$$ US$9–US$15
$$$ more than US$15

Specialities

o **bocas** – a menu of cheap fried snacks (ie appetizers), often served in a bar to accompany beer.

o **casado** – an inexpensive set lunch, usually of rice, black beans, meat, plantain and a small salad. An extremely popular *casado* is the ubiquitous *arroz con pollo*, which is chicken and rice that is usually dressed up with grains, vegetables and a good mix of mild spices.

o **ceviche** – while not traditional Tico fare, *ceviche* is on most menus, and usually contains octopus, tilapia, dorado and/or dolphin (the fish, not Flipper). Raw fish is marinated in lime juice with chilies, tomatoes and herbs. Served chilled, it is a delectable way to enjoy fresh seafood.

o **empanadas** – corn turnovers filled with ground meat, chicken, cheese or sweet fruit.

o **gallo pinto** – the 'spotted rooster' is the national dish – savory rice and black beans. These come in a variety of levels of fanciness and are served with scrambled eggs and fruit, though even at its most basic it is filling and cheap.

o **olla de carne** – a traditional, filling meat stew, filled with a variety of squash (including the *chayote*, a local pear-shaped vegetable).

o **patacones** – fried green plantains cut into thin pieces.

o **sauces** – *Salsa Lizano* is the most popular sauce in the country, and often poured over *gallo pinto* or meat dishes. It's the Tico (Costa Rican) version of Worcestershire sauce. Tabasco, or some kind of vinegar-based hot sauce, is also available.

o **tamales** – steamed cornmeal surrounds a filling of meat and vegetables; these are popular at Christmas time.

can be found in San José and tourist towns.

o Lodges in remote areas that offer all-inclusive meal plans can accommodate vegetarian diets with advance notice.

o Vegans, macrobiotic and raw food–only travelers will have a tougher time as there are fewer outlets accommodating those diets. If you intend to keep to your diet, it's best to choose a lodging where you can prepare food yourself.

Gay & Lesbian Travelers

In Costa Rica, the situation facing gay and lesbian travelers is better than most Central American countries and there are some areas of the country – particularly Quepos and Parque Nacional Manuel Antonino – which have been gay vacation destinations for two decades. Sexual acts between two consenting adults (aged 18 and over) are legal. Still, when it comes to homosexuality, Costa Ricans are tolerant of it mostly only at a 'don't ask, don't tell' level.

Since 1998 there have been laws on the books to protect 'sexual option' and discrimination is generally prohibited in most facets of society, including employment. And though the country becomes increasingly more gay-friendly with the cultural currents of the rest of the world, this traditional culture has not always been quick to adopt equal protection. Legal battles to recognize same-sex partnerships have been a hot topic in the country since 2006 and were a major point of contention in the 2010 presidential race. Current President Laura Chinchilla Miranda opposes gay marriage but has voiced support for legal recognition of same-sex couples.

Same sex couples are unlikely to be the subject of harassment, though public displays of affect might attract unwanted attention. The undisputed gay and lesbian capital of Costa

Rica is Manuel Antonio. The monthly newspaper *Gayness* and the magazine *Gente 10* (in Spanish) are both available at gay bars in San José.

Health

BEFORE YOU GO

○ Since most vaccines don't produce immunity until at least two weeks after they're given, visit a physician four to eight weeks before departure.

○ Bring medications in their original containers, clearly labeled.

○ If carrying syringes or needles, be sure to have a physician's letter documenting their medical necessity.

○ Understand your health coverage abroad and arrange for travel insurance if you do not have it.

INSURANCE

○ A list of medical-evacuation and travel-insurance companies is on the website of the **US State Department** (www.travel.state.gov/medical. html).

○ If your health insurance does not cover medical expenses while you are abroad, consider supplemental insurance.

○ Worldwide travel insurance is available at www. lonelyplanet.com/travel_ services. You can buy, extend and claim online anytime – even if you're already on the road.

AVAILABILITY & COST OF HEALTH CARE

○ Good medical care is available in most major cities, but may be limited in rural areas.

○ For an extensive list of physicians, dentists and hospitals go to the website of the **US embassy** (☏2519-2000; http://costarica. usembassy.gov; Carretera a Pavas).

○ Most pharmacies are well supplied and the pharmacists are licensed to prescribe medication. A handful are open 24 hours. If you're taking any medication on a regular basis, make sure you know its generic (scientific) name, since many pharmaceuticals go under different names in Costa Rica.

INFECTIOUS DISEASES

DENGUE FEVER (BREAKBONE FEVER)

Dengue fever is a viral infection found throughout Central America. In Costa Rica outbreaks involving thousands of people occur every year. Dengue is transmitted by aedes mosquitoes, which often bite during the daytime and are usually found close to human habitations, often indoors. They breed primarily in artificial water containers such as jars, barrels, cans, plastic containers and discarded tires. Dengue is especially common in densely populated, urban environments.

Dengue usually causes flulike symptoms including fever, muscle aches, joint pains, headaches, nausea and vomiting, often followed by a rash. Most cases resolve uneventfully in a few days. Severe cases usually occur in children under the age of 15 who are experiencing their second dengue infection.

There is no treatment for dengue fever except taking analgesics such as acetaminophen/paracetamol (Tylenol) and drinking plenty of fluids. Severe cases may require hospitalization for intravenous fluids and supportive care. There is no vaccine. The key to prevention is taking insect-protection measures.

HEPATITIS A

Hepatitis A is the second-most-common travel-related infection (after traveler's diarrhea). It's a viral infection of the liver that is usually acquired by ingestion of contaminated water, food or ice, though it may also be acquired by direct contact with infected persons. Symptoms may include fever, malaise, jaundice, nausea, vomiting and abdominal pain. Most cases resolve without complications, though hepatitis A occasionally causes severe liver damage. There is no treatment.

The vaccine for hepatitis A is extremely safe and highly effective. You should get vaccinated before you go to Costa Rica. Because the safety of hepatitis A vaccine has not been established for pregnant women or children under the age of two, they should instead be given a gammaglobulin injection.

LEISHMANIASIS

Leishmaniasis occurs in the mountains and jungles of all Central American countries. The infection is transmitted by sand flies, which are about one-third the size of mosquitoes. Most cases occur in newly cleared forest or areas of secondary growth. The highest incidence is in Puerto Viejo de Talamanca. It causes slow-growing ulcers over exposed parts of the body There is no vaccine.

RABIES

Rabies is a viral infection of the brain and spinal cord that is almost always fatal. The rabies virus is carried in the saliva of infected animals and is typically transmitted through an animal bite, though contamination of any break in the skin with infected saliva may result in rabies.

Rabies occurs in all Central American countries. However, in Costa Rica only two cases have been reported over the last 30 years.

TYPHOID

Typhoid fever is caused by ingestion of food or water contaminated by a species of salmonella known as *Salmonella typhi*. Fever occurs in virtually all cases. Other symptoms may include headache, malaise, muscle aches, dizziness, loss of appetite, nausea and abdominal pain. A pretrip vaccination for typoid is recommended, but not required. It's usually given orally, and is also available as an injection.

TRAVELER'S DIARRHEA

Tap water is safe and of a high quality in Costa Rica,

but when you're far off the beaten path it's best to avoid tap water unless it has been boiled, filtered or chemically disinfected (iodine tablets). To prevent diarrhea, be wary of dairy products that might contain unpasteurized milk; and be highly selective when eating food from street vendors.

ENVIRONMENTAL HAZARDS

ANIMAL BITES

Do not attempt to pet, handle or feed any animal, with the exception of domestic animals known to be free of any infectious disease. Most animal injuries are directly related to a person's attempt to touch or feed the animal.

Treat any bite or scratch by a mammal (including bats) promptly by thoroughly cleansing with large amounts of soap and water, followed by application of an antiseptic such as iodine or alcohol, and contact a local health authority.

INSECT BITES

No matter how much you safeguard, getting bitten by

mosquitoes is part of every traveler's experience in the country. While there are outbreaks of dengue fever in Costa Rica, for the most part the greatest worry you will have with bites is the itching and general discomfort.

The best prevention is to stay covered up –wearing long pants, long sleeves, a hat and shoes, not sandals. Unfortunately, Costa Rica's sweltering temperatures make this difficult. The best measure you can take is to invest in a good insect repellent, preferably one containing DEET.

In general, adults and children over the age of 12 can use preparations containing 25% to 35% DEET, which usually lasts about six hours. Children between two and 12 years of age should use preparations containing no more than 10% DEET, applied sparingly, which will usually last about three hours.

Dusk is the worst time for mosquitoes, when it's best to take extra precautions.

SNAKE BITES

Costa Rica is home to all manner of venomous snakes and

Practicalities

○ **Electricity** While Costa Rica uses a 120V/60Hz power system that is compatible with North American devices, power surges and fluctuation are frequent.

○ **Emergency** The local tourism board, Instituto Costarricense de Turismo (ICT), in San José, distributes a helpful brochure with up-to-date emergency numbers for every region. Dialing 911 will contact emergency services and an English-speaking operator, though response time is slow.

○ **Weights & Measures** Costa Ricans use the metric system for weights, distances and measures.

any foray into forested areas will put you at (a very slight) risk of snake bite.

The best prevention is to wear closed, heavy shoes or boots and to keep a watchful eye on the trail. Snakes like to come out to cleared paths for a nap, so watch where you step.

In the event of a venomous snake bite, place the victim at rest, keep the bitten area immobilized and move the victim immediately to the nearest medical facility. Tourniquets are no longer recommended.

SUN EXPOSURE

To protect yourself from excessive sun exposure, you should stay out of the midday sun, wear sunglasses and a wide-brimmed hat, and apply sunblock with SPF 15 or higher, with both UVA and UVB protection. Sunblock should be generously applied to all exposed parts of the body approximately 30 minutes before sun exposure and should be reapplied after swimming or vigorous activity. Travelers should also drink plenty of fluids and avoid strenuous exercise when the temperature is high.

Dollars vs Colones

While colones are the official currency of Costa Rica, US dollars are virtually legal tender. Case in point: most ATMs in large towns and cities will dispense both currencies. However, it pays to know where and when you should be paying with each currency.

You can use US dollars to pay for hotel rooms, midrange to top-end meals, admission fees for sights, tours, domestic flights, international buses, car rental, private shuttle buses and large-ticket purchase items. Local meals and drinks, domestic bus fares, taxis and small-ticket purchase items are better to buy with colones.

Throughout this guide, all of our listings have prices in US dollars.

Internet Access

○ Costa Rica has plenty of internet cafes, and many businesses have wi-fi.

○ Expect to pay US$1 to US$2 per hour in San José and tourist towns.

○ Wi-fi is nearly ubiquitous at all mid- and top-end hotels throughout Costa Rica.

Legal Matters

○ If you are arrested your embassy can offer limited assistance. Embassy officials will not bail you out and you are subject to Costa Rican laws, not the laws of your own country.

○ Keep in mind that travelers may be subject to the laws of their own country in regard to sexual relations.

DRIVERS & DRIVING ACCIDENTS

○ Drivers should carry their passport and driver's license at all times.

○ If you have an accident, call the police immediately to make a report (required for insurance purposes).

○ Leave the vehicles in place until the report has been made and do not make any statements except to members of law-enforcement agencies.

Bargaining

○ A high standard of living along with a steady stream of international tourist traffic means that the Latin American tradition of haggling is unpopular in Costa Rica.

○ Do not try to bargain for hotel room rates, as it is very uncommon.

○ Negotiating prices at outdoor markets is acceptable, and bargaining is accepted when hiring long-distance taxis.

● ● ●
Money

ATMS

○ Cajeros automáticos (ATMs) are ubiquitous in all but Costa Rica's smallest towns.

○ Most ATMs dispense both US dollars and Costa Rican colones.

CASH & CURRENCY

○ The Costa Rican currency is the colón (plural colones, ₡), named after Cristóbal Colón (Christopher Columbus).

○ Bills come in 500, 1000, 5000, 10,000, 20,000 and 50,000 notes, while coins come in denominations of five, 10, 20, 25, 50 and 100.

○ Paying for things in US dollars is common, and at times is encouraged since the currency is viewed as being more stable than colones.

○ Newer US dollars (ie big heads) are preferred throughout Costa Rica.

○ When paying in US dollars at a local restaurant, bar or shop, the exchange rate can be unfavorable.

EXCHANGING MONEY

All banks will exchange US dollars, and some will exchange euros and British pounds; other currencies are more difficult. Most banks have excruciatingly long lines, especially at the state-run institutions (Banco Nacional, Banco de Costa Rica, Banco Popular), though they don't charge commission on cash exchanges. Private banks (Banex, Banco Interfin, Scotiabank) tend to be faster.

Reserving by Credit Card

○ Some pricier hotels will require confirmation of a reservation with a credit card. Before doing so, note that some top-end hotels require a 50% to 100% payment upfront when you reserve. This rule is not always clearly communicated. In addition, many hotels charge a hefty service fee for credit card use.

○ In most cases advance reservations can be canceled and refunded with enough notice. Ask the hotel about its cancellation policy before booking. (In Costa Rica it's a lot easier to make the reservation than to unmake it.)

○ Have the hotel fax or email you a confirmation. Hotels often get overbooked, and if you don't have confirmation, you could be out of a room.

Make sure the bills you want to exchange are in good condition or they may be refused.

Safe Travel

For the latest official reports on travel to Costa Rica see the websites of the **US State Department** (www.travel.state.gov/medical.html) or the **UK Foreign & Commonwealth Office** (www.fco.gov.uk).

EARTHQUAKES & VOLCANIC ERUPTIONS

Costa Rica lies on the edge of active tectonic plates, so it is decidedly earthquake-prone. Recent major quakes occurred in 1990 (7.1 on the Richter scale) and 1991 (7.4). Smaller quakes and tremors happen quite often – particularly on the Península de Nicoya – cracking roads and knocking down telephone lines. The volcanoes in Costa Rica are not really dangerous as long as you stay on designated trails and don't

try to peer into the crater of an active volcano. As a precaution, always check with park rangers before setting out in the vicinity of active volcanoes.

HIKING HAZARDS

Hikers setting out into the wilderness should be adequately prepared for their trips.

○ Know your limits and don't set out to do a hike you can't reasonably complete.

○ Carry plenty of water, even on very short trips.

○ Carry maps, extra food and a compass.

○ Let someone know where you are going, so they can narrow the search area in the event of an emergency.

○ Be aware that Costa Rica's wildlife can pose a threat to hikers, particularly in Parque Nacional Corcovado.

OCEAN HAZARDS

Approximately 200 drownings a year occur in Costa Rican waters, 90% of which are

Credit Cards

⊙ Expect a transaction fee on all international credit-card purchases.

⊙ Holders of credit and debit cards can buy colones and sometimes US dollars in some banks, with a high transaction fee.

⊙ All car-rental agencies require drivers to have a credit card.

caused by riptides, which are strong currents that pull the swimmer out to sea. Many deaths in riptides are caused by panicked swimmers struggling to the point of exhaustion. If you are caught in a riptide, do not struggle. Simply float and let the tide carry you out beyond the breakers, after which the rip-tide will dissipate, then swim parallel to the beach and allow the surf to carry you back in.

RIVER-RAFTING HAZARDS

River-rafting expeditions may be particularly risky during periods of heavy rain – flash floods have been known to capsize rafts. Reputable tour operators will ensure conditions are safe before setting out.

THEFTS & MUGGINGS

The biggest danger that most travelers face is theft, prima-rily from pickpockets. There is a lot of petty crime in Costa Rica so keep your wits about you at all times and don't let your guard down. See also boxed text, p369.

Telephone

⊙ Cellular service now covers most of the country and nearly all of the country which is accessible to tourists.

⊙ To call Costa Rica from abroad, use the country code (☎506) before the eight-digit number.

⊙ The entire country has one area code so it is not necessary to dial 506 when placing a call within the country; simply dial the eight-digit number.

Public Holidays

Días feriados (national holidays) are taken seriously in Costa Rica. Banks, public offices and many stores close. During these times public transport is tight and hotels are heavily booked. Many festivals coincide with public holidays.

⊙ **New Year's Day** January 1

⊙ **Semana Santa** (Holy Week; March or April) The Thursday and Friday before Easter Sunday is the official holiday, though most businesses shut down for the whole week. From Thursday to Sunday bars are closed and alcohol sales are prohibited; on Thursday and Friday buses stop running.

⊙ **Día de Juan Santamaría** (April 11) Honors the national hero who died fighting William Walker in 1856; major events are held in Alajuela, his hometown.

⊙ **Labor Day** May 1

⊙ **Día de la Madre** (Mother's Day; August 15) Coincides with the annual Catholic feast of the Assumption.

⊙ **Independence Day** September 15

⊙ **Día de la Raza** Columbus' Day; October 12

⊙ **Christmas Day** (December 25) Christmas Eve is also an unofficial holiday.

⊙ **Last week in December** The week between Christmas and New Year is an unofficial holiday; businesses close and beach hotels are crowded.

●●● Time

Costa Rica is six hours behind GMT, so Costa Rican time is equivalent to Central Time in North America. There is no daylight-saving time.

●●● Tourist Information

o The government-run tourism board, the **Instituto Costarricense de Turismo** (ICT; ☎2222-1090, in USA & Canada 866-267-8274, in USA toll free 800-343-6332; www. visitcostarica.com; Plaza de la Cultura, Calle 5 btwn Avs Central & 2), has an office in the capital. The ICT can provide free maps, a master bus schedule (which can also be downloaded online) and information on road conditions in the hinterlands. English is spoken, and travelers can consult the ICT's flashy English-language website for information. Brochures and information are also available by calling the ICT's toll-free number from the USA.

●●● Travelers with Disabilities

Although Costa Rica has an equal-opportunity law for disabled people, the law applies only to new or newly remodeled businesses and is loosely enforced. Therefore, very few hotels

and restaurants have features specifically suited to wheelchair use. Many don't have ramps, while room or bathroom doors are rarely wide enough to accommodate a wheelchair.

●●● Visas

Passport-carrying nationals of the following countries are allowed 90 days' stay with no visa: Argentina, Canada, Israel, Japan, Panama, the USA and most Western European countries. Citizens of Australia, Iceland, Ireland, Mexico, New Zealand, Russia, South Africa and Venezuela are allowed to stay for 30 days with no visa. Others require a visa from a Costa Rican embassy or consulate.

For the latest information on visa requirements, check the website of the ICT or the **Costa Rican embassy** (www.costarica-embassy.org) in Washington, DC.

EXTENSIONS

o Extending your stay beyond the authorized 30 or 90 days is time-consuming, making it easier to leave the country for 72 hours and then re-enter.

Passport

o Citizens of all nations are required to have a passport that is valid for at least six months beyond the dates of your trip.

o When you arrive your passport will be stamped.

o Though seldomly enforced, the law requires that you carry your passport at all times.

o * Extensions can be handled by the office of **Migración** (Immigration; ☎2220-0355; ⏰8am-4pm) in San José, opposite Channel 6, about 4km north of Parque Metropolitano La Sabana.

o Requirements for extensions change, so allow several working days.

●●● Women Travelers

Most female travelers experience little more than a '*mi amor*' ('my love') or an appreciative hiss from the local men in Costa Rica. But in general, Costa Rican men consider foreign women to have looser morals and to be easier conquests than Ticas (female Costa Ricans). Men will often make flirtatious comments to single women, particularly blondes. Women traveling together are not exempt from this. The best way to deal with this is to do what the Ticas do – ignore it completely. Women who firmly resist unwanted verbal advances from men are normally treated with respect.

Transport

Getting There & Away

ENTERING THE COUNTRY

o Entering Costa Rica is mostly free of hassle, with the exception of some long queues at the airport.

o The vast majority of travelers enter the country by plane, and the vast majority of international flights arrive at Aeropuerto Internacional Juan Santamaría, outside San Jose.

o Liberia is a growing destination for international flights. It is in the Guanacaste Province and serves travelers heading to the Península de Nicoya.

o Overland border crossings are straightforward and travelers can move freely between Panama to the south and Nicaragua to the north.

o Some foreign nationals will require a visa. Be aware that you can not get a visa at the border. See also Visas for more information.

 AIR

Costa Rica is well connected by air to other Central and South American countries, as well as to the USA.

o International flights arrive at Aeropuerto Internacional Juan Santamaría (p71), 17km northwest of San José, in the town of Alajuela.

o Aeropuerto Internacional Daniel Oduber Quirós in Liberia also receives international flights from the USA, the Americas and Canada. It serves a number of American and Canadian airlines and some charters from London. Flights into Liberia have increased since the 2012 opening of a new terminal.

o The US Federal Aviation Administration has assessed Costa Rica's aviation authorities to be in compliance with international safety standards.

 SEA

o Cruise ships stop in Costa Rican ports and enable passengers to make a quick foray into the country. Typically, ships dock at either the Pacific port of Puerto de Caldera or the Caribbean port of Puerto Limón.

o It is also possible to arrive in Costa Rica by private yacht.

 Getting Around

 AIR

SCHEDULED FLIGHTS

o Costa Rica's domestic airlines are **NatureAir** (☎ 2220-3054; www.natureair. com) and **Sansa** (☎ 2290-4100; www.flysansa.com).

o Both airlines fly small passenger planes, and you're allocated a baggage allowance of no more than 12kg.

o Space is limited and demand is high in the dry season (December to April), so reserve and pay for tickets in advance.

o In Costa Rica schedules change constantly and delays are frequent because of inclement weather. You should not arrange a domestic flight that makes a tight connection with an international flight back home.

o All domestic flights originate or terminate at San José. Destinations reached from San José include Bahía Drake, Barra del Colorado, Golfito, Liberia, Neily, Palmar

Departure & Arrival Tax

o There is a US$26 departure tax on all international outbound flights, payable in cash.

o At the Juan Santamaría and Liberia airports this tax can be paid in cash or by credit card, and Banco de Costa Rica has an ATM (on the Plus system) by the departure-tax station.

o Travelers will not be allowed through airport security without paying.

Domestic Air Routes

High season scheduled flights with Sansa or NatureAir
Some connecting flights with Sansa or NatureAir
• Some airports for light charter planes
Flights subject to change, especially in low season

Sur, Playa Nosara, Playa Sámara, Playa Carrillo, Playa Tamarindo, Puerto Jiménez, Quepos, Tambor and Tortuguero.

CHARTERS

○ Travelers on a larger budget or in a larger party should consider chartering a private plane as it is by far the quickest way to travel around the country.

○ It takes under 90 minutes to fly to most destinations, though weather conditions can significantly speed up or delay travel time.

○ The two most reputable charters in the country are NatureAir and **Alfa Romeo Aero Taxi** (www.alfaromeoair. com). Both can be booked directly through the company, through a tour agency or some high-end accommodations.

○ Luggage space on charters is extremely limited.

BOAT

○ Ferries cross the Golfo de Nicoya connecting the central Pacific coast with the southern tip of Península de Nicoya.

○ The **Countermark ferry** (☏2661-1069) links the port of Puntarenas with Playa Naranjo four times daily. The **Ferry**

Peninsular (☏2641-0118) travels between Puntarenas and Paquera every two hours, for a bus connection to Montezuma.

○ On the Golfo Dulce, a daily passenger ferry links Golfito with Puerto Jiménez on the Península de Osa, and a weekday water taxi travels to and from Playa Zancudo. On the other side of the Península de Osa, water taxis connect Bahía Drake with Sierpe.

○ On the Caribbean coast, there is a bus and boat service that runs several times a day, linking Cariari and Tortuguero, while another links Parismina and Siquirres.

Climate Change & Travel

Every form of transport that relies on carbon-based fuel generates CO_2, the main cause of human-induced climate change. Modern travel is dependent on airplanes, which might use less fuel per kilometer per person than most cars but travel much greater distances. The altitude at which aircraft emit gases (including CO_2) and particles also contributes to their climate change impact. Many websites offer 'carbon calculators' that allow people to estimate the carbon emissions generated by their journey and, for those who wish to do so, to offset the impact of the greenhouse gases emitted with contributions to portfolios of climate-friendly initiatives throughout the world. Lonely Planet offsets the carbon footprint of all staff and author travel.

○ Boats ply the canals that run along the coast from Moín to Tortuguero, although no regular service exists. A daily water taxi connects Puerto Viejo de Sarapiquí with Trinidad on the Río San Juan. The San Juan is Nicaraguan territory, so take your passport. You can try to arrange boat transportation in any of these towns for Barra del Colorado.

 BUS

LOCAL BUSES

○ Local buses are a cheap and reliable way of getting around Costa Rica; the longest domestic journey out of San José costing less than US$20.

○ San José is the transportation center for the country, though there is no central terminal. Bus offices are scattered around the city: some large bus companies have big terminals that sell tickets in advance, while others have little more than a stop – sometimes unmarked.

○ Buses can be very crowded, but don't usually pass up passengers on account of being too full.

○ There are two types of bus: *directo* (direct) and *colectivo* (shared minibus). The *directo* buses should go from one destination to the next with few stops, the *colectivos* make more stops and are very slow going.

○ Bus schedules fluctuate wildly, so always confirm the time when you buy your ticket. If you are catching a bus that picks you up somewhere along a road, get to the roadside early.

○ For information on departures from San José, pay a visit to the Instituto Costarricense de Turismo (p365) office to pick up the reasonably up-to-date copy of the master schedule, which is also available online.

SHUTTLE BUSES

The tourist-van shuttle services are an alternative to the standard intercity buses. Shuttles are provided by **Grayline's Fantasy Bus** (☏ 2220-2126; www.grayline-costarica.com) and **Interbus** (☏ 2283-5573; www.interbu-sonline.com). Both companies run overland transportation from San José to the most popular destinations, as well as directly between other destinations. These services will pick you up at your hotel and reservations can be made online, or through local travel agencies and hotel owners.

 CAR

○ Drivers in Costa Rica are required to have a valid driver's license from their home country. Many places will also accept an International Driving Permit (IDP), issued by the automobile association in your country of origin. After 90 days, however, you will need to get a Costa Rican driver's license.

○ Gasoline (petrol) and diesel are widely available, and 24-hour service stations are along the Interamericana. At the time of writing, fuel prices averaged US$1.25 per liter.

○ In more remote areas, fuel will be more expensive and might be sold at the neighborhood *pulpería* (corner grocery store).

RENTAL & INSURANCE

○ There are car-rental agencies in San José and in popular tourist destinations on the Pacific coast.

○ All of the major international car-rental agencies have outlets in Costa Rica, though you can sometimes get better deals from local companies.

○ Due to road conditions, it is necessary to invest in a 4WD unless travel is limited only to the Interamericana.

○ Many agencies will insist on 4WD in the rainy season,

when driving through rivers is a matter of course.

○ To rent a car you need a valid driver's license, a major credit card and a passport. The minimum age for car rental is 21.

○ Carefully inspect rented cars for minor damage and make sure that any damage is noted on the rental agreement. If your car breaks down, call the rental company. Don't attempt to get the car fixed yourself – most companies won't reimburse expenses without prior authorization.

○ Costa Rican insurance is mandatory, even if you have insurance at home. Expect to pay about US$15 to US$25 per day. Many rental companies won't rent you a car without it. The basic insurance that all drivers must buy is from a government monopoly, the Instituto Nacional de Seguros. It is legal to drive only with this insurance, but can be difficult to negotiate with a rental agency to allow you to drive away with only this minimum standard. Full insurance through the rental agency can be up to US$50 a day.

○ The roads in Costa Rica are rough and rugged, meaning that minor accidents or car damage are common.

○ Note that if you pay basic insurance with a gold or platinum credit card, the company will usually take responsibility for damages to the car, in which case you can forego the cost of the full insurance. Make sure you verify this with your credit-card company ahead of time.

○ Most insurance policies do not cover damages caused by flooding or driving through a river, so be aware of the extent of your policy.

○ Rental rates fluctuate wildly, so shop around. Some agencies offer discounts for extended rentals. Note that rental offices at the airport charge a 12% fee in addition to regular rates.

○ Motorcycles (including Harleys) can be rented in San José and Escazú.

ROAD CONDITIONS & HAZARDS

○ The quality of roads vary from the quite smoothly paved Interamericana to the barely passable rural back roads. Any can suffer from landslides, sudden flooding and fog.

○ Most roads are single lane and winding, lacking hard shoulders; others are dirt-and-mud affairs that climb mountains and traverse rivers.

○ Drive defensively and expect a variety of obstructions in the roadway – from cyclists and pedestrians to broken down cars and cattle. Unsigned speed bumps are placed on some stretches of road without warning.

○ Roads around major tourist areas are adequately marked, all others are not.

ROAD RULES

○ There are speed limits of 100km/h or less on all primary roads and 60km/h or less on secondary roads.

○ Tickets are issued to drivers operating vehicles without a seat belt.

○ It's illegal to stop in an intersection or make a right turn on a red.

○ At unmarked intersections, yield to the car on your right.

Flat Tire Scam

For years Aeropuerto Internacional Juan Santamaría has suffered from a scam involving sudden flat tires on rental cars. Many readers have reported similar incidents and it is commonly reported, but it continues to happen.

It happens like this: after picking up a rental car and driving out of the city, the car gets a flat. As the driver pulls over to fix it, the disabled vehicle is approached by a group of locals, ostensibly to help. There is inevitably some confusion while changing the tire, and in the commotion the driver gets relieved of their wallet, luggage or other valuables.

This incident has happened enough times to suggest it might be an inside job on the part of someone at the desk of the rental agencies who 'facilitates' these flat tires. It certainly suggests that travelers should be very wary – and aware – if somebody pulls over to help after getting a flat on a recently rented car.

Driving Through Rivers

Driving in Costa Rica will likely necessitate a river crossing at some point. Unfortunately, too many travelers have picked up their off-road skills from watching TV, and every season Ticos (Costa Ricans) get a good chuckle out of the number of dead vehicles they help fish out of waterways for wayward travelers. If you're driving through water, follow the rules below:

○ **Only do this in a 4WD** Don't drive through a river in a car. (It may seem ridiculous to have to say this, but it's done all the time.) Getting out of a steep gravel riverbed requires a 4WD. Besides, car engines flood very easily.

○ **Check the depth of the water before driving through** To accommodate an average rental 4WD, the water should be no deeper than above the knee. In a sturdier vehicle (Toyota 4-Runner or equivalent), water can be waist deep.

○ **The water should be calm** If the river is gushing so that there are white crests on the water, do not try to cross. Not only will the force of the water flood the engine, it could sweep the car away.

○ **Drive very, very slowly** The pressure of driving through a river too quickly will send the water right into the engine and will impair the electrical system. Keep steady pressure on the accelerator so that the tail pipe doesn't fill with water, but go slow.

○ **Err on the side of caution** Car-rental agencies in Costa Rica do not insure for water damage, so ruining a car in a river can come at an extremely high cost.

○ Drive on the right and passing is allowed only on the left.

○ If you are issued with a ticket, you have to pay the fine at a bank; instructions are given on the ticket. If you are driving a rental car, the rental company may be able to arrange your payment for you – the amount of the fine should be on the ticket. A portion of the money from these fines goes to a children's charity.

○ If you are driving and see oncoming cars with headlights flashing, it often means that there is a road problem or a radar speed trap ahead. Slow down immediately.

LOCAL TRANSPORTATION

BUS

Local buses operate chiefly in San José, Puntarenas, San Isidro, Golfito and Puerto Limón, connecting urban and suburban areas. Most local buses pick up passengers on the street and on main roads. For years, these buses were converted school buses imported from the USA, but they have slowly been upgraded and now many include coach buses.

TAXI

In San José taxis have meters, called *marías*. Note that it is illegal for a driver not to use the meter. Outside of San José, however, most taxis don't have meters and fares tend to be agreed upon in advance. Bargaining is quite acceptable.

In rural areas, 4WD jeeps are often used as taxis and are a popular means for surfers (and their boards) to travel from their accommodations to the break. Prices vary wildly depending on how touristy the area is, though generally speaking a 10-minute ride should cost between US$5 and US$15.

Taxi drivers are not normally tipped unless they assist with your luggage or have provided an above-average service.

Language

Spanish pronunciation is not difficult as most of the sounds are also found in English. You can read our pronunciation guides below as if they were English and you'll be understood just fine. And if you pronounce 'kh' in our guides as a throaty sound and remember to roll the 'r,' you'll even sound like a real Costa Rican.

To enhance your trip with a phrasebook, visit lonelyplanet.com. Lonely Planet iPhone phrasebooks are available through the Apple App store.

BASICS

Hello.
Hola.   o·la
How are you?
¿Cómo está? (pol)   ko·mo es·ta
¿Cómo estás? (inf)   ko·mo es·tas
I'm fine, thanks.
Bien, gracias.   byen gra·syas
Excuse me. (to get attention)
Con permiso.   kon per·mee·so
Yes./No.
Sí./No.   see/no
Thank you.
Gracias.   gra·syas
You're welcome./That's fine.
Con mucho gusto.   kon moo·cho goo·sto
Goodbye./See you later.
Adiós./Nos vemos.   a·dyos/nos ve·mos
Do you speak English?
¿Habla inglés? (pol)   a·bla een·gles
¿Hablas inglés? (inf)   a·blas een·gles
I don't understand.
No entiendo.   no en·tyen·do
How much is this?
¿Cuánto cuesta?   kwan·to kwes·ta
Can you reduce the price a little?
¿Podría bajarle el   po·dree·a ba·khar·le
el precio?   el pre·syo

ACCOMMODATIONS

I'd like to make a booking.
Quisiera reservar   kee·sye·ra re·ser·var
una habitación.   oo·na a·bee·ta·syon
Do you have a room available?
¿Tiene una habitación?   tye·ne oo·na a·bee·ta·syon
How much is it per night?
¿Cuánto es por noche?   kwan·to es por no·che

EATING & DRINKING

I'd like ..., please.
Quisiera . . ., por favor.   kee·sye·ra . . . por fa·vor
That was delicious!
¡Estuvo delicioso!   es·too·vo de·lee·syo·so
Bring the bill/check, please.
La cuenta, por favor.   la kwen·ta por fa·vor
I'm allergic to ...
Soy alérgico/a al . . . (m/f)   soy a·ler·khee·ko/a al . . .

I don't eat ...
No como . . .   no ko·mo . . .
   chicken   *pollo*   po·yo
   fish   *pescado*   pes·ka·do
   (red) meat   *carne (roja)*   kar·ne (ro·kha)

EMERGENCIES

I'm ill.
Estoy enfermo/a. (m/f)   es·toy en·fer·mo/a
Help!
¡Socorro!   so·ko·ro
Call a doctor!
¡Llame a un doctor!   ya·me a oon dok·tor
Call the police!
¡Llame a la policía!   ya·me a la po·lee·see·a

DIRECTIONS

Where's a/the ...?
¿Dónde está . . .?   don·de es·ta . . .
   bank
   el banco   el ban·ko
   ... embassy
   la embajada de . . . la em·ba·kha·da de . . .
   market
   el mercado   el mer·ka·do
   museum
   el museo   el moo·se·o
   restaurant
   un restaurante   oon res·tow·ran·te
   toilet
   el baño   el ba·nyo
   tourist office
   la oficina de   la o·fee·see·na de
   turismo   too·rees·mo

Behind the Scenes

Our Readers

Many thanks to the travelers who used the last edition and wrote to us with helpful hints, useful advice and interesting anecdotes:

Joelle Etienne, Jan Franck, Jos Molema, Mark Stackhouse

Author Thanks

NATE CAVALIERI

My fervent thanks go to Felipe Pardo, a Manuel Antonio guide and godsend, who found and returned notes for this guide after I dropped them on a trail in Manuel Antonio Park. For the information and the companionship while on the road, thanks to Jorge Picado, Matt Sulkis, Carlos Meneo and Jenny Shrum. Thanks also to Cat Craddock and Kellie Langdon for their careful editing and patience and David Carroll and the Christo team at Lonely Planet for their support.

Acknowledgments

Climate map data adapted from Peel MC, Finlayson BL & McMahon TA (2007) 'Updated World Map of the Köppen-Geiger Climate Classification', *Hydrology and Earth System Sciences*, 11, 163344.
Cover photographs
Front: Rafting on Río Pacuare, Jesus Ochoa ©
Back: Chestnut-mandibled toucan, Alfredo Maiquez / Getty Images ©

This Book

This 2nd edition of Lonely Planet's *Discover Costa Rica* was written by Nate Cavalieri, Adam Skolnick and Wendy Yanagihara. The previous edition was written and coordinated by Matthew Firestone, Carolina Miranda and César Soriano.

This guidebook was commissioned in Lonely Planet's Oakland office, and produced by the following:

Commissioning Editor Catherine Craddock-Carrillo
Coordinating Editors Kellie Langdon, Kate Mathews
Coordinating Cartographer Anthony Phelan
Coordinating Layout Designer Nicholas Colicchia
Managing Editors Brigitte Ellemor, Bruce Evans
Managing Cartographers Alison Lyall, Adrian Persoglia
Managing Layout Designer Chris Girdler
Assisting Editors Briohny Hooper, Bella Li, Charlotte Orr, Catherine Naghten, Gina Tsarouhas
Cover Research Naomi Parker
Internal Image Research Aude Vauconsant
Language Content Branislava Vladisavljevic
Thanks to Dan Austin, Laura Crawford, Ryan Evans, Larissa Frost, Jouve India, Asha Ioculari, Trent Paton, Averil Robertson, Silvia Rosas, Fiona Siseman, Andrew Stapleton, Gerard Walker

Index

A

accommodations 49, 333, 356-7, *see also individual locations*
activities 335-9, *see also individual activities*
air travel 366, 366-7
Alajuela 88-91, **89**
Amighetti, Francisco 342
amphibians 351, *see also* frogs
animals, 349-52, *see also individual animals*
archaeological sites
Alma Ata Archaeological Park 162-3
Monumento Nacional Arqueológico Guayabo 82, 102
petroglyphs 160
turtle trap 229
Arenal Observatory Lodge 111, 128
art galleries, *see also* museums
Museo de Arte y Diseño Contemporáneo 342
Museo Islita 190
arts & crafts 354
ATMs 48, *see also* money
Auditorio Nacional 63
Aviarios del Caribe Sloth Sanctuary 314

B

Bahía Drake 248, 254-8, **256**
accommodations 255-6, 258
activities 254-5, 257-8
food 255-6
sights 257-8
banana industry 265, 325-7
Barrio Bird Walking Tours 70
Barva 83, 95-7
Basílica de Nuestra Señora de Los Ángeles 83, 96, 97
bats 158
Beach Break 186
beaches 18
Costañera Sur 235-6
Dominical 210, 211, 231-5
Dominicalito 211
Islita area 190
Jacó 218-21
Mal País 199-203
Manuel Antonio 209
Montezuma 15, 172, 194-8
Nosara area 188-91
Parque Nacional Marino Ballena 237
Pavones 248, 266-8, 338
Playa Avellana 186-8
Playa Bahía Uvita 237
Playa Barrigona 192
Playa Brasilito 180-1
Playa Camaronal 190
Playa Cocalito 254, 257
Playa Cocles 312
Playa Conchal 173, 181
Playa del Coco 173, 178
Playa El Carmen 199-200
Playa Espadilla Sur 229
Playa Grande 181-2
Playa Guiones 26, 189-91
Playa Hermosa 211, 213, 221-2, 338
Playa Las Caletas 254
Playa Llorona 263
Playa Manuel Antonio 229
Playa Manzanillo 199
Playa Nancite 159
Playa Naranjo 159
Playa Negra (Nicoya) 186-8
Playa Portero Grande 159
Playa Puerto Escondido 229
Playa Sámara 24, 172, 192-4
Playa San Josecito 254
Playa Tamarindo 183-6
Playa Tortuga 238
Punta Uvita 237
Playa Ventanas 181
Salsa Brava 289
Santa Teresa 199-203
Zancudo 249
belief systems 320
bird-watching 21, 339, 348-9
Ara Project 101
Barrio Bird Walking Tours 70
Hacienda Baru National Wildlife Refuge 230-1
Parque Nacional Carara 30, 218
Parque Nacional Chirripó 272-3
Parque Nacional Los Quetzales 274-5
Parque Nacional Manuel Antonio 229
Parque Nacional Palo Verde 163
Parque Nacional Santa Rosa 158
Parque Nacional Tortuguero 303-4
Parque Nacional Volcán Arenal 111, 126
Puentes Colgantes de Arenal 130
Puerto Viejo de Sarapiquí 164
Refugio Nacional de Fauna Silvestre Ostional 193
Refugio Nacional de Vida Silvestre Gandoca-Manzanillo 317
Reserva Biológica Bosque Nuboso Monteverde 109, 147
Reserva Santa Elena 148
San Gerardo de Dota 274

Tirimbina Rainforest Center 162

Wilson Botanical Garden 278

Black Virgin 83, 93

boat travel 367-8

boat trips 297, 298, 304, *see also* canoeing, kayaking

books 47, 71, 341-2

Bosque Eterno de los Niños 109, 139

budget 49, 356

bus travel 368, 370

butterfly gardens 101, 127, 135, 164, 224, 231

C

Cabo Matapalo 262-3

Cacao Trails 310

Café Britt Finca 96-7

Cahuita 289, 305-9, **306-7**

  accommodations 307-8

  food 308-9

  sights 306-7

caimans 16, 182, 249, 266, 304

Canales de Tortuguero 302

canoeing, *see also* boat trips, kayaking

  Bahía Drake 255

  La Fortuna 121

  Parque Nacional Tortuguero 16, 297, 304

  Puerto Viejo de Sarapiquí 164

canopy tours 335-6

  El Castillo 127

  Hacienda Barú National Wildlife Refuge 214, 231

  Jacó 219

  La Fortuna 121

  Los Angeles Cloud Forest 93

  Monteverde & Santa Elena 17, 109, 139-41

  Montezuma 195

  Nosara 188

  Playa Sámara 192

  Rainforest Aerial Tram 300

canyoning 121

capuchins, *see* monkeys

car travel 48, 368-70

  driver's licenses 368-9

  insurance 368-9

  rental 368-9

  road rules 369-70

  safety 362, 369

Carate 262-3

Cariari 296

Caribbean coast 24, 283-317, 345, **38, 284-5, 292, 295, 306-7**

  highlights 286-89, 290-1

  itineraries 39, 292-3, **38, 292**

  planning 291

  tours 294, 298

Cartago 83, 97-8

Catarata de Río Celeste 156-7

Catarata La Cangreja 155

Catarata San Luis 152

cathedrals, *see* churches

central Pacific coast 205-39, **36, 40, 206-7, 216, 219, 228**

  highlights 208-13, 214-5

  itineraries 36-7, 40-1, 216-17, **36, 40, 216**

  planning 215

  tourist information 215

  tours 230, 231, 232-3

central valley 21, 77-103, **78-9, 86, 89, 94**

  highlights 80-5

  historical sites 84

  itineraries 86-7, **86**

  planning 85

  tours 101-2

Cerro Chato 12, 119, 128

Cerro Chirripó 19, 245, 271-3

Cerro de la Muerte 100-101

Children's Eternal Forest 109, 139

children, travel with 30, 332-4

  Jacó 221

  Quepos 223

Chinchilla, Laura 330-1

churches

  Basílica de Nuestra Señora de Los Ángeles 83, 96, 97

  Iglesia de la Inmaculada Concepción 93

  Iglesia La Agonía 88

  Iglesia San Bartolomé 95

cinemas 238

climate 48, 49, 357-8

Cloudbridge Nature Preserve 275

coatis 147, 148, 230, 350

coffee 323, 325, 353

  Café Britt Finca 96

  plantations 21, 138-9

colonial parks 330

Columbus, Christopher 322-3

Corcovado *see* Parque Nacional Corcovado

Coronado, Juan Vásquez de 323, 325

Costa Rican Independence Day 44

credit cards 48, 363, 364

crocodiles 163, 164, 182, 218

culture 320-1

curassow 163

currency 48, 362, 363

cycling 183, 195

D

dance 342

Día de Guanacaste 44

Día de la Raza 44

Día de los Muertos 45

Día de San Pedro & San Pablo 43

Día del Boyero 43

diving 338-9

  Caribbean coast 287

  Parque Nacional Isla del Cocos 268

  Parque Nacional Marino Ballena 237

  Peninsula de Nicoya 173, 178, 183, 192

Puerto Viejo de Talamanca 312-3
Quepos 222
Reserva Biológica Isla del Caño 255
dolphin-watching 238, 255, 287, 351
Dominical 28, 210-11, 213, 231-5
  accommodations 233-4
  activities 46, 210, 211, 213, 231, 232, 233
  drinking 234-5
  festivals 232
  food 234-5
  tours 232-3
Dominicalito 211
driving, see car travel

E

Easter Blossom 346
Ecocentro Danaus 155
ecolodges 25, 251, 345
economy 320-1, 341
El Castillo 127-9
El Fortín 93
emergencies 59
environment 343-7
environmental hazards 361-2
Envision Festival 43
Escazú 57, 74-5
events 42-5
exchange rates 49

F

Fallas, Carlos Luis 341
family travel, see children, travel with
Feria de la Mascarada 43
Fernández, Juan Mora 324
Ferrer, José Figueres 328-9
ferries 367-8
Festival Imperial 43

festivals & events 42-5, see also individual festivals
Fiesta Cívica de Liberia 42
Fiesta de la Virgen del Mar 44
Fiesta de los Diablitos 42
Fiesta de Santa Cruz 42
Fila Urán 245, 272
films 47, 238
Finca Cántaros 279
Fincas Naturales 209, 224
fishing
  Playa del Coco 179
  Playa Tamarindo 183
  Quepos 222
  San Gerardo de Dota 274
  San Gerardo de Rivas 270
Flutterby House 46
food, see individual regions
Friends Meeting House 143
frogs 127, 135, 224, 351, 352

G

Galería Namu 70
gardens
  ATEC 296
  Butterfly Botanical Gardens 209
  Cacao Trails 310
  Catie 101
  Ecofinca Andar 296
  INBioparque 94
  Jardín Botánico Las Cusingas 296
  Jardín de Orquídeas 137-8
  Lankester Gardens 101
  Mariposario de Cahuita 306-7
  Montezuma Gardens 195
  Sarapiquís Gardens 162
  Tree of Life 309
  Veragua Rainforest Research & Adventure Park 309
  Wilson Botanical Garden 278
gay travelers 227
geology 346
golf 179

Golfito 265-6
Golfo Dulce 27, 247, 265
Guardia, President Rafael Ángel Calderón 328

H

Hacienda Barú National Wildlife Refuge 214, 230-1
handicrafts 145, 354
hanging bridges 130, 141-2, 162, 165
health 360-62
Heredia 93-5, **94**
hiking 336-7
  Bahía Drake 255
  Bosque Eterno de los Niños 139
  Catarata San Luis 152
  Cerro Chato 119
  Monteverde & Santa Elena 109, 139, 147
  Montezuma 195
  Parque Nacional Cahuita 311
  Parque Nacional Chirripó 19, 272, 273
  Parque Nacional Los Quetzales 274
  Parque Nacional Manuel Antonio 229
  Parque Nacional Rincón de la Vieja 154
  Parque Nacional Santa Rosa 159
  Parque Nacional Volcán Arenal 110, 111, 126-7
  Parque Nacional Volcán Tenorio 156-7
  Puerto Viejo de Sarapiquí 164
  Puerto Viejo de Talamanca 313
  Southern Costa Rica 244, 245
  Tortuguero 298
historic sites 329, see also archaeological sites
  El Fortín 93
  La Casona 158

history 322-31
    Battle of Santa Rosa 158-9
    Columbus, Christopher 322-3
    pre-Columbian 55, 63, 82, 102, 326
    Quakers 143, 146, 147
    Spanish colony 323-4
horseback riding
    Catarata San Luis 152
    El Castillo 127
    La Fortuna 121
    Monteverde & Santa Elena 142
hot springs 161, *see also* spas
    Aguas Termales 157
    El Guayacán 153
    La Fortuna 24
    Parque Nacional Rincón de la Vieja 155
    Río Negro 46
    Tabacón Hot Springs 25, 118-19
    Termales Miravalles 153
    Thermo Manía 153
howler monkeys, *see* monkeys

I

Iglesia de la Inmaculada Concepción 93
Iglesia La Agonía 88
Iglesia San Bartolomé 95
iguanas 351
INBioparque 94
indigenous culture 162, 326, 354
indigenous reserves
    Reserva Indígena Boruca 275-7
    Reserva Indígena Guaymí de Coto Brus 277
infectious diseases 360
insects 110
insurance 360
internet access 48, 362
internet resources 47, 85, 115, 175, 215, 251, 291

Isla Ballena 237
Isla del Caño 247, 255
Isla del Cocos 268-9
Islita 190
itineraries 32-41, **33**, **34**, **36**, **38**, **40**, *see also individual regions*

J

Jacó 31, 212, 218-21, **219**
jaguars 349
Juan Santamaría Day 43

K

kayaking 338, *see also* boat trips, canoeing
    Bahía Drake 255
    Dominical 213, 233
    Golfo Dulce 27, 247
    Jacó 219
    La Fortuna 121
    La Virgen 113, 160-1
    Nosara 188
    Puerto Viejo de Sarapiquí 164
    Río Sarapiquí 161
keel-billed toucans 339, 349
kitesurfing 132

L

La Casona 158
La Fortuna 25, 112, 118-125, **119**, **120**
    accommodations 122-3
    activities 118-19, 121
    food 123-4
    sights 118-19
    tours 121
La Negrita 83, 96, 97
La Virgen 113, 160-4
La Virgen de los Ángeles 44
Laguna de Arenal 112, 129-31
languages 48, 372
Las Fiestas de Palmares 42
Las Fiestas de Zapote 45

lesbian travelers 227
Liberia 148-53, **150-1**
    accommodations 149-50
    drinking 151
    food 150-1
    sights 149
Limón Carnival 45
literature 341-2, *see also* books
Little Hawaii 186
Little Theatre Group 63
Llanos de Cortés Waterfall 159
Los Ángeles Cloud Forest Adventure Park 93
Los Yoses 57, 73-4

M

macaws 30, 163, 214, 218-39, 247, 257, 258, 263, 101
Mal País 18, 199-203
    accommodations 202
    activities 199-200
Manuel Antonio 208, 209, 223-5, **228**, *see also* Parque Nacional Manuel Antonio
    accommodations 224
    activities 224, 229-30
    drinking 225
    food 224-5
    sights 224
Manzanillo 286-7, 315-17
Maracatu 211
marine mammals 350-1
markets 75
    Mercado Artesanal 75
    Mercado Borbón 75
    Mercado Central 56, 71
    Mercado Central Annex 75
Matapalo 247
medical services 181, *see also* health
Mercado Central 56, 71
Mesoamerican Biological Corridor 281
Mogensen, Karen 198
Moín 296

money 48, 49, 363
  credit cards 48, 363, 364
  currency 48, 362, 363
  exchange rates 49
monkeys 349-50
  capuchins 147, 148, 227, 230, 258, 263, 272-3, 304, 350
  howler monkeys 126, 147, 304, 349
  spider monkeys 272-3, 304
  squirrel monkeys 214, 350
Monteverde Cheese Factory 138
Monteverde Cloud Forest 17, 109, 135, 146
Monteverde & Santa Elena 11, 108, 135-46, **136-7**
  accommodations 142-4
  activities 17, 109, 139-42, 147
  drinking 145
  entertainment 145
  food 144-5
  shopping 145
  sights 135-42
Montezuma 15, 172, 194-8, **194**
  accommodations 196
  activities 194, 195
  festivals 195-6
  food 197
  sights 195
Montezuma Waterfall 196
Monumento Nacional Arqueológico Guayabo 82, 102
mountain biking 183, *see also* cycling
mountain lodges 127
Museo de Arte Costarricense 46
Museo de Arte y Diseño Contemporáneo 55, 66, 342
Museo de Jade 55
Museo de Oro Precolombino y Numismática 55
Museo Nacional de Costa Rica 55, 66

museums 54
  Casa de la Cultura 94
  Museo de Arte Costarricense 46
  Museo de Arte y Diseño Contemporáneo 55, 66, 342
  Museo de Cultura Popular 96
  Museo de Insectos 73
  Museo de Jade 66
  Museo de los Niños & Galería Nacional 66
  Museo de Oro Precolombino y Numismática 63
  Museo Islita 190
  Museo Juan Santamaría 88
  Museo Nacional de Costa Rica 55, 66
music 47, 342

N

Naranjo, Carmen 342
national parks & reserves 14, 199, 266, 345-6, *see also* wildlife refuges, wildlife reserves
  Bosque Eterno de los Niños 109, 139
  Cloudbridge Nature Preserve 275
  Ecocentro Danaus 155
  Hacienda Barú National Wildlife Refuge 214, 230-1
  Humedal Nacional Térraba-Sierpe 266
  Las Baulas National Marine Park 182
  Los Ángeles Cloud Forest Adventure Park 93
  Parque Internacional La Amistad 19, 281
  Parque Nacional Barra Honda Caverns 199
  Parque Nacional Braulio Carrillo 303
  Parque Nacional Cahuita 309-11
  Parque Nacional Carara 30, 212, 218

Parque Nacional Chirripó 19, 245, 271-3
Parque Nacional Corcovado 16, 245, 246-7, 257-8, 263-5
Parque Nacional Guanacaste 155
Parque Nacional Isla del Cocos 268-9
Parque Nacional Los Quetzales 249, 274-5
Parque Nacional Manuel Antonio 13, 225-30, 238
Parque Nacional Marino Ballena 213, 237-8
Parque Nacional Marino Las Baulas de Guanacaste 181, 182-3
Parque Nacional Palo Verde 163
Parque Nacional Piedras Blancas 268
Parque Nacional Rincón de la Vieja 154-6
Parque Nacional Santa Rosa 28, 113, 158-60
Parque Nacional Tapantí-Macizo Cerro de la Muerte 100-1
Parque Nacional Tortuguero 16, 288, 297, 302-5
Parque Nacional Volcán Arenal 110, 111, 125-7
Parque Nacional Volcán Irazú 98-9
Parque Nacional Volcán Poás 90
Parque Nacional Volcán Tenorio 113, 156-8
National Stadium 46
northern Costa Rica 105-65, **106-7, 116, 119, 120, 136-7**
  highlights 108-13, 114-5
  itineraries 116-17, **116**
  planning 115
  tours 121
Nosara 26, 188-91
Nuevo Arenal 129, 131-2, 132-3

000 Map pages

O

Ojochal 238-9
Ollie's Point 113, 159, 337
orchids 137-8, *see also* plants
Osa Wild 46, 258-9
outdoor activities 335-9, *see also individual activities*

P

Pacheco, Fausto 342
Pacific coast 343-4
Palmares 93
Pantano Punta Mona 317
Papaya 46, 202
Parque España 62
Parque Internacional La Amistad 19, 281
Parque Metropolitano La Sabana 56, 63
Parque Morazán 63
Parque Nacional Braulio Carrillo 303
Parque Nacional Cahuita 309-11
Parque Nacional Carara 30, 212, 218
Parque Nacional Chirripó 245, 271-3
Parque Nacional Corcovado 16, 245, 246-7, 257-8, 263-5
Parque Nacional Guanacaste 155
Parque Nacional Isla del Cocos 268-9
Parque Nacional Los Quetzales 249, 274-5
Parque Nacional Manuel Antonio 13, 225-30, 238
Parque Nacional Marino Ballena 213, 237-8
Parque Nacional Marino Las Baulas de Guanacaste 181, 182-3
Parque Nacional Palo Verde 163
Parque Nacional Piedras Blancas 268

Parque Nacional Rincón de la Vieja 154-6
Parque Nacional Santa Rosa 28, 113, 158-60
Parque Nacional Tapantí-Macizo Cerro de la Muerte 100-1
Parque Nacional Tortuguero 16, 288, 297, 302-5
Parque Nacional Volcán Arenal 110, 111, 125-7
Parque Nacional Volcan Irazú 98-9
Parque Nacional Volcán Poás 90
Parque Nacional Volcán Tenorio 113, 156-8
Parque Vargas 294
Path of the Tapir 230-1
Pavones 29, 248, 266-8, 338
Península de Nicoya 167-203, **168-9, 176, 194**
   highlights 170-5
   itineraries 176-7, **176**
   planning 175
Península de Osa 247
people 340-2
petroglyphs 160
planning
   budgeting 49
   calendar of events 42-5
   Costa Rica basics 48-9
   itineraries 32-41, **33**, **34**, **36**, **38**, **40**
   repeat visitors 46
   resources 47
   travel seasons 42-5, 48
plantations 21, 138-9
plants 278, 346-7, *see also individual species*
Playa Avellana 173, 186-8
Playa Brasilito 180-1
Playa Camaronal 190
Playa Cocalito 254, 257
Playa Cocles 312
Playa Conchal 173, 181
Playa del Coco 173, 178-80

Playa El Carmen 199-200, 201-3
Playa Espadilla Sur 229
Playa Grande 20, 181-2
Playa Guiones 26, 189-91
Playa Hermosa 211, 213, 221-2, 338
Playa Las Caletas 254
Playa Manuel Antonio 229
Playa Manzanillo 199
Playa Nancite 159
Playa Naranjo 158, 159
Playa Negra (Caribbean) 307-8, 309, 312
Playa Negra (Nicoya) 173, 186-8
Playa Pelada 26, 191
Playa Portero Grande 159
Playa Puerto Escondido 229
Playa Sámara 24, 172, 192-4
Playa San Josecito 254
Playa Santa Teresa, *see* Santa Teresa
Playa Tamarindo 183-6, **184**
Playa Tortuga 238
Playa Ventanas 181
Plaza de la Cultura 57, 63
Porras, Juan Rafael Mora 158, 325
pre-Columbian history 55, 63, 82, 102, 326
Proyecto Geotérmico Miravalles 153
Puentes Colgantes de Arenal 130
Puerto Jiménez 249, 258-61, **259**
Puerto Limón 294-6, **295**
Puerto Viejo de Sarapiquí 162-5
Puerto Viejo de Talamanca 288, 311-15, **312**
   accommodations 313-14
   activities 311-13
   food 314-15
Punta Catedral 229
Punta Islita 190
Punta Mona 287
Punta Río Claro Wildlife Refuge 257-8

Q

Quakers 143, 146, 147
Quepos 222-5
quetzals 135, 147, 249, 274-5, 348-9
Quirós, Teodorico 342

R

Rafiki Safari Lodge 226
rafting, see white-water rafting
Rainforest Aerial Tram 289, 300
Ranario 135
Refugio Nacional de Fauna Silvestre Ostional 193
Refugio Nacional de Vida Silvestre Bahía Junquillal 155
Refugio Nacional de Vida Silvestre Camaronal 190
Refugio Nacional de Vida Silvestre Caño Negro 155
Refugio Nacional de Vida Silvestre Curú 199
Refugio Nacional de Vida Silvestre Gandoca-Manzanillo 287, 317
religion 320
reptiles 351-2
Reserva Absoluta Nicolás Wessburg 195, 198
Reserva Biológica Bosque Nuboso Monteverde 109, 146, 147
Reserva Biológica Dúrika 266
Reserva Biológica Hitoy-Cerere 299
Reserva Biológica Isla del Caño 255
Reserva Biológica Nosara 199
Reserva Indígena Boruca 275-7
Reserva Natural Absoluta Cabo Blanco 198-9
Reserva Santa Elena 109, 148
Reserva Sendero Tranquilo 139

reserves, see national parks & reserves
Río Celeste 113, 156-8
Río Chirripó 270
Río Claro 257
Río Naranjo 209
Río Pacuare 15, 81, 86, 100
Río Sarapiquí 160, 161, 164
Río Savegre 274
Río Sierpe 258
road trips 129
Roca Bruja, see Witch's Rock
rock-climbing 46
ruins, see archaeological sites

S

safe travel 363-4
Salsa Brava 289, 311, 316
San Gerardo de Dota 273-4
San Gerardo de Rivas 270-1
San Isidro de El General 269-70, **269**
San Isidro Labrador's Day 43
San José 20, 51-75, **53**, **64-5**, **68-9**
    accommodations 67-8, 73-4, 74-5
    children, travel with 67
    entertainment 58, 70, 74
    Escazú 74-5
    food 59, 68-9, 73-4, 74-5
    highlights 54-9
    itineraries 60-1
    Los Yoses & San Pedro 73-4
    planning 59
    shopping 58, 70-1, 75
    sights 62, 73
    travel to/from 71-3
    travel within 71-3, 74, 75
San Pedro 57, 73-4
San Vito 277-80
Sánchez, José León 342
Sánchez, Oscar Arias 330
Santa Elena, see Monteverde & Santa Elena

Santa Juana Mountain Village 209
Santa Teresa 18, 199-203
Santuario Ecológico 139
Sarapiquí Valley 23
Sarchí 83, 91-3
scarlet macaws, see macaws, bird-watching
scenic flights 192, 219
scuba diving, see diving
sea turtles 350
Sendero Valle Escondido 139
Serpentario 161
sharks 268
shopping 353-4, see also individual regions
Sierpe 258
sloths 314, 339, 349
snake bites 362-2
snakes 350, 351-2
    Serpentario (La Virgen) 161
    Serpentario (Santa Elena) 135-6
    World of Snakes 101
snorkeling 338-9, see also diving
    Bahía Drake 254
    Manzanillo 287, 312
    Parque Nacional Cahuita 311
    Parque Nacional Marino Ballena 237
    Playa Conchal 173
    Playa del Coco 178
    Quepos 222
Society of Friends 143
Solórzano, Rodolfo Salazar 149
South Caribbean Music & Arts Festival 43
southern Costa Rica 241-81, **242-3**, **252**, **256**, **259**, **269**
    highlights 244-51
    itineraries 252-3, **252**
    planning 251
    tours 258-9, 269
spas 155, 181, 224, see also hot springs

spider monkeys 349
sportfishing 274, *see also* fishing
squirrel monkeys 350-1
squirrels 147
surfing 29, 337-8
  Beach Break 186
  Dominical 46, 210, 211, 231, 232
  Dominicalito 211
  Jacó 218-19
  lessons 232
  Little Hawaii 186
  Mal País & Santa Teresa 199-200
  Montezuma 194
  Nosara area 188
  Ollie's Point 113, 159, 337
  Pavones 29, 248, 266-8
  Península de Nicoya 170, 171
  Playa Avellana & Playa Negra 173, 186
  Playa Cocles 312
  Playa Colonia 237
  Playa del Coco 179
  Playa El Carmen 199-200
  Playa Grande 20
  Playa Hermosa 211, 213, 214, 221-2, 338
  Playa Manzanillo 199
  Playa Naranjo 158, 159
  Playa Portero Grande 159
  Playa Santa Teresa 199
  Playas Avellana & Negra 186
  Playa Tamarindo 183
  Playa Tortuga 238
  Punta Banco 267
  Salsa Brava 289, 311, 316
  Witch's Rock 28, 113, 158, 159
suspension bridges, *see* hanging bridges
swimming
  Bahía Drake 254
  Parque Nacional Cahuita 311
  Parque Nacional Manuel Antonio 229

Puerto Viejo de Talamanca 312
  safety 363-4

T

Tabacón Hot Springs 25, 118-19
tapirs 214, 230-1, 350
taxis 370
Teatro La Máscara 63
Teatro Melico Salazar 63
Teatro Nacional 55, 63, 70
Termales Miravalles 153
theaters 54, 63
thermal pools, *see* hot springs
Thermo Manía 153
Ticos 340-2
Tilarán 132-5
tipping 48
Tirimbina Rainforest Center 162
Tortilla Flats 211
Tortuguero Village 296-302, **297**
  accommodations 298-300
  activities 297, 298
  food 300
  sights 297
  tours 298
toucans 339, 349
tourism industry 320-1
train rides 141-2
tram rides 141-2
trekking, *see* hiking
Turrialba 15, 81, 101-3
turtles 350-1
turtle-watching
  Islita 190
  Nosara 189
  Parque Nacional Marino Ballena 238
  Parque Nacional Marino Las Baulas de Guanacaste 182
  Parque Nacional Santa Rosa 158-9
  Refugio Nacional de Fauna Silvestre Ostional 193
Turtuguero 296-7, 302-3

U

Unión Area 130-1
Uvita 213, 235-7

V

Valle de Orosi 99
venomous creatures 351
Villa Deevena 46, 189
visas 48, 365
visual arts 342
volcanoes 344, 346
  Volcán Arenal 12, 110, 111, 125-7, 128
  Volcán Chato 111, 119
  Volcán Irazú 82, 84, 98-9
  Volcán Miravalles 153-4
  Volcán Poás 90
  Volcán Rincón de la Vieja 154-6
  Volcán Santa María 154
  Volcán Tenorio 113, 156-8

W

wakeboarding 132
Walker, William 158
water (drinking) 333
waterfalls
  Catarata de Río Celeste 156-7
  Catarata La Cangreja 155
  Catarata San Luis 152
  La Catarata de la Fortuna 119
  Llanos de Cortés Waterfall 159
  Montezuma Waterfall 196
weather 48, 357-8
websites 47, 85, 115, 175, 215, 251, 291
Wessburg, Nicholas Olof 198
whales 350
whale-watching
  Bahía Drake 255
  Parque Nacional Marino Ballena 214, 238
  Uvita 235

white-water rafting 338
  Central Valley 100
  Dominical 232
  La Fortuna 121
  Río Sarapiquí 161
  Parque Nacional Manuel
    Antonio 209, 224
  Turrialba 16, 80-1, 101-2
wi-fi 48, 362
wildlife 348-52, *see also
  individual plants, birds &
  animals*
wildlife refuges 101
  Hacienda Baru National
    Wildlife Refuge 230-1
  Jaguar Centro de Rescate
    309
  Punta Río Claro Wildlife
    Refuge 257-8
  Refugio Nacional de Fauna
    Silvestre Golfito 266
  Refugio Nacional de Fauna
    Silvestre Ostional 193
  Refugio Nacional de Vida Sil-
    vestre Bahía Junquillal 155
  Refugio Nacional de Vida
    Silvestre Camaronal 190
  Refugio Nacional de Vida
    Silvestre Caño Negro 155
  Refugio Nacional de Vida
    Silvestre Curú 199
  Refugio Nacional de Vida
    Silvestre Gandoca-
    Manzanillo 287, 317
wildlife reserves, *see also
  national parks & reserves,
  zoos*
  Africa Mía 149
  Aviarios del Caribe Sloth
    Sanctuary 314

El Castillo-Arenal Butterfly
    Conservatory 127
  Reserva Biológica Bosque
    Nuboso Monteverde 109,
    146
  Reserva Biológica Dúrika
    266
  Reserva Biológica Hitoy-
    Cerere 299
  Reserva Biológica Isla del
    Caño 255
  Reserva Biológica Nosara
    199
  Reserva Indígena Boruca
    275-7
  Reserva Natural Absoluta
    Cabo Blanco 198-9
  Reserva Santa Elena 109, 148
  Serpentario (La Virgen) 161
  Serpentario (Santa Elena)
    135-7
  Tirimbina Rainforest Center
    162
wildlife-watching 21, 214,
  250, 339, 348-50, *see also
  canopy tours, individual
  animals & birds*
  Bahía Drake 257
  Monteverde & Santa Elena
    109, 139
  Parque Nacional Chirripó
    272-3
  Parque Nacional Corcovado
    263
  Parque Nacional Isla del
    Cocos 268
  Parque Nacional Los
    Quetzales 249, 274-5
  Parque Nacional Manuel
    Antonio 230, 238

Parque Nacional Marino Las
    Baulas de Guanacaste 182
  Parque Nacional Palo Verde
    163
  Parque Nacional Santa Rosa
    158-9
  Parque Nacional Tortuguero
    303-4
  Parque Nacional Volcán
    Arenal 111, 126
  Puerto Viejo de Sarapiquí 164
  Reserva Biológica Bosque
    Nuboso Monteverde 147
  Reserva Santa Elena 148
Wilson Botanical Garden 278
windsurfing 132
Witch's Rock 28, 113, 158, 159,
  337-8
Wong, Isídro Con 342
World of Snakes 101

Y

yoga 188-9, 200, 232

Z

Zancudo 249, 266-8
zip lining, *see* canopy tours
Zona Protectora Miravalles 153
zoos, *see also* wildlife reserves
  El Jardín de las Mariposas
    135
  Parque Zoológico Nacional
    Simón Bolívar 67
  Ranario 135
  Serpentario (La Virgen) 161
  Serpentario (Santa Elena)
    135-7